Julian Steward and the Great Basin

Julian Steward and the Great Basin

The Making of an Anthropologist

Edited by

Richard O. Clemmer

L. Daniel Myers

Mary Elizabeth Rudden

The University of Utah Press
Salt Lake City

Library of Congress Cataloging-in-Publication Data

Julian Steward and the Great Basin : the making of an anthropologist / edited by Richard O. Clemmer, L. Daniel Myers, Mary Elizabeth Rudden.

p. cm.

Includes bibliographical references.

ISBN 978-0-87480-949-7 (alk. paper)

1. Steward, Julian Haynes, 1902–1972. 2. Anthropologists—Great Basin—Biography. 3. Archaeologists—Great Basin—Biography. 4. Indians of North America—Great Basin—Antiquities. 5. Human ecology—Great Basin. 6. Human geography—Great Basin. 7. Hunting and gathering societies—Great Basin. 8. Great Basin—Antiquities. I. Clemmer, Richard O. II. Myers, L. Daniel, 1949– . III. Rudden, Mary Elizabeth, 1974–

E76.45.S74J85 1999

979′.03′092—dc21 99–13657

Contents

A Note on Orthography

The editors have not endeavored to standardize the spelling or writing of indigenous words or designations. Rather, we have kept the spellings initially used by the authors. For the most part, Steward spelled "Shoshoni" with an "i," and some authors in this volume have done the same. Others have opted for "Shoshone" or "Newe," the latter a term meaning "people" in the Western dialect that Shoshones use for themselves. Others prefer the term "Numa," which is both the putative proto-Numic designation and also the one used in Paiute dialects. Similarly, "Paiute" is sometimes written "Piute," and so forth. If readers find any of these designations puzzling or unfamiliar, we refer them to the "Synonymy" sections of the *Handbook of North American Indians,* Volume 11, *Great Basin,* published by the Smithsonian Institution in 1986.

Acknowledgments

Many thanks to Shannon Thompson, graduate work-study student in the Department of Anthropology, University of Denver, for undertaking the tedious task of entering copyediting changes and retyping the references to create a uniform style. We thank Amanda Kershner, assistant to Deward Walker Jr. in the Anthropology Department, University of Colorado, Boulder, and Lorraine Herbst (MA, University of Denver, 1997) for editing and typing assistance. We are also grateful to various reviewers, known and anonymous, for helpful suggestions and comments on drafts of various chapters at various stages of revision.

Introduction

Richard O. Clemmer and L. Daniel Myers

The message of this book is that Steward the social-scientific theorist cannot be separated from Steward the historically conditioned man and Steward the anthropologically trained academic. Steward's Great Basin work stands as a metaphor for much of what American anthropology was in the middle decades of the twentieth century: struggling to come to grips with functionalism, materialism, and neo-evolutionism while balancing those against psychologism, concepts of sociocultural change from sociology, and the residues of Boasian relativism; witnessing the dissolution of anthropology into its constituent subfields; warily birthing applied anthropology; and becoming involved in legal and political issues for which few anthropologists were prepared. Thus we present a critique as well as an appraisal of Steward. We treat him and his work not so much as a lone individual pursuing a career, but rather as a bundle of professional training, socially informed attitudes, paradigmatic biases, and methodological concerns that were certainly innovative and unique but also reflective of general trends and developing issues in anthropological theory and method.

Among the many distinctions of Steward's academic career, his writings based on his Great Basin experiences (1918–1943) are most impressive for the number of papers and studies published and the substantial achievements advanced during this period. In the space of about 20 years, Steward proposed a systematic scheme for interpreting the social organization of hunters and gatherers, generated the concept of "cultural ecology," proposed culture histories for the southwestern Puebloan and Great Basin peoples, and (rightly or wrongly) put behavioral anchors into the definition of the "Great Basin culture area." These accomplishments founded what would become two of the more productive and invigorating topical areas of study in American anthropology in succeeding years: ecological anthropology and the anthropology of hunters and gatherers.

Equally important, however, was Steward's astute ability to analytically describe and systematically synthesize large sets of data, which few before him had attempted to do on such a grand scale (see Patterson and Lauria-Perricelli, chapter 14). As a descriptive functional analysis, his monograph *Basin-Plateau Aboriginal Sociopolitical Groups* (1970a [1938]) stands as an exemplar of his momentous synthetic facility. Therefore, as we approach the twenty-first century, this examination of one of the most influential minds in anthropology represents a final salute as well as a critical appraisal of Steward's impact.

STEWARD THE ANTHROPOLOGIST

Julian Haynes Steward was born in Washington, D.C., in 1902, and lived there until, at age 16, his parents sent him to Deep Springs Preparatory School. Located on the high desert to the east of the Sierra Nevada, the school allowed Steward to study the geography, flora, fauna, people, and cultures of two starkly different areas: Death Valley and Owens Valley. Surely the contrast between these areas and the opportunity to become intimately familiar with high desert ecosystems (see Kerns, chapter 1) stimulated Steward's interest in how physical environments could affect cultures. In fact, Steward may have maintained a certain nostalgia for the rugged "man-against-nature" image of life in the more sparsely inhabited parts of the Great Basin, such as Death Valley.

Following graduation he enrolled in the University of California, Berkeley, but stayed only one year. He instead transferred to Cornell University, where he earned his bachelor's degree in zoology and geology in 1925. Steward immediately returned to Berkeley and took up graduate studies in anthropology under Alfred Kroeber and Robert Lowie. Robert Murphy (1970: 154), one of Steward's students from Columbia and one of the few who continued Steward's Great Basin work, has characterized Kroeber and Lowie as being "steeped in the historicism, and sometimes nominalism, of the Boas group." Steward does not particularly reflect that historicism. However, Kroeber and Lowie were also students of hunters and gatherers, and Murphy has suggested that Steward "took with him the environmental orientation of Kroeber and Lowie's lifelong interest in social organization."

The impact and influence of Kroeber's and Lowie's work on Steward's research efforts cannot be underestimated or overemphasized (Murphy 1977:3; Shimkin 1964:2–3; see Myers, chapter 9). Steward's dissertation was entitled "The Ceremonial Buffoon of the American Indian" (Steward 1991 [1929]). As Robert Murphy (1977:4) notes, the topic is totally out of character in terms of what Steward is known for: Steward the ecologist and evolutionist wrote his dissertation on ritual and ceremony and framed it as an inquiry into the psychology of humor! The dissertation undoubtedly reflects Kroeber's keen interest in psychology, rather than Steward's. (Kroeber had undergone psychoanalysis under one of Freud's disciplines in Vienna after the death of his friend and informant Ishi, the "last wild Indian," and maintained a psychoanalytic practice out of his home from 1919 to 1923 [Steward 1973:11–12]). However, Murphy's characterization of the work as a "library dissertation" is not quite correct. Steward did spend a couple of weeks in 1927 and 1928 observing masked dances on the Hopi mesas at which clowns would have performed (Steward 1931b).

While still a graduate student, in 1926 Steward joined William Duncan Strong in archaeological excavations along the Columbia River. Steward (1933a:233, 1936d) made two visits of about six weeks each to Owens Valley and Mono Lake during the summers of 1927 and 1928 and another short visit in December 1931. These ethnographic stints resulted in his well-known *Ethnography of the Owens Valley Paiute* as well as a corpus of myths and a life history.

Steward was an innovator. In the fall of 1928 he became the first instructor in anthropology at the University of Michigan. Two years later he moved to the University of Utah and established anthropology as an academic discipline there. His appointment included a mandate to initiate an archaeological research program in the state. However, he left Utah after only three years, perhaps to end an unhappy marriage and to take up a new life with Jane Cannon, whom he met in Utah and married following his divorce. In 1934 Steward returned to the University of California, Berkeley, where he took a temporary teaching position. During his first year of teaching at Berkeley Steward wrote two of his most influential papers.

"The Economic and Social Basis of Primitive Bands" concerned the ecology of hunters and gatherers and postulated a cross-cultural similarity of causes for the emergence of bands (Manners 1973:890; Murphy 1977:24). Its thesis gave rise to the notion of three band types: patrilineal, composite, and matrilineal. The first two types were viable; Steward felt the last was hypothetical in terms of the ethnographic present but that it could have existed in the past. He would later call for modification of the band concept and disavow his earlier attempt at taxonomy; instead he favored a search for causes of similar forms of social organization and an empirical "case-by-case" approach (Steward 1969c:187, 289). However, the essay represents "the first attempt [in American anthropology] to apply the concept of cultural ecology comparatively" (Shimkin 1964:4) and is the first systematic treatment of hunters and gatherers as a distinctive subject. "Primitive Bands" must therefore be viewed as a landmark in the field of hunter-gatherer studies and as one of the cornerstones for Steward's (1949b, 1953a, 1955b) evolutionary theory. It was also a direct stimulus to the 1966 "Man the Hunter" symposium (Lee and Devore 1968).

During the 1934–1935 academic year, Steward (1937f) also wrote "Ecological Aspects of Southwestern Society," which Murphy (1977:26) calls "one of the most original and creative works ever published in archaeology." As one of the earliest analytical discussions of settlement patterns in the New World that utilized archaeological data (Shimkin 1964:4), this essay combines North American archaeology and ethnology into a synthesis of prehistoric social organization in Pueblo society (Manners 1973:890; Murphy 1977:5, 26–27; Shimkin 1964:4). Here again Steward has produced a landmark in North American historic reconstruction.

Together these two essays provide an excellent example of cultural ecological research on synchronic and diachronic levels. However, a number of American journals rejected both papers because of their great analytical and synthetic propensities, or as Manners (1973:890) says, "because of their novelty." "Primitive Bands" was eventually included in a Festschrift to Kroeber in 1936; *Anthropos,* an annual Viennese journal, published "Ecological Aspects."

In 1935 Kroeber put Steward to work (whether Steward volunteered or took the job due to a cash-flow dilemma, no one knows for sure) on his massive "culture-element distribution" (CED) research project, assigning to him the Western, Northern, and Gosiute Shoshone and some Paiute groups. Steward spent six months in the field, largely in Nevada, and interviewed 46 people. Steward appears to have changed his mind over the years on the utility of the CED approach. In 1941 (Steward 1941b:209) he concurred "with Kroeber that they are a real advance as a technique for field work and for presentation of data." The intrinsic merit of the lists, he averred, lay in "the extensive use of tabulation." However, after 30 years of reflection he found it to be "wholly unsuited for an account of the structure of the social groups and of the cultural ecological adaptation involved" (Steward 1973:46). Relationships and interrelations on any level were missing and the method could not account for much of the symbolic and nonmaterial aspects of culture (see Myers, chapter 9).

Steward evidently did not limit himself to interviewing consultants according to the checklist; he also gathered information that would enable him to write *Basin-Plateau Aboriginal Sociopolitical Groups,* a work that fully explicated the paradigm of cultural ecology in anthropology. Steward obtained permanent employment in the latter part of 1935 with the Bureau of American Ethnology (BAE), which published *Basin-Plateau* in 1938. This appointment as associate anthropologist allowed him to return to the Great Basin for four months in 1936 to complete the element lists for the Northern and

Gosiute Shoshone (Shimkin 1964:4). The Bureau also loaned him out to the newly formed Applied Anthropology Unit of the Bureau of Indian Affairs (BIA). However, whether Steward did any separate or special data collection at this point is unclear; he may have simply continued to gather material for his CEDs and for *Basin-Plateau.* The BIA had hired Steward to produce a report entitled "Shoshonean Tribes" that would evaluate their contemporary situation with regard to implementation of the Indian Reorganization Act. However, Elmer Rusco (chapter 6) expresses doubt that Steward did any separate research for this report. Rather, following his return to Washington, D.C., in the fall of 1936, Steward probably wrote the report on the basis of informal observations and ad hoc conversations with Indians in the course of his CED and *Basin-Plateau* research.

Basin-Plateau stands as the classic empirical analysis of social structure and cultural ecology in the Great Basin. Steward used 25 of the 26 groups and/or localities delineated in the CED surveys. Although empirical, the work is highly deductive. Steward clearly intended it to demonstrate the application of the cultural ecological method. Yet, in its frustratingly telegraphic, synoptic way, along with the CED surveys, *Basin-Plateau* constitutes the only close-to-comprehensive summary of historic and protohistoric cultural systems for large portions of the Basin-Plateau areas.

During the years 1937–1939 Steward did a lot of writing: several items for the BAE and more than 10 reviews per year (Manners 1973:898–899). In 1940, the BAE published "Native Cultures of the Intermontane (Great Basin) Area," a synthesis of over a decade of geographical, geological, archaeological, and ethnographic data. Steward continued his accelerated publishing pace well into the 1940s, but in 1940 he was assigned to head the BAE's *Handbook of South American Indians* project. Over three years Steward secured commitments from authors and saw the handbook through to the editing of all six volumes. However, Steward made only one brief trip to South America during his tenure on the project; poor health apparently made the trip disagreeable for him.

In the fall of 1946 Steward took a teaching position at Columbia University, where he inspired and trained many students whose influence in anthropology has become legendary (Murphy 1977:8–10). Most followed in Steward's materialist footsteps, although Robert Murphy was an exception. (Murphy took a number of psychology courses at Columbia and gravitated toward a critical brand of social psychology, although not before producing some very materialist studies.) It was during Steward's teaching years at Columbia, which lasted only until 1952, that he wrote arguably his most important theoretical contributions: "Cultural Causality and Law: A Trial Formulation of the Development of Early Civilizations" (1949b), "Area Research: Theory and

Practice" (1950), "Levels of Sociocultural Integration" (1951), "Evolution and Process" (1953a), and "The Cultural Study of Contemporary Societies: Puerto Rico" (Steward and Manners 1953).

Altogether, the publications released between 1949 and 1953 represent nearly the entire gamut of Steward's broad range of interests: from cultural evolution, prehistory, and archaeology to the search for causality and cultural "laws" to area studies, the study of contemporary societies, and the relationship of local cultural systems to national ones. In much of this work, Steward's approach to his Great Basin studies, which might be characterized as a perspective that people are in large part defined by what they do for a living, can be seen in his growing interest in studying the transformation of slash-and-burn horticulturists into national proletariats in South America. However, two items printed and released after he left Columbia reflect a little-known aspect of Steward's work, one that brought him back to the study of Great Basin societies that he had left 15 years earlier. These were "Aboriginal and Historic Groups of the Ute Indians of Utah: An Analysis and Native Components of the White River Ute Indians" (1953b) and "The Northern Paiute Indians" (Steward and Wheeler-Voegelin 1954). Both were printed in mimeo by the Department of Justice and distributed only to a handful of people and agencies. Steward originally produced these and another item, "The Concept and Method of Cultural Ecology" (later a chapter in *Theory of Culture Change;* Steward 1955b) as part of his expert witness testimony on the government's side in two Indian Claims Commission (ICC) cases: the Confederated Ute case and the Northern Paiute case. It is also likely that Steward developed some elements of his "levels of sociocultural integration" concept as part of his Ute testimony and introduced them again in the Northern Paiute case (see Ronaasen et al., chapter 12). After the ICC rendered its decisions in the 1970s, when only the precise amounts were yet to be determined, the proposed findings of defendants as well as the findings of the commission were released into the public domain as government documents. (The plaintiff's proposed findings and testimony were not released without the tribes' consent.) The Clearwater and Garland companies published many of these findings, including the testimony, supporting papers, and monographs produced by the expert witnesses. In the case of the Northern Paiutes, these publications included the testimony of Julian Steward and Erminie Wheeler-Voegelin.

Although his move to the University of Illinois in 1952 marked the end of his active work with Great Basin materials, Steward continued to have an interest in the position of his Great Basin work in anthropology. Steward still served on doctoral committees, but he never again took on the kind of intensive student mentoring that he had done at Columbia. Much of his effort went into establishing the research and publication series *Contemporary Change in Traditional Societies.* Steward's publishing continued to be impressive through 1969. However, in 1967 his health took a marked turn for the worse. Steward retired in 1968 and died in 1972, just short of putting the finishing touches on a short book on his mentor, Alfred Kroeber; Jane Cannon Steward finished it and the book was published in 1973.

STEWARD THE GREAT BASINIST

It is Virginia Kerns (chapter 1) who perhaps sheds the most light on Steward's Basinist motivations. What grabbed Steward's interest in the Great Basin was the land itself and a way of life based in it: He saw Numic land-based subsistence giving way to a ranching life based in the market economy. Steward's enthusiasm for starting the archaeological research program in Utah, according to what Joel Janetski (chapter 3) rightly calls "a very busy research schedule," can be interpreted as equally motivated by Steward's enthusiasm for working in and with the land itself. Steven Crum (chapter 8), critiquing Steward's interpretation of Numic life as "gastric," offers a more intellectual and expressive interpretation of that life. As Clemmer argues in chapter 10, Steward surely recognized these symbolic, nonmaterial aspects of Numic culture, but regarded them as unimportant because they did not put food in the basket or in the belly.

It is almost as if Steward himself had a "gastric" orientation—a keen appreciation for the biological contingencies of life, which as a sickly child he might have come to appreciate more than the less material aspects. In fact, it is somewhat perplexing that in the ICC proceedings (see Ronaasen et al., chapter 12) the attorneys for the Northern Paiute seem to have depended completely on Omer Stewart's conceptualization of the Northern Paiute territory as band owned to demonstrate aboriginal possession, rather than turning Steward's own analysis on itself: Surely people who were so "gastrically" oriented would have been so dependent on land that depriving them of occupation and use—the primary criteria for determining aboriginal possession—would have been tantamount to depriving them of life. As Steward documented, the fact that Paiutes formed "predatory" bands to protect their territory from white encroachment would seem to reinforce the Paiutes' possessory imperative and thus their ownership rights. Yet, as Ronaasen et al. show (chapter 12), the question of variation in Native North American land-tenure systems and their validity in comparison to state-level property conceptualizations seems to have come out only in a post hoc symposium on the ICC proceedings at the American Anthropological Association meetings in 1954, which included not only Omer Stewart and Julian Steward but also Alfred Kroeber.

The late 1960s and early 1970s brought a resurgence of a debate between Steward and his former student, Omer C. Stewart, over aboriginal sociopolitical organization. One of Steward's last publications (Steward 1970b) was a lively and extremely well-argued rebuttal to some of Stewart's (1939) conclusions. Thus, it can be said that Steward never really moved completely away from Great Basin studies. The last two decades of his life brought him recognition for grand schemes and sweeping generalizations, such as those in "South American Cultures: An Interpretive Summary" (1949a), "Cultural Causality and Law: A Trial Formulation of the Development of Early Civilizations" (1949b), and "Area Research: Theory and Practice" (1950). However, Steward's "cultural ecological" model of human adaptation in the Great Basin was also influential. It inspired much of the archaeological work in the Archaic and Woodland periods of desert, basin-and-range, and high plains areas of North America and in the Early Puebloan period of the Northern Puebloan Periphery as discussed by Janetski, Arkush, and Walker (chapters 2, 3, and 5, respectively). As Crum (chapter 8) notes, Steward's characterizations of Great Basin Shoshoneans as a "stage" of North American Indian sociocultural evolution have been reproduced in textbooks and popular history books in a manner that Steward would probably find unacceptably uninformed and insupportable due to the typological rigidity of "examples" taken out of context and the attempt to turn what he regarded as methodological concepts into unquestioned "facts" (cf. Steward in Manners 1973:887).

Both L. Daniel Myers (chapter 9) and Deward Walker Jr. (chapter 5) discuss Steward's influence in promoting a somewhat rigid circumscription of the Great Basin as a "culture area." Although Kroeber, of course, had initiated the designation, use of the culture-area approach as the primary organizing framework for the *Handbook of North American Indians* undoubtedly was influenced by Steward's success in organizing the ethnography of South American Indians into culture areas in the 1940s. Steward (Steward 1955a:55 [1951]; Steward and Wheeler-Voegelin 1954, 1974) was not comfortable with the concept of distinct "tribes" or "bands" (see Ronaasen et al., chapter 12), preferring to see borderlands, gradations, and dialects where others saw boundaries, distinctions, and discrete languages. However, Steward ultimately found that he had to make some delineations to have a way of talking about the groups (Steward 1939).

Steward's testimony in the ICC cases, his synthesis of his "methodology of cultural ecology," and the general "theory of culture change," which he tried to achieve in the book by the same title (Steward 1955b), can all be seen as developments coming out of his short but fruitful and intense work on defining "areas" and "area studies." Steward saw the Great Basin culture area and part of the Plateau as being integrated socially by interactions among individuals and small groups whose primary activities and "core culture" were organized and largely conditioned by the food quest. It was the environmental characteristics of the area as a *distinct zone of cultural adaptations and geophysical constraints* that, we believe, he saw as the primary way of dealing with aboriginal culture and people in any particular region. In fact, Steward first introduced what J. C. Steward and Murphy (1977:43) call "one of the very few summary statements written by Steward on cultural ecology," which nonetheless "characterized Steward's work more than any of his other interests," as testimony in the Northern Paiute claims case. Although Steward strongly disavowed any role for anthropology as an applied science, as Ronaasen et al. (chapter 12) endeavor to show, it was in the context of considering the practical, legal implications of his methodological work that Steward came to some of his better-known theoretical formulations. The ICC gave him the opportunity to reinterpret, or at least hone his interpretation of, the cultural systems that he had earlier dealt with as adaptations or as clusters of traits as now being various parts of one single adaptive system within an overdetermined *area*. Ronaasen et al. discuss how attorneys for the Northern Paiute, who were operating within a set of power relations like those between anthropologists and the ethnographized "other," were able to use Steward's theory-driven myopia to trounce the government attorneys and win a monetary award for the Northern Paiutes.

STEWARD IN RETROSPECT

When L. Daniel Myers suggested putting together a "Steward Retrospective" symposium for the 1996 Great Basin Anthropological Conference (GBAC), neither of us realized the extent to which Steward's Great Basin work, which constitutes only a tiny portion of his publications, influenced the rest of his work and, in turn, anthropology as a discipline. However, as the abstracts came in, it became clear that even the very definitions of who Basin peoples are and what we call them, as opposed to what they call themselves (see Goss, chapter 6), has been influenced by Steward. Moreover, Steward's work was situated within a framework of colonial power relationships that, as Ned Blackhawk notes (chapter 13), placed virtually all anthropologists as unilaterally authoritative interpreters of Native American cultures. Alice Kehoe observes (chapter 11) that the very people who were struggling to mediate and modify these power relationships in the 1870s, 1880s, 1890s, and even well into the twentieth century, such as Wodziwob, Wovoka (Jack Wilson), and Wuzzie George, are completely missing from Steward's ethnographic work, except for a checkbox in the CED surveys.

As mentioned earlier, these omissions may have stemmed from a part of Steward's self that yearned for the "noble savage" of rugged and undaunted disposition who roamed through the Basin landscape. As Clemmer suggests (chapter 10), Steward seems to have had a great deal of trouble with the concept of "acculturation." He embraced it and used it casually to describe an assumed process of cultural change throughout his writings in the 1930s, 1940s, and 1950s, but never was involved in the discussions and debates coming out of Columbia University that preceded his tenure there. When Steward finally did come to reevaluate the concept in the 1960s, he seemed to reject it as a fuzzy, ill-defined, misapplied concept. However, by that time it was apparently too late for him to reassess his own use of it. As a graduate student at the University of Illinois in the 1960s, Clemmer recalls Steward throwing out his hands in a mild gesture of frustration and saying, "After all the work that has been done, we still do not know just exactly how cultures change."

We probably never will know, but Steward may have been including and critiquing his own work in that statement as much as the work of others. Authors who were unable to participate directly in the GBAC symposium (Virginia Kerns, chapter 1; Sheree Ronaasen, chapter 12; Thomas Patterson and Antonio Lauria-Perricelli, chapter 14) have shed some light on this question. These additional contributions make it clear that Steward saw cultural change as a variable of ecological, economic, demographic, and political factors that allowed for a lot of regional variation, but ultimately acquired a force of their own to which culture was bound to react. For Steward, culture was in the realm of concrete social fact. If culture did not always seem to react predictably to these forces, it was because researchers had either not analyzed situations carefully enough or had defined and used typologies and concepts—in some cases those originating with Steward himself (such as "band")—too rigidly.

Thus, in these revised papers we intend to go beyond what we initially hoped to accomplish in the GBAC symposium. Here we attempt to evaluate Steward's Great Basin work and his contributions to anthropology based on that work in light of two fundamental criteria: Steward's personal history and Steward's relationship to the motivations and the driving forces in American anthropology at the time. For example, Steward assumed that a description of an antelope drive from the late contact period in the desert area inhabited by the Gosiute Shoshone was a plausible model for precontact antelope abundance and frequency of drives (Arkush, chapter 3); however, this must be interpreted in light of Kerns's (chapter 1) recent discoveries in interviews and archival documents about Steward's relationship to the desert areas on the western edge of the Great Basin. The fact that Steward could deny a concept of territoriality to Numic peoples (Ronaasen et al., chapter 12) yet cast into stone names for particular segments of those peoples, suggest boundaries for their territories (Goss, chapter 6), and imply a uniform adaptive strategy characterizing the "Great Basin culture area" (Myers, chapter 9; Walker, chapter 5) surely reflects Kroeber's culture-area-and-distribution obsession as much as it does Steward's interpretation of empirical data. Steward used the concept of acculturation without ever really coming to grips with what it did or did not mean (Clemmer, chapter 10). This must be juxtaposed against his failure—or refusal—to include in his analyses the ways in which Numic individuals were dealing with the political and economic conditions brought about by the globalization of the times (Fowler et al., chapter 4; Kehoe, chapter 11). As Fowler et al. show (chapter 4), Steward either completely missed or chose to ignore important adaptations that Shoshones in Death Valley made to participate in the market economy of the mines and ranches of the West as early as the 1860s, and as Walker (chapter 5) argues, Steward seems to have carried that image to his analysis of some of the more cornucopian ecotones of the Basin-Plateau region. That refusal, in turn, must be viewed along with the general assumption about Native Americans during most of the first six decades of the twentieth century, namely, that they had been vanquished, were powerless, and were doomed to disappear as sociopolitical entities (Blackhawk, chapter 13). As Rusco (chapter 7) makes clear, Steward's obvious ethnocentrism and bias against the idea that Numic cultures deserve collective rights to territory, political recognition, and sovereignty, no matter how limited (Crum, chapter 8; Ronaasen et al., chapter 12), were really mainstream American assumptions and arguments for the status quo.

STEWARD THE CITIZEN

Steward certainly knew about the movement among the Western Shoshone for recognition of treaty rights (Clemmer, chapter 10; Crum, chapter 8). However, his intellectual confrontation with the BIA over moves to reinstitute a special status for Indian nations and to uniformly refer to them with the term used in the U.S. Constitution—"tribes"—was not mere curmudgeonness. It was an expression of a developing trend in American anthropology to study and account for how "traditional" societies were "acculturated" and being absorbed into nation-state political systems and the global market economy. This trend would eventually seize Steward's interest and propel his thinking for more than three decades. It would lead him to write in "Perspectives on Modernization" (Steward 1967b:9, 21; emphasis in original):

> The transition from the traditional to the modernized has entailed conflict between the many earlier patterns of cooperation and sharing and the recent

> goals of maximizing individual profit. . . . The conflict is still evident in the factionalism between the older and younger generations. . . .
>
> [Thus] *assimilation* is subject to certain misunderstandings. A traditional society cannot of course assimilate the totality of a state culture. It may adopt only a limited number of traits, and the adoption always has preconditions. . . . A traditional or native society may retain some degree of ethnic distinctiveness, but, as a special type of rural society or as a subsociety of an urban center, it accommodates to the total institutional and structural framework. . . . A traditional society may so lose its "ethnicity" that it is assimilated into pre-existing segments of the state.

STEWARD THE MENTOR

We see the meshing of perspectives that Steward the "citizen" and "applied anthropologist" made with the perspectives of Steward the "theorist" and "social scientist." As a fledgling student at the University of Illinois, Clemmer signed up for Steward's "Cultural Ecology" seminar. Unfortunately, another bout of bad health hit Steward and he had to cancel his seminar; his health never really recovered, he never offered another class, and died five years later, in 1972. However, during those years of ill health and subsequent retirement, Steward continued to act as a mentor and maintained contact with selected students. Clemmer recalls that several students were guests in Steward's home at various times, where Jane graciously served coffee and cookies and Julian chain-smoked and shared his perspective on various things. A number of these students—Arthur Piper, H. Paige Stevens, John Chance, Steven Auerbach, James Baltaxe, and Clemmer—came up with the idea for a Steward Society modeled on Berkeley's Kroeber Society, which would hold local symposia and publish a modest journal or at least collections of papers from time to time. Thus, the *Steward Journal of Anthropology* was born.

John Chance, editor-in-chief, promptly went off to do fieldwork and the assistant editor announced that he was simply too busy; that left to Clemmer the task of putting together the first two issues. Chance managed to do a splendid interview with Steward before leaving for Oaxaca and Clemmer asked Steward if he would contribute an article. To Clemmer's surprise, Steward wrote a strongly stated critique of applied anthropology that utilized his experience in the BIA's Applied Anthropology Unit in 1936 (Steward 1969b). Also in this first issue was Clemmer's equally strongly stated critique of an anthropology that could not methodologically incorporate the politically significant resistance to acculturation among particular segments of small-scale societies (ones that Steward thought inappropriately designated as "tribal"—he preferred the term "folk"). The issue also included a study of the "rebels" of Reis Tijerina's *Alianza Federal de Mercedes,* which was then hardly known in the academic world. It was quite an issue.

Clemmer did not realize at the time how out of character it was for Steward to have written such an article. Steward's concern with the relationship of anthropologists to science and their primary obligations to the scientific community, rather than to the community they study, had been evident throughout Steward's career. Commitment to scientific objectivity was an important part of how Steward defined himself as a "good citizen" (Manners 1973:891). Steward undoubtedly took a very dim view of Clemmer's call for anthropologists to get involved with the aspirations and issues of the communities they study. However, Steward always seemed happy to receive drafts of papers that Clemmer sent him, politely ignoring what probably did not please him and commenting positively on new information (e.g., "My God! I had no idea that was happening," in response to a draft of a thesis chapter on Peabody Coal Company's strip mine on the Hopi and Navajo Reservations). Clemmer did not then know of "Shoshonean Tribes" (see Blackhawk, chapter 13; Crum, chapter 8; Rusco, chapter 7; the manuscript is not listed in Jane Steward's comprehensive "Bibliography of Julian H. Steward" [Manners 1973:897–903]). Besides "Acculturation and the Indian Problem" (1943d) and the draft of an autobiographical statement prepared for the National Academy of Sciences (Manners 1973:892), which may not have ever circulated to more than a few selected associates, Steward had never revisited his highly politicized assessment of contemporary Great Basin Indians as he had known them in 1936. However, that experience had clearly stayed with him for more than 30 years. John Collier, commissioner of Indian Affairs when Steward had done his ill-fated applied work for the BIA, had died two years earlier. Perhaps Steward had purposely waited until Collier's death to resurrect his critique of Collier and his policies; he asked Clemmer point blank if Mary Collier, John's widow, had raised any objections. Of course, she had not.

CONCLUSION

Perhaps Steward held a certain nostalgia for what he saw as the nobly rugged and persevering Numic peoples, only too corrupted by acculturation, for 30 years. That nostalgia may have been the source of the frustration evident in "Shoshonean Tribes": Why couldn't the peaceful, hard-working, close-to-starvation people he thought they must have been, who were constantly on the search for food and sharing what they had with one another, have persisted long enough for Steward to experience them in the flesh, rather than merely in historic conjecture? Why did they have to change? Numic culture had clearly been successful because it had resulted in long-term adaptation and endurance. However, as Clemmer notes in his discussion of Steward's uneasy relationship with the concept and process of acculturation (chapter 10), Steward regarded culture as potentially "dangerous": Modernized and industrialized Euro-American, European, and Asian cultures that were zealously pursuing nuclear armament would probably result in the termination of human adaptation.

The history of anthropological theory—and of social-scientific theory in general—is as much a history of how the wind blows at particular times in particular disciplines and how national and global political and economic events condition and contextualize "social science as usual" and paradigm shifts as it is a history of how individuals generating grand ideas and the accumulation of data come to influence and constitute an academic discipline. We hope that this first effort to evaluate the early work of one of the dolmens of American anthropology will encourage other broad evaluations not only of Steward, but of other theorists as well.

1

Learning the Land

Virginia Kerns

Contrary to Robert Murphy's suggestion that the Northern Paiute and Shoshone acted as the "catalyst" for Julian Steward's theory and method of cultural ecology, Kerns's suggestion is that his most meaningful encounter with landscape and ecology began years earlier. Steward left the East at age 16 and traveled alone to Deep Springs Valley, near the Nevada border in California, and spent three years there in a private boarding school. He learned much from his early and direct engagement with the land there. The valley offered visible lessons about the significance of technology (the irrigation system), the organization of labor (the students who cooperated to keep the system in working order), and a limited environmental resource (water). In many respects, Deep Springs offered an experience with many parallels to ethnographic fieldwork and constituted the laboratory of Steward's cultural ecology. In making this case, Kerns draws on Steward's own words and photographs, the memories of several people who knew him well, and her own observations of the school and valley.

Julian Steward emerged as a distinctive voice in mid-twentieth-century anthropology, in part for the attention he gave to the land: to the landscape itself and to the animals, plants, and water that humans use to sustain life. His theory of cultural ecology offered an environmental perspective on culture. Robert Murphy, one of Steward's students at Columbia University during the late 1940s, has stressed that Steward developed a theory of *cultural* ecology (Murphy 1977:22). Here I want to shift the emphasis toward cultural *ecology* and toward Steward's own lived experience as the primary source of his theory.

Steward's work as an anthropologist—ethnographic, archaeological, and theoretical—was deeply rooted in his early life. It grew out of experiences of

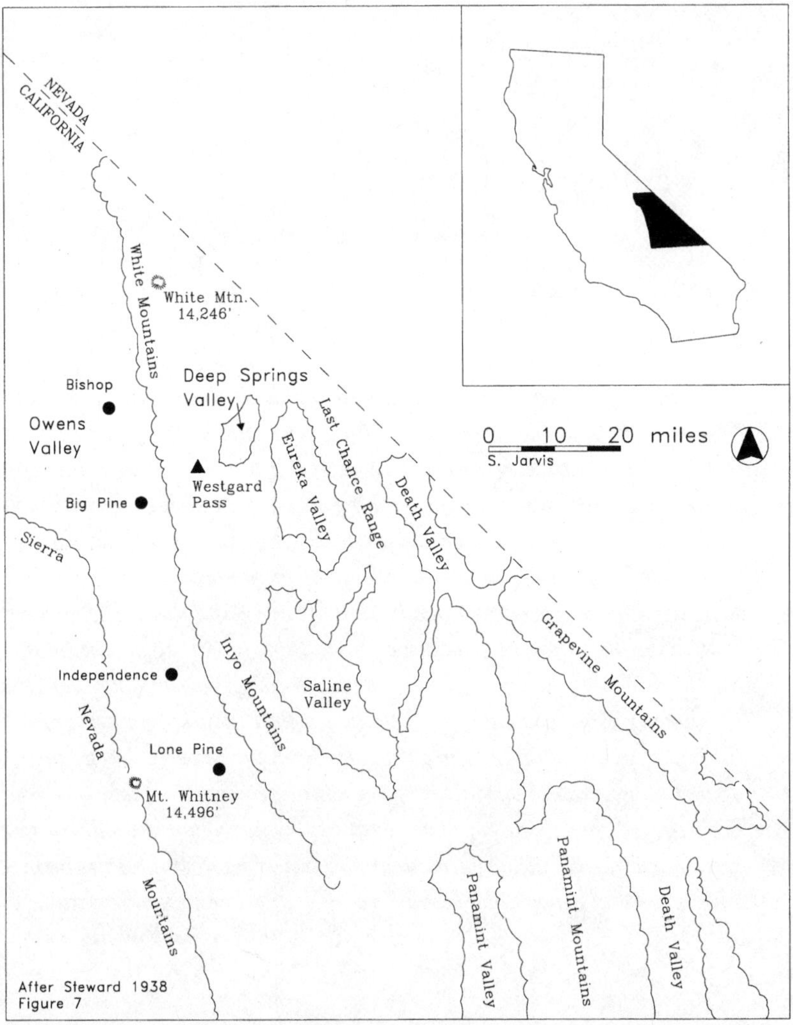

Figure 1.1 Owens Valley and Deep Springs Valley, eastern California.

his childhood and adolescence, including some events that he himself considered defining moments in his life, although he appears never to have seen their specific connections with the content of his intellectual work. These events took place long before his first fieldwork in the Great Basin and before his graduate training at Berkeley, where his courses included several in geography. Many years afterward, when Marvin Harris suggested in print that the geographer Carl Sauer had greatly influenced Steward's work, Steward pointedly denied that Sauer—or even Alfred Kroeber—had influenced the direction of his thought (Harris 1968:662; JHS Boxes 1, 3, 1969). Certainly his most meaningful encounter with landscape and ecology began years before he knew those men, when he left the East at the age of 16 and traveled alone to Deep Springs Valley, near the Nevada border in California. He learned much there from his early and direct engagement with the land, lessons that books and formal study would only reinforce and complement.

As I will show, his first experience of the high desert shares certain parallels with ethnographic fieldwork. Like many a lone ethnographer, the young Julian Steward left behind all that was familiar, traveled thousands of miles by himself, and entered an entirely alien setting, one that bore no resemblance to the place where he had spent the previous years of life. Steward lived there for a prolonged period (1918–1921), had an experience of total immersion in a landscape and social setting that offered new sights and perspectives, and regarded it as pivotal and transforming. The three years that he spent in Deep Springs Valley, from the age of 16 to 19, profoundly influenced the direction of his later intellectual work as an anthropologist. It provided, first of all, an intimate knowledge of a particular landscape and ecology, one that would remain in his mind's eye and influence his thinking for the rest of his life. The intensity of that experience had no rival in the years that followed. The time that he spent afterward actually engaged in ethnographic fieldwork, primarily with the Northern Paiute and Western Shoshone, was surprisingly brief and appears rather pallid by comparison. The strong sense of place that pervades so much of Steward's writing has its roots in the life he led before entering anthropology.

Robert Murphy has suggested that the Northern Paiute and Shoshone acted as the "catalyst" for Steward's theory (Murphy 1977:6, interview 1989). Again shifting the emphasis, I want to show in some detail how the Great Basin, and one particular valley in the basin, provided the theory's crucible. In making this case, I am drawing on a variety of sources that create a consistent and richly textured picture of Steward's experiences at Deep Springs. These include Steward's own words, taken from his letters and unpublished writings; the memories of several people who knew him well, including fellow students at Deep Springs and Jane Cannon Steward, who first visited the valley with her husband in the 1930s; my own observations of the school and the valley and of other places where Steward lived, both in the East and in the West; and photographs taken by Steward during his student days there. The photographs come from an unidentified album that I found at Deep Springs College. I eventually came to think that the album had belonged to Steward, a supposition that Jane Steward confirmed when I showed her copies of the photographs.[1]

STEWARD'S LIFE: THE EARLY YEARS

Steward began life as an Easterner but soon became, in the words of his wife, a "passionate Westerner" (J. C. Steward, interview 1988). He was born in Washington, D.C., in 1902, the second child of Thomas G. and Grace Garriott Steward. Thomas Steward, then in his mid-40s, held degrees in engineering and law and had risen to the position of examiner-in-chief of the U.S. Patent Office. Grace Garriott Steward, who was in her early 30s, had worked briefly as a schoolteacher and then for six years as a federal employee in the Pension Office before her marriage. Both of their children, Julian and his sister Marion, would eventually have careers with the federal government themselves, he at the Smithsonian's Bureau of American Ethnology and Marion at a variety of agencies.[2]

The family moved several times during Steward's early childhood, leaving an apartment in the city for, eventually, a house in a quiet suburban neighborhood. By age 11, Steward lived on Macomb Street in Cleveland Park, among families of Washington's professional and upper-middle class. Later in life, Steward recalled his pleasure in exploring nearby woodlands and ravines, some of which lie within the boundaries of Washington's Rock Creek Park (J. C. Steward, interview 1988; Willey 1988:222). For several summers, he spent a few weeks at a camp on the Chesapeake Bay, away from the city. He was, in his own words, a "mediocre" student, despite having an avid interest in natural history (DSC 1961).

His warmest memories from those years centered on the time he spent outdoors, and perhaps not coincidentally, away from home. By the time Steward was 15, in 1917, his parents' marriage had deteriorated to a point evidently beyond repair. Grace Steward, remembered as an outgoing and deeply religious woman (she converted to Christian Science when her son was nine years old), had married a man with a very different temperament and very different interests in life. Their marital problems led Thomas Steward to withdraw slowly from family life (J. C. Steward, interview 1988). He spent much of his time outside of work at the Cosmos Club, which John Wesley Powell had helped found in 1878 just before becoming the director of the Smithsonian's Bureau of Ethnology (later the Bureau of American Ethnology; see Stegner 1954:242). In 1917, the Cosmos Club's members included many men from Washington's intellectual elite, among them the secretary of the Smithsonian Institution, Charles D. Walcott.

Sometime during that year, perhaps at the point when she and her husband formally separated, Grace Steward learned about Deep Springs, a new college preparatory school for boys. Located in California, on the western edge of the Great Basin, Deep Springs charged no tuition, provided room and board, and awarded college scholarships to many of its students. Founded by a wealthy lawyer and businessman named L. L. Nunn, the school aimed to train a select number of young men—most from professionally prominent Anglo-Saxon families—for careers in public service. The financial benefits, as well as the school's location in the West, appealed greatly to Grace Steward at that juncture. Her impending divorce had introduced a strong element of financial insecurity into her life and evidently into her children's as well. Moreover, although born and reared in the Midwest and long a resident of the East, she was deeply drawn to the West. She urged her son to apply for admission to the school.

Steward wrote a letter of application in early January 1918, a few weeks before his sixteenth birthday (TA 1918). He mentioned Charles Walcott's son in his letter; both the son and Charles Walcott himself knew L. L. Nunn quite well. That connection, as well as Thomas Steward's professional position, may have led Nunn's associates to take note of the letter. One of them soon replied, asking for more information and promising an interview. Four months later, and even before the term had ended at his high school in Washington, D.C., Steward boarded a train and left the East for Deep Springs, where he had just been accepted (Steward 1918b). Marion, who had withdrawn from college after two years of study, soon followed her brother to the West; she transferred from her position as a clerk-typist in Washington, D.C., to a similar one with the War Department at Fort Mason in San Francisco. In late 1918, Grace Steward also moved to the West, having accepted a position that would prove to be short-lived as a government clerk at the Klamath Indian Reservation in southern Oregon. Thomas Steward remained in Washington, D.C. (Steward 1918a, 1918b).

Julian Steward's journey west coincided with what he saw as the disintegration of his family and the loss of his childhood home. With his mother, father, and sister scattered in three different and distant places, and himself in a fourth, he was on his own at the age of 16. More than 35 years later, remembering that time, he wrote, "[I] left my home and family to which I was never to return." Steward called the ensuing years at Deep Springs "the turning point" in his life, and retained vivid memories of the years he spent there (JHS Box 6, 1954a, 1954b). He would return to Deep Springs—both the school and the valley—again and again as an adult. Near the end of his life, after decades spent living in the East and Midwest, he would confess to feeling "terribly homesick" whenever he saw pictures of the desert and the Sierra Nevada (JHS Box 3, 1969).

UNIMAGINED LANDSCAPES

Julian Steward arrived in the high desert of eastern California in late May 1918. Disembarking from a train in Owens Valley, California, he found himself on the western border of the Great Basin, in an arid valley enclosed on two sides by towering mountains. To the west stand the snow-swept peaks of the Sierra Nevada, and to the east the massive White Mountains. At their highest points they rise two vertical miles above the valley floor. He would come to know these ranges well over the next three years, a result of many mountaineering adventures with friends from Deep Springs during holidays. Trips to town to pick up supplies, either in Big Pine or in Bishop, would take him back to Owens Valley again and again, as would hiking excursions into the eastern Sierra. In his later fieldwork with the valley's Northern Paiute Indians, first as a graduate student in the mid-1920s and again in the mid-1930s, he entered familiar territory and renewed contacts that spanned many years.

On the day of his arrival in 1918, he did not linger in Owens Valley. The school had sent a vehicle to pick him up, and the return trip of some 30 miles took him into the White Mountains and through Westgard Pass, at an elevation of more than 7,000 feet, then down into Deep Springs Valley. The dirt road deteriorated to little more than ruts in the sand once he and the driver left the mountains. As they descended 2,000 feet into the valley, Steward caught his first glimpse of what would be his home for the next three years. The valley lay spread out before him, nearly 50 square miles of high desert, a vast sea of sagebrush bordered by mountains and framed by an intensely blue sky. In this arid and open landscape, the eye can see for miles, even to the far end of the valley where cottonwood trees and a few low buildings stand in a cluster. That was the school, which included a working ranch.

L. L. Nunn had previously set up his experimental school on a farm in the East, on the margins of Tidewater, Virginia, a notably flat, forested, and well-watered area. With its broad tidal rivers and bordering creeks and marshlands, the setting would have seemed familiar to Steward from his summers at camp along the nearby Chesapeake Bay, but it could not have differed more from Deep Springs Valley. As it happened, various problems plagued the school in its Virginia location, including the proximity to towns, and L. L. Nunn quickly ordered it closed (Noon 1917).

Nunn relocated it 3,000 miles to the west, having bought an isolated ranch for that purpose. During the first academic year, in 1917–1918, 10 students worked alongside stonemasons to construct the school's few buildings (Reich 1974:1, interview 1989). When Steward arrived in 1918, he found the work still under way. L. L. Nunn quickly assigned the new arrival to assist the elec-

Figure 1.2 The ranch at Deep Springs, ca. 1918.

trician, and when the electrician abruptly quit, the student-assistant had to finish the job. To Steward's own surprise, he did so successfully (J. C. Steward, interview 1988).

Nunn believed in learning by doing, and he considered the best form of education to be a mix of manual and intellectual work carried out at a distance from the distractions of town life. Some of his writings suggest a biblical reverence for the desert, which he had chosen as the new setting for his school. The desert, he said, had "a voice" that great leaders from Moses on had sought and heard. "You can hear it if you listen," he wrote, "but you cannot hear it while in the midst of uproar and strife for material things" (Nunn ca. 1925). The school's location, in a remote desert valley, insured uninterrupted study and work.

Together with his fellow students, Steward spent weekday mornings in classes following a standard curriculum. During his three years at the school, he studied English, history, mathematics, biology, and languages (Steward 1920, 1921a). He also had a course in geology, one that must have gained meaning not only from field trips with the class but from the everyday proximity of the landforms they studied. Whenever he stepped outside the classroom, he saw an open valley ringed by nearby mountains, not the city sidewalks and schoolyard of his Washington, D.C., childhood. Living on the land, as students did at the ranch, also gave an immediacy to anything he learned about the land in class or in books.

His most memorable learning experiences took place outside school walls, while he was working outdoors in the afternoons or during his free time on the weekends. Photographs taken by Steward during these years document

Figure 1.3 Julian Steward (right) branding calves, ca. 1919.

what he saw and what he thought significant enough to record on film. He took dozens of pictures of ranch life, as well as many photographs of its setting: the open and windswept desert, the mountains, the plants and animals new to him. The valley's wildlife included antelope, badgers, coyotes, mountain lions, bighorn sheep, rattlesnakes, gopher snakes, deer, and rabbits, only the last two familiar from the East. He photographed a gopher snake and a dead coyote as well as more accessible animals, especially the ranch's horses, cattle, and sheep. The sparse vegetation, predominantly sagebrush, also attracted his attention.

Steward learned much about the land by careful observation, as his photographs show. He learned perhaps even more through a kind of participant observation, as one who worked the land, cared for the livestock, and tended the ranch's irrigation system. He and the other students spent their afternoons doing a multitude of chores, all needed to keep the ranch running. His photographs document some of those tasks. They show the students rounding up cattle, branding calves, milking the dairy cows, and harvesting the hay. Steward and his fellow students also helped irrigate the fields, sometimes assisting Captain Harry, who served briefly as the ranch's "chief irrigator" (Breiseth and Edmonston 1987:163–164; Reich, interview 1989). Captain

Harry, who was part Shoshone and part Northern Paiute, lived at the ranch with his Northern Paiute wife, Mary, and their daughter and son-in-law. Steward's first contact with Indians was with this family.

Keeping the ranch's system of flood irrigation in working order preoccupied the students, including Steward. When he purchased the ranch, Nunn had bought the water rights to Wyman Creek, the source of most of the valley's fresh water. The creek, which was located some distance to the northeast, provided the water that made life possible at the ranch. The cattle drank the water; the corn and alfalfa, which sustained the cattle when other feed was scarce, grew in the valley only under irrigation; and the people who lived at the school and ranch, nearly all of the inhabitants of the valley at that time, needed the water for drinking, cooking, and washing.

The ranch's system of flood irrigation had certain peculiarities that the students remembered in vivid detail even many years after leaving Deep Springs. One of them, Harvey Mansfield, recalled that the water flowed down the creek bed to a small dam. There a portion of it was diverted into a "pressure box." The purpose of the box, a rectangular structure made of wood, was to allow sand and silt to settle; the clear water that left the pressure box entered a pipe that carried it to the school's few buildings. Water in the pipe, itself made of a thin metal, often froze during the winter months, interrupting the school's supply. As Harvey Mansfield remembered, the students then had to dig out sections of pipe, use a blowtorch to thaw the frozen water, and patch any holes they had made in the pipe (Breiseth and Edmonston 1987:332).

Cleaning the screens that kept the pipes from clogging was a daily task, whatever the season. Summer brought its own set of problems. Water from Wyman Creek that flowed to the ranch through irrigation ditches, rather than through pipes, was used for watering the cattle and irrigating the alfalfa fields. One of the students, Herbert Reich, recalled seeing a field covered with water, then glancing away, only to find minutes later that the water had disappeared and was spilling out of gopher holes in an adjacent field (Breiseth and Edmonston 1987:162; Reich, interview 1989).

The problem of water—coping with a limited supply, transporting it where needed, and controlling its use—was inescapable at Deep Springs. Every day offered another vivid lesson in how the scarcity of water and the use of water affected plants, animals, and people. The alfalfa fields, a brilliant green in late spring, had the look of an oasis in a desert of sagebrush and sand. Cattle left the valley for the lush pastures that bordered the upper reaches of Wyman Creek in summer, grazing and fattening there. The creek itself attracted all manner of wildlife as well. The students, most of them Easterners, quickly

Figure 1.4 Captain Harry (left), ca. 1918.

learned to carry along water whenever they left the ranch to work at a distance or to hike in the mountains. (Jane Steward [interview 1988] remembered that years later she and her husband spent some time calculating the weight of water and trying to determine how far people might range from their water source if they had to carry their own supply for drinking.)

The scarcity of water in that dry land affected how people lived and where they lived, where cattle ranged, and where crops grew. It clearly affected human activity as well as the distribution and abundance of wild plants and animals. How humans *used* the water, with the help of technology, also influenced all of these. For three years Steward saw this on a daily basis. He also learned from firsthand experience about ranching, farming, and living in an arid environment. Most days he worked for many hours outdoors, directly engaged with the ranch animals, fields, and water system.

Steward spent his free time outside as well, exploring the valley and the surrounding mountains, a rugged landscape where humans had made little mark. In contrast to the ranch and its immediate environs and to the East that he remembered, the landscape retained the look of wilderness. He photographed it again and again, capturing the wide sweep of the valley and the rugged mountains that enclosed it. One of his hikes, to the top of a mountain not far from the school, afforded a view of Eureka Valley, waterless and uninhabited—true desert wilderness. Steward lived, in other words, within view of a natural world that appeared untransformed by human effort. It provided a striking counterpoint to the ranch, which was a center of human technology and productive work.

Deep Springs Valley and the adjacent areas of the Great Basin, with their vertical landscapes, offered a view of the natural world that Steward had not seen in the coastal flatlands of his eastern childhood. Changes in elevation meant changes in plant life, and these were clearly visible from the valley floors, at 4,000 to 5,000 feet, where sagebrush predominates. Pinyon pines, once a major food source for the Indians, grew at 6,500 feet, along with juniper. Other trees and plants grew at the upper reaches, with timberline at about 11,000 feet (Schoenherr 1992:12, 167, 187ff.).

Jane Steward recalled her husband's claim that he had climbed all of the peaks in the surrounding mountains during his student days at Deep Springs. His photographs testify to hiking trips in the White Mountains. Other trips probably took him into the Inyo Mountains, Eureka Valley, and perhaps the Panamint Range near Death Valley; he also climbed many peaks in the eastern Sierra Nevada. As it happens, this region encompasses one of the world's most compact areas of variation in climate and plant geography. Death Valley, the lowest point in North America at 282 feet below sea level, is also one of the hottest places on earth. Not far to the west stands Mount Whitney, at 14,496 feet the highest point in the contiguous United States. In ecological terms, a hike from one point to the other can be compared to a trip from Mexico to the Arctic Circle—but fewer than 90 (direct) miles, not thousands, separate the blistering heat of Death Valley and the frozen peak of Mount Whitney (Schoenherr 1992:11–14).

Given his bent as a naturalist, Steward's excursions into the high desert and mountains of eastern California must have taught him much about ecology, years before he gave serious thought to the term and its application to the human world. From Captain Harry and his wife and family he may have learned something about the traditional subsistence practices of the Northern Paiute and Western Shoshone. Petroglyphs that he saw and photographed not far from the ranch attested to the Indians' long presence in the valley. Steward also collected arrowheads, and he probably saw fragments of pottery and flint scattered on the ground near some rock shelters by Wyman Creek. (As a graduate student, he later returned to Deep Springs Valley to study the potsherds and the petroglyphs; see Steward 1928b, 1929.)

During his student days at Deep Springs, he also photographed the remains of an abandoned mining settlement that stood about four miles from the ranch. White miners who had tried to exploit the mineral resources of the valley in the mid-nineteenth century had been replaced by white ranchers, who introduced grazing livestock. Throughout the Great Basin, as Steward (1970a:7 [1938]) would later note, the introduction of livestock always produced a change in ecology because the animals decimated the native plants that had nourished generations of people. By 1918, when he arrived at Deep Springs as a student, only remnants of the precontact past remained. Nearly everyone living in the valley at that point—the few Indians as well as the white students, teachers, and staff—depended on the ranch for their water and for much or all of their food supply.

Thus, the valley offered very visible evidence about how new technologies, ranging from irrigation systems to automobiles, brought with them changes in settlement pattern and social organization—in other words, cultural change. Equally important for his future theory of cultural ecology was the lesson, reinforced each day that he worked on the ranch, about the significance of technology (the irrigation system) and its relationship to the organization of labor (the students who cooperated to keep it in working order) and to limited environmental resource (in this case water). The ranch existed in the same environment where Indians had lived a very different way of life, based on other technologies and a different sort of social organization.

When Steward left Deep Springs Valley in 1921 to attend college, he carried with him much of the "raw data" that would later help him develop his theoretical perspective. He never seems to have made a conscious and specific connection between those experiences and his theory. Throughout his life, however, he did emphasize the intellectual importance of his years at Deep Springs. Both in letters and in his conversations with several people who were close to him, he credited the experience with bringing about an "intellectual awakening." At Deep Springs, he said, he had learned that he could think and that he could think for himself (Steward 1954b, 1961; J. C. Steward, interview 1988).

AFTER DEEP SPRINGS

In late June 1921, after cooperating with several other students to harvest the hay, Steward and three of his friends left Deep Springs Valley for San Francisco. Eschewing travel by train or automobile, they chose to walk. Their overland trek, with two burros in tow to carry their gear, took them across the Sierra Nevada and through Yosemite National Park. After 15 days and more than 200 miles, they reached San Francisco (Steward 1921b). In the fall, at age 19, Steward entered the University of California, Berkeley.

In the spring of 1922, Steward took his first course in anthropology, "General Anthropology: Origin and Development of Civilization." Many years later Steward remembered that it had been taught by Alfred Kroeber, Robert Lowie, and Edward Gifford, curator of the university's Museum of Anthropology. The university catalog, which listed only Kroeber as the instructor, described the course as covering the "source and growth of institutions, arts, customs, industries, language, and religion" (Steward 1925, 1954b).

At the end of the semester, having been awarded a scholarship by Telluride Association, another of L. L. Nunn's educational ventures, he transferred to Cornell University in Ithaca, New York. There he joined many of his former classmates from Deep Springs. Cornell offered no courses in anthropology, a fact that did not seem to trouble Steward. After considering several majors, including law, he chose geology and zoology, "to satisfy my scientific interests," he later wrote (JHS Box 6, ca. 1954; TA Steward to F. C. Noon, 1922). He graduated in 1925 with a bachelor's degree (Steward 1921b; UCMDA Box 43, 1925).

Unlike Deep Springs, Cornell's location in upstate New York made little lasting impression upon Steward. Immersed in his studies and social life at Telluride House, a rather lavish residence that L. L. Nunn had had built for his students, he evidently lived a very indoor life during his three years there. Surrounded by the broad green lawns and winding roadways of campus, Telluride House represented a different sort of educational experience than Deep Springs. Also, the area around Ithaca could scarcely differ more from the arid high desert of eastern California. Known for its overcast skies and surrounded by cascading streams and lakes, Ithaca and the environs are well watered and profusely vegetated. Those very differences may have reinforced what Steward had observed about the arid landscape around Deep Springs.

Steward had ample opportunity to witness the contrasts between East and West during that period in his life. Between 1918, when he left Washington, D.C., and 1925, when he graduated from Cornell and returned to California, Steward made five overland trips across the United States during summer months, usually traveling by train—this at a time when many people never traveled far from their region of origin (TA miscellaneous correspondence, 1918–1925). Each trip began and ended in two radically different landscapes: the luxuriantly green woodlands of the East and the arid, open reaches of the West.

Returning to California in 1925, Steward entered Berkeley's graduate program in anthropology. He had applied only to Berkeley, a public institution, because its tuition was far lower than that of Columbia and the few other private universities that offered graduate study in anthropology. Despite his social origins in Washington's professional class, Steward spent a decade, from the young age of 16 to 26, patching together a living. Until he found full-time employment in 1928, he depended on fellowships, loans from a private benefactor and from the Telluride Association, and some meager income that he earned. Letters from this period show that subsistence was a pressing issue in his personal life, soon to emerge as an intellectual issue in his research. Against a backdrop of the era's general prosperity, supporting himself and helping his mother financially remained a chronic worry for him in the 1920s.

Steward undertook field research in archaeology and ethnography during several summers in the mid-1920s. Like other students of Kroeber and Lowie, he received no training in field methods, perhaps a legacy of their own training with Franz Boas. Almost 30 years later, Steward remembered his first efforts at archaeology as "improvised" and "unbelievably bad" (Steward 1954b). When he left Berkeley in 1928 to accept a position at the University of Michigan, he found himself living in the forested upper Midwest for two years. Like upstate New York, the place itself made no lasting impression on him. He returned briefly to Berkeley in 1929 to defend his dissertation, one based on library research, as was common at the time.

Steward returned to the West in 1930 to marry an educational psychologist named Dorothy Nyswander who taught at the University of Utah. During the three years of their married life, Steward taught there as well. He also worked at archaeological sites throughout Utah (see Janetski, chapter 2) and briefly with Uintah Ute Indians; the latter included a collaborative project with his wife (Nyswander, interview 1996; UCMDA Box 43, 1931). After separating from Dorothy Nyswander in 1933, he resigned from the University of Utah but remained in the West. He returned to California, newly married to Jane Cannon Steward, whom he had met in Utah, and held a temporary teaching position at Berkeley in 1934. During those Depression years, new positions in anthropology had dwindled to a near-vanishing point.

In the spring of 1935, still without regular employment, he began field research in the Great Basin under the auspices of Kroeber's "Culture Element Distribution" survey (see Myers, chapter 9). That work would result in several publications, most notably *Basin-Plateau Aboriginal Sociopolitical Groups,* a book that drew on places and people Steward had known for many years. His field research began in the high desert of eastern California, and Captain Harry's widow, Mary, served as one of his informants in Owens Valley (JJJS 1934–1936; J. C. Steward, interview 1988). Some of the ideas that Steward pursued had had a long gestation. Seven years earlier, as a graduate student, he had returned to Owens Valley during the summer for fieldwork. Steward spent several weeks mapping Northern Paiute settlements, hunting territories, and seasonal camps; studying the distribution of plants; and investigating irrigation practices of the Indians (UCMDA Box 43, 1928). Also, seven years before that, in 1921, he had passed through Owens Valley on his way to the Pacific Coast and college, after having spent three transforming years in an adjacent high desert valley. Owens Valley, still irrigated and green in 1921, would revert to high desert during the next decade, with most of its water carried away by the Los Angeles aqueduct (Kahrl 1982). Steward had witnessed the dramatic transformation of Owens Valley during the 1920s and 1930s; it undoubtedly reinforced what he had learned years earlier at Deep Springs. During his time as a student there he had come to know a once-alien landscape very well. He had seen the effects of water scarcity on the land; observed how a particular technology, irrigation, led to changes in land-use and settlement patterns in the valley; and worked collectively with others, managing and using a variety of resources, from water to crops to cattle, to help sustain life on the ranch.

THE LEGACY OF DEEP SPRINGS

For some 50 years after Steward left Deep Springs, until the end of his life, his memories of the place remained vivid and clear, renewed by occasional visits. These memories evidently helped guide his thoughts as he set about constructing a theoretical perspective, one that would help him to make sense of his first observations in the high desert. His later research took him to all corners of the Great Basin during five months in 1935 and again in 1936. Still later, he traveled in the Andes and visited the Gran Chaco in South America, supervised a research project in Puerto Rico (Lauria-Perricelli 1989), and saw other parts of the world. However, with one exception, these later travels did not involve ethnographic fieldwork. Moreover, his research in the Great Basin during 1935 and 1936 was based largely on formal interviews with the aim of reconstructing a way of life that had almost vanished. Hence, he scarcely used participant observation and learned rather little about the daily social lives of the Shoshone and Northern Paiute men and women he interviewed. He appears to have spent as much time, and perhaps more, traveling from place to place and observing the land as he did interviewing people about how to wrest a living from it (JJJS 1934–1936; J. C. Steward, interview 1988).

In summary, Deep Springs—the place (the valley) *and* the social setting (the school and ranch)—constituted the laboratory of Steward's cultural ecology. The three years he lived there offered an experience with many parallels to ethnographic fieldwork as it came to be practiced after Steward was trained at Berkeley. He entered an entirely alien setting and stayed there for a prolonged period of time; he learned to live in the new setting and, by taking part in daily life over the course of years, he developed a deep familiarity and an intimacy with the people, plants and animals, and land around him.

Returning home to the East to attend Cornell, like so many ethnographers returning from fieldwork, Steward may have found that the once-familiar home setting now assumed greater salience, providing vivid contrasts between "here" and the remembered "there." Most ethnographers would note cultural contrasts above all. To the young Julian Steward, however, who had just spent three years living with peers who shared his social background, the differences between "here" and "there" probably pertained more to landscape and other features of the natural world. At Cornell, he chose to study geology and zoology, which undoubtedly helped him to see the contrasts between the landscapes of East and West in a systematic way.

His ethnographic research between 1927 and 1936, which was based largely on formal interviews, was brief. His work in 1927 and 1928 with Northern Paiute Indians in Owens Valley took him back to familiar territory. But in many respects, the time he spent in ethnographic research lacked the intensity and depth of his experience in Deep Springs Valley during his student days. His own comments, in letters and in conversations with each of his wives, suggest that the Deep Springs years had no parallel in his adult life (Dorothy Nyswander, interview 1996; J. C. Steward, interview 1988; Steward 1954a, 1954b).

Like many other anthropologists, Steward was indelibly marked by his first field experience. However, that experience predated his formal entry into anthropology and its focus was more environmental than cultural. It involved an encounter with a profoundly different landscape; an active engagement with various technologies, from irrigation to electricity, all vital to ranch life in that arid and isolated setting; and cooperative work with his peers, caring for the animals and tending the irrigation system that provided life-sustaining water for them all. That work was carried out—unremittingly, day by day and season by season, over the course of three years—in a place where intriguing traces of another way of life remained.

Those traces took various forms and perhaps provided Steward's first glimpse of material evidence about cultural change, the focus of so much of his later theoretical work as an anthropologist. Besides the potsherds and arrowheads that he picked up during his free time, he first saw petroglyphs in the valley. They drew his interest for many years (see Steward 1929). He also saw living evidence of another way of life, in the persons of Captain Harry and his family. All of this offered a striking contrast to ranch life and especially to its technological and productive base. The surrounding landscape—nature nearly unmodified by culture, by human effort—also presented a highly visible counterpoint to the ranch, where technology and the labor of men had transformed the nearby desert.

These contrasts, as well as regional ones, clearly made a deep impression on the mind of the young Julian Steward. They influenced the direction of his research as an anthropologist and they resurfaced again and again in the monographs and papers that he wrote. Sidney Mintz, who studied with Steward at Columbia in the late 1940s, has noted, for example, that Steward stressed in his published work "the way environments are *made* into human landscapes" (Mintz 1979:18; emphasis in original). Moreover, Steward never treated water as a given (Mintz 1979:18).

I find no evidence in his unpublished writings that Steward ever saw any of the specific links I have identified here between his early years in the West and his theoretical perspective as an anthropologist. He thought of himself as a scientist and described the trajectory of his research in terms of a scientific quest. But the evidence of his life suggests to me that his own experiences, more than just a commitment to science, provided the source of his most distinctive ideas.

What Steward saw and experienced in Deep Springs Valley, in the *Anglo*-American West, found expression repeatedly in his later writings about American Indians and cultural ecology. Land, water, food, technology, and the work of men: these were to be enduring themes of his intellectual work. These were a legacy of the last years of his boyhood, of three defining years that he spent learning and working in California's high desert.

NOTES

1. I am grateful to the Virginia Foundation for the Humanities and Public Policy and the College of William and Mary for financial support of this project. Since I began research for a book about Julian Steward, many people have assisted me in my work at various archives and during visits to Deep Springs Valley and Berkeley. Although they are too numerous to

name here, I wish to thank them collectively for their help. My deepest gratitude is to the late Jane Cannon Steward and Dorothy B. Nyswander for their generosity and patience. Steward's academic records (DSC) were used with the permission of Jane C. Steward.

2. I have used a variety of sources to reconstruct the early years of Steward's life and to trace the work histories of his mother, father, and sister. These include census records; city directories for Washington, D.C., and San Francisco; records of the Cosmos Club and of the First Church of Christ, Scientist; and federal employee records.

2

Julian Steward and Utah Archaeology

Joel C. Janetski

Steward's influence on archaeological research in Utah was greatest following the 1938 publication of his Basin-Plateau Aboriginal Sociopolitical Groups. *What is not generally known is that Steward held a faculty position at the University of Utah from 1930 to 1933. During that brief period, and for the only time during his professional career, Steward's field focus was archaeology. Several publications resulted from his research. However, Steward's most lasting legacy for archaeology, the theory of cultural ecology, is not readily apparent in these early, mostly descriptive reports. But in some ways, these reports structured archaeological inquiry into Utah's distant past for several decades thereafter. Most important was his construction of a variant model for the Northern Periphery based on material trait distributions. Joel Janetski reevaluates this model in light of the last 60 years of archaeological research and theorizing.*

Julian H. Steward left an enduring legacy in anthropology. His pioneering contributions in the revival of evolutionary thought and his cultural ecological approach have secured his place in history (see Harris 1968; Willey and Sabloff 1993). The bulk of Steward's anthropological research was ethnological, but his interests and experiences were certainly much broader. Robert Murphy (1977:3) describes Steward as being "as much an archaeologist as cultural anthropologist" early in his career and notes that fully one-third of his publications from 1927 to 1939 were in archaeology. However, Steward spent only a small portion of his professional life doing archaeology. As a young man still in graduate school, he worked with William Duncan Strong in the Dalles of the Columbia River (Manners 1973), but much of his archaeological field experience came while he was at the University of Utah in the early 1930s. This paper reviews Steward's fieldwork and publications for that period and discusses the impact these have had on Utah archaeology.

STEWARD'S UTAH PERIOD

Julian Steward's interest in the Great Basin began at age 16 when he traveled from his home in Washington, D.C., to the Deep Springs Preparatory School near Owens Valley. Here, according to Robert F. Murphy (1977:2), he formed a lasting attachment to the West and was first introduced to the Paiute and Shoshone people whom he later studied in depth. Steward began his university career at the University of California, Berkeley, but transferred to Cornell University, where he completed his undergraduate work. He returned to Berkeley for graduate study under Alfred L. Kroeber and Robert H. Lowie (both of whom had a demonstrated interest in the Great Basin) and earned his Ph.D. in 1929. Steward spent two years at the University of Michigan (1928–1929), where he preceded fellow evolutionist Leslie A. White.

In 1930 Steward took a position at the University of Utah. His appointment included a mandate to initiate an archaeological research program in the state, which he lost no time in doing. Over the next three years (1930–1933), he excavated numerous "Puebloan" mounds and several caves, spent time exploring the Glen Canyon area, and documented numerous "Anasazi" sites east of Kanab. With the exception of the cave excavations, Steward's choice of fieldwork locations largely mirrored that of Neil Judd; between 1915 and 1920, Judd also dug in mounds along the Wasatch Front and investigated Anasazi sites near Kanab and on the Arizona Strip (Judd 1926). Judd's influence is clear in Steward's publications: Both men were interested in the relationship between the many mounds in central Utah and the "Anasazi" remains to the south. Steward followed Judd's pioneering work by maintaining a Puebloan perspective in his reports; however, these went beyond those produced by Judd in a number of ways, as will be noted in this chapter.

Archaeological Fieldwork in Utah

Steward did his archaeological fieldwork from 1930 until 1932. Cave excavations were interspersed with research at mound sites and trips to the south. Table 2.1 provides a chronology of what was a very busy research schedule.

In his publication *Pueblo Material Culture in Western Utah* (Steward 1936a), Steward states that the article presents data on research carried out between 1930 and 1933, but I can find no documentation of fieldwork being done in 1933. Because he had already accumulated abundant data, it appears that he decided to take a season to write up the findings. In fact, two articles came

TABLE 2.1. JULIAN STEWARD'S ARCHAEOLOGICAL FIELDWORK IN UTAH BETWEEN 1930 AND 1933

Year	*Places Worked*
1930	1. Excavated caves around the Great Salt Lake 2. Sevier Desert; brief trip to Grantsville mounds (fall) 3. Excavated mounds at Kanosh (probably in winter of 1930–1931 because photos of houses are snow covered and article on Kanosh came out in 1931; Figure 2.1 (Steward 1931)
1931	1. Excavated mounds near Grantsville (two weeks in the summer) 2. Excavated mounds at Provo 3. Excavations in the Uintah Basin 4. More excavation of caves around the Great Salt Lake
1932	1. Survey of Johnson's Canyon and the lower Paria river 2. Glen Canyon boat trip and survey 3. Brief trip to Grantsville mounds 4. Excavation of mounds at Willard (spring and summer)
1933	No fieldwork

out in 1933, one essentially descriptive (Steward 1933a), the other more synthetic (Steward 1933b).

MOUND RESEARCH

As noted, Steward's mound research focused on relationships between the occupants of the mounds and the Puebloan societies of the Southwest. He discussed architecture and portable material culture to resolve this issue. During the course of this research, he excavated at Willard (near Ogden), Grantsville, Provo, Kanosh, Sevier Lake, and in the Uintah Basin. In all of these places, Steward found what are now considered to be classic Fremont houses, mostly rectangular pit structures, as well as adobe-walled houses (Table 2.2). The most interesting architecture described was found in Mound 5 at Kanosh, which, according to Steward, was "nearer to being a communal dwelling than any of the small houses north of Kanosh" (Steward 1933b:21; Figure 2.1). The structures consisted of an adobe-walled house with a fire hearth and at least nine adobe-walled rooms without hearths, all arranged neatly in a "court."

Steward primarily presented details on his mound research in two publications: *Early Inhabitants of Western Utah: I. Mounds and House Types* (Steward

Table 2.2. Findings of Steward's Mound Research

Locale	*Mound/Site*	*Number of Houses*	*Other Finds*
Willard	Mound 1	one pit lodge	three caches
	Mound 2	none	one large cache, burial
	Mound 3	none	two caches
	Mound 4	two superimposed houses: one pit lodge, one adobe-walled house on top	
Grantsville	House 1	one house	burial
	House 2	square pithouse	
	Site 3	square pithouse	burial in corner
	Site 4	none	cache of charred corn in a pit
	Site 5	square house	
	House 6	house present, but no details	nine crushed pots in one corner
	House 7	square pithouse	burned human bone on floor; two subfloor caches of painted bowls
	House 8	circular pit structure; "kiva"(?)	
	House 9	square house	
Provo	Mound 1	rectangular pithouse, kivalike	
	Mound 2	two rectangular adobe-walled rooms	
	Benson Mound	none identified	burial
	Rollins Mound	none	Promontory pottery

TABLE 2.2. FINDINGS OF STEWARD'S MOUND RESEARCH, CONT'D

Locale	*Mound/Site*	*Number of Houses*	*Other Finds*
Kanosh	Mounds 1–4	two rooms in each, rectangular, adobe-walled	stone hatch covers; brief occupation
	Mound 5	multiple surface houses making a court, "communal"(?) dwelling	exterior rimmed hearth in court area
	Site/Mound 6	two "kivas," pithouses	no mounds; roofed tunnel
Sevier Lake	Site 1	none	pottery
	Site 2	none	campsites, sherds
	Site 3	none	sherds, painted ware
	Site 4	house, pit lodge	pottery
Uintah Basin	Mound 1	rectangular pithouse	
	Mound 2	disintegrated	
	Mound 3	rectangular, shallow pithouse	
	Rock Wall House	masonry, against cliff	fireplace present

Figure 2.1 Excavating adobe-walled houses at Kanosh, Utah, winter of 1931 (University Archives, University of Illinois Urbana-Champaign).

1933b) and *Pueblo Material Culture in Western Utah* (Steward 1936a). Steward made it clear in the introduction of *Early Inhabitants* that he intended to write a second part. In fact, in the introduction he alludes to a section in the table of contents that was supposed to list "remaining topics" (presumably material culture; Steward 1933b:5), but that in fact does not appear in the table of contents. The second part never appeared in the University of Utah Bulletin; instead the material culture article came out in 1936 in the University of New Mexico Bulletin.

Always one to state objectives clearly, Steward presented the goal of his mound excavations in the introduction to *Early Inhabitants:* "The purpose of this paper is to place on record information relative to the early Pueblo cultures of western and northwestern Utah, i.e., of the Great Salt Lake and Sevier Desert regions" (Steward 1933b:5). Certainly, this was a very descriptive goal. However, in the conclusions of *Pueblo Material Culture* he spent several pages pondering the relationship between the builders of the mound structures in western Utah and the Anasazi and the fate of the farmers of the Northern Periphery. In an almost Childe-like culture-history fashion (see Childe 1951), Steward outlined the fate of the Puebloan culture and the relationship between these farmers and the subsequent Promontory and ethnographic Shoshonean culture in terms of diffusion, migration, "hostile invaders," and abandonment and buttressed his argument with telling traits such as ceramics, figurines, metates, and diet. This historic narrative anticipates a somewhat more detailed, empirically based, culture-history scenario as a consequence of his cave research (see below).

Steward's Puebloan view of the farming sites north of the Colorado and Virgin Rivers had been held for a long time. It began at least as early as Edward Palmer, who dug in mounds in Payson in 1876 and concluded that the occupants were related to the "Pueblo tribe" (Palmer 1876). As noted, Judd (1926) also held this perspective when Steward arrived in Utah. This influence is most evident in Steward's work at Kanosh, where he found both pithouses and surface, adobe-walled granaries. Steward concluded that the former were kivas and the latter were houses, which he labeled the "Kanosh type," as opposed to the pit lodges found to the north at Willard and Grantsville. Ever cautious, Steward maintained that the Wasatch Front farmers possessed "some traits in common with the Basket Maker and Pueblo peoples of southern and southeastern Utah and some distinctive traits" (Steward 1936a: 57). The Puebloan view of the Fremont persisted with John Gillin, Steward's successor at the University of Utah, and others into the 1950s (see Rudy 1953).

Great Salt Lake Caves: The Promontory Culture

In 1930 and 1931 Steward completely excavated two large caves on Promontory Point (Promontory 1 and 2) on the north shore of the Great Salt Lake and did extensive testing at Black Rock Cave on the south shore (Figure 2.2). Complete excavations (at least of upper levels) were considered necessary because "amateur enthusiasm" was so great that Steward doubted that either would survive another year (Steward 1937a:3). He examined at least eight other cave sites in more cursory fashion. These caves were the first in the state to be examined by a professional archaeologist. Steward's purpose was "discovering ancient cultures which could be dated by reference to the chronology of the [Great Salt] lake," which is a very different goal from that purported for the mound research, but still very much focused on history. Steward excavated these caves by levels identified on the stratigraphic profile accompanying his report (Steward 1937a:9).

The findings in the Promontory caves, especially Cave 1, were most significant for the recovery and definition of a distinctive kind of pottery that Steward found in the upper levels of all the caves examined. Steward labeled the ceramics Promontory ware and described it in some detail: "This pottery is distinguished by the general crudeness and blackness of its finish, its coarse white temper, its lack of painted decoration, the use of 'fingernail,' incised, and punched decoration on olla exteriors, thickened and decorated lips, and the great preponderance of soot-encrusted olla sherds" (Steward 1937a:3).

Figure 2.2 Excavation crew at Promontory Cave (University Archives, University of Illinois Urbana-Champaign).

Steward documented the association of this pottery with other diagnostic artifacts: side-notched arrow points and distinctive, pucker-toed moccasins, some decorated with porcupine quills on the gusset (Steward 1937a:122). Relying on these and a number of other finds, Steward defined the Promontory culture, which he concluded was the most recent of the archaeological cultures in the region based on stratigraphic relationships. He extended the distribution of the Promontory culture south to the Provo area, where similar pottery had been found by himself and by Albert Reagan (1935). Despite the stratigraphic placement of the Promontory culture at the top of the cave deposits, Steward did not assume that it had been left by the ancestors of the Shoshone who had lived in the area. He stated that the Promontory culture "cannot be positively attributed to modern tribes of the region, for it possesses a curious combination of traits of northern and southern origin" (Steward 1937a:122).

Finally, Steward concluded that the Promontory culture was subsequent to the Puebloan, although no Puebloan occupations were recognized in the caves (for more on this topic see Contributions to Utah Archaeology below). Instead, the deposits underlying the Promontory contained few distinguishing materials other than quartzite dart points. Because this cultural debris did not resemble the well-known Basket Maker material recovered in the Four Corners area, Steward was unable to make a statement about temporal relationships.

Surveys in Southeastern Utah: Efforts to Find the Origin of the Northern Periphery

Steward took two trips into southern Utah and northern Arizona in 1932: one into the Johnson Canyon and lower Paria River country east of Kanab and the other by boat down the Colorado River between the mouth of the Dirty Devil and Lee's Ferry in northern Arizona. The purpose of these efforts was "to discover the place and manner in which those culture elements [of the Northern Periphery of the Puebloan culture area] . . . had become blended into a single culture and spread northward into the Northern Periphery" (Steward 1941a:281). In other words, Steward was looking for the origins of the builders of the mound structures in central and northern Utah, a quest he considered the "outstanding problem" of the Northern Periphery. Field efforts were focused on surveys rather than excavations, although he did do some excavating.

The Johnson Canyon–Paria River work was considerably more productive than the Glen Canyon research. The latter was more of a junket headed up by Charles Kelly (Figure 2.3), although Steward carefully collected data during the trip. The result of this fieldwork was a highly detailed report of 170 sites visited: 142 in the Johnson Canyon–Paria River area and 28 along the Colorado River. Included in the report are regional maps with sites plotted, detailed individual site maps, quantities of ceramics types (which Steward named and defined) by site, drawings of artifacts, documentation of rock art, details of architectural masonry, room dimensions, and measurements of corn cobs and counts of rows of kernels.

Steward's research in southern Utah was a settlement study, the first in the state. Based on estimates of site numbers, sizes, and ages, he argued for demographic change and settlement shifts from Basket Maker through Puebloan times. Using architecture and ceramics for temporal placement, Steward calculated the numbers of sites from early and late and concluded that "a marked population increase is indicated, a doubling at least" (Steward 1941a:353). Other observations are more explicitly ecological. He noted that early sites in the uplands may be better positioned for hunting, whereas later sites (which were "no doubt . . . coupled with increasing importance of horticulture") are located in canyon bottoms close to arable land (Steward 1941a:354).

Steward's conclusions reflect the essentially historic question posed at the outset: Was this region the place of origin for the Northern Periphery culture? His answer was negative: "The cultural inventory of southern Utah does not

Figure 2.3 Julian Steward (far left) and crew on the Colorado River, 1932 (Utah State Historical Society collections, gift of Charles Kelly).

correspond with that of the Northern Periphery" (Steward 1941a:355). Nor was there evidence for much contact between the two areas. An important consequence of this research is the contribution it made to Steward's "Ecological Aspects of Southwestern Society" (1937f), a work that Murphy (1977:5) calls "path-breaking" in that Steward argued for an integration of ethnography and archaeology.

CONTRIBUTIONS TO UTAH ARCHAEOLOGY: CULTURE-HISTORY AND FREMONT-VARIANT MODELS

In the introduction to *Evolution and Ecology* (J. C. Steward and Murphy 1977), Robert Murphy passes quickly over Steward's Utah archaeological work: "[Steward] did some cave archaeology in northern Utah, but most of his efforts were directed toward the southwestern part of the state, an area into which the classical Anasazi variety of Puebloan culture had extended" (Murphy 1977:5). Murphy then moves to praise the insights of Steward's "Ecological Aspects of Southwestern Society" (1937f). Likewise, Manners (1973:889) treats the Utah period in a series of subordinate clauses: "[Steward] remained at Michigan until 1930 when he went to the University of Utah where he taught until 1933 and conducted considerable archaeological research in Puebloid cultures."

From the perspective of scholars of Utah archaeology, these comments require some minor clarification. Both Murphy and Manners, for example, sweep the mound and Anasazi research into the same Puebloan pile. As is clear from the above discussions, mound sites along the Wasatch Front were usually labeled Puebloan until after the 1950s; therefore, the characterization of Steward's mound excavation as being on the "Puebloan culture" is understandable. However, these sites from Kanosh north would now be labeled "Fremont." In fact, Steward himself noted the departure of the southern Utah material from the cultural inventory of the Northern Periphery. Another minor point is that Steward's "Anasazi" research was done mostly in the Johnson's Canyon area east of Kanab in *southern* (Kayenta Anasazi region) rather than *southwestern* (Virgin region) Utah.

Steward maintained his southwestern perspective as he pondered historic issues such as the origins and demise of the Northern Periphery farmers as well as the cultural relationships of prefarming cultures whose remains were encountered in the Great Salt Lake caves. The reasons for this are simple: With its well-known sequence of basketmaker to cliff-dweller, the Southwest was the best frame of reference available for comparative study.

Like Palmer, Judd, and Alfred Kidder, Steward looked to the Southwest for the origins, analogues, and dating of the Fremont. The Puebloan perspective prevailed until the 1950s, when Rudy (1953), Wormington (1955), and Jennings (1956:104) reemphasized (following Morss 1931) the uniqueness of the Fremont pattern as distinct from the "Anasazi." (For more discussion on this point see Jennings 1978:155.) They rejected the notion of the Fremont as a culture peripheral to the Southwest and simply a "diluted" version of the "Anasazi." It should be pointed out, however, that Steward did not see the Northern Periphery as "diluted Anasazi" and, in fact, proposed that it be regarded as "a discrete, single subdivision of the Southwest" (Steward 1933b:3). It was for this reason that he refrained from assigning Pecos terms (Basket Maker III, Pueblo I, etc.) to Fremont sites.

Steward's most lasting contributions to Utah archaeology based on his *archaeological* research are in the realm of culture-history and Fremont-variant models.

Culture History: The Views of Steward and Others

In 1940 Steward published a synthesis of the culture history of the Intermontane area in which he characterized the archaeological remains for the Northern Periphery (and other regions) and guess-dated the timing. His Figure 30 is reproduced here (Figure 2.4; Steward 1940a:455). In essence, Steward proposed a sequence of hunter-gatherer to farming to hunter-gatherer that covered about the last 2,000 years. According to the scheme, Puebloan influence arrived sometime after A.D. 500 and persisted until shortly after A.D. 1000. In the northern portion of the Northern Periphery, Puebloan farmers coexisted briefly with an intrusive group of hunters, the Promontory culture. The Promontory "people" persisted for only a short time, after which they were replaced by the Ute and Shoshone. Steward's position on the temporal priority of the Puebloan over the Promontory culture is made a number of times. This position is based on Steward's own research and that of Albert Reagan at open sites in Utah Valley, where Promontory ceramics were found overlying "Puebloan" (Fremont) material culture. Steward concluded that the two cultures were not contemporary for very long and they clearly represented different peoples.

Over two decades after Steward's synthesis, Aikens (1966) challenged a portion of this reconstruction based on excavations around the Great Salt Lake. The recovery of both Promontory and ceramic types now labeled as Fremont (Steward's "Puebloan") in the same levels at Injun Creek near Ogden and at several other sites around the Great Salt Lake, combined with a radiocarbon date of "A.D. 1110 ± 75" on a Promontory moccasin from the Promontory caves, led Aikens to suggest that "Promontory does not in fact represent a cultural grouping distinct from the Fremont, [rather] the 'Promontory culture' is an artifact of archaeological misinterpretation of a few variant items of material culture from seasonal Fremont hunting camps" (Aikens 1966:74). Aikens's reconstruction of the local culture history stood for two decades.

However, researchers working at single-component sites near Brigham City (Simms and Heath 1990) and around Utah Lake (Janetski and Madsen 1990) in the 1980s dated Promontory-style pottery and associated material culture, such as the distinctive Desert side-notched arrow points, to A.D. 1400–1600. These data led Janetski (1994) to conclude that Steward was correct in placing Promontory subsequent to the Fremont. However, if Promontory pottery, Desert side-notched points, and pucker-toed moccasins are contemporary (as maintained by Steward), Aikens's date on the moccasin is troublesome. The discrepancy is lessened somewhat once the moccasin date is calibrated. Aikens does not give radiocarbon years, only an A.D. date. However, using 840 B.P. as the raw date, the calibration of the Promontory moccasin age is A.D. 1212 with a 2σ range of A.D. 1029–1278 (Stuiver and Reamer 1987). This overlaps with the 2σ range of dates from Heron Springs (A.D. 1255–1485), a site in Utah Valley with Promontory ceramics and Desert side-notched points (Janetski and Madsen 1990:242). These dates from Heron Springs also overlap with other Promontory sites in Utah Valley and the Brigham City site. This issue could perhaps be further clarified with additional dating of Promontory moccasins.

Thus, the most recent work on Fremont-Promontory relationships suggests that Steward's original reconstruction of the local culture-history se-

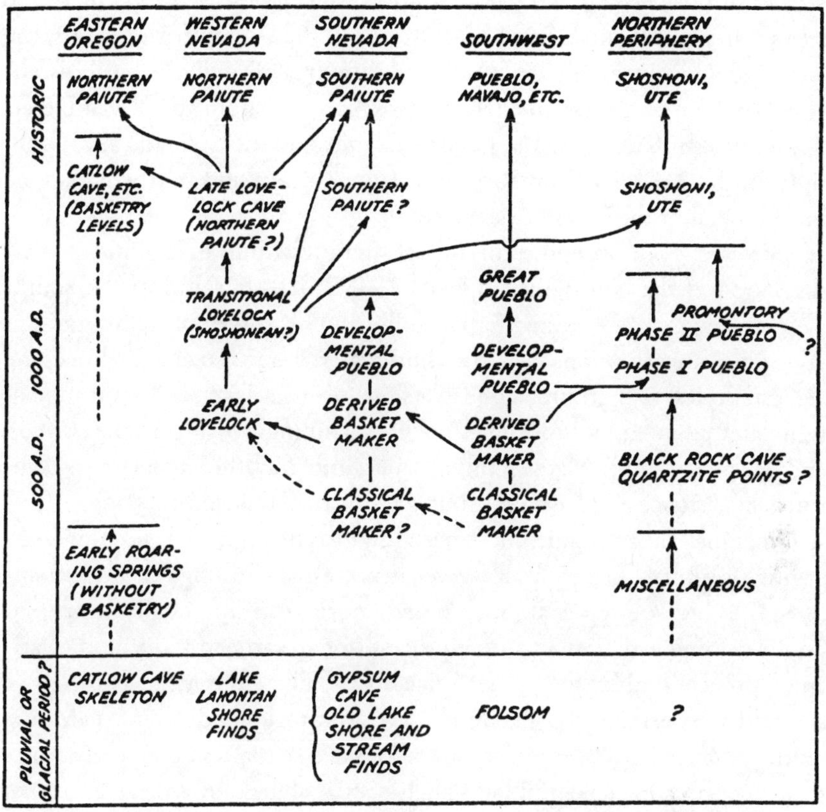

Figure 2.4 Cultural development in the Intermontane area (from Steward 1940a:55).

quence for the recent period still holds. Differences are primarily in dating and in the explanations of the changes that occurred; however, Steward's guess-dating of the sequence was amazingly close to the current view.

Fremont Regional-Variant Models

One of Steward's most enduring ideas was a regional-variant model for the Northern Periphery based on artifact differences. The history of variant models has been well reviewed by Marwitt (1970) and Anderson (1983); therefore, this treatment will be brief.

Variability in the Northern Periphery was recognized early on by Morss (1931), who contrasted his Fremont River culture with the "Puebloan" remains reported by Judd (1926) along the Wasatch Front. Steward formalized that variability by dividing the Northern Periphery into four regions (Steward 1933b): Area 1, the Colorado Plateau north of the Colorado River, which was further subdivided into Area 1A or the Fremont (following Morss 1931), the area south of the Uintah Basin, and Area 1B in the Uintah Basin; Area 2, the Great Salt Lake including Utah Valley and the area north in the northeastern Great Basin; Area 3, western Utah south of Area 2 including the Sevier Desert down to Cedar City; and Area 4, the region north of the Colorado River from the mouth of the San Juan River into Saint George and northern Arizona including all of the Virgin Anasazi country.

Steward (1933b) proposed his model after presenting an argument for the derivation of the Northern Periphery from BMIII–Pueblo I of the Southwest, a view he later rejected in part following his survey of Johnson's Canyon. The area definitions were based on material traits such as architecture, ceramic styles, and ground stone. Versions of material-trait variant models were later adopted by Wormington (1955), Jennings (1956), Ambler (1966), and Marwitt (1970). Madsen (1979) later simplified the model and substituted subsistence emphasis and strategies for material culture.

Regional-variant models have been useful as descriptive devices for comparative, regional discussions. However, in some cases, sorting sites into variant categories became the goal. Such overtly normative interests lend little to understanding variation or culture process (for an earlier critique of the variant approach see Hogan and Sebastian 1980). Therefore, variant models as an end have been largely abandoned. Fremont regional differences are currently more realistically perceived as unbounded spatial and temporal adjustments to shifts in ecological (and likely social) change (Madsen 1982, 1989; Simms 1986), although Madsen's (1979) emphasis on subsistence rather than artifact types remains. Interestingly, Steward explained the variation in the Northern Periphery in terms of differential diffusion, amalgamation, independent invention, and the adaptation of certain traits to a "diversified environment" (Steward 1933b:3). Such statements anticipate his ecological, multilinear evolutionary, and area-studies approach to understanding cultural systems and foreshadow the current explanations for Fremont variability mentioned above.

CONCLUSIONS

Steward's influence on Utah archaeology prevailed for nearly half a century. During that period, like Steward, Utah archaeologists dwelled mostly on culture history and taxonomy. Although the details of Steward's culture history have been modified with the advantage of absolute dating techniques, as have the shape and content of variant models (see Madsen 1989:14), the essentials of Steward's conclusions remain valid. A shift away from history toward subsistence and behavioral studies has changed the direction of Utah archaeology, although Steward's basic interests in culture history and regional variation remain important. In fact, discussions of internal Fremont variability continue to be a major focus of research in the state (Madsen 1982; Simms 1986, 1990). However, interest in historic connections between the "Anasazi" and the Fremont as espoused by Steward and Judd were largely abandoned by the 1960s (for an exception, see Gunnerson 1962). As a consequence, Fremont research has benefitted in the realms of understanding regional differences in material culture, architecture, and subsistence, but issues of internal and external trade, social and political organization, and ideology have lain dormant for several decades (for an exception see Gunnerson 1969). However, the 1990s has seen a resurgence in these interests (see Janetski et al. 1996).

Of course, Steward's primary contribution to archaeology was his concept of cultural ecology, a concept that matured during his ethnographic study of the Great Basin aboriginal societies (Steward 1970a [1938]). However, there are hints of ecological interests in the Utah archaeological research: Steward's settlement study of Johnson's Canyon and his suggestion that variation could be understood as a process of adaptation to differing environments clearly anticipate a cultural ecological approach for archaeology.

Steward's explicit emphasis on ecology in *Basin-Plateau Aboriginal Sociopolitical Groups* had a significant impact on the most enduring model in Great Basin prehistory, the Desert culture proposed by Jennings (1957). Jennings cites Steward regularly in the implications section of the Danger Cave report while laying out the argument for a "simple substratum" in the Great Basin and surrounding areas. Fowler (1977:22) has stated that Steward's data are so tightly interwoven with Jennings's that it is hard to separate them. She labels the Desert culture an integrative model because it combined both archaeological and ethnographic data for its arguments. Interestingly, such an integration is precisely what Steward proposed for archaeology in the 1940s (Murphy 1977:27). One would imagine that such thinking influenced Jennings (1957), although he does not cite the critical articles (e.g., Steward 1942; Steward and Setzler 1938) in the Danger Cave report.

The integration of ethnography and archaeology continues in Great Basin anthropology, and cultural ecology is still a primary theme in Utah archaeology. Recent volumes that include empirical data from Utah and that carry explicit ecological emphases include *Man and Environment in the Great Basin* (Madsen and O'Connell 1982) and *Wetland Adaptations in the Great Basin* (Janetski and Madsen 1990). Certainly, ecological studies have moved beyond Steward's descriptive approach (for a discussion of the limitations of descriptive ecology see Madsen and O'Connell 1982) to evolutionary and behavioral ecology (e.g., see Simms 1986). However, Kelly (1995:51) notes that behavioral ecology does not take the place of cultural ecology; it simply adds the concept of natural selection. Steward's legacy remains and will continue to influence the way archaeology is done in Utah for the foreseeable future.

3

Numic Pronghorn Exploitation: A Reassessment of Stewardian-Derived Models of Big-Game Hunting in the Great Basin

Brooke S. Arkush

In his 1938 Basin-Plateau Aboriginal Sociopolitical Groups, *Steward implied that successful communal pronghorn hunts typically resulted in significant reductions among local antelope populations and that a number of years were required to restore the herds before group hunts were once again feasible. It seems that Steward based this implication on descriptions of postcontact pronghorn drives in relatively marginal environmental settings (such as that provided by Howard Egan for the Deep Creek Gosiute) that were not representative of precontact pronghorn populations in more optimal locales. Brooke Arkush shows that archaeological, historic, and ethnographic data support the proposition that during late prehistoric and protohistoric times, many parts of the Great Basin supported relatively large pronghorn herds that would have allowed many Numic groups to practice annual drives without decimating local pronghorn populations.*

In his seminal publication concerning Basin-Plateau aboriginal groups, Julian Steward (1970a:33 [1938]) indicated that pronghorn antelope *(Antilocapra americana)* were among the most common big-game animals in the Great Basin and, as such, were the focus of important communal hunts throughout much of this vast region. Pronghorn are grassland- and shrubland-oriented artiodactyls that form large herds during late fall, winter, and early spring and then typically disperse into smaller groups during late spring and summer. Although lone hunters might obtain one or two animals by stalking or ambushing small herds, it was much more productive to conduct large-scale, communal hunts in which portions of larger herds were driven into elaborate rock and/or wood traps. These traps often consisted of two long, converging drift fences that funneled animals into large circular or ovate corrals (Figure 3.1).

Steward (1970a:33 [1938]) believed that successful pronghorn drives often resulted in substantial reductions of local animal populations and that a number of years might be required before herds regained sufficient numbers, thus making it feasible to drive them once again. However, there is good reason to doubt that such a scenario applies to most precontact Great Basin Native groups. A comprehensive review of ethnographic and ethnohistoric literature indicates that the "pronghorn-depletion" concept stems from one or two postcontact accounts of Gosiute Shoshone drives, when populations were no longer representative of prehistoric herds in productive, ungrazed valley and foothill settings.

The rapid influx of Euro-American emigrants and settlers throughout much of the Great Basin during the mid to late nineteenth century initiated the process of uncontrolled livestock grazing and nonnative ungulate competition (Christensen and Johnson 1964; Young et al. 1976), which significantly decreased the precontact pronghorn range carrying capacity (Tsukamoto 1983:10; Yoakum 1978:114). Establishment of agricultural fields and winter pasturage areas further reduced key pronghorn habitats, and fences restricted their movement between seasonally specific ranges (e.g. Harper 1986; Tsukamoto 1983). Increased human predation in the forms of market and sport hunting exerted additional pressures upon these animals, and by the late 1800s, pronghorn had been extirpated from various Great Basin valleys, especially those associated with mining districts in Nevada and eastern California (e.g., Wedertz 1978:172; Yoakum 1986:78). It appears that many researchers have largely ignored the devastating effects of early historic nonnative land-use practices upon Great Basin pronghorn populations when assessing the sizes of Late Archaic period (ca. A.D. 500–1750) and Protohistoric period (ca. A.D. 1750–1850) herds and the frequency of communal hunts during those times.

THE HISTORIC BIAS

Steward's notion of the long-term depopulating effect of a single communal pronghorn hunt seems to stem from the well-known account provided by Howard Egan, an early Mormon settler who witnessed a Deep Creek Gosiute Shoshone pronghorn drive in the northern Antelope Valley of eastern Nevada "about twenty miles northwest of Deep Creek" (Egan

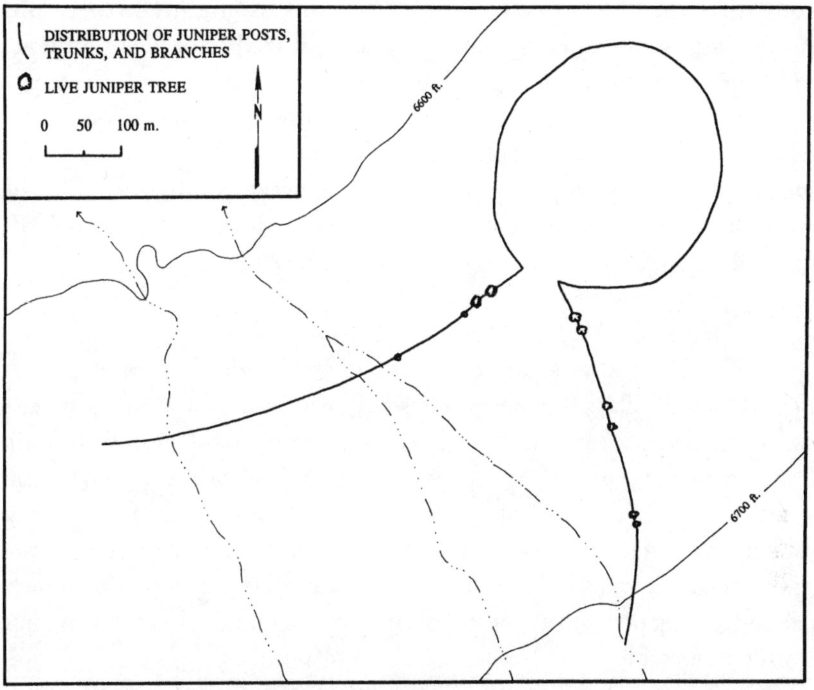

Figure 3.1 Map of the central pronghorn trap (Trap 2) at Site CA-Mno-2122. The configuration is common to many late-prehistoric Great Basin wing traps.

1917:238) during the late 1860s or early 1870s. After providing excellent descriptions of the wing trap and pronghorn drive in which about 25 animals were captured, Egan (1917:240) included the following information: "The Indians told me that the last drive, before this one at this place, was nearly 12 years ago and the old men never expected to see another at this place, for it would take many years for the animals to increase in sufficient numbers to make it pay to drive. These drives are mostly in the desert valleys, where the poor horseless natives live."

Steward (1970a:34–35 [1938]) presented the vast majority of Egan's three-page account of this drive, and this one historic account appears to have heavily influenced his perspective of communal Great Basin pronghorn hunting. I know of no other firsthand accounts of historic Numic pronghorn drives that include information regarding the frequency of this activity. Steward apparently thought that the postcontact usage pattern of one trap in one part of the Great Basin more or less reflected the frequency of precontact pronghorn drives throughout much of the Intermontane West. Various Great Basin archaeologists and ethnohistorians have incorporated this view of communal pronghorn hunting into their interpretations of late prehistoric and protohistoric subsistence systems, producing what I believe are dubious models or scenarios of precontact Numic pronghorn drives and perpetuating what Martin Wobst (1978) refers to as "a worm's eye view of reality." The archaeological record offers a broader view of reality and gives a basis for reassessing and perhaps rejecting some of these Stewardian-driven models of pronghorn as a resource and the frequency with which they were hunted, especially in the central and western Great Basin.

THE ARCHAEOLOGICAL RECORD

Until recently, the documentation of prehistoric Great Basin pronghorn traps and kill or butchering sites has been minimal. Within the last decade, however, various archaeological projects in east-central California (Arkush 1986:247–249, 1995), west-central Nevada (Hall 1990; Hall and Dansie 1990; Parr 1989; Wilke 1986), and northeastern Nevada (Arkush 1998; Murphy and Frampton 1986; Stearns and Peterson 1987) have been devoted to locating and documenting such sites. As a result of these investigations, our knowledge concerning prehistoric communal pronghorn hunting in these areas has grown considerably.

As part of my Ph.D. research, I documented and studied three pronghorn traps at a large, multicomponent site (CA-Mno-2122) in the eastern Mono Lake Basin (Figure 3.2). One of these features (Trap 4) most likely dates between A.D. 500 and A.D. 1300 (Arkush 1995:23), and the remaining two traps (Traps 1 and 2) are securely dated between A.D. 1350 and A.D. 1800 (Arkush 1995:20–21).

East and northeast of CA-Mno-2122 in west-central Nevada are two other pronghorn trap complexes: 26-Mn-589, located in an upland valley south of Huntoon Valley (Figure 3.2), and 26-Mn-5, located at the northern end of Little Whisky Flat (Figure 3.2). Site 26-Mn-589 consists of an older, Rosegate series component corral within a younger, Desert series component corral (Parr 1989:32–61). The older structure most likely dates between A.D. 500 and A.D. 1300, whereas the younger trap probably dates between A.D. 1600 and A.D. 1800. Immediately south of Site 26-Mn-589 lies a circular concentration of some 180 catastrophically broken projectile points (26-Mn-736; Figure 3.2). Most diagnostic points are either Elko series or Humboldt Basal-notched specimens; Parr (1989:144–145) therefore interprets this site as a Middle Archaic period pronghorn kill dating between about 1300 B.C. and A.D. 600. The Little Whisky Flat trap and associated rock rings yielded a time-sensitive artifact assemblage of mostly Desert series arrow points and glass trade

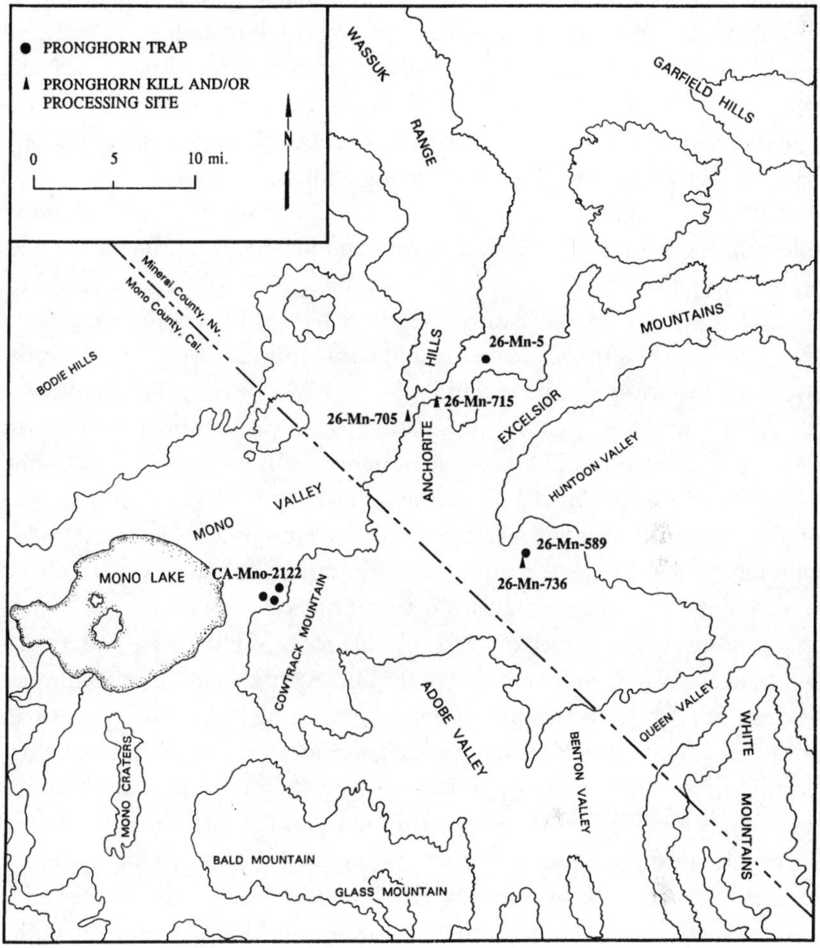

Figure 3.2 Distribution of known pronghorn traps and processing locales in the greater Mono Basin and Excelsior Mountains regions of east-central California and west-central Nevada.

beads, which led Wilke (1986) to assign a terminal Late Archaic and Protohistoric period time range (ca. A.D. 1650–1850) for construction and use of the trap.

The Anchorite Pass area just southwest of Little Whisky Flat (Figure 3.2) contains two Middle Archaic period pronghorn kill and/or butchering sites (26-Mn-705 and 26-Mn-715). Site 26-Mn-705 yielded some 150 Elko series and Humboldt Basal-notched projectile point fragments that apparently were broken by ballistic impact. Hall (1990:450–451, 463) interpreted this site as a pronghorn kill dating between about 500 B.C. and A.D. 600. Site 26-Mn-715 appears to have functioned mostly as a pronghorn butchering site and consists of a large scatter of prehistoric cultural materials, several rock rings, and one midden/hearth area. Over 300 diagnostic projectile points were recovered there, most of which were classifiable as either Elko series and Humboldt Basal-notched dart points or Rose Spring and Eastgate arrow points (Hall 1990:569; Hall and Dansie 1990). Excavations at two of the rock rings resulted in recovery of over 20,000 complete and fragmentary pronghorn bones representing the remains of at least 21 animals, and two radiocarbon dates bracket the use of these features between 1800 B.P. and 1640 B.P. Hall (1990:577) believes that primary use and occupation of 26-Mn-715 dates between about A.D. 150 and A.D. 550.

As of 1997, 19 pronghorn traps dating to late prehistoric, protohistoric, or early historic times had been documented within the Bureau of Land Management's Elko District in northeastern Nevada (Figure 3.3). Fourteen of these structures previously were described by Murphy and Frampton (1986), who believe that none of them date any earlier than about A.D. 1600 and several may have been used as late as 1870 or 1880.

A recent surface survey of nearly 530 ha in the White Horse Pass area of southeastern Elko County resulted in the documentation of three prehistoric wooden wing traps and several associated processing loci (Figure 3.4) as well as various lithic scatters, several of which appear to be game monitoring stations (Arkush 1998). The occurrence of time-sensitive artifacts (Shoshone brown ware ceramics) at Site 26-Ek-6156 and the presence of butchered pronghorn bone in surface and near-surface contexts at Site 26-Ek-6158 strongly suggest that two of these traps postdate A.D. 1000. Although time-sensitive cultural materials were not encountered at Site 26-Ek-6157 during its initial study, most of the feature's construction elements are well preserved and it seems quite likely that this wing trap postdates A.D. 1000. All three of these traps occur within a 400-ha area and comprise the White Horse Pass Pronghorn Trap complex. Such a tight cluster of wing traps indicates that White Horse Pass was a commonly used pronghorn migration corridor and suggests that the Antelope Valley–Goshute Valley region supported a substantial pronghorn population during late prehistoric times. At present, White Horse Pass contains one of the highest known densities of aboriginal wing traps in the entire Great Basin.

The final archaeological site discussed here is located in the southern portion of Clover Valley, Nevada (Figure 3.3), near several of the Elko County pronghorn traps mentioned above. Site 26-Ek-2789, which is confined to the

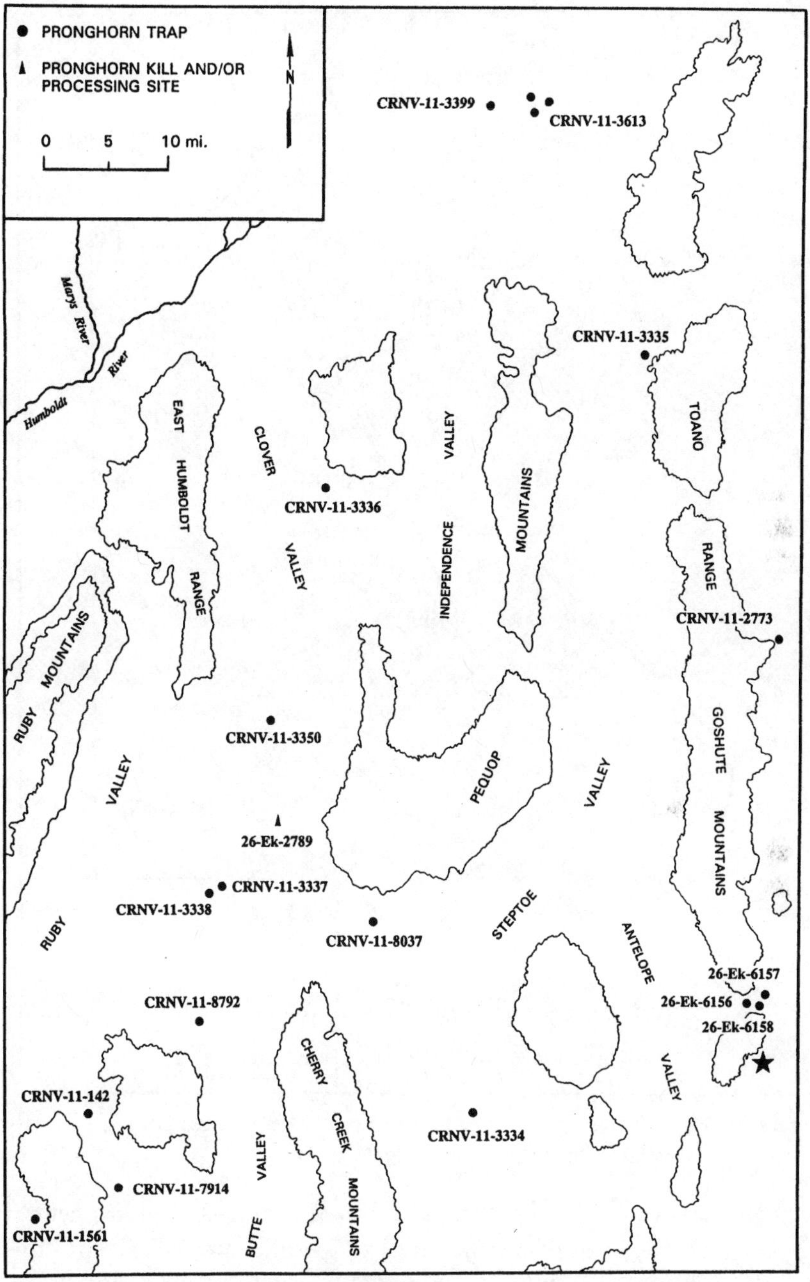

Figure 3.3 Distribution of known pronghorn traps and probable kill site in northeastern Nevada. A star in the eastern Antelope Valley area marks the approximate location of the historic wing trap described by Egan (1917).

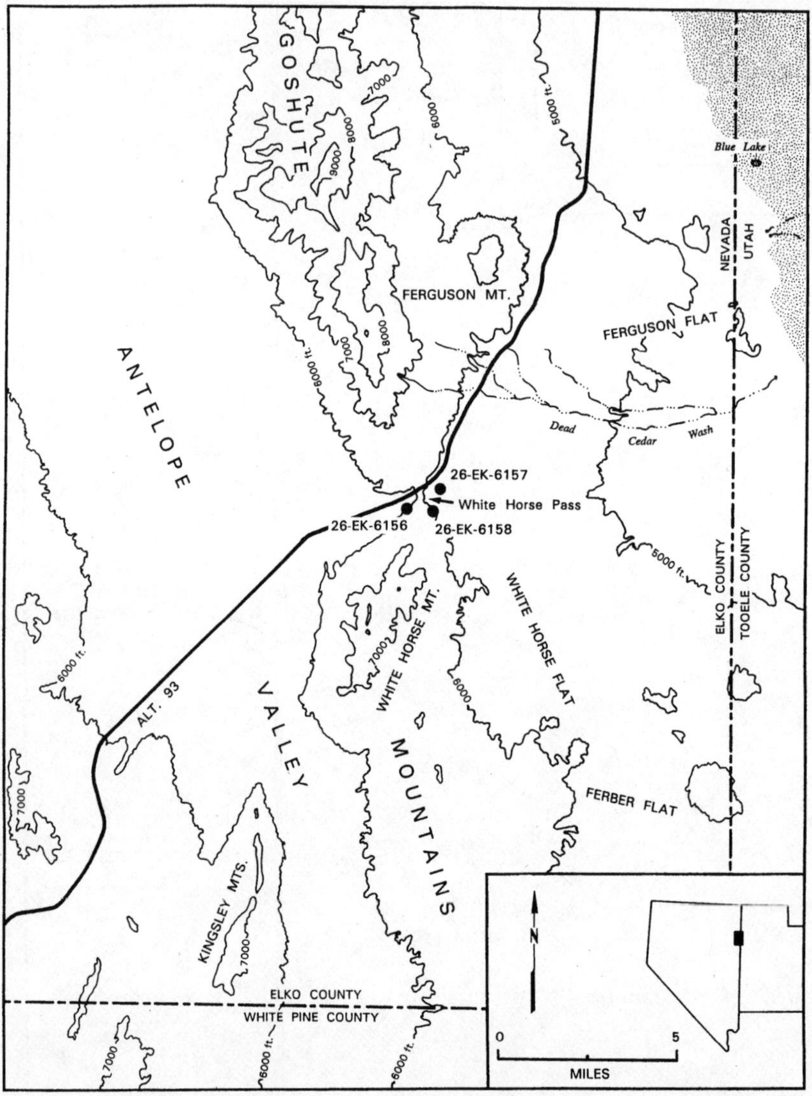

Figure 3.4 Map of the greater White Horse Pass area of southeastern Elko County, Nevada, showing locations of Sites 26-Ek-6156, 26-Ek-6157, and 26-Ek-6158.

crest and flanks of a small knoll, yielded over 250 complete and fragmentary projectile points, most of which belong to the Elko and Humboldt series (Stearns and Peterson 1987:15). Stearns and Peterson believe that this site represents an Early Archaic or Middle Archaic period (ca. 6000 B.C.–A.D. 500) communal pronghorn kill where prehistoric hunters used some type of trap to drive animals onto the knoll and then dispatched them there with atlatls and darts. If a wood-and-brush pronghorn trap was used at Site 26-Ek-2789 (or at 26-Mn-705 and 26-Mn-736), most of the elements would have decayed long ago, leaving little or no trace of its existence.

The above data indicate that eastern California and western and eastern Nevada contain clusters of communal pronghorn hunting sites consisting of Late Archaic and Protohistoric period traps and associated butchering areas, and Early Archaic and Middle Archaic period kill and butchering sites. In all likelihood, many other portions of the Great Basin contain similar densities of such sites, but they have not been found either because these areas have not been intensively surveyed or people have not recognized these sites. At the very least, the distribution of known Great Basin pronghorn traps suggests that these complex features are relatively common aspects of the Numic archaeological record and most intact traps less than about 500 years old should be fairly visible.

ETHNOGRAPHIC DATA

Various ethnographic descriptions of pronghorn hunting suggest that communal hunts occurred throughout much of the Great Basin on an annual basis, and several specific accounts reported by Steward himself indicate that some Numic groups conducted two pronghorn drives during a given year. One of Steward's Grouse Creek Shoshone consultants stated that "A new antelope corral was built each year. Hunts were held when antelope went south in the fall, and in early spring" (Steward 1970a:175 [1938]). In his discussion concerning the subsistence practices of Nevada Shoshone groups, Steward (1941b:219) reported that "Most antelope hunting was communal, large numbers of persons assembling from considerable distances once or twice a year for that purpose."

One of Isabel Kelly's (1932:85) Northern Paiute consultants reported that "sometimes two hundred [pronghorn] were killed and divided evenly among all." Such a large number for a single drive seems somewhat unlikely; also, Kelly (1932:69) mentioned that this individual remembered "virtually nothing of the old life." The average successful precontact Great Basin pronghorn drive may have resulted in the capture of between 30 and 50 animals. A Surprise Valley Paiute who provided "good information" mentioned that her great uncle had participated in a drive in which "forty or fifty antelope" were captured (Kelly 1932:85). The potentially adverse effects of pronghorn drives probably were partially mitigated by the fact that approximately 90 percent of does give birth to twins after their first breeding cycle (Hoover et al. 1959; Larsen 1964; Yoakum 1978:105; Zeveloff 1988:335), and yearlings often were set free at the conclusion of a hunt by Numic groups who could afford to do so

(Stewart 1942:335, 1943a:267). In general, it seems that pronghorn reproductive trends allowed prehistoric herds to rebound relatively quickly from a successful drive episode, and some Great Basin groups incorporated conservation practices to help maintain local pronghorn populations.

PRONGHORN EVOLUTION, POPULATION DENSITY, AND ECOLOGY

Antilocapra americana is the sole surviving species of a formerly diverse North American ungulate family, the Antilocapridae, which seems to be most closely allied to the living family Cervidae (Byers 1997:6, 13). Traditionally, the Antilocapridae are divided into two subfamilies: the Merycodontinae and the Antilocaprinae (Webb 1973). The smaller Merycodontinae existed from the mid to late Miocene and apparently gave rise to, and were replaced by, the larger Antilocaprinae (Byers 1997:13; Janis 1982). As a group, the Antilocapridae developed a specialized adaptation to grassland-savanna habitats that covered much of North America during the late Tertiary (Webb 1977). Although the specific ancestry of *A. americana* is not clearly known (Hibbard and Dalquest 1960), the living pronghorn most likely is a remnant of a clade of Antilocaprinae that first appeared during mid Pliocene times (Byers 1997:13).

The prehistoric pronghorn population of western North America has been estimated at 30 to 40 million (Cahalane 1947:69; Yoakum 1978:103, 1986:78). Today, many wildlife biologists view this estimate as an extremely conservative one and maintain that 60 to 80 million animals is more of a reasonable estimate for the prehistoric pronghorn population of western North America (David W. Kitchen, personal communication 1993).

James Yoakum is a veteran wildlife biologist who has studied Great Basin pronghorn herds for some 40 years. He believes that in prehistoric times, somewhere between 100,000 and 200,000 pronghorn inhabited the hydrographic Great Basin. Yoakum (personal communication 1993) admits that this is a conservative figure, which is based on the assumption that carrying capacity was less than one animal per square mile. Don Beale (personal communication 1993) and David W. Kitchen (personal communication 1993) also are pronghorn specialists who contend prehistoric Great Basin grasslands were capable of supporting three to four animals per square mile. This estimate translates into a maximum population of approximately 250,000 to 350,000 animals for the hydrographic Great Basin and approximately 650,000 to 900,000 animals for the cultural Great Basin.

These estimations are based upon the assumption that during relatively lengthy precontact intervals, the hydrographic Great Basin supported at least

85,000 square miles of grasslands and relatively moist high desert shrublands, whereas the cultural Great Basin supported at least 220,000 square miles of these two biomes. Pronghorn thrive in lush grassland biomes such as those in Montana and Wyoming, where they attain densities approaching 20 animals per square mile (David W. Kitchen, personal communication 1993). Shrubland biomes do support pronghorn populations, but densities in this setting are much lower than those of grassland biomes.

Pronghorn are selective feeders that harvest individual leaves, flowers, and fruits from a wide variety of plants (Byers 1997:28). In spring, pronghorn eat new leaves and shoots, and this is the only time of year when large amounts of grasses are consumed (Byers 1997:29). Overall, grasses form a minor part of their diet (Smith and Beale 1980:10; Yoakum, personal communication 1993). During mid to late spring and early summer, pronghorn prefer to feed upon succulent forbs such as vetches (*Astragalus* spp.), hawksbeard (*Crepis* spp.), buckwheat (*Eriogonum* spp.), spurge *(Euphorbia ocellata),* bursage *(Franseria acanthicarpa),* poverty sumpweed *(Iva axillaris),* biscuitroot (*Lomatium* spp.), and phlox (*Phlox* spp.). Forbs commonly grow in both grassland and shrubland settings (Tsukamoto 1983:6; Yoakum, personal communication 1993; Zeveloff 1988:335), but are more prevalent in grassland ecosystems, which typically receive greater amounts of precipitation than shrublands. In many parts of the Great Basin, shrubs such as sagebrush (*Artemisia* spp.), saltbush (*Atriplex* spp.), and bitterbrush (*Purshia* spp.) dominate the diet of pronghorn (e.g. Mason 1952:387; Smith and Beale 1980:10) and are especially important during late fall and winter.

Dietary research conducted over an eight-year period by Beale and Smith (1970) on the U.S. Forest Service Desert Experimental Range in Pine Valley, southwestern Utah, indicated that during summers of above-average rainfall, forbs provided over 90 percent of the pronghorn diet during peak production. Computation of fawn:doe ratios and fawn mortality rates indicated that the increased consumption of forbs had both direct and indirect effects on reproductive success. When summer and fall diets were high in forb content, pronghorn does produced more fawns, and high forb consumption by fawns typically resulted in superior physical condition and lower mortality rates than during years when there were few succulent forbs (Beale and Smith 1970:581).

DIETARY COMPETITION BETWEEN PRONGHORN AND DOMESTIC SHEEP

Domestic sheep are the primary livestock competitors for pronghorn because they consume many of the same plants that pronghorn feed upon (Hanley and Hanley 1982). This is especially true of shrubs such as sagebrush, which form the critical fall and winter dietary component for pronghorn (W. Sue Fairbanks, personal communication 1998; Michael Hess, personal communication 1998). Cattle are viewed as minor competitors because they mostly eat grasses (Hanley and Hanley 1982), and dietary overlap with pronghorn typically occurs only in early spring (W. Sue Fairbanks, personal communication 1998).

To evaluate rangeland competition between sheep and pronghorn, a controlled study was conducted by Smith and Beale (1980) within an enclosed 17-m^2 portion of the Desert Experimental Range. At an early stage of the project, it became apparent that both pronghorn and sheep were consuming large amounts of black sagebrush (big sagebrush did not occur within the study area), with sheep utilizing three times as much of this species as pronghorn (Smith and Beale 1980:25, Table 8). Once sheep had grazed the study area, most available shrubs had been heavily browsed and pronghorn were forced to search out sufficient forage in the more remote and steep areas of the experimental range where sheep had not grazed (Smith and Beale 1980:34).

HISTORIC MODIFICATIONS OF GREAT BASIN PRONGHORN HABITATS AND POPULATIONS

Among the numerous cultural and ecological changes that occurred in the Great Basin after about A.D. 1850, three postcontact developments proved to be especially disastrous for pronghorn habitats and populations. One of these modifications was the rapid and dramatic change in valley and foothill plant communities that resulted from a marked decrease in the frequency and size of wildfires. Prior to Euro-American settlement, many Great Basin native peoples intentionally set fire to lowland areas to check the expansion of shrubs, such as sagebrush and rabbitbrush, and to promote the growth of seed-bearing grasses and forbs (Harper 1986:53; Stewart 1955; Young et al. 1976). With the establishment of early Anglo settlements came the near-complete suppression of this aboriginal resource-management practice, and shrubs began to proliferate at the expense of native grasses and broad-leaved herbs throughout much of the Intermontane West (Barrett 1980; Sauer 1950). Although the cessation of native-ignited range fires increased the availability of winter browse in the form of shrubs, it almost certainly resulted in a dramatic decrease in forbs, which comprise important spring and summer food sources for pronghorn (Yoakum 1978:110).

The early historic period also was associated with significant increases in regional pronghorn mortality rates due to marked increases in human predation. In a synopsis of pronghorn population trends of the mid to late nineteenth century, Yoakum (1986:78) reported that "Through relentless year-long hunting of all sexes and ages by thrill seekers, sportsmen, and commercial hunters, populations in some areas were completely decimated within a ten-year period. In other areas, the slaughter continued for several decades. In less than 50 years, most remaining pronghorn populations were small isolated herds. So ended the 19th century for the American pronghorn." During the first decade of this century, the American pronghorn population was at a historic low of approximately 13,000 (Hoover et al. 1959). Within a 50-year period, these animals had experienced a catastrophic reduction in numbers from at least 30 million to "less than a fraction of one percent" (< .05 percent; Yoakum 1978:113, 1986:78).

Because of its favorable habitat, western Wyoming probably supported one of the larger late prehistoric and protohistoric pronghorn populations in the cultural Great Basin. Market hunters became active in this portion of Wyoming between 1860 and 1870 and accounted for a substantial reduction in pronghorn numbers during the third quarter of the nineteenth century. In 1881, more than 55,000 animals were slaughtered in northwestern Wyoming and southwestern Montana and their hides shipped down the Yellowstone River to St. Louis (Thomas 1966:13). During 1895, market hunters were "killing wagon loads of antelope along the Green River" in southwestern Wyoming (Creek 1967:1). Early wildlife biologists estimated that the Big Sandy River region of southwestern Wyoming supported a population of some 30,000 animals in 1885. By 1924, the entire state of Wyoming contained no more than 8,000 pronghorn (Nelson 1925:57).

Although historic fire-suppression and hunting practices certainly had adverse impacts upon Great Basin pronghorn herds, it appears that the development and maintenance of the livestock industry had the most detrimental impact upon these animals. Beginning in the 1850s, key pronghorn habitats in lowland portions of Utah, Nevada, and eastern California were settled and used for livestock pasturage, hay production, and open-range grazing. "Early livestock grazing protection resulted in an increase of native shrubs undesirable for browsing, a drastic reduction in native grasses and forbs, and a significant invasion of alien weeds highly adapted to intensive grazing. The depletion of native ranges had an almost immediate adverse impact by decreasing the pronghorn range carrying capacity" (Tsukamoto 1983:10).

Intensive early historic Anglo exploitation of the natural resources of northern Nevada began in the late 1840s, as emigrants and their livestock moved westward along the Humboldt branch of the California Trail (e.g., Clemmer 1987). Mass migration along the Humboldt River severely impacted native plant and animal foods, exhausted supplies of firewood, and fouled waterholes (Fowler and Liljeblad 1986:456). Widespread degradation of the

Humboldt River corridor and its associated pronghorn habitat by livestock competitors began in the early 1850s, when sheep and cattle were driven along the California Trail in response to demand created by the California gold rush.

During the first recorded sheep drive across northern Nevada in 1852, Richers L. Wooten drove 9,000 head; Christopher "Kit" Carson and Lucien B. Maxwell drove 13,000 head of sheep along this same route the following year (Georgetta 1972). Between 1853 and 1860, an estimated 500,000 sheep were trailed across the Intermontane region to California and Oregon (Georgetta 1972). By 1870, resident livestock in Nevada had grown considerably and included 33,000 sheep. Ten years later, the number of sheep in Nevada had skyrocketed to nearly 260,000 (Short 1965).

Christensen and Johnson (1964) have reported on the widespread ecological changes caused by early historic livestock overgrazing in Juab, Round, and Pavant Valleys of central Utah. A number of Mormon families had established small ranches in these three contiguous valleys by the mid-1850s, and 10 to 15 years after initial Anglo settlement, the Church of Jesus Christ of Latter-day Saints began to use the region as winter pasture for much of its stock. Accordingly, large numbers of cattle, sheep, and horses were driven southward from the Great Salt Lake region into central Utah. By the mid-1880s, Juab Valley had become a popular winter range for sheep, and one observer reported the presence of 200,000 sheep near the town of Nephi in 1887 (Worthington 1958:60–61). As elsewhere in the Great Basin, uncontrolled grazing in central Utah caused major shifts in the vegetational composition of lowland areas. Extensive stands of wheatgrass, bluegrass, and ricegrass were overgrazed and largely replaced by sagebrush and nonnative weeds (Christensen and Johnson 1964:13–14). Shortly after this dramatic ecological shift, juniper trees began to invade the upper portions of the former grassland-sagebrush zone. By 1870, sand dunes began to migrate into the lower Pavant Valley (Christensen and Johnson 1964:14).

DISCUSSION

A number of historic sources and wildlife management–related research clearly indicate that domestic sheep grazing and other Euro-American land-use activities forever altered critical pronghorn habitat in many Great Basin valleys and significantly reduced precontact range carrying capacities. Because of this, pronghorn populations declined markedly throughout the Intermontane West, especially in fertile lowlands used by the livestock industry for winter pasturage and hay production (e.g. Tsukamoto 1983:10). Traditionalist models concerning the frequency of precontact Numic pronghorn drives are largely based on the assumption that late prehistoric Great

Basin pronghorn populations were similar to early historic populations, and this perspective is implied in much of the archaeological and ethnohistoric literature. However, empirical data do not lend much support to this proposition. The occurrence of various late prehistoric wing traps in the western and central Great Basin and the rapid and widespread degradation of pronghorn habitats before 1875 provide a good deal of support for the alternative proposition that prior to 1850, frequent communal hunts were possible in many portions of the Great Basin.

Before the arrival of Euro-Americans and livestock competitors, most Great Basin grasslands probably supported relatively large pronghorn herds that could be driven annually or biennially without decimation. Healthy grasslands provide adequate forage for pronghorn populations to recover from naturally and culturally induced catastrophes, whereas shrublands oftentimes do not (Yoakum, personal communication 1993). It may be that infrequent precontact pronghorn drives were the rule in the more southerly Great Basin valleys that received minimal amounts of precipitation and typically never supported large herds.

My main point here is that a single postcontact account regarding the frequency of communal pronghorn hunting in one portion of the Great Basin should not be applied uncritically to an entire culture area. If the locality where Howard Egan witnessed the historic Deep Creek Gosiute pronghorn drive supported such a paucity of pronghorn, then why do three late prehistoric–aged pronghorn traps (the White Horse Pass complex) occur some 10 miles north of it? Furthermore, a number of Steward's (1970a [1938]) settlement and subsistence maps suggest that protohistoric pronghorn drive sites are a common archaeological component of many Great Basin valleys. However, Michael Hess (personal communication 1998), a longtime big-game biologist with the Nevada Division of Wildlife, reports that pronghorn have not been seen in many of the communal hunting areas on Steward's maps "for many years" (perhaps for as long as a century or more). It appears that historic land-use practices, especially those relating to the livestock industry, have had such an adverse impact on Great Basin range conditions that many areas where pronghorn formerly flourished are no longer capable of supporting even modest populations.

In all likelihood, the Gosiute pronghorn drive witnessed by Howard Egan occurred at least 20 years after Anglo settlement of the Deep Creek area, which began in 1852 when the first of several Mormon ranches were established at Ibapah (Malouf 1974:85). The early 1850s marked the beginning of livestock grazing within the greater Deep Creek area. During the following two decades, a number of developments arose that further degraded range conditions and impacted traditional native plant and animal foods. In 1854, a private mail route was opened through Ibapah by Howard Egan and George Chorpening (Malouf 1974:86–87). This enterprise established an east-west communications corridor that was soon followed by the Pony Express and Overland Mail and Stage Route (established in 1860 and 1861, respectively). As the Overland Stage stations, settlers, and livestock continued to adversely impact the Gosiute's subsistence base in the early 1860s, natives turned to organized attacks upon stage stations and ranches to repel the interlopers. Many local natives also raided livestock in an attempt to replace traditional food resources that had been reduced and/or depleted by Anglo hunting and land-use practices. These activities resulted in U.S. Army detachments being sent into the Gosiute homeland to protect stage stations and ranches and to carry out punitive expeditions against local native groups (e.g., Malouf 1974:101–105).

Therefore, it appears that the communal hunting episode witnessed by Egan occurred during a time when the Deep Creek Gosiute were pursuing remnants of a much-depleted local pronghorn population. Archaeological evidence indicates that during late prehistoric times, the greater Goshute Valley–Antelope Valley region of northeastern Nevada supported relatively large numbers of pronghorn; natives undoubtedly pursued these herds through communal hunts whenever it was feasible to do so.

Both Thomas (1983a:51) and Murphy and Frampton (1986:2, 13) have suggested that many Great Basin archaeological surveys have overlooked the remains of pronghorn traps because they were not oriented to the possibility of encountering these extensive, but often subtle, features. Historic and ethnographic sources indicate that many valley and foothill areas of the Great Basin contain pronghorn traps. Future survey projects in these settings should be designed accordingly to locate them. Recent investigations have shown that late prehistoric pronghorn traps are far more common than previously thought, and we are just beginning to understand their true role in precontact Numic subsistence regimes.

The contradictory views of Numic pronghorn hunting provided by Steward are puzzling. On one hand, he maintained that communal drives were relatively infrequent events, while on the other hand, various native consultants provided him with information concerning biannual, annual, and semiannual hunts as well as the locations of many traditional drive areas. All of us are aware of the potential problems associated with using ethnographic data to interpret prehistoric phenomena and reconstruct aspects of prehistoric societies (e.g., Trigger 1981; Wobst 1978). Throughout much of western North America, cultural reconstructions produced from salvage ethnographies probably do not accurately describe many aspects of pristine, precontact cultural systems (e.g. Trigger 1981:12).

Compounding this problem is the temporal distortion and cultural distance resulting from memory culture, in which consultants who had experienced a good deal of acculturation provided anthropologists with filtered information that had been transmitted to them by parents, grandparents, and other elders. Taken together, these factors produce an ethnographic present that is part fact and part fiction, thereby presenting major difficulties for the prehistorian who is trying to interpret archaeological data via ethnographic analogs.

The sometimes-muddled ethnographic picture of aboriginal society is the fault of neither the native consultant nor the early ethnographer. These accounts were the best that could be produced under those circumstances. Julian Steward was an amazingly productive researcher who amassed a great deal of information concerning Great Basin native peoples during the course of his career. Today, we have access to a much more extensive archaeological database than Steward and his contemporaries had, which allows us to more effectively assess the accuracy of ethnographically and historically derived models of Numic pronghorn hunting.

In view of the above information, the notion that most Great Basin pronghorn drives seriously depleted local herds, which then required many years to recover (Egan 1917; Shimkin 1947; Steward 1970a [1938]), should mostly be applied to early historic herds in shrubland biomes and not to prehistoric herds in grassland biomes. During precontact times, the plains and grasslands of the Great Basin culture area probably supported substantial pronghorn populations, making annual drives possible for many groups during favorable climatic periods. I believe that with adequate precipitation and appropriate anthropogenic burning, most Great Basin grasslands were capable of supporting relatively large pronghorn herds prior to postcontact impacts from emigrants, settlers, and livestock.

CONCLUSION

Our current understanding of the antiquity and regularity of Numic pronghorn drives is woefully incomplete. Fluctuations in the sizes of local pronghorn herds, the availability of other food resources, and the extent of interaction with adjacent native groups probably caused both regional and temporal variations in the frequency of communal pronghorn hunts and the number of animals taken during any one drive. Pronghorn drives not only provided large amounts of meat, marrow, and bone grease as well as other important animal products such as hides and sinew, but were a major component of Numic ceremonial systems and appear to have been one of the few group activities of Great Basin peoples that were highly ritualized (e.g. Murphy and Frampton 1986; Steward 1970a [1938]).

Recent research by Lubinski (1997) argues convincingly for the intensified utilization of pronghorn in the Wyoming Basin after about A.D. 1300, a pattern that may be associated with late prehistoric Numic expansion into the northeastern Great Basin. In an overview of pronghorn hunting on the northwestern Great Plains, Frison (1991:241) noted that most known communal pronghorn kills there date to late prehistoric and protohistoric times, although he acknowledges that the practice probably has a much greater time depth. Within the Great Basin, most wood-and-brush pronghorn traps built before approximately A.D. 500 most likely are poorly preserved and have little or no archaeological visibility. However, the clustered occurrence of catastrophically broken dart points (e.g., Hall 1990; Hall and Dansie 1990; Parr 1989) and isolated bone beds (e.g., Lubinski 1997) in various lowland settings of the Intermontane West imply that for millennia Great Basin native peoples have conducted communal pronghorn hunts via intercept facilities and surround strategies.

Various archaeological sites and ethnographic sources suggest that pronghorn comprised an important big-game resource throughout much of the prehistoric Great Basin. When combined with favorable environmental conditions, pronghorns' tendency to have twin births probably allowed local populations to rebound from large-scale drives within a relatively short period of time. Our present understanding indicates that communal pronghorn hunting was an important aspect of Numic subsistence and ceremonial systems. Also, the socioeconomic benefits of this activity would have encouraged people to conduct group hunts whenever and wherever possible. The discovery and investigation of additional pronghorn wing traps and kill/processing sites will provide greater resolution to prevailing models of Great Basin native subsistence systems. By focusing on the archaeological record of Numic pronghorn hunting, we can begin to distance ourselves from the historically biased interpretations that have unduly influenced our views of prehistory.

NOTE

The structure and content of this chapter have benefitted from conversations with Don Beale, Richard Clemmer, Sue Fairbanks, Mike Hess, David Kitchen, Pat Lubinski, Jim Yoakum, and Sam Zeveloff and from the comments of two anonymous reviewers. To these individuals I extend my thanks and appreciation.

4

In the Field in Death Valley: Julian Steward's Panamint Shoshone Fieldwork

Catherine S. Fowler, Molly Dufort, Mary K. Rusco, and Pauline Esteves

In the early 1930s, Julian Steward visited or recorded data about several winter and temporary camps in Death, Panamint, and Saline Valleys as part of various projects on Shoshonean ethnography. In addition to locations for these camps, Steward also elicited data on subsistence rounds, sociopolitical structure, permanent and seasonal residents, interconnections, and much more. He also gathered extensive place-name data for the region, in some cases duplicating existing recordings, but in most cases providing the first data on ethnogeography. In the 1990s, as part of projects for the Timbisha Shoshone Tribe of Death Valley and the National Park Service Applied Ethnography Program, the authors of this chapter reexamined Steward's data with present-day tribal members, usually finding them accurate and of great value to the people, but sometimes finding them flawed by Steward's "ethnographic-present" approach. The potential uses of these data in modern land-use studies are examined, as well as the level of recall of place names among today's tribal members.

Julian Steward was a man with many interests and accomplishments, a complex individual whose career and contributions spanned more than 40 years of active involvement in anthropology. He was a fieldworker in ethnography and archaeology; a synthesizer of complex areal data; a theorist who made significant contributions to cultural evolution, cultural ecology, culture change, and applied anthropology; an organizer and administrator of complex projects; and a teacher who left a significant intellectual legacy (Murphy 1977). Steward was also a person of strong opinions, but one who admitted when he had reached a wrong conclusion (e.g., on the predictive value of anthropology in certain applied situations; Steward 1969b). In short, Steward remains a major figure in the history of anthropology in general as well as one of the key figures in Great Basin studies (Harris 1968).

However, it is to some of the more detailed aspects of Steward's contributions that we turn our attention: specifically to his fieldwork among the Panamint or Timbisha Shoshone people of Death Valley and vicinity and the contributions that some of these data can still make to present-day tribal concerns, such as land-based issues. In recent years we have participated in various studies involving the Timbisha Shoshone Tribe: a land-use study of Death Valley and vicinity for the National Park Service (Fowler, Dufort, Rusco, and the Historic Preservation Committee, Timbisha Shoshone Tribe 1995), a traditional cultural properties study for the tribe (Parker and King 1990), and a project to define the extent and historic uses of the broader aboriginal territory of the Koso-Panamint-Timbisha people for tribal land-restoration purposes (Fowler, Dufort, and Rusco 1995). Although the "survey" nature of Steward's fieldwork among the Timbisha people was not conducive to in-depth ethnography, the details he was able to gather in a few short visits are remarkable and have proven invaluable for all of our studies. However, we can also see problems with some of the assumptions Steward made about the data he was recording in the 1930s. In particular, as others have also suggested (e.g., Service 1962; Stewart 1980), Steward seems not fully aware of the changes that had arisen among the people due to nearly 100 years of Euro-American contact. At times this led him to present data as more representative of "precontact" conditions than perhaps was warranted. This assessment is based on the opportunity for more in-depth ethnographic and ethnohistoric studies than Steward was afforded, as well as certain clarifications by Timbisha people.

STEWARD IN THE FIELD

Little is known about Steward's actual fieldwork schedule among the Shoshone peoples of the Great Basin; he simply stated that he spent six months during 1935 and four months during 1936 in the region (Murphy 1977:5; Steward 1970a:ix [1938]). The purpose of these field trips was to collect data for Alfred L. Kroeber's culture-element distribution survey, a task noted for its brief field stays in any one specific area (i.e., two to three days, sometimes a week). A good deal of Steward's field time was likely spent in locating people, who were at this time scattered on ranches, near active and inactive mining camps, and only sometimes living in or next to small Nevada towns. Because Steward also collected data on sociopolitical structures and their seeming environmental correlatives, as Kroeber notes, Steward prefaces his Nevada Shoshone element lists with a much longer ethnographic discussion than was usual in survey reporting. It was also because of this extensive data collection that Steward wrote his seminal monograph *Basin-Plateau Aboriginal Sociopolitical Groups.* From his 10 months in the field, Steward ultimately published 25 element-survey lists with appended discussions (Steward 1941b, 1943a), his major monograph (hereafter *Basin-Plateau*), a small collection of Shoshone myths and tales (Steward 1943a), and various theoretical discussions (e.g., Steward 1955b, 1970b). Of the data-oriented publications, *Basin-Plateau* provides the most useful materials for contemporary Timbisha Shoshone land concerns, specifically by documenting in some detail various winter and summer camps with the names of their inhabitants, place names, and subsistence and ceremonial activities.

Exactly when and how Steward visited the Timbisha people is not clear, but it appears that the visits were made in 1935 and that altogether they lasted less than a month. We have been able to identify by name nine of Steward's 11 consultants (he normally identified them in his published reports by initials only). Although all of these individuals are long deceased, present-day Timbisha people are comfortable with their credentials and know them to have been honest and knowledgeable about the region. Steward seems to have interviewed several of them in Beatty, Nevada, although it is possible he also got to Grapevine Springs in northern Death Valley and perhaps Little Lake and Darwin in southern California. He mentions interviewing one individual in Lone Pine in Owens Valley regarding Saline Valley (Steward 1943b:253); it is possible that he either obtained the Darwin and Little Lake data from that person or directly visited with other people in those areas. It is doubtful that Steward personally visited many of the other places he lists, including Furnace Creek in central Death Valley, Panamint Valley, Saline Valley, and the mountain sites on Hunter Mountain and in the Panamint Range, which makes his documentation of them through absentee individuals all the more remarkable. We assume that Steward had maps that at least showed major mountain ranges and springs in these areas, although he did not state this or provide any references.

TIMBISHA SITES AND LAND-USE PATTERNS

From information obtained from his various consultants, Steward defined both specific settlement and land-use patterns as well as his more general model of Shoshonean lifeways (Steward 1955b, 1970a [1938]). For Death

Valley proper, he defined and located four primary winter-camp areas on the floor of the valley, two sites in Panamint Valley, four in the Saline Valley district and surrounding mountains, four in the Little Lake and Koso district, and four to five in Lida and vicinity. All of these sites probably do indeed have a precontact or aboriginal component for the Timbisha-Panamint people because they have good water sources and are close to valley mesquite groves. However, some of them also have a significant historic component that Steward seems to have completely missed or failed to fully assess.

For example, Steward received conflicting reports as to the age of the Furnace Creek camp in central Death Valley, the modern headquarters of the Timbisha Shoshone Tribe. One consultant remembered an old Shoshone camp there, whereas the other felt that the first Shoshone resident was "Bill Bullen" (actually Bill Boland, Pauline Esteves's grandfather), who came there with his son and five daughters from Hunter Mountain to work (Steward 1970a:92 [1938]). In reality, both statements are partly true because there is ample archaeological evidence of both old and historic camps at Furnace Creek (Tagg 1984) and Bill Boland and his family figure prominently in the ranching history of the area (he worked at Greenland Ranch). However, Steward failed to follow up on this interesting history, probably because he did not visit the area himself or talk directly to any of the inhabitants. By 1935, there was significant activity taking place at Furnace Creek, with a population of 50 or more people resident. However, Steward seems more concerned about the ethnicity of the area (Kawaiisu or Shoshone) and ultimately awarded the whole of Death Valley south of Furnace Creek to the Kawaiisu, although he notes a few Shoshone place names for the area (Steward 1970a:93 [1938]).

With reference to this southern area, Steward (1970a:92–93 [1938]) was told by a consultant from Beatty that he remembered three families that camped about 15 miles south of Furnace Creek and spent "some time during winter" at the Borax works (Eagle Borax) and Bennetts Well and the rest of the year at "Hungry Bill's Ranch" at the 1,525-m level in the Panamint Range. The consultant gave a native place name for the ranch along with a list of 17 residents. Interestingly, present-day family tradition suggests that this site was indeed first occupied by people "from the south," including three brothers (later known as Panamint Tom, Panamint Bill, and Panamint John), their sister, and mother and that they came there sometime between 1820 and 1830 to avoid the Spanish. They married locally and developed the site into a well-watered gardening area, which ultimately featured fruit trees, grapes, hay, and a large vegetable garden. When visited in 1860, the site flourished with garden crops and it continued to grow sufficient food for trade in local mining camps (Birnie 1876; Lingenfelter 1986). Panamint or "Hungry" Bill applied for formal allotment of the land in 1907 as an Indian homestead, something that was not granted until after his death some years later (Fowler, Dufort, and Rusco 1995). Although Steward was probably correct that at least some of this area in southern Death Valley was historically Kawaiisu, he had no idea about its much more interesting and complex ethnic history. The data in *Basin-Plateau* are presented as if this site is of the same "precontact" type as the other camps on the floor of Death Valley.

Steward makes a similar error with the Saline Valley site of the Hunter-Caesar Ranch, which was also an aboriginal camp called "Koˀo." By 1935, when Steward recorded his data, this site had been a patented Indian homestead for more than 40 years (Fowler, Dufort, and Rusco 1995). When visited in 1891, the families here had over 40 ha in alfalfa, melons, squashes, corn, beans, barley, and wheat and were supplying a borax company a mile away with these products (Nelson 1891). The families were using mowing machines and plows to carry out the work. Although subsistence on mesquite, pinyon, and rabbits had not ceased, reconstructing an aboriginal subsistence pattern for this site even in the 1930s would have been difficult (Steward suggested such a pattern; 1970a:77–79 [1938]). Probably by the 1880s, families at the ranch would have had enough stores of nonindigenous vegetable products to have altered their seasonal pattern of movements and augmented their population. Although Steward would have had to do some original documentary research to find the homestead papers, he later cites one of the key references for the area (Nelson 1891), but not about this site (Steward 1970a:84 [1938]). If Steward had actually visited the area, he might have learned more of the actual history of this and similar sites. The families at this property put in an extensive irrigation system for their crops, channeling the flow of one of the mountain creeks into a stone reservoir and from there into multiple feeder ditches. All of this was in place prior to 1891.

George Hanson, who served as a consultant to Steward, had a similar, extensively developed ranch at Warm Springs in the Panamint Valley. Steward's (1970a:84 [1938]) only comment about Hanson's Indian Ranch was that it probably was not occupied until "recently" when a well was dug. By 1935, Indian Ranch had been occupied for nearly 50 years, again being the site of extensive Indian-built irrigation works, fruit orchards, and gardens—all of which were well documented in 1891 (Coville 1892). Exactly how this area figured into a precontact subsistence round is open to speculation, but certainly Hanson was a very sophisticated farmer by 1935.

Steward also seems to have misread the seasonal round for central Death Valley, again probably because he did not actually visit the area. He did record from consultants that the people from central Death Valley went to named spring sites in the Panamint Mountains (at Wildrose) and used that range predominantly for their subsistence. Steward did note that there were mesquite groves near Furnace Creek, but made little of this. In actuality, the Furnace Creek subsistence pattern was decidedly a dual one, in which seasonal movements between fairly fixed sites were practiced. From December through early June, people lived in camps in the valley, ultimately harvesting and storing a large mesquite crop. In mid-June, they went to the mountains, where summer seeds and roots were harvested, and remained through November, living on pinyon and bighorn sheep. The arrows on Steward's map (see his Figure 7, 1970a [1938]) indicate the patterns of movement from valley floor to the mountains, but his text does not really document the extent of the seasonal migration patterns that existed in this and other areas.

PLACE NAMES AND SEASONAL CAMPS

Steward, along with C. H. Merriam before him (see Grosscup 1977; Merriam 1955, 1963), recorded nearly 150 place names for the Panamint-Timbisha country, many of them still reconstructible today and of use for land-claims purposes. Unfortunately, either Steward had not had much linguistic training or was unskilled in transcription, because his renderings are often not very accurate. However, pronouncing them as best we can to fluent Timbisha speakers has led to a significant recovery of these data, as well as the addition of new forms. Without these names as prompts, it is doubtful that one-quarter of them could be recovered from memory alone today. However, with even a basic prompt, Timbisha speakers can then recall these and others that they have heard that coincide with additional sites in these areas. As noted earlier, given that Steward seemingly did not visit most of these sites with his consultants, he must have worked carefully with some type of maps to which his consultants could relate. His consultants also had to know the Anglo names for many of these springs and canyons to have them appear as accurate as they do today (see Fowler, Dufort, Rusco, and the Historic Preservation Committee of the Timbisha Shoshone Tribe 1995:Appendix B).

KINSHIP

Steward's detailed data on camp residents and kinship connections are often difficult for present-day Timbisha people to interpret. However, with effort, they can usually tell whom he is referring to or consulting. Individuals he actually names (Anglo or native names) are more easily recognized than more vague references. For example, in one passage Steward refers to Kittie, sister of Tule George of Grapevine (in northern Death Valley), who married a man from Beatty and had a daughter, who married an Italian and had seven children (Steward 1970a:87 [1938]). The latter grouping is obviously the Strozzi family, who are well known in the region and have several living descendants. Pete Sam, whom Steward (1970a:80 [1938]) mentions in connection with Hunter Mountain, is the maternal grandfather of Melvin Checo of Lone Pine, California, whom we interviewed about the Hunter Mountain and Darwin areas. Pete Sam also had a camp and garden at "China Garden" near Darwin Falls until he was pushed out by a white man in the 1920s. Given that Steward's (1970a:81 [1938]) data are poor for the Darwin area, he did not learn about Pete Sam's other activities, although he correctly recorded the place name for Darwin Falls near his garden site. Steward also correctly assessed that all of the Panamint-Timbisha groups were linked by kinship. These links have continued to the present time. However, he probably could have done even more with these patterns if he had constructed actual genealogies for the families of the different areas. Although some of the details Steward does give on marriage and descent relationships for specific families are often confusing to present-day Timbisha people, it is probably inappropriate to suggest that Steward's data on these topics are flawed. Multiple marriages; cultural patterns that require, at least in theory, that the names of the dead not be remembered; and nearly 60 years of intervening time since the recordings have also come into play.

CONCLUSION

Steward's record thus remains valuable to Timbisha Shoshone people today because of its on-the-land detail. We only wish that there were more information and that Steward had spent longer in the field and visited more areas. Although he clearly failed to explicitly account for the effects of nearly 100 years of contact on the people and their patterns, Steward nonetheless did a great service for modern generations by recording what he did. With careful analysis and reinterpretation in the light of history, the data can be made even more valuable for practical purposes. However, the data should not be taken literally as representing precontact conditions, or even 1870s conditions in some instances, and further use of the data in theoretical models for the region should be judicious. However, Steward's remain the most valuable detailed data on the Timbisha homeland and there will be few more to match them.

5

A Revisionist View of Julian Steward and the Great Basin Paradigm from the North

DEWARD E. WALKER JR.

Based on continuing ethnographic investigation among northern Great Basin peoples since the 1950s, Walker makes several suggestions for revision of Steward's interpretive models. Steward's subsistence models are too impoverished to account for the relative affluence of the various groups possessing access to anadromous fish, bison, and other large-game animal resources. Steward's kinship and political models are too simplified to account for developments during the equestrian period. Steward's failure to understand the relative affluence and social complexity of northern Great Basin peoples led him to omit the emerging regional task groupings and associated patterns of political leadership similar to those seen among eastern Plateau and western Plains groups during the equestrian period. Finally, the acceptance of Steward's ethnographic models and images as revealed truth among linguists and archaeologists has led to further interpretive distortions by prehistorians.

Culture-area characterizations have largely determined both the organization of anthropological information and the development of anthropological theory and research in North America. Schools of anthropologists are identified with culture areas in ways similar to theoretical schools in other academic disciplines. Great Basin culture-area characterizations have been developed by figures such as Alfred L. Kroeber, Julian Steward, Jesse Jennings, Sydney Lamb, and their students. Nevertheless, culture areas have inherent limitations that have been long recognized, especially in how well they deal with groups located on the borders of culture areas and their divergence from the defining criteria for the culture area (d'Azevedo 1986; d'Azevedo et al. 1966). Extensive Plains influences can be seen in the eastern parts of both the Plateau and Great Basin, especially during the protohistoric and historic periods. Likewise, we see ancient Plateau influences among the northern Numic in the Snake River drainage groups in the similarity of their riparian settlement patterns and dependency on big game, aquatic resources, and abundant root resources such as camas. In fact, based only on subsistence orientation, it would be relatively easy to reassign the Numic-speaking groups considered here (Northern Paiute, Northern Shoshone, Shoshone-Bannock, and Eastern Shoshone) to the Plateau culture area. Various scholars have advanced supporting evidence for such reassignment (Anastasio 1972; Green 1992; Hewes 1947, 1973; Moe 1982; Walker 1967, 1993a).

In this chapter I propose not only that the northern Numic groups can be easily grouped with Plateau cultural systems, but also that Steward's ethnographic model for these groups must be revisited. The subsistence, kinship, economic, and political components of his model are too simplified to account for the relative affluence of various northern Numic groups and the emerging regional task groups (composite bands) with their associated patterns of political leadership during the equestrian period and probably before. These patterns resemble those seen among eastern Plateau and western Plains groups. I begin with a few criticisms of the Great Basin culture-area paradigm.

THE GREAT BASIN RESEARCH PARADIGM

Jennings's Desert Culture and Lamb's Linguistic Hypothesis

Research and theory development in the Great Basin has been driven by a three-pronged anthropological research paradigm strongly influenced by Julian Steward's environmentally based, simplified ethnography (Steward 1955b, 1970a [1938]), Jennings's Desert culture concept (Jennings 1953, 1968), and Lamb's (1958) hypothesis of a late prehistoric Numic spread.[1]

Even though Jennings himself disavowed the Desert culture concept (Jennings 1973), his idea that the Great Basin is basically a desert has influenced the thinking of a generation of archaeologists and others who continue to regard Great Basin cultures as primarily desert adapted, a view encouraged by Steward's earlier Shoshone ethnographic model (Fowler 1972; Fowler et al. 1973). Coupled with Jennings's Desert culture concept has been the idea that northern Numic groups were marginal, not only to the Great Basin but also at the terminus of a prehistoric Numic spread that originated far to the south in the desert environment of the central and southern Great Basin.

Although Kroeber earlier identified the fan-shaped distribution of Numic languages, he did not attribute a chronology to the pattern; it was left to his student, Julian Steward, to add this component to the paradigm.

Swanson was among the first archaeologists to challenge this paradigm as it affected the northern Numic-speaking groups:

> A salient feature of the Northern Shoshoni is their geographic position in the Northern and Central Rocky Mountains, a fact which tends to disappear when, as usually happens, they are placed in the Great Basin culture area (Kroeber 1939; Steward 1938). The traditional view is that the Northern Shoshoni were in a marginal position and, if one starts in the center of the Great Basin, then indeed they were. However, if one starts with the Rocky Mountain ecological system (Daubenmire 1943) which encompasses the intermountain region and regulates plant and animal distribution for food-collecting people, then the Great Basin is internally marginal to the flanking mountains. In this situation the Northern Shoshoni are on the center line of the system (Swanson 1966). The consequence is that the Northern Shoshoni and related peoples spread away from rather than toward the Rocky Mountains. It is more probable that their origins are on this axis than in the margin. . . . All of the cultural groups mentioned speak dialects of the Shoshone-Comanche [Numic] languages. This is a division of the Numic family, one of a series of independent families of Utaztekan stock (Lamb 1958). Lexicostatistical studies have indicated slight time differences for the separation of Numic languages (e.g., Goss 1968; Lamb 1958; Miller 1966; Voegelin et al. 1962). The apparently small time involved in separation of Numic languages from one another, as compared with greater time differences for other Utaztekan families, has suggested to some that various Shoshoni groups spread northeastward from the Great Basin at a late time. . . . *This assumption may be questioned since the time differences can be equally explained in terms of a spread from the Northern Rocky Mountains to the south and west.* (Swanson 1972:9–11; emphasis added)

Swanson's proposal that the Numic expansion was from north to south was intended to directly contradict the Lamb model of an expansion from the southwest to the northeast. Although the southwest-to-northeast expansion model derives primarily from Lamb (as well as Steward), not all linguists accept his hypothesis, even though many archaeologists still adhere to it while rejecting Swanson's north-to-south counter proposal (see Madsen and Rhode 1994).

The assumption of a recent Ute-Aztecan expansion (Lamb's "Numic spread"; Hopkins 1965) into the northern Great Basin from the southwest based on linguistic arguments was forcefully rejected 20 years ago by Goss

(1977). He notes that from Lamb's view, northern Numic groups are recent arrivals from a desert environment to the south and are thought to have brought with them a core of diagnostic Great Basin cultural traits of the type described by Jennings and his students in their Desert culture concept. Goss (1977) believes that Lamb's linguistic hypothesis has become the "pet model" for many Great Basin prehistorians and is largely responsible for the recent-arrival hypothesis that continues to cloud most interpretations of southern Idaho prehistory, history, ethnography, and language (cf. Butler 1978:69–75, 1981:14–15, 1986; Holmer et al. 1986:276–280). Goss (1977:60) summarizes his objections to the Lamb hypothesis as follows: "I feel we have been seriously detoured by our blind acceptance of the Lamb hypothesis and the resultant reluctance to look at the counter interpretations the data keep throwing at us. Lamb has been a Judas-goat to a generation of Great Basin prehistorians. It is probably meaningful to note that he didn't do any more with the model, after he did it to us."

Goss concludes that a recent arrival of Ute-Aztecans in southern Idaho and adjacent areas remains highly speculative at best. In his rejection of the Lamb hypothesis, Goss agrees with Swanson (1972) and concludes that the available evidence points instead to an ancient Ute-Aztecan presence in all of the Great Basin for perhaps as long as 10,000 years (including southern Idaho). Goss then recites Kroeber's (1925) doubts about the "Numic spread," and calls for a rejection of the recent-arrival hypothesis espoused by scholars such as linguist Wick Miller (1986:98–103) and others who have attempted to codify the Lamb hypothesis in the Great Basin volume of the *Handbook of North American Indians* (d'Azevedo 1986).

Lamb based his hypothesis on the methodology of lexicostatistics, now a largely discredited method for determining the age of separation among related languages assumed to be descended from a common ancestral language. This method is based on several questionable assumptions. One is that all languages have "culture-free" core vocabularies such as pronouns, numerals, and words for body parts. Another assumption is that the core vocabulary of any particular language will change very slowly over time because there would be little need to acquire a new word for something that "is always with us" (Eastman 1990:89). A third assumption is that over long periods of time, parts of this core vocabulary do change through random historic events and that the rate of "loss" is the same for all languages, 19 percent per 1,000 years. These assumptions are based on studies of Indo-European languages for which time depth is known. Lexicostatistical procedures involve comparing lists of core vocabularies from two or more languages to find words that are cognates on the basis of sound and meaning. The time depth is then computed by solving for t in the following equation (Eastman 1990:89):

$$t = \log c$$
$$t = 2 \log r$$

Core vocabularies of Numic languages were compared with native languages of southern California such as Serrano, Cahuilla, and Gabrieleno believed to be the Ute-Aztecan languages most closely related to Numic (Goss 1977). Because they were found to be close, a time depth of ca. 1,000 years of separation was postulated, as had been done for Indo-European languages for which this method was developed. A recent example of linguistic interpretation in the Great Basin is seen in Miller's description of the Numic languages in the Great Basin volume of the *Handbook of North American Indians:*

> Sven Liljeblad (1971) has compared certain semantic domains of the Shoshone and Northern Paiute speakers in Idaho with those of the neighboring Nez Perce. His best example is with "fish." He finds that the Shoshone and Northern Paiute have only two root words for fish, and the many kinds of fish found in southern Idaho are given compound and descriptive names, such as Shoshone *ca'ppenkwi* "trout" (literally "good fish"), *patokwa* "lamprey" (literally "water snake"), and Northern Paiute *pissappakkwi* "trout" (literally "good fish") and *pakkwi pap^{ʔ}i* "sturgeon" (literally "the big brother of the fishes"). In all these instances, Nez Perce has a single, unanalyzable word. *These facts again point to a recent arrival by the desert-dwelling Numic peoples, as opposed to the Nez Perce who lived in this environment for a greater period of time.* (Miller 1986:103; emphasis added)

Liljeblad is also cited in another source (Meatte 1986:42; emphasis added), in which he is alleged to support the recent-arrival hypothesis for northern Great Basin groups:

> Old speakers of this language [Northern Shoshoni], whom I interviewed in the 1940's, still remembered having heard about this animal [caribou], which they call *tsuugwi* or in English "reindeer." One informant added that the caribou formerly was found toward the Montana side. The word *tsuugwi* is reminiscent of the general Shoshoni term *tsuugwe* which means "mule deer." *Since it is highly doubtful that Shoshoni was spoken in this locality before the fifteenth century, Shoshone emigrants from the Great Basin toward the north often applied the terminology formerly used for botanical and animal food to new but similar species in their new habitats.*

Here Liljeblad was not comparing culture-free vocabulary, but making a comparison of domains of meaning between two languages spoken in the

Basin and Plateau. His assumption that culturally significant words would more likely be independent words, rather than words modified by other words being coupled with them, is questionable as is his assumption that northern Great Basin peoples had not occupied the region long enough to form independent words. He also fails to take into account the Ute-Aztecan practice of using descriptive terms for subobjects.

The continuing power of this paradigm is also seen in recent interpretations of Shoshone-Bannock culture history (Holmer et al. 1986). Although the Holmer study makes valuable contributions to our understanding of Shoshone-Bannock riparian adaptations, Holmer's much more ancient linking of the ethnographic Shoshone-Bannock to a specific archaeological assemblage remains speculative. I have argued that his resulting effort to employ the Numic-spread concept to interpret Shoshone-Bannock prehistory by use of various tool types is valid only if the Numic-spread idea is valid, if specific archaeological assemblages can be linked to specific ethnographic groups, and if changes in tool types can be shown to mark changes in the cultures represented (Walker 1993a). In this regard, it is useful to recall Miller's (1986:100) own admonition that language groups rarely correspond to ethnographic groups or divisions in the Great Basin. In fact, there are not always clear-cut territorial divisions between languages, as pointed out by Steward (1970b:124), for the Shoshone and Northern Paiute, where there can be an overlap zone of bilingualism, intermarriage, and other cultural mixing as much as 100 miles wide. Thus the linking of specific tool assemblages with particular ethnographic/linguistic groupings is suspect.

Because this linking is evident in the Madsen and Rhode collection of papers (Madsen and Rhode 1994), it is possible to argue that the Desert culture concept and Lamb's Numic-spread concept have produced a distorted image of northern Ute-Aztecans. Further, in disputing the evidence for a Numic spread out of the central or southern Great Basin, Kroeber (1963) has also suggested that such a diffusionary-migratory model is theoretically untenable. Theoretical expectation would normally be that such diffusion proceeds outward from more complex cultural centers toward less complex cultural margins, the reverse of the situation encountered when comparing the central to the northern Great Basin. Although Julian Steward's ethnographic model of the Great Basin Shoshone has also been employed to characterize northern Numic groups, it fails to accurately represent them.

Steward's Shoshone Ethnographic Model

Based on his earlier research, Steward summarizes his Shoshone ethnographic model in his *Theory of Culture Change* (Steward 1955b), a collection of method papers dealing with multilinear evolution. Based in a theoretical commitment to a subsistence and environmentally determined cultural core, Steward (1955b:102) describes his model as "essentially a condensation" of his 1938 *Basin-Plateau Aboriginal Sociopolitical Groups.* The model stresses the primacy of the family, "the nuclear, biological or bilateral family, consisting of mother, father and children," which Steward asserts is the functioning unit of Great Basin Shoshone society. Based primarily on field research in the central and southern Great Basin during the 1930s (Steward 1970a [1938]) and rearticulated in *Theory of Culture Change,* Steward's model may be summarized as follows. The steppe environment of the Great Basin was so limited in natural resources that the Shoshone population was extremely sparse (one person per 20 or 30 square miles), and the Shoshone were constantly on the verge of starvation, especially in the winter. Natural resources in the Great Basin were highly dispersed, unpredictable, and had a socially fragmenting effect (family separatism), requiring extensive travel to secure adequate subsistence resources. The Shoshone possessed a very limited subsistence technology for gathering and storing food resources and no opportunity for the development of semipermanent settlements around fishing or other resources similar to those of the Northwest. The nuclear family was the primary social grouping, with few social structures above the level of the nuclear family. Rights to ownership of resources were based on usufruct. There were no property claims by local groups to delimitable areas of natural resources upon which work had not been expended. Despite various forms of collective action including cooperative hunting, dancing, gambling, visitation, and occasional limited feuding, the Shoshone did not possess the same leaders on successive occasions, nor did the same families cooperate in such activities from year to year. Shamans had little authority beyond their specific ritual duties, and even in the most permanent groupings—the winter villages—there was no permanent membership or leadership. It was only in the few locations of uncommonly abundant food resources that true villages and village chiefs were present. Under aboriginal conditions horses had little value because they consumed the very plants upon which the Shoshone depended while contributing little to the hunting of rabbits, antelope, or deer. Religion served to integrate society only to a minor degree. Relationships with the supernatural were largely an individual matter. Food-named groups such as "Grass Seed Eaters" or "Pine-nut Eaters" were not permanent social groupings, but instead referred to those Shoshone who happened to be in a particular food resource area at any one time (see Crum, chapter 8). They were designations of social groups only in a very temporary sense. According to Steward, Omer Stewart confused food-named groups with aboriginal social groups.[2] Shoshone kinship consisted of widely connected nuclear families such that most Shoshone were ultimately interconnected in ramifying networks that cut across local groups. No kinship-based bands or communities were formed under these conditions. Only after whites introduced livestock and irrigation agriculture into the Great Basin did the Shoshone begin to live by predatory raiding. Steward observes that bison hunting and warfare of the Plains type were adopted in the northeastern Great Basin by A.D. 1800, but he fails to describe this process for other groups in the Great Basin. He claims that there was no national warfare or intertribal warfare among the Great Basin Shoshone.

The Shoshone model also satisfies the "simplest of all cultures" part of Steward's theoretical formulation on general cultural evolution (Steward 1955b). Such an elementary form of human society has also been a convenient construct for neo-evolutionists such as Sahlins and Service (1960) and Harris (1968).[3] Widespread theoretical use of Steward's Shoshone model has probably discouraged critical ethnographic evaluation. For example, in the Great Basin volume of the new *Handbook of North American Indians,* Murphy and Murphy (1986) continue to adhere to Steward's Shoshone ethnographic model in dealing with the Shoshone-Bannock. This approach is especially evident in matters of social organization, as Murphy and Murphy (1986:287) describe the Shoshone-Bannock in a manner typical of Steward's simplified descriptions of Great Basin Shoshoneans: "The rubric of Northern Shoshone [Shoshone-Bannock], then, did not refer to a stable or social aggregate, but to a locus of population, a center of gravity so to speak, in the Snake River plains and the mountains to the north." Elsewhere Murphy and Murphy (1986:289; emphasis added) observe that "The chief characteristic of Northern Shoshone and Bannock social life was a looseness and lack of definition of groups *that bespoke the Basin origins of the people.* . . . The Bannock exerted leadership functions disproportionate to their number in the buffalo-hunting bands, whereas the institution of chieftaincy was almost absent among the purely Shoshone groups farther west." They continue:

> the Northern Shoshone and Bannock evidenced a wide range of types of political organization and groupings, from the bands of Fort Hall and Lemhi valley through the large villages of the Boise River to the scattered groups composed of a few foot-going families living in the Sawtooths and south of the Snake River. The need for cooperation in economic activities and war underlay the mode of organization and leadership, but beneath this was the basic Shoshone characteristic of loose and shifting association and individual autonomy. . . . Perhaps their very lack of large, stable political groups made the Shoshone a "people" in the truest sense of the word, for the social

networks of individuals were widely ramified, and interlocking. (Murphy and Murphy 1986:291–292)

What strikes Murphy and Murphy as looseness and lack of definition in social organization may be better regarded as flexibility in social organization. The strong leadership patterns exerted by bison-hunting Bannock in the mixed Bannock-Shoshone bands of southern Idaho, as well as the leadership and organization of economic groups and activities among Boise Valley groups, argue for an alternative view more similar to the large task groupings described by Anastasio (1972) for the Plateau, a view also less influenced by Indian Claims Commission (ICC) litigation.[4]

A NORTHERN NUMIC ETHNOGRAPHIC MODEL: AN ALTERNATIVE VIEW OF NATURAL ENVIRONMENT AND ECONOMY

A growing body of archaeological evidence from southern Idaho demonstrates that the area has enjoyed relatively affluent subsistence resources for millennia, a condition not predictable from either Jennings's Desert culture concept or Steward's Shoshone ethnographic model. The prehistoric abundance of large game, fish, and vegetal resources in the region has been well documented by various researchers (Ames 1982; Dominguez and Walker 1981; Green 1982; Moe 1982; Pavesic 1987, 1988, 1997; Plew 1980; Rudolph 1995; Statham 1982; Walker 1993b).

The natural environment of southern Idaho is distinctive from that of the central and southern Great Basin, where Steward's ethnographic model has the best fit. The Snake River and its many tributaries, including the Payette, Lemhi, Salmon, Boise, Weiser, Owyhee, Malheur, and others, form a primarily riverine foundation for permanent villages in southern Idaho. In contrast to Steward's Shoshone model, rivers form the basis for permanent villages and provide abundant aquatic resources in both resident and anadromous fish (Stewart 1991; Walker 1993b). Although areas intervening between the rich river valleys are classified as steppe by Steward (Steward 1970a [1938]), the river valleys as well as the many upland areas of southern Idaho (Dominguez and Walker 1981; Wright et al. 1980) provide easy access to subsistence vegetal and large-game resources. They also provide well-watered areas for the large horse herds that became central to the northern Numic economy and society during the equestrian period.

Steward's description of Great Basin natural resources as highly dispersed is also misleading for southern Idaho, where such resources were generally concentrated and quite abundant. Not only were there seasonally lush camas fields and productive fisheries, but there were also bison and mountain sheep populations of great subsistence value prehistorically as well as historically. The concentration of such resources permitted an aggregation of the population in a series of locations, with a well-marked seasonal round of subsistence and associated social activities. Bison hunting; intercepting the anadromous fish runs; hunting for deer, antelope, and elk; and digging roots all entailed seasonally large gatherings during the equestrian period and probably before. Technology for these activities was sophisticated and resembled that seen in the Plateau and Plains, again contradicting the image conveyed in Steward's ethnographic model.

Social Structure during the Equestrian Period

To understand the limitations of Steward's model in southern Idaho, it is necessary to understand that during the equestrian period northern Numic groups underwent confederation into larger, more inclusive social, economic, political, and territorial systems (Liljeblad 1957:40–115). A similar process of confederation has been documented by Verne Ray for the Columbia Basin and is seen in the protohistoric and historic emergence of what he has termed the Columbia Confederacy (Ray 1960). He has also documented the tribalizing effects of the horse in the central and eastern Plateau as the easternmost groups underwent a transformation toward patterns of tribal organization during the protohistoric and historic periods. As in southern Idaho, there was less tribalization or confederation in the West as one moved farther from Plains influences (Ray 1939). A further Plateau parallelism is evident in the Great Basin Shoshone-Bannock villages of the Boise Valley region, which closely resembled Plateau Sahaptian and Chinookan groups residing in the mid-Columbia region, such as the Wayam and Wishram of the Dalles-Celilo mid-Columbia (Anastasio 1972; Walker 1992, 1993b).

A continuing failure to recognize the emerging confederation of the various Northern Shoshone and Northern Paiute subgroups also stems from confusion surrounding the older, food-based local groups. At the beginning of the historic period, such groups were being rapidly incorporated into larger composite bands and tribal structures throughout southern Idaho, with the possible exception of a few Northern Paiute groups. Food-based local groups were remembered at the beginning of the nineteenth century in southern Idaho; however, other more complicated structures had long since taken their place, according to Omer Stewart (1965). Contradicting Steward, he observes correctly that prehorse, northern hunting districts (occupied by food-named groups) formed the basis of the prehorse society (pre-1700). With the adoption of the horse, such food-named local groups were quickly absorbed into larger composite bands. However, these group names probably survived as the "hunting districts" named in the Fort Bridger Shoshone-Bannock Treaty of 1868 and continue to be regarded by certain ethnographers as permanent social groupings (Madsen 1980, 1986; Walker 1993a). Omer Stewart (1965:4) ably describes this evolution of social organization among northern Numic groups following adoption of the horse and links the process to an emergent class structure:

> I wish to propose that the difficulty and the uncertainty in regard to the sub-divisions of the Northern Shoshoni result from the fact that the ancient local groupings and food-named bands [hunting districts] had been entirely superseded and, in general, replaced by a new socio-political structure which included all of the Northern Shoshoni of Idaho, Wyoming, and Northern Utah, but that these Indians were [also] subdivided into a class structure made up of individuals from the entire northern area. Furthermore, the Bannock Indians, a Northern Paiute-speaking group from Oregon, had also been integrated into this new class structure of the Northern Shoshoni. [This equestrian class served to unify the various local groupings into one social system dominated by the Bannock.] Some memory of the ancient, pre-horse subdivisions [described as hunting districts but not as local groups in the Fort Bridger Shoshone-Bannock Treaty of 1868] persisted among the very poor and aged who had remained tied to the soil, subsisting on small game and seeds which had constituted the pre-horse basis of survival of these Shoshoni. [These continued to be important food resources during the equestrian period.] The majority, however, had become participants in the larger structure, in which those with many horses and sufficient goods to travel widely formed the upper class. In the middle class were those having a few horses and participating partially in the nomadic life of the upper class, or the more fortunate fishermen settled at very productive spots. Finally, in the lower class were [also] individuals who remained without transportation and had to depend upon the gifts or generosity of the wealthy Shoshoni and upon their own hunting of rodents and gathering of roots, seeds, and insects in the ancient fashion on foot.

Concerning the emerging confederation of northern Numic groups, Stewart then concludes:

> The actual history of the northern Shoshoni Indians from 1805 to 1870 suggests that the ancient territorial food-named bands, with slight need for political leadership, were overlaid by a widespread, simple democratic *tribal structure* by which the wealthy horse owners of all ancient local bands combined and followed the chief they wished. The larger groups combined or broke up as individual Shoshoni Indians elected to give allegiance to one chief or another [see also Liljeblad 1957]. This loose democratic government

> of wide geographical extent was the product of a single, unified upper class of horse-using Indians. The older, local, food-named bands thus became, in fact, lower class people who lived in a small area which could be exploited on foot. [It is clear that few, if any, of the subgroups comprising the Shoshone-Bannock existed as such a "lower class."] The sedentary Shoshoni, living beside the productive salmon fisheries, appear to be a middle class, intermediate between the poor Shoshocoes or Root Diggers and the "real Shoshoni" or Buffalo hunters. [A similar ranking system based on subsistence orientation has been described for the Nez Perce (Walker 1968b).] (Stewart 1965:28; emphasis added)

Thus, Stewart argues that for most northern Ute-Aztecans, there was integration into a unified social, economic, political, and territorial system during the equestrian period. Raymond Wood (Wood and Liberty 1980) also documents their integration into a wide-ranging system of trade and exchange linking the Plateau, Plains, and Great Basin. Stewart's analysis also has the virtue of documenting the rapid evolution of northern Ute-Aztecan social structure during the equestrian period, in which complex, integrative social arrangements well above Steward's family level of sociocultural integration came into being. As noted elsewhere, this process was also evident during the Plateau equestrian period (Anastasio 1972; Ray 1939, 1960; Walker 1968b, 1978).

In addition to the emerging system of classes that cross-cut local groups, other large-scale groups were formed as needed and corresponded to similar structures in the Plateau that Anastasio (1972) has termed "task groups," structures closely resembling Steward's "composite bands" (Steward 1955b). These groups were activated as needed, composed of large numbers, and led by semi-permanent leaders (Shimkin 1986; Trenholm and Carley 1964). Their most important function was military. The explosive expansion of the Shoshone-Bannock and eastern Plateau groups onto the Plains after A.D. 1700, as well as the invasion of their territory by non-Indians after A.D. 1800, required a military capacity and response. In contrast to Steward's Shoshone model, the northern Numic equestrian system of warfare called for corresponding political structures and leaders of unprecedented power and authority (Madsen 1986). This view contradicts both the Murphys' Great Basin–derived image of Shoshone-Bannock social organization and Steward's Shoshone model.

Warfare and Sociocultural Integration

Steward's Shoshone ethnographic model asserts that there was no national warfare in the Great Basin. Although interfamily feuding existed everywhere in the Great Basin, there is no doubt that equestrian warfare was present on a large scale in southern Idaho. Documented examples of such warfare begin with Lewis and Clark in 1805 (Walker 1993a) in which northern Ute-Aztecans had driven Sahaptians onto the north bank of the Columbia River on the border of present Oregon and Washington. Simultaneously, Ute-Aztecans were seen on the western Plains, presenting an effective challenge to the Blackfeet and Sioux in their competition for dominance over the regional bison herds. The integrative effect of this continuing intertribal warfare, as well as the ceremonial integration stemming from adoption of such Plains traits as the Sun Dance, strengthened both the spiritual and political power and authority of leaders. Again, this picture contrasts sharply with the image of weak, temporary, and changing leaders described in Steward's model. Steward affirms the presence of predatory bands in the Great Basin, but believes they were dependent solely on the raiding of whites. This characterization is both incorrect and overly simplistic (Walker 1993a).

CONCLUSION

In this chapter I have presented a brief, selective assessment of the Great Basin research paradigm and Steward's Shoshone ethnographic model. The principal findings are that the natural environment and resources of southern Idaho were relatively abundant, were frequently concentrated, and provided for semipermanent villages that aggregated the population into riverine-defined settlement patterns similar to Plateau patterns; the equestrian period brought rapid cultural change to the northern Ute-Aztecans, producing a more complex social system involving social stratification and composite bands; the northern Numic groups were very similar to eastern Plateau and western Plains groups, especially during the equestrian period; and Julian Steward's Shoshone ethnographic model has little applicability in southern Idaho during the equestrian period and may also diverge from local patterns of the prehistoric period as well.

It is to Steward's credit that he recognized some overlap between the Basin and Plateau culture areas in his 1938 work. However, his ethnographic model for the area was incorrect in that it was drawn from data pertaining to a way of life far to the south—perhaps as far to the south as Death Valley—with which Steward had become intimately familiar 20 years earlier. By contrast, he completed very little field research in the northern Great Basin and southern Idaho, which is too often ignored by archaeologists, linguists, and ethnographers who continue to uncritically employ Steward's Shoshone ethnographic model in this complex region that has many cultural similarities to the Plateau.

NOTES

This is a revised version of a paper presented at the 1996 Annual Meeting of the Great Basin Anthropological Conference in a session organized by Richard Clemmer and L. Daniel Myers. It reflects my own research among northern Great Basin groups begun in 1958. I am indebted both to Theodore Stern and to Ruth Gruhn (1987) for reminding me that the Northern Shoshone, Paiute, Bannock, and Lemhi Shoshone are not located within the physiographic Great Basin; instead they are in the Snake River drainage (see Grayson 1993). Nevertheless, most descriptions of the Great Basin culture area continue to consider them as Great Basin groups.

1. Julian Steward's work in the Great Basin has become part of a three-pronged research and interpretive paradigm, including especially the later work of Jennings, Lamb, and their students. A combination of these three influences may be seen in most anthropological research publications from the Great Basin during the last several decades. It is difficult to separate one part of this emergent paradigm from another because archaeologists, linguists, and ethnographers generally rely on all three of these interpretive traditions. Madsen and Rhode (1994) have performed a valuable service in their *Across the West,* whose various papers reveal extensive diversity of opinion concerning Numic origins and the antiquity of their occupation of various parts of the Great Basin culture area.

2. The very brief ethnographic research by Julian Steward among northern Numic groups must be viewed only as ethnographic reconnaissance, rather than the sustained, long-term ethnographic research typical of Omer Stewart or Sven Liljeblad.

3. The theoretical need for a "simplest form of human society" is evident in most neo-evolutionary anthropological writing since the mid-twentieth century. Not only are the Great Basin Shoshoneans regarded in this manner, but they are sometimes grouped with the Bushmen, who are thought to occupy a similarly lower evolutionary position.

4. In a personal communication in 1970, Omer Stewart stated that Julian Steward and his students were employed by the federal government to defeat his (Stewart's) testimony given in support of various Shoshone, Paiute, and Ute groups of the Great Basin mostly through the law firm of Wilkinson, Cragun, and Barker (Stewart 1959). It is clear that Julian Steward's Shoshone ethnographic model was a useful tool for Department of Justice attorneys, who sought to minimize tribal territorial claims, especially because under ICC rules, tribes were required to prove exclusive ownership of lands to receive any monetary compensation. It is the opinion of various tribal leaders and attorneys of my acquaintance that the net effect of Julian Steward's involvement in the claims cases was to minimize significantly tribal claims awards. His ethnographic model emphasizing a paucity of territoriality, overlapping land-use practices, and relatively underdeveloped property concepts among Great Basin peoples was a major tool employed by the federal government in minimizing tribal claims. Another effect of Steward's work with the ICC was to leave the title to large portions of land unresolved or potentially still under tribal ownership in the northern Great Basin and especially southwestern Idaho and adjacent regions of Oregon (cf. Ronaasen et al., Chapter 12).

6

The Yamparika—Shoshones, Comanches, or Utes—or Does It Matter?

James A. Goss

Goss rereads Steward's analysis of Ute historic groups in the context of his previous theoretical works and in light of linguistic data and selected ethnohistoric material from the Spanish era. As Goss notes, a critical reassessment of labels and designations of these groups is long overdue. Goss's reinterpretation raises new questions about the Utes of the Colorado and Utah mountains, particularly on the peoples' view of their adaptation and territories, social interrelationships, and relationships to Shoshones, Comanches, and other neighbors. He points out an unfortunate tendency not only in Great Basin anthropology, but also in political-legal circles, to reify labels that confuse linguistic and cultural groups. For example, the Goshute differ from the Western Shoshone only in details of history and slightly in terms of dialect. Yet the Goshute became politically separated from the Western Shoshone when commissioners decided to negotiate two separate treaties in 1863: one with the Goshute at Deep Creek and one with Shoshones in Ruby Valley. Similarly, "Bannock" is a term that historically referred to mounted Northern Paiutes, who were distinguishable from other Northern Paiutes not on the basis of language but only in their close association with Shoshones and, after the 1878–1879 Bannock War, their hostility toward local non-Indian settlers. Culturally, the Bannock were identical to the Shoshones with whom they are associated. Thus, in one instance anthropological usage divides two culturally and linguistically similar groups, whereas in the other usage divides one group from linguistically similar groups, but also divides them in terms of labeling from the group to which they are culturally most similar. Steward ascribed very little importance to boundaries and noted that "along the whole area of Northern Paiute–Western Shoshoni contact there were bilingualism and intermarriage in a zone up to 100 miles wide" (Steward 1970b:124, 126, 128). He thought the only legitimate way of determining the distinction between Southern Paiutes and Utes might be through word lists, but cautioned against using linguistic evidence to demonstrate "tribal" distinctiveness. Yet Steward found it heuristically impossible not to carve up and label Great Basin groups. (Steward 1937c). The criteria he used were generated by research undertaken within the "culture-element distribution" framework (see Myers, chapter 9). Steward did not consider that there might be other ways of making distinctions among groups that would be more meaningful to the Newe themselves. Goss suggests that it is more complicated, but also more useful, to try to discover a linguistic system that generates a dynamic model reflecting the behavior of the studied groups than it is to merely replicate, generation after generation, the behavior of anthropologists of long ago.

A rereading of Julian Steward's analyses of historic Ute groups in the context of his theoretical works quickly makes it obvious that a critical reassessment is long overdue. This reinterpretation will shed new light on the antiquity of the Utes in their Colorado and Utah mountains, *their* view of *their* adaptations and *their* territories, *their* view of *their* social interrelationships, and *their* relationship to the Shoshonis, Comanches, and other neighbors. I shall begin this reinterpretation with Steward's views on what he regarded as the inaccurate emic designations of solid political groupings that the people themselves used and proceed to a reanalysis of these Stewardian names-turned-into-things.

STEWARD ON IDENTITIES

In 1939 Julian Steward wrote that certain scholarly conflicts regarding ethnic identities in the Shoshonean portion of the Great Basin area were "unreal" and could be dispelled by proper interpretation of the facts. He went on to write: "Definitions do not, of course, matter so long as they are consistently used." Then, getting down to specifics, he wrote: "There is danger, then, in using the term band, because its usual connotation of group solidarity is likely to lead to the effort to name and localize groups with a fictitious exactness. It is, in fact, the attempt to impose exactness upon the extremely inexact groupings native to this area that has led to the apparent conflicts in findings. Thus, native usage, not the writers', is in conflict" (Steward 1939:261).

After essentially rejecting peoples' emic classifications of themselves or others as inaccurate, he went on to elaborate:

> Native identification of peoples was very crude: people occupying a region were, if identified at all, usually named for some salient characteristic of that area (see Goss 1964). In the northern half of the area it was most often a local food which was considered remarkable either for its abundance or for some peculiarity. . . . People of neighboring localities, moreover, might be impressed by different features of an area and name it differently. Or the same name might be assigned to widely separated areas. The emphasis, I think, is clearly upon the territory rather than upon any unified group of people occupying it. . . . Furthermore, several names might be used for the same people. This system of nomenclature served in a crude way to identify people by their habitat. Upon moving to new localities, they acquired new names. (Steward 1939:262)

Steward lamented that "It helps little to seek the name used by people for themselves because this was generally nuwu or numu, meaning people. Other names for localities were usually first applied by neighbors" (Steward 1939:263). He went on to warn us that "It is probable . . . that discrepancies in recording the boundaries between most of the divisions of the Shoshoneans are unimportant. There was so much intermarriage and intermixture that the zones of contact were very broad belts, not sharp lines" (Steward 1939:264).

At this point, Steward could not have been clearer in his warnings to his intellectual descendants not to draw sharp lines marking Basin-Plateau-group territories and not to consider the names to indicate persistent band units. He also could not have been clearer in telling us that he devalued clear attempts by these people to define themselves. He calls them "crude" in their self-identification and in their insistence on all calling themselves "numu," "The People." He simply followed the clearly colonial policy of defining them by the accounts of neighbors or outsiders and turned a deaf ear to the peoples' insistence that all of the "Basin-Plateau aboriginal sociopolitical groups" call themselves by slight variations of the same term and consider themselves to be all the same people.

Many of the problems that have become our burden would have been solved if Steward had listened to "The People" and started his study by basically respecting the right of "The People" to define themselves, perhaps retitling his original study, "The Numu People and Their Lands." Also, we all know that, with the establishment of the Indian Claims Commission within the next decade, Steward built a career on external definitions of these people at the government's insistence. This work continues to have a serious impact on the quality of life of the descendants of "The People" (Steward said that because there were no clear boundaries, the lack of territoriality made claims impossible; see Ronaasen et al., chapter 12). In trying to justify his part in this, in one of his last epistles to us Steward wrote: "The concept of tribes among Shoshoneans is an anthropologist's fiction. . . . There is no scientific definition by which all of these groups can be classed as tribes. As plaintiffs in the claims cases, however, a sense of identification has been enhanced. . . . While specific potential benefits are at stake in tribal claims, the new trend is increasingly . . . pan-Indian" (Steward 1970b:147–148).

Steward may have been correct in this, but the fact that they were not originally tribes does not mean that they had no collective self-designated nations at all. His interpretation is that, by drawing lines and separating different groups of The People into "tribes" accepted as legitimate units, the government has enhanced the self-identifications of "The People" as ethnically defined "tribes." Yet, Steward still did not acknowledge the ability and the right of The People to define themselves without the help of anthropologists and government agents. The "People," the "Numu," have always known who they are, who they have been for thousands of years, and who they will be in the future dynamic. They have always been "supra-tribal," open, and "pan-Numu," inclusive. We could have learned so much from them, if we had only listened. However, it is not too late. There is another generation of Basin anthropologists coming that is learning by our mistakes.

NAMES TURNED INTO THINGS

Eric Wolf has asked us "Why do we persist in turning dynamic, interconnected phenomena into static, disconnected things?" (Wolf 1982:4). He wrote that "concepts like 'nation,' 'society,' and 'culture' [we could add 'band' and 'tribe'] name bits and threaten to turn names into things" (Wolf 1982:3), and that "by turning names into things we create false models of reality" (Wolf 1982:6). Basin anthropologists—three generations of us—have built careers on playing with names and have created false models of reality that have had a deep effect on the quality of life of The Numu People. This false modeling started with the first Spanish contacts, continued through the Anglo-American domination, through the work of anthropological giants like Julian Steward, and into the present, notably marked by our most current "Basin Bible," volume 11 of the *Handbook of North American Indians* (d'Azevedo 1986). The absurdity of our "naming game" is well illustrated by the "Synonomies" sections of that volume.

Let us look at some of these names that we have turned into "things," names like Utes, Southern Paiutes, Shoshones, and Comanches. These are the names for our most current false models as presented in the chapter titles of the handbook. These are not the names that these people have for themselves. They are all external labels and the models they invoke are "outsider" not "insider" constructs. Utes call themselves "nunwi," "nuuci," or "nuutsi," "nuuciyu" in plural. Southern Paiutes call themselves "numi," "numici," "numincimi," or "nuutsiyu" in plural. Shoshones call themselves "nuwu," "newe," or "nenewe," "nuwuni" in plural. Comanches call themselves "numu," or "numunu" in plural.

It should be noted that the handbook introduces the names that these people have for themselves only at the ends of the synonymies, as a sort of afterthought. We have not even taken the first step in respecting the right of The Numu People to *define themselves.* We would think that anthropologists would long ago have insisted that these people have the basic right of self-definition. Instead, we continue to define them, as if we know better than they who they are.

The terms that they have for themselves are all cognate and closely related to the first-person plural pronoun in all of these closely related dialects. It is because of this congruency that linguists made the decision 30 years ago to name their language family "Numic." It is clear that The People are telling us that they are all one people—"We," as opposed to "others," "We, The People." It is quite probable that they have viewed themselves as one people in our Intermontane West for at least the last 10,000 years, even before acquiring Numic languages. Although local group relations have been affected by "the continuing fission and fusion process, which we would expect in this complex, variable, and varying environment" (Goss 1977:62), the capability of self-identity through use of a single root word for "we" raises some interesting questions about the internal identity-divisions within this larger pan-Numic identity. To begin to investigate these questions, let us consider the legacy of the Spanish colonial era in terms of labels and identities.

NAMES, IDENTITIES, AND STEREOTYPES: PRODUCTS OF THE SPANISH COLONIAL POLITICAL AGENDA

There is good evidence that we have misread the ethnohistoric scenarios that led to the confusing labeling and modeling that we find in the *Handbook of North American Indians.* We simply have not listened to The People or respected them as the *owners of their own history.* Also, we have confused language and cultural units and ignored the dynamics of the system. We have added to the negative stereotyping of these people. In our attempt to be "helpful" we have actually stood in the way of the attempt of these people to tell their own story.

The Nuutsiyu people consider their name to refer to a language group, the people that speak "Nuu-apagai" or "Nungwi-apagai," "The Numu language." All the Numu-speaking consultants that I have spent time with over the past 35 years have agreed that they are defined by their language. Of course, they recognize dialectical differences in the different regions, but they always emphasize the commonalities.

My view of Numu relations started with my work with the descendants of the Nuutsiyu people of the Spanish frontier, who now live on the Southern Ute Reservation of Colorado. It is always important for us to start by defining our "view from." This is especially true in working with The Numu People, because they always view their relatives and neighbors from the perspective of their own local area. In 1961 people on the Southern Ute Reservation noted that the dialects of the groups that we anthropologists call "Shoshones" and "Utes" are different enough to cause some problems in communication, and referred to those people as "Kumantsi," or "Kumantsiyu" in the plural. The Nuutsiyu recognize the Kumantsiyu as their close relatives, but they note that they are different enough to be called "The Others." The derivation of and the dynamics of the use of this word "Kumantsi" is really a key to understanding the social dynamic of The Numu People.

This word Kumantsi is derived from the root "kuma-," "the left," "the left hand." In the context of Nuutsiyu usage, as I found in 1961, the meaning of "Kumantsi" may also be interpreted as "the left-handed ones," "the backward ones," "the ones that do not have our valued mountain adaptation, but live in the more arid basins and plains that surround us." The view from the Colorado mountains is that the Kumantsi are "poor folk," our "shirt-tail relatives" who often have to resort to digging roots and dressing in rabbit skins. Confusion develops for anthropologists who have jumped to the conclusion that all Kumantsi are "Shoshoni" speakers. It does not bother the Nuutsiyu that the "Gosi-Ute" and the "Weber Ute" speak Shoshoni and that they call some of the "Southern Paiutes" Kumantsi, even though they speak dialects essentially indistinguishable from the Nuutsiyu dialects.

The Nuutsiyu are not confused, or "in conflict," either with the philosophical system they use to designate others or with the logic of that system, which can be more easily recognized than Steward alleged. They define themselves and their relatives by language and cultural affinities. Most importantly, they know who they are and know the logical dynamic in process. We anthropologists have known neither. Marvin Opler (1943) and Wallace and Hoebel (1952) firmly established an unfortunate misinterpretation when they stated, authoritatively, that "Comanche" means "enemy" not in Spanish but in Ute.

In Ute, the word is more exactly rendered "Komantcia," which in a fuller sense means "anyone who wants to fight with me all of the time" (Wallace and Hoebel 1952:4). Wallace and Hoebel further stated that "generically the Utes applied this term to Comanches, Arapahoes, Cheyennes, and Kiowas—all of whom they fought" (1952:4–5).

Marvin Opler, who was with the Ute for only one summer field season in 1937, was not with the Nuutstiyu long enough to get into the finer nuances of usage. I have no evidence that Wallace or Hoebel ever talked to a Ute, but I do know that their interpretation is just plain wrong. In Nuutsiyu "Kumantsi" was not a generic term for enemy—it was a term for their "other" relatives. They now and then did have squabbles with their relatives, but they never generically labeled them enemies. The Nuutsiyu did consider the Arapahoes and Cheyennes to be enemies, and they called them "Sari-tikatsi" or "Dog-eaters."

It is helpful that Wallace and Hoebel (1954) tell us that this misinterpretation was taught to the anthropologists by the Spanish, who first equated "Comanche" with "The Enemy." The reference always seems to go back to the journal of the Dominguez-Escalante tour into the heart of Numu country in 1776 (Warner 1976). We ethnohistorians should never make the mistake of supposing that Escalante was meeting the Numu in a pristine state, untouched by European influences. For 175 years, or over seven generations, there had been contact between the Nuutsiyu and the Spanish on their frontier. There had been several generations of *genizaros,* the frontier population of mixed Nuutsiyu and Spanish heritage. This population had produced cultural brokers and traders that were at home with both languages and on both sides of the frontier. That is, by 1776 the Nuutsiyu had become very sophisticated in their dealings with the Spanish. Before the Pueblo Revolt of 1680, the Spanish had treaty and trading agreements with the Nuutsiyu and valued them as a buffer and an ally against the more northerly groups and the French incursions. The Nuutstiyu did not join the revolt and did not break their agreements with the Spanish. During the DeVargas reconquest, the Nuutsiyu were recontacted by the expedition in the San Luis Valley in 1694 and the Utes were invited back to their market relations at Abiquiu, Taos, Santa Fe, and Pecos (Colville 1996). Between 1694 and 1776 there had been continuous, although poorly documented, interaction between the Nuutsiyu and the Spanish of this frontier.

When the padres entered Nuutsiyu country in 1776, they were being given a guided tour by bilingual *genizaro* guides from the frontier settlements of Bernalillo, Embudo, and Abiquiu. The padres called the Nuutsiyu by the term "Yuta," which was the Spanish corruption of the Hopi and possibly the Jemez name for "The People." Of course, this is the term that we still perpetuate in "Utah," "Utaw," and "Ute." Father Escalante recorded for the first time the names that the guides were using for the people that they met: Yutas Tabehuachis, Yutas Muhuachis, Yutas Sabuaganas, Yutas Payuchis, and Yutas Timpanogotzis. It is clear that these people were all considered part of the same great Yuta nation by the Spanish. The interpretation of the names as units of political persistence, and the baseline for tracing "Ute band" affiliations, came later. Thus began our misinterpretation.

Tabehuachi probably means "Sun people," or "people of the east"; Muhuaches "cedar bark people," "those that live in cedar bark huts"; Sabuaganas "those that live in brush houses"; Payuches "those near the water"; and Timpanogotzis "those that live at the mouth of the canyon or the river." Notice that these are merely descriptions of what sort of houses local groups were living in or where they mainly lived. It is a giant and unjustified step to the conclusion that these terms represented any kind of persistent political units, a point that Steward (1939, 1970b) noted but did not choose to interpret in terms of The People's system of identity logic.

On August 27, 1776, the padres met on the Uncompahgre River of western Colorado: *"un yuta nombrado El Zurdo con su familia"* ("a Ute named the Left-Handed One with his family"; Warner 1976:145). This is undoubtedly their first meeting with an individual referred to as a Kumantsi, interpreted as "the Left-Handed One." Notice the interpreters identify him as a "yuta," but also as one of the "others." The padres did not find any of the information that he had very useful.

On August 28, in a parley with five Yutas Sabuaganas, the padres heard of quarrels with the Comanches Yamparikas and were cautioned, with exaggerations of their brutality, not to go farther. However, when they did go on, the Comanches Yamparikas evaporated and the padres found only more Yutas. The Comanches had gone *"mas alla,"* farther on.

The Spanish equation of "Comanche" with "The Enemy" was probably finally cemented in 1779 by the de Anza campaign to punish the Comanches for their transgressions. De Anza had taken command as governor and commander in New Mexico only in 1778, and this was his first contact with the Yuta frontier. He had to depend on his bilingual guides to sort out the Apaches from the Yutas and from the Comanches. In his journal, de Anza uses the terms "enemy," "savages," and "Comanches" interchangeably.

de Anza marched north into what is now Colorado with 600 men and 400 horses to punish the perpetrators of depredations on the northern frontier of the New Mexico colonies. Of course, the Nuutsiyu always referred to the raiders as Kumantsi, "The Others," to divert the vengeance of the Spanish to those *"mas alla,"* farther on. This expedition firmly established the Kumantsi as an outlaw political unit in Spanish frontier policy.

On August 19, 1779, on the Rio de los Pinos just south of present Antonito, Colorado, de Anza met a combined force of 200 Apaches and Yutas. There could have been a violent conflict there, but several of the Yuta leaders of this defensive group were known to de Anza and his interpreters. They had been to Santa Fe to negotiate market agreements with the new de Anza administration. In the parley, it was settled that these Apaches and Yutas were not the enemy. The enemy was the Kumantsi that were *"mas alla,"* farther on. In the parley, the 200 Apaches and Yutas joined the Spanish in their punitive raid on the Kumantsi, now the common "Enemy," bringing the combined force to 800 men and 2,400 horses.

The column then moved northward through the San Luis Valley, stopping at several friendly Yuta campsites, then through Poncha Pass on through South Park and down Ute Pass by the present site of Colorado Springs. South of Colorado Springs on Fountain Creek, near the present community of Wigwam, they attacked the first camp that they considered to be "hostile" Comanche, killing 18 men and capturing 30 women, 34 children, and 500 horses. On the next day, September 1, 1779, most of the Yutas left, moving back up the Arkansas River, near present Pueblo, Colorado. Their job was done. They had scapegoated their poor relatives in a small camp on Fountain Creek (Kessler 1994).

de Anza's column, however, moved south to try to intercept the leader of the "hostile" group, who had been away during the first attack. They confronted the leader, Greenhorn, with a small party of his followers. In the ensuing skirmish on September 3, "Cuerno Verde perished, with his firstborn son, the heir to his command, four of his most famous captains, a medicine man who preached that he was immortal, and 10 more" (Kessler 1994:30).

On the punitive expedition, de Anza's forces had killed or taken prisoner 133 "Comanches." But more importantly, they had turned the name "Kumantsi," "others," into a "thing," a hostile political unit. Some of The People have suffered from this labeling ever since. Undoubtedly, the Yutas with de Anza had relatives in the "Comanche" group that was attacked and slaughtered. The Yutas immediately made every attempt to disassociate themselves from the attack. Even Greenhorn had been considered a Nuutsiyu before the attack. However, after the attack, he had become a Comanche leader that the Spanish had killed to stop the raids.

Although official history records Cuerno Verde as a Comanche leader, it is important to note that the Southern Ute people recorded his name in the list of their heroic leaders in their own official history (Jefferson et al. 1972:97).

All this time, the Nuutsiyu have known that Cuerno Verde was scapegoated and that he and his people were part of them.

The groups that we have come to know as Comanches, then, are the Numu groups that the Spanish and the frontier Nuutsiyu conspired to keep out of the New Mexico trading and raiding business. These are the groups that were labeled outlaw by the Spanish and Mexican administrations. The American administration continued this policy in trying to outlaw the "Comanchero" trade.

These are the groups that were forced to fight their last-ditch battle for survival on the southern Plains, as they were caught in the closing vise of the Spanish to the south and west, the Cheyenne and Arapahoes to the north, and the Texans to the east. As the vise closed and their survival resource, the buffalo, was destroyed, their Nuutsiyu cousins even helped the United States to contain them and force them onto a reservation in Oklahoma.

CONCLUSION

Steward warned us about the dangers of turning names and definitions into things. In practice, however, Steward ignored his own warnings. A generation of Basin anthropologists followed the lead of his practice to the theater of the absurd, which is represented in the *Handbook of North American Indians.* We have better information from The People themselves to begin the reinterpretation from their point of view. In fact, we have this responsibility. It is not enough to add a minor addendum to the handbook telling what they call themselves and how they view their history. This is obviously only the beginning point. The anthropological models have started at the wrong place and are upside down and backwards. We have a new generation of Basin anthropologists that now includes historians and cultural consultants that are members of the Numu community. Therefore, Basin anthropology can make a real new beginning and have a bright future.

However, there is much to do. Everything has to be taken apart and redone from the perspective of The People. The contact dynamic must be reinterpreted from this perspective. Only if we take it all apart and put it back together can we begin to have an "inside" view of the present dynamic and, possibly, help with the future dynamic options. The key now is to get past our own false models and to listen to The People. *We must allow them to define themselves.* They have always known who they were, who they are, what has been done to them, and where they are going. Our job is to help them tell their history as they would like it to be told, not to create a history for them to suit our own purposes.

Yamparika—Shoshones, Comanches, or Utes—or does it matter? It is clear that The People have understood anthropologists much better than anthropologists have understood The People. For anthropologists it has been an academic game—for The People it has been *survival.* What matters to them now, and has mattered in the past, is the historic context in which the processes of identity and culture have been constantly socially constructed by the participants in those processes.

In July 1997 I was camping with Clifford Duncan, a Yamparika spiritual leader and cultural consultant, in the Flat Tops Wilderness of Colorado. I asked him whether he was a Nuutsi or a Kumantsi. He said "Nuutsi." I told him that I had heard that the early-nineteenth-century explorer, trapper, and mountain man Jim Bridger had been married to a Yamparika woman. He said "Yes," that was true. I asked if she had been a Nuutsi or a Kumantsi. He said that it did not matter, "We are all The Same People."

7

Julian Steward, the Western Shoshones, and the Bureau of Indian Affairs: A Failure to Communicate

Elmer R. Rusco

In 1936 Julian Steward, at the time employed to assist the Bureau of Indian Affairs in its work on behalf of Indians, was asked to prepare a report on the current status of the Western Shoshones. He did no fieldwork specifically for this purpose and his ill-tempered report was so hostile toward the Western Shoshones that the Bureau of Indian Affairs attempted to suppress it. Rusco explores the reasons for this incident in the light of theories about relations between scholars and practitioners dealing with Native American populations during the 1930s.

In 1936, as a temporary employee of the Bureau of Indian Affairs (BIA), Julian Steward wrote a special report on the Western Shoshones. This report was considered so unsatisfactory by bureau officials that they made an attempt to suppress it; the local superintendent in Nevada thought she could not show it to the Shoshones at all. The BIA objected to the report partly because its recommendations for action conflicted with its own plans. The principal problem, however, was the very negative view of the Western Shoshones expressed in this document. This report and how Steward prepared it are examined here in an attempt to explain why he and the BIA misunderstood each other so radically.

Several elements contributed to the failure to communicate: differences between the fundamental orientations of scholars and administrators, differing values and goals (including the fact that Steward apparently did not see there was a conflict), and different conceptions of political organization among the Western Shoshones in the nineteenth century and the 1930s. The incident sheds light on several ongoing questions, including how anthropologists and government officials may cooperate and how to understand the political aspects of Native American life.

Julian Haynes Steward has been appraised along with Ruth Benedict and Leslie White as one of the most important anthropologists working in the United States during the first two-thirds of the twentieth century (Hatch 1973a). Steward, who was a graduate student at the University of California, Berkeley, from 1925 until he received his Ph.D. there in 1929, himself said that he was a "student" but not a "disciple" of Kroeber (Steward 1973:vi). The obvious major reason for this statement is that although Kroeber did not search for causal laws, believing that they were either nonexistent or unknowable, Steward from the beginning was interested in "a search for causes" (Chance 1969:ii). For this reason, Harris (1968) also treats Steward, along with Leslie White, as one of the most important leaders in the "nomothetic revival," or the twentieth-century return to earlier attempts to understand human behavior in scientific terms. Steward also differed from Kroeber in that he devoted almost all of his attention to the material environment in which human societies exist and to economic, rather than symbolic, human behavior. Harris has no hesitation in describing Steward as a "cultural materialist," someone who believes in the "principles of techno-environmental and techno-economic determinism" (Harris 1968:2, 4–5), although, from at least 1952, Steward preferred to describe himself as a "cultural evolutionist" (Hatch 1973a:117).

Steward's most important early theoretical work was *Basin-Plateau Aboriginal Sociopolitical Groups* (hereafter *Basin-Plateau*). *Basin-Plateau* embodies the results of his most extensive fieldwork. In this paper I shall consider only the portions of this work dealing with the Western Shoshones, based on data initially gathered during six months of fieldwork in 1935 "financed by the University of California and a grant-in-aid from the Social Science Research Council" (Steward 1936e:561). Support from the University of California was based partly on his work in compiling culture-element distribution lists for the Western Shoshones, the Northern Shoshones, and the Goshute, a project being promoted at the time by Kroeber. Some aspects of Steward's conclusions, which were expanded in a later theoretical work dealing with the Northern Paiutes that he coauthored with Erminie Wheeler-Voegelin (Steward and Wheeler-Voegelin 1974), also need to be discussed here.

ABORIGINAL POLITICS: STEWARD'S ASSERTIONS ABOUT SOCIOPOLITICAL ORGANIZATION AND LEADERSHIP

The conclusions of *Basin-Plateau,* Steward tells us, were derived from interviews with informants in 27 Western Shoshone "villages" or "valleys," which included two Gosiute locations because Steward considered these people to be Western Shoshones. (He also visited several Northern Paiute or Southern Paiute locations, but these are not noted here.) Steward tells us that "a list of informants is given with the element lists elsewhere" (Steward 1970a: ix–xi [1938]). The actual informants are listed (in code for Nevada Shoshones and by name for Gosiutes) in his culture-element distribution reports for Nevada Shoshones and Northern and Gosiute Shoshones. In these lists there are 40 informants with some Shoshone ancestry (Steward 1941b:212–214, 1943a:263–265). However, the principal subject of this paper is a report that Steward made to his temporary employer, John Collier, head of the BIA. In this 1936 report, Steward says that he talked with 50 "Nevada Shoshone families" (Steward 1936b:1).

In *Basin-Plateau,* Steward insists that because of the nature of the harsh environment in which the Western Shoshones lived, combined with the level of technological development in their culture, the members of this society before Euro-American intrusion had highly decentralized sociopolitical structures. In fact, he says, "The individual [extended] family was in most respects . . . the independent economic unit" (Steward 1970a:230 [1938]). He recognized that some economic activities—such as antelope hunts or rabbit drives—brought together several families on a temporary basis, that festivals (often annual events, but sometimes held two or three times a year) brought several families together occasionally, and that sometimes several families would live together in winter villages. But he insisted that at most no more than 15 or 20 families "could congregate in a true village" (Steward 1970a:232 [1938]).

Steward's main point was to deny that "bands" existed among the Western Shoshones in precontact times. In these larger villages there were "headmen," but the authority of these men was very limited. In fact, the title of headman, he wrote, "means 'talker' and truly designates his most important function. 'Chief' usually connotes extensive authority and perhaps should not be applied to these men, though it has been used in this paper" (Steward 1970a:247 [1938]). That is, the headman gave information and advice to the village, which often followed this advice, but could not issue commands because "any family was at liberty to pursue an independent course at any time" (Steward 1970a:247 [1938]).

Moreover, above the village level, during periods when several families came together, leadership was both temporary and task limited. One man might direct a rabbit drive, an antelope shaman might lead an antelope hunt, and various talkers might organize dances and give advice at festivals. "In some instances, a village headman was also antelope shaman, dance director, or rabbit-drive leader. But his special authority was restricted to the communal activity and ceased at its conclusion" (Steward 1970a:247 [1938]). Steward described the Western Shoshone people as a whole as living within an interlocking network of village relationships, without political authority above the village level. He explicitly denied the existence of bands among the aboriginal Western Shoshones (Steward 1970a:246 [1938]).

Steward does not discuss systematically the crucial area of self-identification. He does not attempt to say how the people identified themselves, except to note that people living in various areas were known to others by names that identified a principal food source within their area or a key feature of their principal area of residence. (That is, a group would be known as "mentzelia-eaters," the name of residents of what is now called Reese River Valley, or "white-knife" because they used for their tools the distinctive white stone found at the "white-knife" Tosawihi quarry north of present Carlin, Nevada.) Steward does not make it clear whether a particular group felt themselves to be different from other Shoshone-speaking groups.

Steward's View of Postcontact Changes

Steward's description in *Basin-Plateau* of political changes that arose in Western Shoshone country as a result of Euro-American intrusion sheds light on his concept of "band" and also deals with questions relevant to the political structure of Western Shoshone society when he was doing his fieldwork, about which *Basin-Plateau* is almost entirely silent. Steward wrote that after the arrival of Euro-Americans the Western Shoshones went through four different political phases.

First, between about 1850 and 1870, the Western Shoshones acquired horses for the first time, at the same time that their aboriginal food base was being destroyed. The result was the development in parts of Western Shoshone territory of a process that is described in great detail for their neighbors, the Northern Paiutes, in Steward and Wheeler-Voegelin (1974). Bands developed to resist Euro-American intrusion, and the leaders of these groups exercised greater political authority than any leaders before this period. However, Steward wrote in *Basin-Plateau* that "neither the [new] organization nor discipline was strict, and the composition of fighting groups constantly changed" (Steward 1970a:248 [1938]).

Although Steward explains the development of some bands out of the new period of armed conflict, in other cases he describes a similar process as arising among groups that remained peaceful. For example, in the Humboldt River region, "people began to amalgamate in groups of increasing size . . . [even though] they remained peaceful" (Steward 1970a:246 [1938]).

One of the most important of these new leaders was Chief Temoak (Tumok), who "became the so-called chief of people who had lived along the central part of the Humboldt Valley, South Fork, Huntington, and Ruby Valley and a few neighboring valleys." Steward suggests that Temoak's efforts "probably more than anything else preserved peace in this area" (Steward 1970a:249 [1938]). This development turned out to be of substantial importance for the subsequent history of the Western Shoshones because it was during this time that the federal government negotiated treaties with all the Shoshone groups, including the Western Shoshones. Steward all but dismissed the significance of the treaty-making process, however: "In 1863 Tumok and other men who were said to represent the Indians of various valleys signed a treaty embracing a huge area. It is doubtful whether the supposed constituents of these signatories had formally chosen them as their representatives or, indeed, if many even knew what was occurring. Formal delegation of power to enter agreements binding upon everyone was utterly foreign to native political institutions" (Steward 1970a:249 [1938]). In other words, in Steward's view the authority of the new band chiefs was severely limited.

Moreover, according to Steward, the era of band organization did not last long. He wrote that because the areas of the bands were so poorly delineated and so changeable, "The office [of chief] and its duties, having no precedence in native institution and concerning principally warfare and negotiations with the white man, were limited in scope and duration" (Steward 1970a:249 [1938]). In Steward's view, the bands therefore rather quickly died out.

Furthermore, extensive economic changes brought about by Euro-American intrusion began about 1870 to change fundamentally Western Shoshone life and therefore political structures. The combination of destruction of native food sources with the creation of new economic possibilities fundamentally altered Western Shoshone life. As Steward put it, in this stage the Western Shoshones "began to attach themselves in small family groups to ranches, where they worked as hands, and in large colonies to ranch towns and to the rapidly booming mining towns where their labor was in demand" (Steward 1970a:249 [1938]).

These economic changes in turn produced political changes. First, the Shoshones became relatively settled, no longer moving about seasonally from place to place within their territory. Second, "there was little need for political control on the ranches" (Steward 1970a:249–250 [1938]). Presumably, then, even such leadership patterns as had existed in aboriginal times died out. Third, with better transportation, the festivals could and did attract larger numbers of people. "For example, people of the general region of Smoky Valley, Ralston Valley, Tonopah, Hot Creek, the Kawich Mountains, and even Lida began to abandon their local festivals to attend the huge festival at the mining town of Belmont, where many families had gone to live" (Steward 1970a:250 [1938]).

In other words, the new conditions permitted wider social structures. One would think that this would have opened the possibility for the development of leaders with a wider following than would have been possible with smaller units. Steward apparently thought this did not happen, although he did note that "Kawich, a person of evident prestige, become [*sic*] one of the main leaders of the Belmont festival" (Steward 1970a:250 [1938]).

However, the main reason that new native leaders did not develop was that "native political control in these colonies did not extend beyond native communal affairs." That is, the Western Shoshones came under the control of Euro-American political structures, "largely subject to [the white man's] organization and laws" (Steward 1970a:250 [1938]). Although Steward notes that this also increased the need for native leadership in dealing with the new Euro-American control structures, he apparently thought that this factor was not very strong. "The only function of headmen, beyond directing native activities, was to deal with the white man, because the Indian was still but slightly assimilated culturally or linguistically" (Steward 1970a:250 [1938]).

Steward pays scant attention to the complex changes brought about by reservations, presumably because before the 1930s only one lasting reservation—Duck Valley—had been created for the Western Shoshones. Steward devoted only one sentence to reservations, noting that "during this time, of course, many Indians had gone to reservations, where somewhat artificial institutions were at once imposed upon them" (Steward 1970a:250 [1938]).

According to Steward, the third stage dated from 1880 in the Humboldt Valley to 1900 in "isolated parts of southern Nevada." This stage was marked by "a general collapse of all political institutions brought about by accelerated deculturation. Although assimilation is nowhere complete even today, it had [*sic*] progressed sufficiently to destroy most distinctively Indian political institutions." He wrote that communal hunting had been abandoned and that festivals continued only on reservations, "where deculturation has been slower, where large numbers of people make them more expedient, and where embarrassment because of the white man's criticism of native practices carries less weight" (Steward 1970a:250 [1938]). This stage presumably extended into the 1930s, when Steward was writing.

The final comment Steward made about conditions in the 1930s was that "the present trend of those not on reservations is toward physical and cultural assimilation . . . [partly because] assimilation is a goal . . . [particularly for] the younger generation who desire to avoid the handicaps imposed by race prejudice" (Steward 1970a:250 [1938]). This trend would constitute the fourth stage. However, he also noted a "contrary trend" persisting from the second stage, in which bands had developed. "In order to win fulfillment of treaty obligations and other advantages, different persons with varying degrees of support have fought the Indian cause. . . . More recently organizations of white people have backed and encouraged such activities." (Steward 1970a:250 [1938])

Discussion

This much detail has been devoted to Steward's theories about the nature of political structures among the Western Shoshones at various stages from aboriginal conditions to the 1930s for several reasons. First, it is evident that he displayed little interest in this aspect of Western Shoshone life. After the initial part of *Basin-Plateau,* in which Steward outlines his materialist theory, almost the entire book (in the portion dealing with the Western Shoshones, which is most of the work) is devoted to detailed description of pre-Euro-American conditions (1970a:50–230 [1938]) interspersed with only a few occasional comments about events since then. Appendices (dealing with tribal distributions, linguistics, kinship terms and names for plants) are also oriented toward the precontact period. Only at the end of the book (1970a:230–262 [1938]) does Steward give the general conclusions noted above. Second, in these sections Steward provides very little data, in contrast with the extensive documentation provided in most of the book.

I will not attempt to say how accurately Steward has described pre-Euro-American political structures and practices among the Western Shoshones and the changes produced by Euro-American intrusion. Steven J. Crum has published a thorough account of these matters (Crum 1994). However, it was necessary to describe Steward's treatment of this issue because it has direct bearing on the main subject of this chapter, which is a report to the BIA on conditions among the Western Shoshones during the 1930s that Steward wrote after doing the research for *Basin-Plateau.*

"SHOSHONEAN TRIBES": STEWARD'S REPORT ON CURRENT CONDITIONS AND BUREAU OF INDIAN AFFAIRS POLICY

In late 1936, in his role as a consultant to the BIA for the Bureau of American Ethnology (BAE), Steward produced a report entitled "Shoshonean Tribes: Utah, Idaho, Nevada, Eastern California" (Steward 1936b; hereafter "Shoshonean Tribes"). It is not clear when the report was completed, but the Commissioner of Indian Affairs, John Collier, had received it before the end of December 1936 (see below). Almost all of this report deals with the Western Shoshones, so the treatment of it here considers only this group.

There is strong evidence that Steward conducted no separate fieldwork in connection with this report. For one thing, his six months in Nevada the previous year had been completed before he was hired to produce the 1936 report. Although Steward took a civil-service examination for "ethnologist" in June 1935 (receiving the highest score among 17 who took the test), there was no agreement that the BAE would hire him for this work until almost the end of December 1935. Apparently Steward did not go to work until January 1936. (Further details about his employment are given below.) During 1936 Steward spent four months in Idaho and Utah doing research that eventually was reported in *Basin-Plateau,* but his employment with the BAE ceased in June 1936 (JHS folder "Applied Anthropology—1935–36/American Indians"). His papers contain no field notes for either his 1935 or 1936 trip.

This is an important point, because it means that unlike questions dealing with culture-element distribution lists and his interest in reconstructing Western Shoshone life before Euro-American intrusion, Steward did not inquire systematically about current political conditions among the Western Shoshones, but acquired such information only in the course of unrelated work. In his 1936 report he wrote, "Although these trips [in 1935 and 1936] were primarily for ethnographic purposes, I always discussed modern problems at some length with the Indians." (Steward 1936b:1). The structure of the report also supports the conclusion that Steward made no systematic inquiries about current conditions; in contrast to the bulk of *Basin-Plateau,* which quotes individual informants on many points, the 1936 report gives no specific sources at all for most of its assertions.

Steward also says in his 1936 report that he thought identifying himself as a BIA employee would have reduced his prospects for obtaining accurate information on some subjects. He wrote that many Indians were not candid with "persons whom they presume to be in a position to procure them benefits and with whom they often agree merely as a matter of policy" (1936b:1). Later in the report, Steward stated that often people he wished to question would first inquire whether he was connected with the BIA. Reporting on one conversation with an informant, Steward wrote that "When I had satisfied him that I was not, he replied, 'All right, then I will talk to you'" (Steward 1936b:1, 10).

Steward also asserted that some observers had "inadvertently contacted 'poor samples', who do not entirely represent tribal opinion, which means that there is a lack of homogeneity within the groups" (Steward 1936b:1). Presumably this means that he tried to contact people with differing points of view, meaning that his sample was not random. However, nowhere does Steward describe his sampling procedure, so we have no way to know how he located informants and determined to interview them. In any case, his total (of either 40 or 50) informants is too small to be an accurate sample. The minimum sample number to allow reasonable assurance that the characteristics of the sample mirror those of the universe is well above 40, unless the sample is carefully stratified or unless the universe is very small. If interviews were confined to Western Shoshone adults, Steward's universe would have totaled probably somewhere around 1,000.

A strong argument could be made that studies of political structure cannot be done without including important political leaders in the list of informants. Nevada Agency Superintendent Alida C. Bowler complained twice (see below) that Steward had not talked with Muchach Temoak, who was a principal leader of some of the Western Shoshones at this time. Another group who should have been consulted were the BIA employees who had been conducting organizational work in Western Shoshone country for several months before Steward did his research and were still carrying on such activities in 1936. There is no evidence from the 1936 report that Steward contacted agency employees at all; in fact, Superintendent Bowler asserted flatly that he had not done so. In other words, Steward's conclusions about organizational efforts of the BIA were based on no direct evidence.

Steward's Report and the Bureau of Indian Affair's Goals

With this background, Steward's report can now be discussed. Steward began his report with an assertion that he was "fully in accord with [the] objectives of the Indian Office," which he stated to be the development of plans aiming "to give the Indians economic independence and cultural integration." However, in fact, he disagreed fundamentally with the goals of the BIA under the leadership of John Collier, although there is good reason to believe that Steward did not fully understand Collier's orientation. Steward began by asserting that the "Present reservation grouping does not coincide with . . . native differences and has, in some instances, produced friction" (Steward 1970a:1 [1938]). His example was the Duck Valley Reservation, on which had been settled the Western Shoshones (about two-thirds of whom were members of the White Knife band) and several groups of Northern Paiutes (Crum 1994:35–38). Although Steward was correct about Duck Valley, most Western Shoshones at this time did not live on any reservation. There were colonies at Battle Mountain, Elko, and Ely, but these were merely residential sites that lacked land or other resources for economic development (Crum 1994:59–84).

Because there was only one significantly large reservation with a sizable proportion of Western Shoshones—Duck Valley (cf. Crum 1994:99–103)—the BIA's primary organizational efforts necessarily focused on organizing new reservations and governments for them. South Fork, Odger's Ranch, Duckwater, and Yomba Reservations were created within Western Shoshone country during the Indian New Deal.

Early on, Superintendent Bowler had believed that establishing a single, very large reservation was the appropriate way to increase trust lands in the area. But soon she discovered that most Western Shoshone groups wanted smaller reservations in or near their existing homelands. As noted above, ultimately four new reservations were set up for the Western Shoshones, although the net increase in agricultural land was insufficient for more than a minority of Western Shoshone households not currently living on reservations (Crum 1994:97). The BIA sought to establish other reservations and to enlarge the new ones, but was frustrated by inadequate funding and, in some areas, a shortage of lands available for purchase even if funds had been available.

New constitutions and charters were not actively under way at the planned reservations when Steward was doing his research for *Basin-Plateau,* although possibly such efforts had begun at the Duck Valley Reservation. However, Superintendent Bowler launched a significant organizational effort on the belief that most of the Western Shoshones of northeastern Nevada were united under the leadership of Muchach Temoak. Ultimately, the result was the organization of the Te-Moak Bands of Western Shoshone Indians, which was planned as a political unit that would ultimately include the Western Shoshones on several reservations and colonies (Crum 1994:103–108; Rusco 1982). Steward does not mention this effort; whether he knew of it is unclear.

Steward's comments on constitution-writing (e.g., Steward 1936b:3) could have been based on what was happening at the Duck Valley Reservation, but even in this case the process was not complete until mid-1936. It is highly likely, therefore, that Steward's comments on the organizational effort derive chiefly from his observation of the process in other areas.

In any case, Steward charged that neither the Indian Reorganization Act (IRA) nor "the constitutions already drawn up are understood by the Indians. Many who cannot speak English scarcely know they exist. Those who are literate are baffled by the ponderous terminology." Further, he asserted, "most of the basic concepts are foreign to native thinking" (Steward 1936b:3). Admitting that much of the reason for the failure of Indians to understand these documents and their principles resulted from "necessary haste" and "insufficient field personnel," Steward nevertheless asserted that the consequence was that "organization is accepted on faith (if at all) by the majority of the Indians and with only a glimmering of understanding by the remainder" (Steward 1936b:3). Moreover, he asserted, the chief consequence of this fact was that "The operation of organization is left in the hands of the small minority (I suspect that it is more often in the hands of the Superintendent) who, by virtue of superior education and experience are able to comprehend it in some degree" (Steward 1936b:3). Moreover, Steward asserted that the few Indians who understood the constitutions could not be trusted to act on behalf of the "general welfare" of their communities. "As a matter of fact, they are usually so far removed from the native point of view and so bitterly opposed to the old generation that father is often set against son, and they are so strongly motivated by desire for personal gain that only the safeguards in the constitutions and strings held by the Federal government will protect their constituents" (Steward 1936b:3).

In defense of this statement, Steward asserted that "sincere devotion to the common good" was not found often among "white men" either, but that there were two reasons why this attitude was unusually weak among the Western Shoshones. First, "their native culture made them even more individualistic than most Indians. As they possessed nothing which required cooperation in communal enterprises . . . their philosophy was every man for himself and family" (Steward 1936b:4). Second, "their association with white persons unfortunately has often made selfishness, even dishonesty, a virtue" (Steward 1936b:4). Steward also buttressed this with an argument that his point about not trusting Indians involved in constitution-making had general applicability. "As long as any organized reservation does not proceed on the basis of share and share alike for all, but allows rewards for individual initiative and effort, it seems inevitable that a great many of the less astute members will be pretty well fleeced. There is some reason to believe that this is the inevitable concomitant of any democracy, that it applies also to Indians, and that nothing can be done about it" (Steward 1936b:4).

Steward's next point was that, apart from the differences between native groups noted earlier (which were the consequence of Euro-American decisions to put people from different "tribes" on the same reservation), Native Americans were also deeply divided by the "extraordinarily great . . . variation in individual competency" and by the fact that various groups differed in the degree to which they still possessed "native culture" (Steward 1936b:4). Steward identified three groups by the latter criterion: the "old, non-English-speaking fullbloods who still possess native patterns of thought and behavior and who generally have told me that they consider Organization [*sic*] much too puzzling even to try to understand," and whose main concern was to have treaty obligations fulfilled; "young mixed-bloods and persons who have been through high school, perhaps college, who wish to be done with Indian ways and compete with whites on an equal basis"; and "middle-aged and partially assimilated individuals who possess confused and conflicting attitudes and motives" (Steward 1936b:4–5).

His point was that "ties of former culture, of common residence on a reservation, even of family fail to unite such widely differing groups. Their problems are as unlike as those of rich and poor, rural and urban, educated and illiterate whites" (Steward 1936b:5). Consequently, a "single solution" will not do for all Indians. Again, Steward argued that this was also true for whites, but whites, he asserted, at least to some degree possessed a common culture, whereas Indians were divided along cultural lines. "Some Indians have the 'civilized' attitudes of Whites, while others, perhaps their relatives, are still largely stamped with a fundamentally and completely different culture, and still others are simply demoralized" (Steward 1936b:5).

Steward then in effect outlined his own program of "remedial measures" for each of these groups. He thought the situation of the "old persons" hopeless; they should be "peacefully retired with some form of old age pension or annuity." For the younger group, he suggested that since very few "are equipped to handle the responsibilities now being offered them . . . technical education in the concepts of business and self-government as well as in sound economic pursuits must surpass what has been provided Indians in the past" (Steward 1936b:5). He then went on to say that "as for the intermediate generation, the mixed-bloods and semi-assimilated middle-aged persons, I confess some skepticism as to the possibility of any real reintegration. It is worth considering the possibility that clashes of races and cultures involve some conflicts in which there is no possible reconciliation, matters in which one group or another succumbs. . . . Perhaps, the only answer to their problem is that most of them will fare badly, whether it be under Organization or some other program or under no program" (Steward 1936b:6).

Collier's Indian Reorganization Act Policy Versus Steward's Assimilationist Views

The relevance of all of this to specific Western Shoshone conditions is obscure at best. Steward was outlining a general, alternative basic strategy to that outlined in the IRA and attempted by the Collier administration. The administration premised its plan on the need to empower Native American societies to strengthen their authority to govern themselves so that these societies could then make decisions for themselves about how they wished to live. Behind this program was the passionate commitment of Collier, evident from the early 1920s, to find ways to allow traditional societies (particularly the southwestern Pueblos) to preserve cultures and sociopolitical structures still fundamentally different from those of the wider society (Philp 1977; Rusco 1996). Collier understood that not all Indians agreed on these basic questions; his program was designed to allow Indians, not the federal government, to make the crucial decisions on the ultimate development of Native American societies.

Steward, in contrast, did not share the basic values of the Collier administration at a fundamental level. Rather, Steward saw assimilation as an inevitable result of modernization and modernization as a distinctly industrially driven process (see Clemmer, chapter 10; Patterson and Lauria-Perricelli, chapter 14). This view became even clearer later in his report, when Steward discussed assimilation. In a section on "assimilation to white culture" he asserted that assimilation was more important for the Western Shoshones than for most Indians. "Close association with the Shoshonean peoples has forced me to the conclusion that assimilation is not only the inevitable and not distant goal, but is essential for the achievement of Indian Office objectives" (Steward 1936b:6). In other words, Steward thought only a single alternative was available to them, and it was not organization into "tribes."

Steward asserted that very few aspects of Western Shoshone aboriginal culture had survived to the 1930s; he named only "shamanism, a little dancing, gambling, seed gathering and other minor features" (Steward 1936b:7). In his culture-element report on the Western Shoshones (the research for which was conducted primarily during the six months he spent in Western Shoshone country in 1936), he came to a similar conclusion: "Though most of the culture has broken down today, fragments of it survive—mainly, shamanism, pine-nut and some general seed gathering, rabbit-blanket and basket weaving, language, mythology, and some family life" (Steward 1941b:210).

Steward believed that complete replacement of Western Shoshone with Euro-American culture was inevitable: "White patterns of thought and behavior are growing relentlessly and, though their progress is faltering and their acceptance fraught with grief, it is impossible to stem them." In support of this conclusion, he asserted that "The common desire of the younger generation is, moreover, to become White as soon as possible" (Steward 1936b:7).

He also argued that even what had survived of Western Shoshone culture had almost nothing of value worth preserving:

> Their native culture was so meager and their sociopolitical groupings so tenuous that no well-defined and stable patterns had emerged. Shoshoneans had a loose society, in which an individual's social horizon extended scarcely beyond his family and in which his motivation was largely the acquisition of subsistence from day to day. . . . These people possessed virtually nothing

> which win them the admiration, sympathy or support of Whites. Anything distinctively Indian about them merely brands them as queer and "inferior" (rarely as picturesque) and enhances difficulties flowing from race prejudice. I have known the White people of this region too long and heard too much of the contempt they hold for "The squalid Indian" to have any doubt of this. (Steward 1936b:7)

Specifically, Steward held that attempting to provide income from Western Shoshone arts and crafts was futile, because they "were conspicuous for their lack of products which appeal to Whites" and because their former arts and crafts, which he saw as almost entirely gone anyway, "were superficial and unlinked with anything that could give them vigor and persistence" (Steward 1936b:8). Later he was even more explicit about his perception of the quality of Western Shoshone arts and crafts, asserting that they "were among the poorest in America" (Steward 1936b:11). He described their pottery as "execrable" and their basketry as "exceptionally poor, except in Death Valley where it was exceptionally good" (Steward 1936b:11–12). Moreover, Steward said that trying to encourage production of these items or gloves, which he said was "the most common craft today," was not advisable because the compensation for such work, on an hourly basis, was low and could not be raised significantly without destroying the market for the gloves (Steward 1936b:12).

According to Steward, Western Shoshone music was also not worth preserving. He asserted that all young Indians were "outraged" when, under Collier, it was introduced into the schools. However, he did suggest that "cooperative marketing thorough a competent and *trusted* person should be established" to improve Indian income from sales of arts and crafts products and that sale of pine nuts might be a significant source of income for the Western Shoshones (Steward 1936b:12; emphasis in original).

In the last part of his report, Steward offered specific comments on various Shoshonean peoples; here only his references to the Western Shoshones are noted. Essentially, he repeated the conclusions of *Basin-Plateau* and reiterated his "stage" characterization of Western Shoshone sociopolitical history noted earlier. This stage characterization denied that "true bands" had ever existed among the Western Shoshones or that "Te-Moak's band" had been a reality for longer than a few years (see also Crum, chapter 8).

Steward's Suggestions

Although Steward noted some cooperation among the Western Shoshones during the 1930s based on their view of the treaty, he denied that this had significance, saying: "That the people within this area are at the present time cooperating in their effort to obtain advantages promised by this treaty is, of course, no proof whatever that there is any fundamental unity among them" (Steward 1970a:10 [1938]). Rather than seeing these efforts as a possible important future development because it was being organized by Shoshones themselves, he took the more cynical view that Shoshones could be easily manipulated (for contrasting views see Clemmer 1972, 1974, 1996; Crum 1994).

For example, Steward asserted that the "acquiescence of the present councilmen who are a party to the 'Temoak's band' plan" could be explained because they "appear to regard this as Hobson's choice" (Steward 1936b:10). Although this remark was not explained, perhaps Steward meant that Indians had agreed to the plans to get the aid connected with organization. He asserted that "The alleged Temoak's band . . . is clearly a rationalization of the present plans, not a justification of it" (Steward 1936b:10). He further asserted that it would be easy for the BIA "to bring together under a single plan the people signatory to the [Ruby Valley] treaty and exclude others," because there was "little in native culture to prevent it. The amorphous nature of native groupings holds the potentiality of almost any present form" (Steward 1936b:10). However, Steward recommended that the groupings of the Western Shoshones be limited in size and distance as much as possible.

Steward suggested that large groups owning land would bring on the evil effects of "segregation" and would make them "competitors with whites." This competition would increase the racial prejudice of whites toward Indians. The "effect of segregating the Shoshoni in larger groups owning land will be to lessen the difficulties of assimilation" and would slow the inevitable and desirable process of assimilation. Finally, "the great distances between the groups within this area will, so long as the Indians travel in ramshackle automobiles and rarely have money for gasoline, prevent effective cooperation" (Steward 1936b:10, 11).

Steward suggested instead that one of two other plans be followed. First, there could be organization for "a series of smaller groups, based upon the present geographical distribution of the people, in which actual neighbors and kinsmen would cooperate in Organization and new land units" (Steward 1936b:10). He suggested combination of Ely with Duckwater, each separately, or Elko with Wells and Diamond Valley (Steward 1970a:10 [1938]). Second, Steward suggested land could be bought for individual Indians. "Make the land inalienable, provide the wherewithal to develop it, give advice when necessary, and put the Indians on their own responsibility" (Steward 1936b:11). His strongest recommendation therefore was: "Do not segregate them as a racial group, do not complicate and endanger them with a tribal council, do not baffle them with a constitution and charter, do not make them wards of the government, which the younger persons consider humiliation, and do not force a single solution on Indians with all degrees of assimilation" (Steward 1936b:11).

Steward offered both negative and positive reasons for his ideas of dealing with the Western Shoshones on an individual basis without trust lands or tribal governments. He said that the Western Shoshones still retained much of their "native resourcefulness. Their standard of living is often incredibly low, even for Indians, they have always been forced to care for themselves and they are reasonably self-reliant and willing to work. They are experienced as laborers, having worked on roads and at many odd jobs, and most of them are fairly competent ranch hands. In fact, they would probably be unusually successful in operating their own lands if they had them" (Steward 1936b:10–11).

DISCUSSION

Steward's recommendations reinforce the conclusion that he was in fundamental disagreement with the basic policy orientation of the Collier administration, whether or not he was aware of this fact. Collier's primary purpose was to make it possible for Native Americans to preserve their traditional cultures, which Collier thought superior to that of the general society. In contrast, Steward was convinced both that Western Shoshone culture was not worth preserving and that total assimilation of the Western Shoshones to the culture of the general American society was both desirable and inevitable.

Moreover, his advocacy of individual ownership, without trust-status protection, harks back to the allotment policy that dominated national Indian policy from 1887 to 1934. However, not just Collier, but the IRA, reversed this policy because from at least the publication of the Meriam Report in the late 1920s it had been clear that the chief effect of this policy had been a wholesale loss of Indian lands. In addition, Collier passionately wished to preserve the trust status of Indian lands and Indian control of them so that cultures still based on communal ownership of such lands could preserve these practices.

Bureau Reaction to Steward's Report

Given the assumptions embodied in Steward's report as well as the openly expressed negative opinions about Western Shoshone culture and character, it was inevitable that the BIA reacted strongly against the report and limited its circulation. However, more was involved than this. Although no definitive report of relations between the BIA and anthropologists has yet been published, both Graham Taylor (1975) and Lawrence Kelly (1980) have pointed out conflict between some bureau officials (notably Allan Harper and Walter V. Woehlke) and anthropologists working for the BIA, on various grounds. More comment on this subject is included below. Moreover, Superintendent Bowler was skeptical of Steward's work even before she received the report. In a confidential letter to Commissioner Collier in March 1936, Superintendent Bowler wrote that "I do regret it but I feel that I ought to say to you that I am unshakably skeptical about the scientific thoroughness of Dr. Steward's work. I am of the opinion that he is not one of your true scientists, humble in his knowledge of how little he really knows" (Bowler 1936b). After saying that she understood that other anthropologists did not think well of Steward's work on petroglyphs and that she was also skeptical of the work of "many of these young anthropologists," Bowler stated her opinion that Steward was naive about Indians. "You know as well as I do that there are lots of Indians who would never admit that they did not know the answer to a question. If an anthropologist asks such an Indian something he is going to get an answer. I know that Dr. Steward did part of his work with just such Indians" (Bowler 1936b).

She then complained that Steward had told her at a meeting in Denver that he had not talked with Muchach Temoak, who, she said, "stands out both among Indians and white people as a thoroughly honorable, reliable Indian." She also asserted that "One remark that Dr. Steward made in an open meeting at Denver about the Paiute people, for instance, led me to immediately question in my mind the depth that he reached in his studies among the Paiutes. I do not have time to get acquainted with these people but even I had run across some very striking evidence of some very real spirit beliefs in direct conflict with the statement which Dr. Steward made" (Bowler 1936b). In effect, this seems to be a complaint that Steward neglected ideological aspects of Indian cultures, as well as Indians' opinions on their history, culture, and future, which Bowler thought were important.

Bowler ended this letter by asking Collier to keep it confidential, because she stated her belief that it was necessary to maintain cooperative relationships with Steward and other anthropologists. Nevertheless, it is obvious that she was predisposed to be skeptical about the value of his work (Bowler 1936b).

Suppression of Steward's Report

After Steward's report had reached her, Bowler wrote a seven-page memorandum to Commissioner Collier that analyzed the report and in effect recommended that it should be suppressed (Bowler 1937). Her first comments questioned the adequacy of the information contained in Steward's report. She said that it "presents a minimum of so-called 'facts' and a maximum of 'interpretation' and recommendations based upon personal opinion." Because the facts alleged in the report differed from those provided by her own field organization, "in instance after instance," she suggested that if further use was to be made of the report, Steward should be asked to provide a list of his informants and the dates on which they were interviewed, so that the Carson Agency could comment on his sources. Of course, he did not do so; once again it is worth noting that he probably did no specific interviewing for the report.

Bowler then said again that she had learned from Steward that he had not interviewed Muchach Temoak. Bowler wrote that "our experience leads us to consider Muchache [*sic*] one of the finest, most reliable Indians it has been our luck to meet. He is so regarded by both whites and Indians. He exerts, through no conscious effort on his part, a natural leadership upon which large numbers of his people depend." She also said that she had "gained an impression," which she believed to be correct, that one of Steward's principal informants was a man from Ely. She described this man as "all that Muchache [*sic*] is not," asserting that he "represents the poorest type to be found among his people, the self-centered, self-seeking, the unreliable, who will make a great show of knowledge, much of which may be faked, if it seems likely to bring them the attention, or the remuneration, that they crave" (Bowler 1937).

On a specific point, she disputed Steward's conclusions about current population data, saying that "for the locations shown the figures on population are just about 35% correct on the basis of the census we have just been taking by house to house visitation by a young Shoshone employed for organization purposes" (Bowler 1937). Undoubtedly she was referring to William Joaquin Jr. of Battle Mountain (see Crum 1994:68). Bowler also asserted that the dates of interviews with informants were important because she believed Western Shoshone attitudes toward the BIA had changed recently "due in large part to our efforts to inform them about the program of the present administration." She reported that there had been a serious attempt at a number of meetings to explain the IRA and that "Its main features . . . seem to be catching the interest of the natural leaders who are usually selected as their committeemen by the different groups" (Bowler 1937).

She also said that since the previous September the "young Shoshone" mentioned earlier had "spent all of his time in Shoshone country, in the Agency employ, canvassing the individual families, talking to families, larger groups, about organization and its meaning, its opportunities for self-help" (Bowler 1937). She asserted that Steward knew nothing of these efforts and had "made no contacts at the Agency to inquire into the program or to learn what we had hoped to accomplish or how we proposed to go about it." She said she did not know where he had acquired his information about the agency programs but would like to know his sources.

On the crucial question of whether bands had existed in aboriginal times among the Western Shoshones, Bowler wrote that the argument was partly over terms. Bowler said that she would use a different term if Steward or Scudder Mekeel (the head of the Applied Anthropology Unit within the BIA) would suggest one, but that "We use it to mean a group of Indian families banded together for mutual aid in combatting the elements, in gathering food, fuel, and other subsistence items from a cruelly hostile environment, and in defense against enemy peoples—in other words a primitive self-help association, in relation to maintaining existence, probably without any political organization" (Bowler 1937). Although this definition would fit the way Steward used "village," she then indicated that the word "band" had been used in the Ruby Valley Treaty and, in her view, referred again to the special significance of Temoak. She wrote that "The first signer for the Shoshone was Te-Moak, whose name has always stood out in stories of those early days in such a way as to lead us to believe that he was, in fact, the principal chief to whom a considerable number of 'bands' or groups looked for help in negotiating with the strange white man" (Bowler 1937).

In other words, apart from terminological confusion (about which neither was precise), Bowler was differing with Steward on the nature of political organization in northeastern Nevada. Her perception of the leadership position of Temoak and his descendant Muchach Temoak among a number of Western Shoshone groups lay behind the bureau's strategy in attempting to organize a multigroup "Te-Moak Bands" structure. In speaking of northeastern Nevada, she said that "In a way the proposed organization of a sort of Federated Council with elected members from the several scattered Shoshone communities, with local self-government, is patterned after that old loose affiliation. The primary purpose of the general council of Shoshone would be to negotiate with the white man's Government, local, State, and Federal, on behalf of the Shoshone people, and through such negotiations to obtain for them land, credit, and other implements with which to help their people to a better life" (Bowler 1937). She then said that because there was no "political organization" in former days was no reason why there could not be one now. "We are strongly of the opinion that there was in the old days enough of a feeling of inter-dependence for mutual help to warrant organization now for those same purposes."

Bowler then went on to argue that the only alternatives to this policy were both undesirable. First, the colonies living near towns could be organized. But these, she said, "certainly have no traditional significance" because they were purchased for "'homeless Indians of Nevada'. . . . To them drifted those who did not succeed in establishing themselves elsewhere." Second, land for new reservations could be purchased first and then the people moved to them could be organized. (This was, in fact, the policy pursued later by the Carson Agency.) Her objection to this was that she wanted to use organized governments to speed up this process. She wrote that "it had been hoped that the Tribe . . . could be organized now, so that credit might be obtained to enable them to move on to use the land. Otherwise other means of help for the actual resettlement program will have to be sought" (Bowler 1937).

Bowler suggested that Steward was unclear about what the BIA's land plans were and may have thought that the plan was to create "one big reservation." She suggested that Steward might have got this impression from "the tentative reports, hastily prepared on short notice, for the old Submarginal Land organization or the National Resources Board" (Bowler 1937). In 1934, shortly after she became superintendent, Bowler had believed that the proper strategy to pursue with the Western Shoshones would be to place "scattered" Indians on a few large reservations. She said that these plans were "extremely tentative" and had already been changed. "We shall no doubt continue to modify plans for the resettlement of the scattered landless Indians for some years to come, as actual conditions, and the preferences of the Indians, warrant" (Bowler 1937). But she asserted that "the only practicable course" was some kind of resettlement program that was somewhere between the concept of one large reservation and the idea of "scattered individual Indian farms" that Steward had advocated in his report.

She then said that the BIA was already "canvassing" Shoshones to find out which of them wanted to move to agricultural reservations and where those who chose this option wished these reservations to be located. "We are quite confident that if the Government will assist these people in the right way they will create some distinctly admirable rural communities where Indian life may flow on, in wholesome, happy, and culturally productive channels" (Bowler 1937).

Bowler disagreed with Steward's low estimate of the value of Western Shoshone culture, writing that "One can only assume that the writer failed to catch many glimpses of the inner life, the heart and soul of the Indian." She admitted that "the culture of this region was quite simple as compared with that of the Pueblo or the Navajo. But we have no reason to conclude that it does not have living values and satisfactions for the people out of whose past it grew" (Bowler 1937). She denied specifically that "all young Indians 'feel outraged that schools should' teach Indian songs," asserting instead that "we find that some of the young, and many of the middle-aged and the old, have not lost all love for their own distinctive musical and rhythmic expression. The courage to show that appreciation and delight openly is something to be fostered" (Bowler 1937).

Bowler asserted that much of the negative attitude toward their own culture that existed among the Western Shoshones had come from "the ignorant white acquisitive horde that over-ran the gold and silver country" and that exposing this "prejudice" while at the same time "letting Indians know of other white people, not too numerous in Nevada, who have respect, appreciation and admiration for distinctive native cultural products" would help Indians regain pride in their heritage.

While saying that she could not comment on whether nonreservation Shoshones had a happier adjustment than reservation Shoshones, Bowler gave her view of the status of nonreservation Indians in general. She said that without "economic resources of their own" their condition was "pitiable." Furthermore, she denied Steward's assertion that the Western Shoshones were largely assimilated. "The Indian in Nevada is not by any means truly 'assimilated' just because he lives outside an Indian group, among white people. He is still discriminated against socially and exploited economically. He is primarily the badly under paid agricultural seasonal laborer upon whom the big cattle and sheep interests depend for cheap labor at certain seasons . . . he lives on a sub-standard level, and his smug white employer asserts that the Indian is perfectly content at that level and neither desires nor deserves a hand up" (Bowler 1937).

Finally, Superintendent Bowler strongly disagreed with Steward's comments about Western Shoshone character. She wrote that "Certainly the experience of the Agency staff would compel them to disagree violently" with Steward's statement that devotion to the common good was totally lacking among these Indians. She said that "We find Indians who are constantly thinking of what will be best for 'our people.' Some of this type, I am happy to report, are being elected as members of the governing bodies in all of our organized Indian communities." Although Bowler admitted that some "self-seekers" were also being elected, she asserted that using this fact as an argument against any organization at all was invalid, as it would be in "any community."

Bowler closed her memorandum with the assertion that "a report of this character could do great damage to the Shoshoni if given circulation." She said that she had been "decidedly disturbed" to learn recently that the report had been given to soil-conservation employees who were planning to go into "Nevada Shoshone country," and ended by writing that "I shall wish to place these comments in the hands of each worker who has read the Steward report, together with a plea that the Unit go to meet the Shoshoni with a perfectly open mind on all questions, expecting neither complete rascals nor superhumans" (Bowler 1937).

Collier agreed with Bowler that the report was objectionable. In a personal note to her written March 26, 1936, Collier referred to her letter of March 21 (i.e., Bowler 1936b). He reminded her that Steward was "assigned by the Bureau of American Ethnology as their liaison officer" and that "Between ourselves, I find that not just a particular anthropologist, but most any and all of them are naive" (Collier 1936a).

On December 22, 1936, Collier (1936b) had written a "rough draft" of a memorandum to Dr. Scudder Mekeel, head of the Applied Anthropology Unit, which handwritten notations indicate was sent also to Superintendent Bowler and, confidentially, to Allan Harper and William Zimmerman of the BIA. Both Harper and Zimmerman were members of an informal group of close advisers to Collier, and Zimmerman was the assistant commissioner.

In this memorandum Collier had made nine quotations from the Steward report, emphasizing the statements denigrating Western Shoshone culture and character. He then wrote: "I am tempted to excerpt other and lengthier dicta from Dr. Julian Steward's report, but the ones which I have quoted indicate most of the reason why the report does not prepossess me either as social philosophy or as factual reporting" (Collier 1936b). He then went on to say that the recording of "atomized facts" was not enough: "In determining Indian Service policies, and in attempting to evaluate human beings and to chart the future of human spirits, there are needed some endowments of enthusiasm, confidence in the human nature one is dealing with, and social philosophy." He asserted that the Steward report was "on a lower level" than an earlier report he had read on the Mississippi Choctaws and that although he thought Steward was "an attractive individual," the "shedding of light upon our complicated Indian problems needs something more. This is another case showing that achievement in a special science, anthropology or any other, provides no assurance of competency to deal with social problems" (Collier 1936b).

Finding the Report

Obviously someone in the Washington, D.C., office of the BIA suppressed the Steward report. When I discovered the Bowler-Collier correspondence quoted in this paper while doing research in the National Archives Building several years ago, I could not locate the Steward report itself. Later Steven J. Crum, then a graduate student, gave me a copy of the report, which he had found in Steward's papers in Urbana, Illinois. Still later I found that there were other copies in various places. Warren L. d'Azevedo of the Anthropology Department of the University of Nevada, Reno, has a copy, and there is one in Special Collections at the University of Nevada Library.

The history of the University of Nevada's copy is instructive. Roy Nash was the superintendent of the Sacramento Agency of the BIA during the time the report came out. Anthropologist W. W. Hill, who said that Steward had given him the report, provided Nash with a copy on February 24, 1937; Hill wrote on the report that "I think Stew is right, but I am afraid I am the only one he will ever convince." Nash shared it with Charles deYoung Elkus, a friend and adviser of Collier's who often gave advice to the Sacramento Agency also, although Nash asked that it be returned when he had read it.

Some time after this, Scudder Mekeel wrote Hill requesting the return of "the original carbon and any other copies that may be circulated" because "this report has not received the sanction of this Office." Hill wrote Nash on March 15, 1937, requesting the return of the report, because "It seems that I have been guilty of dragging out a dead skunk, and presenting it to parties who might be interested."

Nash either did not return the report or made a copy. Moreover, when he retired Nash took this copy with him. Some time later Nash gave it to Neil Humphrey, a friend of his who later became the first president of the University of Nevada, Reno, and then chancellor of the University of Nevada system. Humphrey, then chancellor, gave it to Special Collections on January 22, 1970 (Special Collections, University of Nevada, Reno, Papers of Julian Steward, Collection NC487). Thus, the report remained suppressed and unavailable until 1970, and until another copy was placed in the Steward archives sometime after Steward's death in 1972.

CONCLUSIONS AND THE RELEVANCE TO WIDER PROBLEMS

The Steward report and the response of the BIA to it raise questions that are both intriguing and important. There is no way to provide definitive answers to these questions. Such answers involve making assumptions about both the motivations of key individuals and complex judgements about important historic events and the nature of Western Shoshone political organization from the pre-1850s to the 1930s. Nevertheless, the following questions are raised and I suggest the best answers currently available to me.

First, there can be no doubt that Steward expressed viewpoints about the Western Shoshones that were at best ethnocentric and at worst racist. What can account for these views? Although I know little about Steward personally that could shed light on this, it is apparent that similar personal views have been held by other outstanding figures among early-twentieth-century anthropologists, as the works of George Stocking and the journal he edits document in disturbing detail (Stocking 1983).

The discovery that some leading scholars held personal views that were derogatory about peoples with whom they had worked is the more puzzling. Anthropology is notable because at a conceptual level it was the first academic discipline in the United States to reject white-racist explanations of the differences between European (including Euro-American) society of the late nineteenth and early twentieth centuries and non-Western societies. It is also true that a central concern of U.S. anthropologists (including Steward) for several decades was to preserve knowledge of Native American societies as they had existed before Euro-American contact, which implies that these were considered valuable. Many social scientists in this country held white-racist basic views until the late 1930s or even later. However, both Boas and Kroeber rejected such views from the beginning. It is safe to say that the discipline followed their lead with almost complete unanimity, at a time when many of their colleagues in cognate fields were still adhering to racist views.

Steward was one of the anthropologists who explicitly rejected racism. Not only does his work implicitly reflect this standpoint, but Steward (1962), in a letter to *Science,* repudiated "The older concept of racism [that] clearly stated that the races of mankind—which involved at best a very confused taxonomy of races—could be rated in a scale of genetic capacity." Moreover, he also rejected as scientifically untenable what he called a newer question, "whether the smaller, long-inbreeding groups of mankind—groups much smaller than the conventionally designated races—can be assumed to have behavioral characteristics which are genetically determined" (Steward 1962: 964–965). In other words, Steward stated that there was no scientific basis for assuming that either Native Americans as a whole or the Western Shoshones in particular were inferior to Euro-Americans.

I do not have the answer to Steward's question, but I suspect it proves how deeply ethnocentric and/or racist modes of thinking became embedded among so-called white people in the European and Euro-American nations that participated in the conquest of most of the rest of the world over several centuries. That is, one might know at an intellectual level that the "Indians" were not subjugated and partially exterminated by Western expansionism over several centuries because they were biologically inferior as groups. Yet the notion that their societies were "primitive" and in some sense inferior to the societies of the conquerors might still persist at fundamental and perhaps subconscious psychological levels.[1]

The second question has to do with the difference between the goals of academic scholars and those of administrators. The purpose of scholarly investigation is the pursuit of truth, as determined by the individual scholar within the context of accepted canons of discourse and the existing loose social structure of various scientific communities. The purpose of administrators is to accomplish the mission of the organization, within the context of accepted canons of organizational behavior and the hierarchical structure of public agencies. Scholars may be guided by both moral and organizational goals, but there are possibilities for conflict because neither the two canons nor the background organizational structures are the same.

Steward was operating within the scholarly mode while doing the research for and the writing of *Basin-Plateau* and the other products of his 1935–1936 research, but he was involved in an administrative task while producing his 1936 report. Did Steward perceive conflicts between these two purposes, and do these conflicts help explain the content of the 1936 report? We do not know precisely how Steward viewed his administrative task. However, we do know that he accepted this task only after most of his research was completed. We also know that there is strong evidence that Steward undertook no research specifically designed to provide information for the 1936 report, which he produced to aid the BIA in its organizational and other work.

It makes sense to assume that writing *Basin-Plateau* (and the two culture-element lists that he had also agreed to prepare) was vastly more important to Steward than the duty to prepare a report for the BIA and that Steward saw the BIA report as an unpleasant by-product of his basic work. Making this assumption could explain partially several things about the report. First, it could explain why Steward did no additional research for the report, although the backward-looking orientation of his original research makes it highly unlikely that initially he systematically sought information on current political/governmental matters. Also, after I had presented an earlier version of this paper at the 1986 annual meeting of the Southwestern Anthropological Association, George Foster, who had known Steward during the 1930s and 1940s, told me that Steward found fieldwork so stressful that it literally made him ill (Foster, personal communication 1986). In other words, even if he could have found the time Steward would have found it difficult to undertake another round of interviewing to seek more information on this topic. Second, this assumption could explain why Steward apparently did not seek out employees of the BIA to find out what they knew about political/governmental (and other) matters involving the Western Shoshones. If he thought of the 1936 report as unimportant compared to his fundamental scientific work, Steward might have not been concerned to inform himself about the matters he was required to discuss in it. Third, the hypothesis that Steward saw administrative work as far less important than scientific work suggests that he resented having to write such a report. This could account partially for the fact that its tone was belligerent toward the BIA, even though he was (indirectly) employed by the agency to make such a report, and can also help explain why Steward did not contact bureau employees for information. Finally, the assumption that Steward saw a conflict between the two types of work, both of which he was being compensated to do, could account for the fact that he failed to understand several important aspects of the fundamental viewpoint of the Collier administration toward Indian policy, even though he said at the beginning of the 1936 report that he was in agreement with it. We do not know how much effort the BIA made to explain its viewpoint to the anthropologists who agreed to accept assignments from the agency. However, Steward may also have resisted understanding what he was being told because of hostility to anything but scientific concerns.

A third set of questions suggested by the Steward report has to do with the utilization by Collier's administration of the knowledge and ideas of anthropologists. Collier had been a vigorous (and indeed tireless) advocate of Indian rights for a dozen years before he finally won appointment as Indian commissioner. During this time he systematically sought out advice and other aid from any persons who knew or cared about Native Americans. Clearly the most important group of scholars knowledgeable about Indians of the United States during this period consisted of the small number of anthropologists, most of whom were in academic positions. (At the 1986 Southwestern Anthropological Association meetings, George Foster [1986] gave a paper in which he estimated that there were only about 200 "fully professional anthropologists" in this country in 1930 and only about 300 by 1940.)

From the beginning of Collier's work through the development of the bill, which became the IRA, and the early implementation of the act, Collier sought to secure the support of anthropologists and to learn from them. For example, Collier says in his autobiography that Alfred Kroeber was asked to support his program during the early 1920s and was a supporter of his work from that time on (Collier 1963:216–217).

In the fall of 1933, when planning for the IRA began, the BIA sent out a questionnaire to approximately 100 anthropologists asking them for information about the political/governmental aspects of the various American Indian societies they knew about from personal research. In December 1933 Collier personally attended a meeting of the American Anthropological Association, during which he asked for the help of anthropologists and made some personal contacts (Kelly 1980:8–9). Collier also systematically sought support and advice from the even smaller group of "friends of the Indians," chiefly through two conferences in early 1933 and early 1934 (Rusco 1996).

It is significant that anthropologists and "friends of the Indians" were consulted months before there was any formal consultation with Indians (although a few Indians attended the 1933 and 1934 conferences). Felix Cohen, the principal author of the bill that was presented to Congress in February 1934, persuaded his colleagues in the BIA in January 1934 to seek similar advice and support from Native American societies (Rusco 1996). Undoubtedly this delay occurred partly because Collier had worked with and for several Native American groups (notably the Pueblos of the Southwest) for a number of years and assumed that he knew what Indians wanted and needed in a major legislative revision of Indian statutory law.

When the IRA was approved (in June 1934) the BIA was faced with a severe organizational problem. Its basic appropriated funds had been cut drastically in early 1933 at the same time that its duties had been expanded as a result of several New Deal programs that were administered by the BIA. The bureau had requested specific new appropriations to make possible organizational work called for by the IRA, but did not receive them from Congress.

Moreover, a feature of the IRA that had not been requested by the BIA substantially increased its work load. This was the requirement that Native American societies had to vote for the IRA before it would apply to them. This requirement (which had been introduced as a result of the expressed desires of several tribes to be excluded from the IRA) meant not only that the BIA had to conduct elections on each reservation within a relatively short time (initially one year from passage of the IRA, although later an extension was granted). It also meant that the BIA had to lobby for approval by each society, because initially a number of the most important provisions of the IRA (although not those ending allotment) could not be carried out if a society voted against the IRA as a whole.

This substantial organizational effort, which the BIA had not planned and for which it received no extra moneys, also must have had an important effect in persuading many BIA employees and many Indians that the bureau had an organizational plan that it wished to promote on every reservation or among every Native American society. The bill that went to Congress proposed to undertake organizational work only on those reservations requesting such aid or on which other BIA programs necessitated such efforts. However, after an Organizational Division had been set up to conduct the IRA elections, in practice the BIA proposed organizational efforts to most Native American societies (although a significant number of such societies refused to organize or reorganize).

Given this set of circumstances, the fact that an Applied Anthropology Unit was set up within the BIA's Organization Division indicates clearly the high value placed upon the knowledge and support of anthropologists by the Collier administration. Several brief studies of the operation of this unit have been published, but there has yet to emerge a full-blown study that deals in depth with the relations between anthropologists and administrators in the Indian New Deal (Kelly 1980; Steward 1969b; Taylor 1975).

Steward was one of the two most important anthropologists called upon to aid the BIA during the beginning of this process, although he worked only during the period when this aid was provided by the BAE. William Duncan Strong of the BAE was the first official of this agency to coordinate this early work with the BIA. When Strong found himself too busy at the end of 1935 to continue his work, he was replaced by Steward, who served until June 1936. Anthropologist Scudder Mekeel was hired directly by the BIA in the fall of 1935, but had no employees directly under him until the beginning of the next fiscal year, in July 1936 (JHS folder "Applied Anthropology—1935–36/ American Indians").

The scanty literature on anthropology plus the comments by Collier and Bowler on the 1936 Steward report make it clear that there was substantial conflict between these academics and the administrators, especially in the period when the BAE was providing these services. One of the most obvious sources of such conflict came in the area of the basic goals of the new Indian policy. It is apparent that Steward was not the only anthropologist who did not share these basic assumptions or even clearly grasp them.

This conflict is illustrated not only in the 1936 report, but also in a 1969 article in which Steward discussed the relationship of anthropology to the wider society. Steward began his 1969 paper by asserting, in effect, that there was a conflict between the pursuit of truth by scientific means and action based on values. He rejected the view that "advocates action on the basis of values that one learns from his society, and holds as a human being, which in effect calls for abdication of attempts at scientific understandings" (Steward 1969b:1). He concluded that "mere humanitarianism is a poor guide to action anthropology" (Steward 1969b:2).

The basis for these conclusions is not clearly stated, but apparently they developed out of the philosophical view, introduced into American social science by logical positivism, that values could not be determined by rational means because at root they were simply preferences. However, Steward also asserted that he believed in "a set of basic values that are valid cross-culturally and scientifically and that are not merely humanitarian because the sociologists say so" (Steward 1969b:2). However, these turn out to be merely material values—the overall goal of "survival," which includes "subsidiary goals such as absence of hunger, pain, sickness and many associated psychosomatic ailments." This basic view might help us understand why Steward did not place much emphasis on symbolic values of all sorts: He believed there was no way to study them scientifically.

The major problem in squaring action with pursuit of scientific knowledge, however, was for Steward the difficulty in understanding the basic processes of social change. As he put it, knowledge of "inevitable trends" is insufficient if one does not understand the basic laws of human development that account for these trends.

In this article Steward applied these basic views to the relationship between anthropologists and the Indian New Deal. In his view, at the beginning of the Indian New Deal few anthropologists were opposed to "the aim of assimilation. . . . [Instead,] the manner of assimilation rather than the ultimate goal was questioned" (Steward 1969b:4). He suggested that anthropologists at the beginning of the Indian New Deal were still primarily interested in "the reconstruction of aboriginal cultures" (as he had been when he wrote *Basin-Plateau*) and hardly at all in the "factors, processes and dynamics of change" as a result of European contact (Steward 1969b:5).

This suggests, correctly, that Steward did not consider that Collier's advocacy of traditional Indian cultures was scientifically based. Consequently, Steward wrote, "When the assistance of anthropologists was finally sought by the BIA in 1934, we were unprepared to offer much of value" (Steward 1969b:5). Specifically, he thought anthropologists lacked a theory of culture change that could be used to guide the movement toward assimilation.

However, Steward's main point was that many anthropologists disagreed, as he did, with the goal of the Collier administration, which was to preserve and strengthen Indian cultures rather than to change them. Collier understood that some Indians wanted to assimilate and also that in some cases, notably the case of the Navajo Nation, some Indians would have to leave the reservation for others to be able to stay and practice traditional ways. But there can be no doubt that Collier's deepest concern was to protect the right of Indian societies to resist total assimilation.

According to Steward, the Indian New Deal "not only sought to halt assimilation and to preserve 'Indianhood' but it permitted John Collier to attempt to introduce his own utopian assumptions about native societies" (Steward 1969b:7). As Steward saw it, "This was truly a messianic or revitalization movement, and Collier was its prophet" (Steward 1969b:8). Instead, Steward asserted, most anthropologists accepted the inevitability of assimilation, but were without scientific knowledge of how to make the development bring less pain to Indians. This being the case, Collier administration policy "left us no alternative but to accept its new goals or disassociate ourselves from the entire program" (Steward 1969b:8–9).

This is an important point, because Steward either did not understand or accept the basic nature of governmental bureaucracies in democratic systems as they exist in modern nation-states, radically misunderstood the Collier program, or both. Although his wording suggests that Steward subordinated his own goals to those of the agency, in fact this was not the case, as his 1936 report clearly indicated. This implies that Steward (and other anthropologists, as he saw it, although it is not clear how many others working with the BIA agreed with his views) had the right to work for a governmental agency even though they could not accept its basic orientations.

It is generally accepted in public government in this country that the officials appointed by and responsible to the elected officials have the right to determine the direction of policy pursued by governmental bureaucracies. Even where an official feels that a policy violates basic moral values or his or her most deeply held beliefs, the proper resolution of this conflict is for the official to resign and combat the policy from the outside. Attempting to resist basic bureaucratic policy while employed by an agency controlled by policy-makers chosen ultimately by elected officials violates basic democratic principles, as these are understood in modern democratic states.

Perhaps Steward did not perceive that his differences with Collier on basic policy were at a sufficiently fundamental level to make it impossible for him to serve in the BIA. However, his 1936 report contains evidence that if he did believe this, he was wrong. Not only Collier himself, but the IRA, had abandoned the policy of establishing individual Indian households as owners of property held in fee simple. Also, the IRA clearly embodied the current legal doctrine, which was that Native American societies exercised restricted sovereignty because this sovereignty had never been taken away from them. Finally, Collier clearly wished to preserve for Indians the possibility of refusing to accept assimilation with the general American society. In these respects Steward was so fundamentally at odds with the Indian New Deal that he should have refused to serve or should have resigned when he realized his situation.

At the end of his 1969 article Steward made some specific remarks that suggest that the advice tendered in his 1936 report was rejected for far less basic reasons. He suggested that anthropologists should have been called upon to recommend solutions to Indian problems tailored to the particular circumstances of each Indian society. However, not only did anthropologists lack a theory of culture change that would have made such suggestions possible, but the BIA's views led it to reject most of the recommendations that were made.

In discussing a number of instances of conflict between anthropologists and the leaders of the BIA during the 1930s, Steward stated that "In the Great Basin, arbitrary territorial units became the alleged native basis for self-government, and my own finding based on years [*sic*] of research in the areas was regarded as an attempt to sabotage the program" (Steward 1969b:9). The exact meaning of this comment is difficult to determine, apart from the fact that it speculates about what motivated Collier and Bowler to suppress the report. Steward's analysis of the situation in Western Shoshone country at the time certainly differed in several respects from that of Superintendent Bowler. Originally she had believed that one or more large reservations should be purchased for the Western Shoshones, but she had abandoned this concept by the time Steward wrote his report, although it is not clear whether he knew this. It is clear, however, that he saw no reason to talk the question over with Bowler.

Probably Steward was referring to her decision to proceed with organization of the Te-Moak Bands rather than a series of governments based solely on small reservations. Steward obviously did not agree with this strategy, although he also disagreed with setting up small reservations. My view on this is that Bowler correctly perceived what Richard Clemmer (1972) described later as a "traditional council" loosely led by Muchach Temoak and that she wished to set up a government that would give this incipient council governmental authority and open access to governmental funds and other kinds of support for the various components of this unit. It does not seem to me that this was an impractical goal, although Temoak and other traditionalists did not accept the Te-Moak Bands organization when it was established. In other words, what Bowler was attempting was not achieved, but it is not certain that it could not have been.

We do not know all the reasons why the concept of Te-Moak Bands initially failed. One reason, however, is evident: although Bowler proposed the idea, BIA headquarters in Washington, D.C., ultimately refused to accept the notion that a tribal government could be based on anything but reservations (Rusco 1982). Thus, the council ultimately formed under the Te-Moak Bands structure was inevitably dominated by the South Fork Reservation and the Elko Colony.

It also seems likely to me that neither Bowler nor Steward understood adequately how the "traditionals" viewed the 1863 Ruby Valley Treaty. Although I have not been able to find definitive statements on this point from either Bowler or Steward, it is highly probable that both took it for granted that the Western Shoshones had irrevocably lost ownership of the lands they clearly held before the signing of the treaty, while it was the view of the "traditionals" that this was not the case and that the treaty, if properly construed, would protect their right of ownership. The strength and persistence of this view within Western Shoshone country until 1996, in spite of a U.S. Supreme Court opinion that they lost aboriginal ownership of their lands in 1872, makes it clear how strong this view was, even several decades after Steward's research (Crum 1994:169–183; Rusco 1992).

Finally, there remains the question of how adequately Steward had understood the aboriginal nature of Western Shoshone society and the changes that had taken place since Euro-American contact. It is not certain what a truly adequate study of these matters would conclude, but there are various reasons to suppose that Steward's conceptualization of these complex subjects was not the last word (see Blackhawk, chapter 13; Clemmer, chapter 10; Crum, chapter 8). Perhaps the clearest conclusion from this chapter is that it is very unfortunate that Steward's 10 months in Western Shoshone country came too late for some purposes and that it remains the most extended study of these matters to date.

NOTE

1. In the research I have done on the history of U.S. government policy toward Indians in the 1920s and 1930s, there is an intriguing parallel between Steward's views and those of Oliver LaFarge concerning the Hopi Indians of Arizona. LaFarge had a master's degree in anthropology, was well informed about at least southwestern peoples, and wrote his "Notes for Hopi Administrators" after helping the Hopi to write a constitution during the 1930s. However, in his "Notes" he expresses even more derogatory opinions of the character of Hopis than Steward does of the Western Shoshones in his 1936 report and clearly states on the title page that it should not be shown to Hopis by administrators (who are implicitly assumed not to be Hopis).

8

Julian Steward's Vision of the Great Basin: A Critique and Response

STEVEN J. CRUM

In this chapter, Steven Crum discusses how Steward's "gastric" vision of Great Basin peoples perpetuated and reinforced an already existing image that the Great Basin tribes were perhaps some of the simplest people on earth. Steward's bias caused him to fail to identify Numic peoples' "inner lives" and the deep attachment to the land to which this "inner life" was oriented. It also resulted in the Western Shoshones being placed by other scholars at a "low" position on a neo-evolutionist scale. Crum's exploration of some aspects of the Western Shoshones' "inner lives" and the historic context in which Steward did his work reveals Steward's view of the Great Basin as too general and incomplete.

Over the years, the American anthropological community has come to regard Julian Steward as one of the most influential anthropologists of modern times. For example, Omer Stewart, professor emeritus at the University of Colorado, writes that Julian Steward was a "pre-eminent anthropological scholar" and "world famous as an anthropological theorist" (Stewart 1980). Robert Murphy of Columbia University calls Steward "one of the leading anthropologists of our time" (Murphy 1970), and Catherine Fowler of the University of Nevada, Reno, writes that Steward "left a lasting impression on the discipline of anthropology as well as Great Basin scholarship" (Fowler 1982). In November 1988 Steward was idolized at the annual conference of the American Society for Ethnohistory in a session entitled, "Forefathers and Mothers: Intellectual Legacies" (American Society for Ethnohistory 1988). In short, Julian Steward has found his place among the great scholars in American anthropology.

In the early 1930s Steward came forth with a model (or theory) labeled "cultural ecology." He tested his theory in 1935 by conducting six months of field research among the Western Shoshones and other tribes of the Great Basin; his findings were published in *Basin-Plateau Aboriginal Sociopolitical Groups* (1970a [1938]), which is now regarded as a classic in Great Basin ethnography. Steward maintained that the Great Basin tribes were "simple hunters and gatherers" before white contact. Their "simple culture" lacked elaborate social or political organizations such as bands or clans. Because the dry, harsh environment possessed only limited food resources, the tribes divided themselves into small extended-family groups living over a large area and eking out a bare existence (Thomas 1983b). Essentially, Steward perpetuated and reinforced an already existing image that the Great Basin tribes were perhaps some of the simplest people on earth (Steward 1937d). Owing to his academic prominence and possibly more than any other individual, Julian Steward gave the public a mental image of the Great Basin people.

RECENT CHALLENGES TO STEWARD'S CONCLUSIONS

For many years the academic community accepted Steward's vision. However, in recent years anthropologists began to erode his conclusions. The first was Omer Stewart; in his article "The Temoke Band of Shoshone and the Oasis Concept" (1980), Stewart differs from Steward by refuting the latter's simplistic generalizations. Stewart refuted the argument that the Western Shoshones possessed short-lived band organizations after white contact. Steward implied that the natives were incapable of maintaining larger groupings because of their simpleness. In contrast, Stewart provides solid evidence that the Temoke Band of Ruby Valley did not have a 10-year existence, in the 1850s and early 1860s, but continued to exist into the twentieth century. If Julian Steward produced a negative image of the Great Basin, then Omer Stewart's was positive. Further, Stewart pointed out that the Great Basin was not a vast, monolithic desert where the natives barely survived before white contact. Rather it possessed fertile pockets or "oas[es] in the desert" (Stewart 1980). One of these places was Ruby Valley in northeastern Nevada. The Ruby Mountains provided the valley with sufficient spring runoff, and shallow lakes existed at the time of white contact. There was a variety of food sources, including deer, antelope, pine nuts, and grass seeds. Ruby Valley was therefore able to accommodate a sizable Shoshone population, even after white contact, although the natives were somewhat mobile. That is, these people were not eking out a bare existence as Steward had portrayed (Stewart 1980:246–249).

Anthropologist Catherine Fowler also challenged Julian Steward in her "Settlement Patterns and Subsistence Systems in the Great Basin: The Ethnographic Record" (1982). She maintains that Steward's view of the Basin was too general and incomplete. Fowler wrote: "Curiously, Steward does not include in the monograph *[Basin-Plateau]* a sketch of any of the lakeshore- or riverine-based Northern Paiute groups" (Fowler 1982:124). Of course, Fowler was referring to those Northern Paiutes of western Nevada who traditionally lived along the Truckee River and Pyramid and Walker Lakes, areas that Steward completely excluded in his classic 1938 study. Fowler notes that before white contact, during half of the year the Paiutes relied extensively upon fish as a major food source, thus making them fishermen, hunters, and gatherers, something not quite the same as the hunter-gatherer model produced by Steward. Fowler's position is supported by anthropologist David Hurst Thomas, who also maintains that Steward excluded the "lakeshore-adapted Northern Paiute groups," or those around Pyramid and Walker Lakes. Furthermore, Thomas asserts that Steward produced a "bias in the Basin"—that all the Great Basin tribes were nothing more than "simple hunter-gatherers" (Thomas 1983b:61–62).

My objective in this chapter is to further erode Julian Steward's vision of the Great Basin. I will do so by examining three of Steward's writings: his unpublished 1936 manuscript "Shoshonean Tribes: Utah, Idaho, Nevada, Eastern California"; his classic 1938 study *Basin-Plateau Aboriginal Sociopolitical Groups;* and his 1955 publication *Theory and Culture Change.* I will focus primarily upon the Western Shoshones because I am most familiar with this tribe.

"SHOSHONEAN TRIBES": A FAILURE TO RECOGNIZE ETHNOGRAPHIC REALITY

Steward's unpublished 1936 "Shoshonean Tribes: Utah, Idaho, Nevada, Eastern California" was a report for the Bureau of Indian Affairs (BIA), which was at the time headed by John Collier (Philp 1977:113–162). Collier came to office with a major objective, namely, to halt the bureau's age-old assimilationist policy for Native Americans. He sought to revive native ways and intertwine them with modern life. In short, Collier wanted the tribes to organize communal tribal governments, and this was a basic purpose of the 1934 Indian Reorganization Act (IRA; Taylor 1980). Collier therefore called upon the anthropological community to advance his new policy of cultural revitalization (Kelly 1980; Taylor 1975).

In 1935 Collier got the support of W. Duncan Strong, director of the Bureau of American Ethnology (BAE). However, due to Strong's busy academic schedule, another BAE employee, Julian Steward, was called upon to find "ways and means of applying anthropology to the practical affairs of Indian administration" (Steward 1937b). In early 1936 the Collier administration asked

Steward to produce a report on how the Western Shoshones and other Great Basin tribes might best adapt to the BIA's new policy.

In response, Steward produced an 18-page report sent to Commissioner Collier as well as Alida Bowler, superintendent of the Carson Agency in Nevada. Bowler received a copy because she was expected to carry out Steward's recommendations at the local level (Bowler 1936c; Mekeel 1936a, 1936b, 1938). Unfortunately, Steward's "Shoshonean Tribes" proved to be of no value to the BIA (see Rusco, chapter 7). In his report Steward stressed that Western Shoshone culture was so "low" and so markedly disrupted by white contact that it was not worth preserving in the twentieth century (Steward 1936b). In drawing this conclusion, Steward presented the Western Shoshones (along with other Great Basin tribes) in an extremely negative light.

Steward emphasized that Western Shoshone culture, both past and present, was extremely "low." He called the Great Basin Shoshones "impoverished 'foot Indians.'" Writing further, he noted that the "Nevada and southern Idaho Shoshoni had no bands or other tribal groupings," except for the family, before white contact. However, Steward did point out that immediately following contact, in the 1850s and early 1860s, the Western Shoshones organized short-lived bands to battle the white intruders. However, according to Steward, "such 'bands' dissolved as soon as the wars were over." The bands were "arbitrary and artificial," and their existence lasted only for about 10 years. As for the well-known "Temoak's Band" of Ruby Valley, it too was a "fiction," a product of white pressure. The band was an "artificial union" that quickly died because it lacked indigenous roots. Steward therefore disagreed with the 1873 report drafted by John Wesley Powell and G. W. Ingalls that maintained that the Nevada Shoshones possessed band organizations in the 1870s (Steward 1936b:2, 9; Thomas 1983b:60).

Indirectly, Steward was saying that if the Western Shoshones formed a larger political organization under the IRA, it would quickly fall apart for two reasons: the Western Shoshones did not have a legacy of possessing larger political organizations before white contact, and, in fact, the short-lived band organizations of the mid-nineteenth century had already fallen apart because a legacy had not existed in precontact days. Steward therefore opposed Superintendent Bowler's plans to organize the Western Shoshones under a large confederated organization, similar to the one that existed in the mid-nineteenth century when Chief Temoke brought together several bands first to fight and then to make peace with the whites.

Steward was both right and wrong about the Western Shoshones. It is true that large band organizations did not exist before white contact. However, the postcontact bands continued to exist, even into the twentieth century. The Temoke Band was not a "fiction," but a reality. Its existence has been confirmed by numerous observers, both non-Indian and Shoshone. Levi Gheen, a BIA agent serving the Western Shoshones, talked about "Te-Moak's Band" of the "Ruby Valley and vicinity" (Gheen 1873). Calvin Asbury, superintendent of the Reno Agency, made reference to "Chief Tomoque's band" (Asbury 1912:2). Frederick Snyder, superintendent of the Carson Agency, referred to the "Indians of Ruby Valley, who are the Temoak band of Shoshone" (Snyder 1926a). In 1929 the editor of the *Elko Free Press* made reference to "the Indians of Ruby Valley, known as the Temoak band, a branch of the Western Shoshones" (*Elko Free Press* 1929). Also, Doris Cleveland of Ely and Johnny Thompson of Star Valley, both Shoshones, considered themselves members of the "Temoak band" (Cleveland 1932; Thompson 1932).

The Temoke Band was undoubtedly a living reality going back to the mid-nineteenth century, although before contact it was most likely a family group or perhaps an extended family. After the arrival of the whites, it became a large band organization consisting of numerous families living in northeastern Nevada. The influential Chief Temoke was responsible for bringing together the independent families, and the Temoke Band was indeed an entity that still existed in the twentieth century (Stewart 1980:250, 252–255). Besides the Temoke Band, the Shoshones of central Nevada also had their own division called the "Too Toaina band," named after Chief Tutuwa (or Tootoaina) of the Reese River Valley (*Battle Mountain Scout* 1947; Snyder 1926b). Both bands practiced hereditary leadership. When old Chief Temoke died in 1891, he was replaced by his son Joe Temoke, and ultimately Joe's son Muchuch Temoke became the chief in 1916 (Carson Agency 1927). Old Chief Tutuwa died in 1897 and was replaced by his son Tom, who in turn was replaced by a family relative, Harry Dixon, in 1922 (*Battle Mountain Scout* 1922; *Reese River Reveille* 1897; *Gold Field Weekly News* 1905).

Steward failed to recognize the existence of these political entities because of his preconceived notions as well as his low opinion of the Western Shoshones. He saw the Western Shoshones as not having the ability to maintain a larger grouping, in part because there "are not today any natural bands or major divisions among them" (Steward 1936b:3). However, in 1932, some three years before Steward's ethnographic visit to the Great Basin, the Shoshones in northeastern Nevada formed a treaty council to press claims against the government for unkept treaty promises (U.S. Senate 1934:14847–14854). The Temoke Band was part of this body. Yet, somehow, Steward failed to recognize its existence.

Steward also did not favor the BIA's effort to revive the Great Basin art in the 1930s. He considered Shoshonean art inferior and unrefined and thus not worth preserving. Steward wrote in his report: "Their arts and crafts were among the poorest in America," "meager" and "superficial." Great Basin pottery was "execrable" (extremely inferior) and the "basketry was exceptionally poor, except in Death Valley where it was exceptionally good" (Steward 1936b:8, 11–12).

Although Steward was correct about Death Valley, he was wrong about other Shoshone places, for good quality basketry was widespread in the Great Basin. One significant basketmaker of northeastern Nevada was Mary Hall, who was born in the 1870s and died in 1946. According to biographer Edna Patterson, Mary "was recognized as one of the most skilled basketmakers of the Western Shoshone people" (Patterson 1985:103). Her baskets included traditional geometric designs as well as newly introduced floral designs. Some of her baskets were extremely large—one was even used as a laundry basket by an Anglo family in the 1920s. Mary Hall passed her skills to four daughters who also became gifted artists in their own right.

Because Steward was so wrapped up in his own preconceived vision of the Western Shoshones, he failed to recognize the fine work produced by Mary Hall and other basketmakers in his 1935 field research. It is no surprise, then, that he wrote "it is, therefore, futile to take measures to preserve anything native. . . . These people possessed virtually nothing which win[s] them admiration, sympathy or support of whites" (Steward 1936b:7). Steward did not acknowledge the fact that the biggest admirers and buyers of Shoshone baskets were the wealthy ranch families and townsfolk of Nevada. In his report, he favored an anonymous person's suggestion that "Navajo weaving, Hopi pottery, and other Indian arts be introduced to Shoshoneans" (Steward 1936b:7).

By producing his "Shoshonean Tribes" report, Steward portrayed himself as a "neo-evolutionist," one who rates societies on a scale from the highest to the lowest. He saw the Pueblos of the Southwest as the "highest" form of Native Americans. They lived in close-knit, sedentary villages; produced agricultural crops; and adapted to their desert environments, especially along the Rio Grande in New Mexico. The Pueblos produced beautiful jewelry and pottery with elaborate designs that were rich in symbolism. They were deeply religious people and their colorful ceremonies were markedly evident. All the Pueblo villages were governed by recognized leaders (Gibson 1980:73–75). However, according to Steward, the Western Shoshones of the Great Basin lacked all that the Pueblos possessed, thereby making them the lowest form of Indian. He wrote in his report: "The Shoshoneans are the antithesis of Pueblos. Their native culture was so meager and their socio-political groups so tenuous that no well-defined and stable patterns had emerged" (Steward 1936b:7).

BIA officials, especially Superintendent Bowler, quickly criticized Steward's report, stressing that his work was based on "a minimum of so-called 'facts' and a maximum of 'interpretation' and recommendation based upon personal opinion" (Bowler 1937:5; for a detailed discussion of Bowler's response see Rusco, chapter 7). Bowler was critical of Steward's report because of his assertion that Western Shoshone culture was low and simple. She maintained that although the culture was not complex like that of the Pueblo or Navajo, Great Basin culture was unique in its own way and possessed important facets not readily visible to the non-Indian outsider. Bowler wrote that Steward "failed to catch many glimpses of the inner life, the heart and soul of the Indian." She referred to traditional round-dance music, "of a lyric type, paying tribute to beauty in nature, an aspect of culture that few white people, if any, knew existed" (Bowler 1937:5). On this particular point, Bowler was correct, for Steward failed to appreciate or identify important nonmaterial aspects of Western Shoshone culture.

Julian Steward eventually read Bowler's response and then stated to a colleague: "I find no reason to alter my previous statements . . . based on ten years' observation" (Steward 1937e). However, Steward was not the only anthropologist to oppose the BIA's reorganization efforts of cultural revival. Two years earlier Ralph Linton stressed that the BIA's effort to bring back old tribalism would fail because the tribes of the twentieth century were already too acculturated (Philp 1977:136–137).

BASIN-PLATEAU: A FAILURE TO IDENTIFY "INNER LIFE"

Julian Steward did not alter his views on the Western Shoshones. His book *Basin-Plateau Aboriginal Sociopolitical Groups* (1970a [1938]), which is now regarded as a classic in anthropology, reinforced his earlier conclusions. Steward reiterated that the Western Shoshones and other Great Basin tribes were "simple hunters and gatherers" before contact. The dry, harsh environment kept them at a "base subsistence level." Because of this limitation "imposed by ecology," or the environment, "their culture was meager" (Steward 1970a:1 [1938]), and Steward concluded that the Great Basin culture was "gastric" (Steward 1970a:46 [1938]).

As before, Steward failed to identify the Shoshones' "inner lives," maintaining that the round dances existed for entertainment purposes, or "merely to amuse small portions of the bands" (Steward 1970a:237 [1938]). It is true that the round dances were held for social entertainment, however, they also served a much more important purpose. Rich in lyrics, the round-dance songs were part of the oral tradition, a way of passing down tribal knowledge. Some songs existed to inform the Shoshones that they lived in unison with nature and that the land (or earth) was their lifeblood. The "Early Morning Song" ("Imma Hupia") was an expression of the Shoshones' attachment to the land (B. Crum ca. 1975):

Early Morning Song

Tsaa napuni, tai sokopi,	How beautiful is our land,
tsaa napuni, tai sokopi,	how beautiful is our land,
Oyo paam paa kematu	forever, besides the water, the water,
tsaa napuni, tai sohopi,	how beautiful is our land
Tsaa napuni, tai sokopi,	How beautiful is our land,
tsaa napuni, tai sokopi,	how beautiful is our land,
Soko totsiyama, paa kematu	Earth, with flowers on it, next to the water
tsaa napuni, tai sohopi.	how beautiful is our land.

Other round-dance songs expressed a deep respect for the animals that the Western Shoshones depended upon. All parts of the animal were utilized: the meat for food, the hides for clothing and footwear, and the antlers and bones for eating utensils and digging instruments. The following song acknowledges the existence of the antelope (B. Crum ca. 1975):

Antelope Song

Pia wantsipe toowenene' iten
Pia wantsipe toowenene' iten
Pennan tapai tatawento toowenene' ite

The big antelope buck-pe slowly grazing while standing
The big antelope buck-pe slowly grazing while standing
Sun beams flashing, hitting him while he stands and grazes.

Still other songs emphasized proper behavior for the people. The following song told the listener that if a child misbehaved he was punished by being carried off by Wolf, the principal father figure (B. Crum 1980):

Furry Wolf

Pia Isa pental	Furry Wolf,
penneh kwasi kasunkha	On his tail he carries him away,
plyatekhi	Carries him away,
plyatekhi	Carries him away,
plyatekhi puatusa nooten	Upon his tail he carries the child away.

Still other round-dance songs gave special attention to human gender. Because of their marked importance, females were emphasized in particular songs, including the following ("Uppi Katete"; B. Crum ca. 1975):

THERE, IN A DISTANT PLACE

Uppi katete huunuma,	There, in a distant place,
tepi yantoma, hein	She sits in an arroyo
Uppi katete huunuma,	Winnowing the pine nuts
tepi yantoma, hein.	She sits in an arroyo.
Ainka tempe huutepena,	By the red-rock wooded place,
tepi yantoma, hein.	Winnowing the pine nuts.

Yet, Julian Steward failed to identify the important aspects of song to Western Shoshone life, which reflects his general viewpoint that ideology simply was not important.

THEORY OF CULTURE CHANGE: A FAILURE TO RECOGNIZE RELIGIOUS ATTACHMENT TO THE LAND

Julian Steward never changed his vision of the Great Basin people. In his book *Theory of Cultural Change* (1955b) he included a chapter on the Great Basin tribes. Here he referred to "Shoshonean culture" as a case of "quantitative simplicity" (Steward 1955b:102). In defending his views, Steward wrote: "An 'element list,' which breaks the [Shoshonean] culture down into details such as basket weaves and shapes, religious beliefs, social practices, and other details, includes a total of about 3,000 items. By comparison, the U.S. forces landing at Casa Blanca during World War II unloaded 500,000 items of material equipment alone" (Steward 1955b:102).

Up to the late stages of his academic career, as a professor at the University of Illinois at Urbana-Champaign, Steward continued to compare the Western Shoshones to other cultural groups to reinforce his argument that the Great Basin people were at the bottom of the cultural scale. Because the Shoshones possessed a "low" culture, their religion was a minor, if not insignificant, force. He remarked in *Theory of Culture Change* that Shoshone religion was "largely a matter of individual concern," implying that it had little, if any, impact on the Shoshones as a collective or communal force (Steward 1955b:114).

Steward failed to realize that to the Western Shoshones "religion" was living in unison with the land, which resulted in a deep attachment to that land. In fact, over the years observers have commented on this important aspect of

Western Shoshone life. John Mayhugh, federal agent for the Nevada Shoshones, wrote that they were "strongly attached to the land of their birth and to the hunting-grounds and home of their fathers" (Mayhugh 1884). In 1932, three years before Steward conducted his ethnographic research, an Interior Department official, Louis Cramton, wrote that the Shoshones and Paiutes were "very strongly attached to their present location" (Cramton 1932:14). Also, Omer Stewart argued that the Western Shoshones had a "strong attachment to their home territory very narrowly defined" (Stewart 1974:81). When Steward visited the Western Shoshones in 1935 for his culture-element distribution work (see Myers, chapter 9; Rusco, chapter 7), he identified informants at 18 different places. Yet Steward failed to realize that these people, who possessed a communal identity, were deeply attached to the land. Even further, they had rejected more than one federal effort to gather up all Western Shoshones and place them on a single reservation (*Battle Mountain Messenger* 1880).

CONCLUSION

Julian Steward was not the first academic to argue that the Western Shoshones possessed a "low" culture. He was joined by at least two others: the late-nineteenth-century historian Hubert Howe Bancroft and anthropologist Alfred Kroeber. In volume 1 of his *The Native Races: Wild Tribes* (1883:440–441), Bancroft wrote: "Yet as in all men there stands out some prominent good, so in these, the lowest of humanity, there is one virtue: they are lovers of their country; lovers, not of fair hills and fertile valleys, but of inhospitable mountains and barren plains; these reptile-like humans love their miserable burrowing-places better than all comforts of civilization." Unlike Steward, Bancroft did recognize the Shoshones' deep attachment to their land, although he also saw them as a lower form of being.

Nor was Julian Steward the last scholar to negatively and deprecatingly refer to the Shoshones. Over the years both anthropologists and historians have continued to make comments about the Western Shoshones as possessors of a low culture and also being a low people. In 1939 world-famous anthropologist Alfred Kroeber wrote that the Shoshones were a "negative fact" (Thomas et al. 1986:275). Historian Arrell Morgan Gibson noted in his *The American Indian: Prehistory to the Present* that "because they had little time to contemplate the metaphysical, the Great Basin tribes had the simplest religion" (Gibson 1980:79). Also, historian William Brandon wrote in his *Indians* that the Shoshones were "primitive people" with a distinct "Shoshonean look"—"short legged and dark-skinned" (Brandon 1985:300).

Because of Steward's "scientific endorsement" of the view that the Western Shoshones possess a low culture, his conclusions have had a great impact on the academic community in this century. Unfortunately, Steward's vision remains largely intact today. I am sad to say that even some Shoshones have come to believe Steward's academic view. I know of two middle-aged Shoshones, former students of the once-existing Stewart Indian School (in Stewart, Nevada), who consider themselves to be "low" Indians. I also know a Shoshone who went to college in the early 1970s to study Native Americans. Yet this person chose to study the "magnificent" warriors of the Great Plains rather than the "lowly" Shoshones of the Great Basin. Perhaps a future generation of scholars might one day reevaluate the Great Basin vision advanced by Julian Steward and create a better one by examining their "inner lives."

9

A Frame for Culture: Observations on the Culture-Element Distribution of the Snake River Shoshone

L. Daniel Myers

Myers discusses some of the background to Steward's culture-element distribution list for the "Salmon-Eaters" of the Snake River in terms of the methodology and theory of the time. He also gives a qualitative interpretation of the pertinent aspects of Steward's work and of explicit, implicit, and tacit assumptions and concepts that underlie Steward's work in the Great Basin. While addressing the question of what influence Steward's contribution had on Great Basin anthropology, Myers calls for redefining the Great Basin as a research paradigm, rather than a culture area, and gives reasons for replacing the "gastric" and quantitative model of Great Basin peoples with a qualitative, symbolic-structural one.

Steward's culture-element distributions (CEDs) are conspicuous by their absence in assessments of his early fieldwork experience and his later writings. An interpretation of these surveys is paramount to understanding the major concepts and assumptions underlying his contributions to Great Basin anthropology as well as to the discipline as a whole. Steward's CED work was intimately tied to the work of his mentor, Alfred Kroeber, and was crucial for Joseph Jorgensen's (1980) monumental survey of western Indian tribes. Therefore, key factors of this "trait-list" approach are important for situating Steward in the history of North American anthropology. As an example of Steward's early fieldwork, I will focus on one of these CED groups, the Snake River Shoshone (the Salmon-Eaters) of south-central Idaho, and the effect that such groups had in shaping Steward's contributions to anthropology. This focus is also significant because it further documents one of the least-known groups studied by Steward.

I will begin with a brief historic account of Kroeber's (1922, 1939a, 1939b, 1939c) CED survey program and then describe some of the more prominent features of this particular survey. From this description, I will explore certain basic assumptions and concepts that underlie Steward's method and theory. Accounts of Steward's early fieldwork appear in a variety of sources (Eggan 1980; Fowler 1982; Fowler 1980; Fowler and Jennings 1982; Fowler et al. 1986; Heizer 1978; Jorgensen 1980; Kroeber 1941; Manners 1973; Murphy 1970, 1977, 1981). As an alternative to Steward's approach and to his conceptualization of the Great Basin as a culture area, I will suggest that a more parsimonious "cognitive" approach be taken. By defining culture as "a system of thought and knowledge" and the Great Basin as a *research area,* I suggest that a "symbolic-structural" perspective be applied to Great Basin studies. This perspective demonstrates the conceptually based, symbolically expressed, and logically structured system of Numic culture. Concurrently, it gives access to the symbolic processes and conceptual repertoire that contribute to, maintain, and support such a cultural system.

SCHOLARLY ANTECEDENTS

Two of the most influential scholars to affect Steward's graduate career were Alfred L. Kroeber and Robert H. Lowie. In 1901, Kroeber received his Ph.D. in anthropology under Franz Boas, served as curator for the California Academy of Science, and founded the Anthropology Department at the University of California, Berkeley. In subsequent years, Kroeber did linguistic, archaeological, and ethnographic research involving the California and Great Basin Indians. Lowie also received his Ph.D. from Columbia University under Boas in 1908 and joined the Department of Anthropology at the American Museum of Natural History as an assistant curator in 1909. In the following years, his stay at the museum was interspersed with travels among the Plains tribes. In 1917–1918, Lowie joined Berkeley's Department of Anthropology as a visiting professor. After two years of service in the military, in 1921 Lowie was permanently appointed as associate professor at Berkeley. Both Kroeber and Lowie were "by default students of the North American Indian, Kroeber specializing in California and the Great Basin and Lowie in the Plains. . . . Lowie saw himself as an 'ethnologist' only, though he did publish linguistic notes on the Crow Indians, but Kroeber worked actively in linguistic and archaeology as well as cultural anthropology" (Murphy 1977:2–3). Both men had worked specifically in the Great Basin region with various groups of Shoshoneans. Kroeber (1901, 1907, 1908a, 1908b, 1909a, 1909b, 1941) did linguistics and social research in the far West by focusing on populations of the southern Great Basin. Lowie (1909a, 1909b, 1915, 1919, 1923, 1924a, 1924b, 1930), however, was concerned with social organization and kinship, as well as religion and myth in the northern Great Basin extending into the western Plains region.

Although both men shared a basic focus on Native North America, they differed in their particularist approaches. Kroeber emphasized a culture-history perspective, while Lowie took a slightly divergent approach of diffusionism. The result of these similarities and differences fostered an emphasis at Berkeley on salvage ethnography, in which key consultants are interviewed for the purpose of reconstructing a picture of a past way of life.

By the time Steward entered the graduate program in 1925, Kroeber and Lowie had set into play the future direction of the department (Manners 1973:889; Murphy 1977:2). As Harris notes, "Steward's own interest in environmental factors was first consolidated by fieldwork among the Eastern Mono and Paiute of Owens Valley, California, in 1927 and 1928. Up to the publication of his 'The Economic and Social Basis of Primitive Bands' [1936c], however, Steward's position corresponded essentially to that of a rather large number of anthropologists who regarded the natural environment as a vaguely limiting or enabling factor of *culture history*" (Harris 1968:662; emphasis added).

CULTURE-ELEMENT DISTRIBUTION SURVEYS

Directed by Kroeber, the CED survey was conceived in the early 1920s, but it was not until the mid-1930s that fledgling anthropologists were sent into the field to pursue ethnographic work through ethnologic reconnaissance. Heizer (1978:9–10) gives the following background on Kroeber's CED survey:

> In the mid-1930s Kroeber himself realized that there was very little time remaining to make even a last-moment attempt to fill out the gaps in the ethnographic record. He conceived of the intensive program of investigation that came to be known as the "Culture Element Survey of Native Western North American" [Kroeber 1939a, 1939c]. The culture element surveys entailed locating the most reliable informants possible, sitting down with them, one at a time, and entering on a written list of traits a plus for presence and a minus for its absence. Between May 1934 and July 1938, 13 field investigators made 20 trips and returned with 279 filled-in lists representing 254 separate tribes or groups ranging from Chitchat Tlingit in the north to the Yaqui in the south and extending as far east as the Ute of eastern Colorado.

The CED survey forms resulted in data that a researcher could easily codify and statistically manipulate, although Kroeber never did so. However, Harold

Driver and other students did. Nearly 40 years after the last CED was completed, Joseph Jorgensen used some of the CED data for his work on cultural relationships among Indians of western America. Jorgensen stated that

> Kroeber's colleagues, such as Edward Gifford, and his students, such as Harold Driver, Philip Drucker, Julian Steward, and Homer Barnett, were sent out to collect comparable information on topics ranging from technological items to magical practices. Although the Culture Element Survey was not begun until the mid-1930s, the investigators were told to seek the oldest and best-informed people in each society, and to record information these elders could give about the cultures of their grandparents. In other words, the ethnographers were asked to collect "recall ethnographies" about what native cultures were like prior to European contact.
>
> Because the ethnographers checked off the responses of their informants on long lists of traits, recording pluses for elements that were present, and minuses for elements that were absent, the Culture Element Distributions that were published for each tribe became known as "checklists," though a more popular and pejorative referent used by anthropologists over the years has been "laundry lists." (Jorgensen 1980:10)

Don Fowler also notes the impact that the CED surveys had on American anthropology:

> The 1930s was a most active period for Great Basin ethnographic research. Stimulus was provided in part by the University of California Culture Element Distribution Survey of Western American Indian groups directed by Kroeber [1939a, 1939c]. The thrust of the Survey was two-pronged. One was an attempt to fill in the ethnographic record, especially in California. The second was by means of long trait lists to determine the presence or absence of each trait for each band or tribe. Given the assumption of the historic method about culture as an agglomeration of traits, it was thought that such data could be statistically manipulated. Such a "scientific" approach might elucidate aboriginal "internal history" [Kroeber 1939a, 1939c], that is, it was seen as a device to determine culture relationship, hence, "historic" connection between and among tribes. . . . Perhaps more important than the lists were the extensive annotations published with them. For some Great Basin groups these lists provide the only ethnographic data of the time. (Fowler et al. 1986:25–26)

Culture-Element Distribution of the Snake River Shoshone

In 1933 Steward published the Owens Valley ethnography (1933a) and two years later began his second fieldwork season. Steward spent six months in 1935 and four months in 1936 gathering ethnographic data of various Shoshonean groups (Steward 1941b:209, 1943a:263).[1] Steward's (1941b) CED "list was based on Driver's list for the southern Sierra Nevada and adjacent region" (Kroeber 1941:v). In the preface of the Steward report, Kroeber (1941:v) described a little of Steward's general itinerary: "Dr. Steward's Shoshoni data presented herein represents the first extension of the element survey to the Great Basin area. His list was based on that of Dr. Driver for the southern Sierra Nevada and adjacent regions. Beginning in southern Nevada, he [Steward] modified to suit local conditions as he traveled north. A second season in the field enabled him to fill a similar list among a smaller number of Shoshone groups farther north and east."

As one of 19 districts that Steward addressed, the Snake River Shoshone of southern Idaho had "information applicable to the stretch of river below Twin Falls, in the vicinity of Bruneau. Contacts with some North Fork and Humboldt River Shoshoni during the summer in the highlands near the present Western Shoshoni Reservation; also with Boise Shoshoni and with Fort Hall Shoshoni and Bannock who, a century ago, were traveling down the Snake River on horseback. Informant: CT; interpreter: TP" (Steward 1941b:212).

The Snake River Shoshone element list was supplied by CT, a "full-blood Shoshoni man, born ca. 1874 at Bliss on the Snake River, Idaho; went to Owyhee (Western Shoshoni Reservation) at the age of 26; well-informed, cooperative, very conscientious and one of the best informants but needs interpreter (TP was interpreter); supplied list S-SnRv, attempting to distinguish what he knew to exist on the Snake River from what he had subsequently seen or heard at Owyhee" (Steward 1941b:213). The interpreter TP was another "full-blood Shoshoni man, born ca. 1870 at Owyhee on Western Shoshoni Reservation; went through seven grades at Carlisle and returned to Owyhee; is exceptional interpreter, serving for CT and JP; also supplied some information concerning North Fork (of the Humboldt) Shoshoni learned from his mother who was born there (his father, an Elko Shoshoni)" (Steward 1941b:214).

Except for these summary statements, little more is known of these two key individuals. Yet the entire ethnographic picture of "precontact" Snake River Shoshone was provided by them. Steward (1941b:210) relates that "Three to six days were spent with each principal informant, but, as the lists were not the sole objective of the trip, only two to three days were devoted to each. . . . No less than three days with a good informant is needed in this area." Beside this and certain qualifying statements that Steward makes in reference to the actual list, no mention is made of the number of days or hours spent with CT, the setting, or any other relevant data.

With data collected during six months in 1935, Steward's "Culture Element Distributions: XIII. Nevada Shoshone" (1941b) delineated 2,742 elements divided into 33 major divisions. The Snake River Shoshone group of southern Idaho was one of 19 groups found in the Nevada region: 15 Shoshone groups, three Northern Paiute groups, and one Southern Paiute group. Steward separated his report into 10 sections: "Objectives of the Element List" (pp. 209–210); "Informants and Field Work" (210–214); "The Great Basin Environment" (214–215); "Shoshonean or Great Basin Culture" (215–216); "Element Variability" (216–217); "Ethnographic Discussion" (218–270); "Culture Element Distribution List" (271–326); "Elements Denied by All Informants" (327); "Ethnographic Notes on the Element List" (328–353); and "Summary and Conclusions" (354–357).

Because Steward's (1941b:271–311) list includes a number of disparate elements, expedience makes a two-fold division: material and social. The material elements include subsistence (Elements 1–577), houses (578–770), navigation (771–783), firemaking (784–808), miscellaneous concepts (809–911), skin dressing (912–931), weapons (933–1031), basketry (1032–1134), weaving (1137–1194), pottery (1195–1227), burdens (1228–1243), cradles (1244–1269), mutilations (1271–1321), dress and adornment (1322–1431), garments (1432–1576), games (1577–1887), money (1888–1893), tobacco and smoking (1894–1943), and musical instruments (1944–2017). Under the social division are marriage (Elements 2018–2052), kinship relations (2053–2089), berdaches or transvestites (2090–2110), division of labor (2111–2140), political organization (2141–2164), property (2165–2173a), warfare (2174–2177), birth customs (2178–2303), girl's puberty (2305–2378), boy's puberty (2381–2386), death customs (2387–2468), religion (2469–2613), dances (2614–2719), and miscellaneous (2720–2742).

Although Steward's 1941 list contains 2,742 elements, he added 23 subnumbers as "a," giving a grand total of 2,765 elements.[2] However, Steward left out 105 numbers altogether, giving a final count of 2,660 elements.[3] Of these, 47 are unidentified, making a grand total of 2,613 elements. Of the elements identified, Steward noted 872 presences, 936 absences, 656 blanks, 3 stars, 11 question marks, 66 numbers, 48 letters, and 19 miscellaneous markings (e.g., +?, (?), (+)). The most numerous counts are in three major categories, present, absent, and blank.

The distributional lists give an unqualified, rigid, and incomplete view of the culture of the groups inhabiting or utilizing the middle Snake River area (Northern Paiute, Northern Shoshone, and Bannock). At its time, the CED program promised to give an objective perspective on traits and complexes of traits, their distribution, diffusion, and/or independent invention, as well as areas of climaxes and marginality (Heizer 1978:10; Jorgensen 1980:10–11; cf. Barnett 1937; Chrétien 1945; Driver 1938, 1939; Driver and Kroeber 1932; Kroeber 1922, 1939a, 1939b, 1939c). The information that the lists provided "was analyzed statistically to secure intertribal correlation and cultural groupings" (Heizer 1978:10). To the contrary, however, the program's emphasis on statistics and other methodological problems far outweighs any results or conclusions that it was supposed to achieve. In fact, Steward's emphasis on statistics was minimal (Manners 1973; Murphy 1977). Steward states:

> Although it [Shoshonean culture] was not uniform throughout the area survey, with a list of about 2,500 elements, [it] demonstrates a striking absence of culture centers or climaxes. Differences between adjoining localities were slight. Over wide areas differences were cumulative. Statistical measurement of similarities gives a 0.7 to 0.9 correlation between neighboring localities but only a 0.5 correlation between such distant localities as Death Valley, Calif., and northern Nevada or western Idaho. But there were no cultural frontiers. This accords with the absence of dialectic and political boundaries [Steward 1939, 1970a (1938)].
>
> The low numerical element content of Shoshonean culture and its lack of climaxes also harmonized with its marginal position relative to neighboring areas. A large number of elements, especially those that produced local differences between Shoshoneans, were imported. (Steward 1940a:474–475)

For Steward (1941b:210), the Nevada Shoshone element lists had certain "advantages and dangers." He states:

> Two seasons of field work with element lists—the result of the field only are presented here—have demonstrated their value to me. Although they were first conceived in connection with the need for data amenable to quantitative treatment, I heartily concur with Kroeber [1939a:1–11] [that] they are a real advance as a technique for field work and for presentation of data.
>
> As a method of procuring and presenting data, the distinctive feature of the element list is the extensive use of tabulation. . . . The element list is unique solely in carrying this method to its logical end, namely, in listing all the components of a culture which can be broken down for tabulation. (Steward 1941b:209)

Although the merits of the survey offered a new field technique and the ability to tabulate extensive ethnographic data in a novel, systematic way, the survey did "not purport to be an exhaustive ethnographic description of the area" (Steward 1941b:210). Steward elaborates:

> It is not assumed that the list covers the totality of culture. Language cannot feasibly be included. Myths, which could no doubt be broken down for some

> tabulation, are omitted. There are other aspects of human behavior of interest to some ethnologic which are also omitted. Moreover, all departments of culture are not equally amenable to tabulation. Material objects, many economic activities, and most features of games, rites, and dances may readily be tabulated, though notes are necessary to explain them and to set them in their contextual relationships. Social organization and religion, on the other hand, are almost impossible to tabulate, and require extensive explanatory texts. In short, an element list has the advantage of fullness in many things ordinarily omitted and of compactness but is not a substitute for other descriptive devices. The objection, therefore, that it might merely enumerate elements torn from their context and omit configurations, functional aspects of behavior, and so forth, is beside the point. There never has been a description which did not enumerate; that the list does so concisely is not an inherent fault. It may be annotated and explained ab lib., according to the interest of the investigator. (Steward 1941b:209)

In light of this extended statement, Steward ends by saying that the lists "were procured somewhat incidentally on a trip devoted primarily to an ecological study of Shoshoni society and should consequently be viewed as a reconnaissance of the area previously unknown ethnographically" (1941b:210).

Steward was dissatisfied, or as Manners (1973:889) suggests, "not happy with the Berkeley emphasis on trait listing and descriptive ethnography," as well as the historic particularistic perspective that predominated in American anthropology in the early 1900s. Associated with Franz Boas, this perspective mandated gathering detailed information on all aspects of culture, society, and way of life. Called "historic" because it focused on a particular period in a group's history (the purported "precontact" period), the perspective was called "particularistic" because it encouraged data-gathering in minute detail. Analysis was discouraged until it was certain that a complete picture of a group had emerged. Interpretation or drawing conclusions was strictly not allowed. Jorgensen gives a general explanation of the conditions at the time:

> The lists were collected during the depth of the Great Depression, and many of the fledgling anthropologists found the job distasteful and mindless, a rote procedure leading nowhere, an exercise that robbed culture of everything—its life, its spirit, its intricate connections, and its sentiments. Many accepted their assignments for the modest stipend that was offered. Although many were in disagreement with the speed with which this vast ethnographic salvage project was conducted, some went on to write excellent areal monographs from their field data. (Jorgensen 1980:10)

THE ETHNOGRAPHIC PICTURE OF THE GREAT BASIN

Steward's CED surveys of the Nevada Shoshone (1941b) and Northern and Gosiute Shoshone (1943a) served as the basis for his *Basin-Plateau Aboriginal Sociopolitical Groups* (1970a [1938]). Together these publications provided the first substantive synthesis of the "Basin-Plateau" region, in general, and southern Idaho area, in particular. Steward's (1955b, 1970a [1938]) contributions toward modeling Shoshonean culture would have a lasting impact on succeeding generations of Great Basin anthropologists (Fowler 1982:124). Although he seemed to find much merit in CED surveys as procedural elements, Steward's general dissatisfaction with them, and the American historic/diffusionist/particularist paradigm that prompted the surveys, may have been responsible for *Basin-Plateau* marking a turning point in American anthropology. With this monograph, Steward set the stage for his own functional approach (Hatch 1973a:114–127, 1973b; Murphy 1977:19).

STEWARD'S CULTURAL ECOLOGY

Steward (1936a, 1940a, 1955b, 1970a [1938], 1970b) conceived and coined the phrase "cultural ecology" to refer to the general relationship between man and environment. Considering the role of the environment was not a new idea; its role had been posited, usually in the extremes, prior to Steward's contribution. Steward's theoretical position stems not from a total disavowal of past theoretical stances; on the contrary, it can be seen as a simple elaboration of the diffusionistic or possibilistic approach. The diffusionistic approach, which was closely associated with historic particularism, aimed at determining the geographical origins of particular traits, the patterns of their spread, and what elements in the "receiving" cultures made it possible for those traits to be adopted. Although diffusionists (e.g., Lowie) or possibilists (e.g., Kroeber) had said that the environment allowed certain possibilities, Steward found it more purposeful to measure the latitude of environmental influence or variations and to relate those variations to the exigencies of life. In other words, the cultural ecological approach attempts to measure the limitations of the environment as a basis for understanding the exploitative nature of the society in question.

Steward's *Basin-Plateau* clearly demonstrated his shift to a cultural ecological position from the previous diffusionistic model. Although environmental factors now become prominent to the discussion, they continue to be related in a possibilistic manner. In other words, the environment is limiting and permits certain variations within these limitations. A number of Steward's statements clearly reflect this (e.g., 1970a:[1938] 236, 256, 258).

It could be argued that Steward's treatment of the environment falls within a general "possibilistic" perspective of culture history. Murphy has commented on the place of the environment in a cultural ecological approach: "The environment, *per se,* is not the critical factor, for the 'behavior patterns' required in its exploitation using certain 'economic devices' are the key elements. . . . [Q]uite simply, the theory of cultural ecology is concerned with the process of work, its organization, its cycles and rhythms and its situational modalities" (Murphy 1970:155). Moreover, "that Steward is only secondarily concerned with environment, *per se,* is manifest in his treatment of complex societies" (Murphy 1970:159). The "theory and method of cultural ecology is not a kind of environmental determinism, nor is it even centrally concerned with the environment" (Murphy 1970:183; for an alternative view see Clemmer, chapter 10.)

Steward defined "cultural ecology" as "the exploitation of [a] . . . particular environment by means of the techniques available to them [the population]" (Steward 1955b:119), or "the nature of social interaction required for subsistence in a given environment by means of a given technology" (Steward 1969c:188). Although others would disagree (see Clemmer, chapter 10), the utilization of a cultural ecological approach requires that a focus be made not upon the "dynamic interplay" in man-environment interactions, but rather on the one-way exploitation of the environment by "super-organic factor of culture" (Steward 1955b:31). Although the environment is constant, its influence is permissive within a certain range of variation—the environment is limiting. That is, the environment is secondary; it has no active role, nor can it have one within a cultural ecological framework. Whether Steward would agree with this or any alternative interpretation of his cultural ecological approach is, of course, open to question.

Steward's Cultural Ecology in the Great Basin

Steward's (1955b, 1970a [1938], 1970b) interpretation of Great Basin existence and persistence revolves around the idea of a "seasonal round" in which "family units" or "family clusters" exploited a "multiple subsistence base." For the greater part of this round, a harsh environment precluded the existence of groups larger than the cluster for any extended period of time. A limiting environment is seen as having a "socially fragmenting affect upon Great Basin society" (Steward 1955b:101–121, 1970b:113–151). People move from resource area to resource area according to what is available in a particular season in a particular area.

Thomas's interpretation of Steward's model accurately concludes that "the seasonal round . . . is simply not a fact; it is theory. The facts are statements from informants and its theory is the integrating interpretation placed upon them by Steward" (Thomas 1973:156). Because "Steward interpreted this generalized pattern from many localities and it is not directly applicable to any specific setting within the Great Basin" (Thomas 1973:157), a significant portion of our understanding of Great Basin existence and persistence has been subsumed within Steward's model. Thus, we might find many exceptions to the generalized model (see Walker, chapter 5). Steward concluded that the Shoshoneans or Numic people were "a gastric society" (1955b:46) and concentrated upon the subsistence activity and economic behaviors associated with the acquisition of the food supply. As Steward saw it, the Numa were on the brink of starvation for the majority of the time, and this was deduced and confirmed by his use of regional histories (1970a:3–10 [1938]). Centering on cultural ecological adaptation reduces culture to only those aspects of behavior that involve the food quest. Such a reified concept of culture does little, if anything, to advance a theory antiquated by its own methodology.

AN ALTERNATIVE VIEW

During the last four decades, scholars have presented an alternative approach to viewing anthropology's history (Leone 1972; Stocking 1968; cf. Kuhn 1970 [1962]). Stating that science—including social science—is not an "incremented or accumulative process," such scholars rely upon "the historical record of the research activity itself" (Kuhn 1970:1 [1962]). Kuhn, in particular, used the notion of paradigm to explore the nature of scientific thought and knowledge. Paradigms are "universally recognized scientific achievements that for a time provide model problems and solutions to a community of practitioners" (Kuhn 1970:viii [1962]). Kuhn suggests that "scientific communities can and should be isolated without prior recourse to paradigms," and he sees the scientific community as consisting of "the practitioners of a scientific specialty" (1970:176–177 [1962]). By community, Kuhn means those who have undergone similar educational and professional initiations, employ the same literature and a bounded subject matter, utilize shared examples or exemplars, and have a set of shared goals. Of course, there are many levels of communities, ranging from the most inclusive community of all natural scientists to those who study topical areas within specific subdisciplines. Kuhn also discusses scientific revolutions, the tradition-shattering complements to the tradition-bound activity of normal science (Kuhn 1970:6 [1962]).

When viewed as an area of research activity, Great Basin anthropology offers unique insights into the examination of itself and of anthropology as a whole (Kuhn 1970:176–187 [1962]). The research area, which has an analytic basis, finds its most concrete expression in the activities and achievements of the community of practitioners. It serves to shift the emphasis from a focus of study to its role within the framework of study. In the case of Great Basin anthropology, it is the geographic area itself that is the framework; Steward had much to do with creating this framework as a materialistic, reified one (see Walker, chapter 5).

Despite the heuristic and pedagogical uses of the concept, in reality, the Great Basin culture area is not so easily defined. While assuming a relationship between the geographic basin and its indigenous peoples, past and current definitions have varied according to historic context and scholarly purpose. Of course, much of this can be attributed to the lack of analytic constructs within anthropology. The concept of culture has never been clearly delineated and, lacking any analytic basis, varies according to both approach and scholar. Nor has the relationship between environment and culture ever been clearly conceived. Assumptions, after all, have the habit of sustaining their own existence and once implied are seldom scrutinized—and why should they be? As much as the concept of culture area has been and can be questioned, it has served its purpose well. Expedience is a justification in itself. Given the applicability to theory and method, the utility of the culture-area concept cannot and should not be denied. Its utility has been responsible for the direction taken by anthropologists in both the ethnologic classification of aboriginal North American cultures and in circumscribing specific cultures as a focus of research and study. However, if we view the Great Basin as an area of research activity, instead of a culture area, it suggests a more parsimonious and analytic approach—an approach that takes into account both the negative and positive effects of the culture-area concept, but one that does not burden us with a focus all its own.

As a research area, the Great Basin subsumes and supersedes the notion of the pedagogic or heuristic culture area. Moreover, the notion of the Great Basin as a research area provides a context in which to view the processes of anthropological thought and knowledge as they are focused on a specific cultural population. At this level, Great Basin research is unique; its development has involved an unusual and forceful interrelationship between ethnographic and archaeological research, as well as between ethnographic and ethnologic interpretation. It also represents a relatively unique example of paradigm conception, formation, and articulation as it applies to cultural ecology, on the one hand, and culture or multilinear evolution, on the other. Therefore, a knowledge of Numic culture must be examined within the historic parameters of the research activity in which it was formulated and articulated. Here, as before, this approach implies that a knowledge of Numic speakers be evaluated within that body of concepts, assumptions, and beliefs generated historically by the community of research practitioners. Although I do not wish to deny the significance of the culture-area concept, it appears more expedient to view the concept in its instrumental role, rather than as a focus in itself.

Because Steward's perspective focused on limiting factors, it was limiting in itself. His concentration on exploitative activities and subsistence patterns, which denied factors such as religious rituals, myth, and shamanism, (e.g., Hultkrantz, 1986; Liljeblad 1986; Myers 1987) was one of the major setbacks of his methodology. The fact that these are missing should not be used to negate the formative role that Steward's model played in the development and articulation of cultural ecology. Yet it is important to note that within this context, any attempt to understand the specifics of Numic culture was placed within a cultural ecological context and that current interpretations rest as much on previous interpretations as on original research. Although interpretations of the Great Basin peoples vary to some degree, most assumed Steward's interpretation, which characterized Numic peoples as a "gastric society" and saw their evolutionary development (or more properly, the lack thereof) as due to an unpredictably harsh environment. Within this approach, metaphor has replaced science and analogy has served as a basis for assumptions that, however implicit, border on determinism. The metaphor for Great Basin cultures was the struggling, small cluster of families merely eking out an existence on the brink of starvation. Steward's emphasis on the environment and the limitation that it imposes expresses only one side, the negative side, of the ecological equation. While acknowledging the harshness of the environment and the fragmenting effect it had on the cultural populations, Steward posits a one-way interaction between an ostensibly passive environment and technologically exploitative populations. By so doing, he overshadows any type of intellectual activity within the technological (Levi-Strauss 1966:40–42), as well as the mediating role of cultural conceptualizations and symbolizations of the social group. As a result, the positive aspects of the ecological equation, in which the environment and culture are seen as participating in an interactive process, are missing.

To classify Numic culture as "gastric," as Steward did, only reinforces that the concept of "gastric culture" has a "force and purpose of its own" (Geertz 1973:11). To insure the vitality of the culture concept, Geertz (1973:4) suggests "cutting culture down to size," which would appear to be one of the most productive and far-reaching ways of looking at this preeminent category in anthropology (cf. Durkheim 1915:21–33). By defining culture as "a system of thought and knowledge," it becomes shared, public, and expressed through a universal process of symbolism (e.g., Firth 1973; Geertz 1963, 1973, 1983; Keesing 1974; Levi-Strauss 1963, 1966, 1967, 1969, 1973, 1979, 1981; Sperber 1975, 1982). In this sense, culture is a context by which and through which such things as myths, rituals, values, beliefs, activities, events, traditions, and institutions must be interpreted (Geertz 1973:14).

I have been involved in the study of Numic myth for nearly 20 years (Myers 1987, 1988, 1990a, 1990b, 1992, 1993a, 1993b). By manifesting a content and context, myth allows access to the cognitive processes underlining a culturally prescribed system of Numic thought and knowledge. Through the symbolic process, culture expresses, codifies, and reifies the conceptual order. Symbolism is a process maintained by the group in which reality is conceptual and by which it is acted upon. Juxtaposing certain rituals (e.g., male initiation and female puberty and partition ceremonies) with the content of the mythic subcorpus, I found that the Numa (i.e., Southern Paiute, Western Shoshone, and Northern Paiute) possess a conceptually based, symbolically expressed, and logically structured system of thought and knowledge, that is, a nongastric system of culture.

Much of my work with myths can be traced to an interest in the relationship between people and the biotic components in their environment. To echo the thoughts of Willis (1974), I am interested in the significance of animals to people. I find this relationship to be ecological and posit a significance that is as much intellectual as utilitarian, as much ideational as behavioral. From this ecological perspective, my task in dealing with Numic origin myths is to delineate the conceptual repertoire by which Numic worldview is conceived and expressed. By demonstrating a conceptually based, symbolically expressed, and logically structured system of Numic culture, my studies have been concerned with defining and elaborating the structure underlying the conceptual repertoire and symbolic processes involved with Numic thought and knowledge.

CONCLUSION

Steward's "Culture Element Distributions: XIII. Nevada Shoshone" (1941b) represents a pivotal, though seemingly unwanted, aspect of his fieldwork. Although he was "not happy" with being saddled with the "laundry list" nature of the CED surveys, he nevertheless found it a necessary incidental, much like myth, to fulfill his research position at Berkeley (see Kerns, chapter 1). Steward diligently worked on and published the two CED surveys (1941b, 1943a), as well as two collections of tales (1936b, 1943b) from the various groups of Shoshones. However, the effect of the surveys seems to be antithetical in their impact on Steward's latter contributions. Compared to Berkeley's emphasis on diffusion and cultural history, Steward's emphasis on the environment was a radical shift in approach and perspective.

The breakdown of cultural phenomena into elements and complexes provided a pseudosystematic way of ordering data in the CED survey of the

Snake River Shoshone. Also, at this level, elements or complexes of elements were considered equivalent and, thus, comparable. Finding disparity between traits or trait complexes did not seem to matter much in the CED surveys; only the presence or absence of traits or elements were important. As Harris has noted, "Even 6,000 traits might be inadequate for measured overall similarity if the traits utilized were not systematically identified on the same level of detail. (Polygyny might count for one trait, while the bow and arrow might count for four or five.)" (Harris 1968:376–377).

Steward's "culture ecology" traces its foundations to a simple diffusionist-possibilist perspective, which makes several questionable assumptions. In this perspective, I took to task certain of these assumptions (e.g., culture concept, culture area, seasonal round). Having a more parsimonious concept of culture as a "system of thought and knowledge" and utilizing the notion of the Great Basin as a "research area" rather than a "culture area" will allow us to move beyond Steward's "gastric" metaphor. I concur with Murphy's statement that

> Steward's work will have a lasting impact upon the anthropological profession for another reason. That is that he posed a series of problems around which one can organize substantive field research—and fieldwork is the defining characteristic of anthropology more than any of its theories. More than this, he left to us some of the finest documents on Native American society ever published, his work on the Great Basin Shoshoneans. His fieldwork can never again be duplicated, and it remains a model for future research, as well as his testimonial to the American Indian. (Murphy 1977:37)

Although Murphy's statement is fitting, because Steward is not duplicatable, other recent perspectives or paradigms are changing the nature and scope of modern anthropology. His contributions require a critical reevaluation and reassessment because they have had such long-standing impact on Great Basin research. Steward's contribution can be looked upon as stimulating us, as he did, to question the dominant paradigm.

NOTES

I would like to thank Richard O. Clemmer, David S. Whitley, Gary Hennen, and Deborah J. Gangloff for their advice and suggestions. I give particular thanks to Gary Hennen for his contribution of tabulating and reviewing the Snake River Shoshone CED survey and to Deborah Gangloff for her help with editing and proofreading this manuscript. Of course, I take full responsibility for the content of this chapter.

1. There appears to be disagreement in the dates of the Steward fieldwork. Both Manners (1973:890) and Murphy (1977:5) suggest that the fieldwork was carried out in 1934 and 1935,

yet Eggan (1980:165–166) states that it was between 1935 and 1936. In both the Nevada Shoshone CED survey (1941b:209) and the Northern and Gosiute Shoshone survey (1943a:263) Steward concurs with Eggan.

2. These subnumbers are 28a, 92a, 130a, 297a, 467a, 593a, 684a, 960a, 997a, 1122a, 1180a, 1514a, 1608a, 1767a, 1895a, 2170a, 2173a, 2312a, 2422a, 2508a, 2509a, 2576a, and 2716a.

3. The missing 105 numbers are: 8, 45, 65, 68, 83, 91, 106, 108, 111, 119, 141, 146, 178, 179, 200, 233, 283, 442, 522, 542, 552, 613, 616, 631, 665, 671, 674, 690, 699, 722, 724, 791, 806, 849, 850, 865, 898, 899, 900, 914, 932, 990, 1027, 1030, 1047, 1185, 1207, 1222, 1283, 1311, 1376, 1395, 1402, 1403, 1414, 1416, 1454, 1519, 1548, 1590, 1603, 1631, 1637, 1650, 1704, 1756, 1833, 1854, 1898, 1984, 2054, 2060, 2063, 2067, 2070, 2074, 2077, 2080, 2082, 2083, 2097, 2103, 2105, 2106, 2107, 2108, 2109, 2110, 2176, 2255, 2279, 2304, 2363, 2379, 2380, 2445, 2450, 2452, 2467, 2525, 2586, 2631, 2666, 2687, and 2711.

10

Steward's Gap: Why Steward Did Not Use His Theory of Culture Change to Explain Shoshoni Culture Change

Richard O. Clemmer

Using Steward's own methodology of multilinear evolution to reevaluate two of his conclusions regarding Numic cultural change reveals that Steward's theory of culture change does not account for the actual changes that occurred. In particular, Clemmer asserts that Steward wrongly assessed Western Shoshones as being caught in an acculturative process that would ultimately end in assimilation. Among other things, Steward failed to grasp the significance of the increase in political activity, group ceremonies, and the frequency of communication among various Shoshone individuals and groups, which allowed the development of a distinct sociopolitical adaptation rooted in Shoshones' interpretations of culture. This failure may have been partially due to Steward's political commitment to an integrated, undifferentiated society. However, Clemmer notes that at the time of Steward's fieldwork the concept of acculturation was not well understood and had only recently become a focus of study. Further attention to the development of anthropology and Steward's role in it reveals Steward constantly rethinking his previous (and usually strongly stated) theoretical positions and constantly questioning concepts such as "acculturation."

"Steward's gap" is the discrepancy between Steward's theory of culture change and a body of data to which he could have applied it, but did not. In other words, Steward discusses a case study of culture change without, apparently, having recourse to his own theory. This case is that of the Western Shoshoni, the only Great Basin group that Steward ever discussed in terms of cultural change. I do not mean that this gap is consistent or pervasive in all of Steward's work—it is not. In fact, Steward is known for using data to inform his methodology of multilinear evolution. The gap is evident only in the case in which he returned to the discussion of the Western Shoshoni culture and people, as Steward tried to explain their contemporary situation.

Steward returned three times to the Western Shoshoni, whose ethnographically reconstructed way of life later provided the basis for his theory of cultural ecology: in a confidential report to Commissioner of Indian Affairs John Collier (see Crum, chapter 8; Rusco, chapter 7) written in late 1936; in his ICC testimony (See chapter 12); and in his 1951 article, "Levels of Sociocultural Integration: An Operational Concept." In this latter piece, Steward devoted barely a page specifically to the Western Shoshoni, using them to exemplify the impact of a national sociocultural system on a culture—Western Shoshoni culture—ostensibly integrated at a "family level." It is evident that Steward based this short summary on his earlier detailed report to Collier, although he does not cite it and its existence was virtually unknown (because the Bureau of Indian Affairs suppressed it) until long after Steward's death.

First, I shall discuss what Steward said about Western Shoshoni acculturation and why I think he was wrong. Then, I will summarize the primary characteristics of Steward's theory of culture change and demonstrate how Steward applied it to a case study—the data his students collected in Puerto Rico. Next, I will show how Steward could have applied his theoretical framework to better understand and analyze Western Shoshoni cultural change. Finally, I will offer some suggestions for why Steward seems to have ignored his own advice, in a sense, when analyzing the history and contemporary ethnographic situation of a people he ostensibly knew better than any other. My intentions are to situate "Steward's gap" in Steward's own professional history and also in a more general analysis of how anthropologists use theory, method, and data.

ACCULTURATION

Acculturation is the process whereby an individual or a group adopt cultural characteristics that do not originate from their own enculturation experience, that is, cultural characteristics that are not familiar to them from their upbringing. Acculturation may be coerced or voluntary and it may be additive or substitutive; in other words, cultural traits may be added to those already carried by the individual or group or may replace them. The most common examples of substitutive acculturation are probably religious conversion and the substituting of handmade technological items with industrially manufactured ones. However, it is axiomatic that some individuals will resist acculturation, others will embrace it, and still others will compartmentalize the process, utilizing cultural values and behavior patterns with which they were raised in some contexts and the "new" or "foreign" ones in other contexts.

Acculturation can occur any place where there is information about different ways of life. For example, the replacement of hamburger and hot dog stands by Mexican, Greek, or Middle-Eastern take-out restaurants as some Americans' favorite purveyors of fast food has occurred without many of their patrons ever having been around Mexicans, Greeks, or Middle Easterners. Similarly, the conversion of the T-shirt—initially an American underwear garment—to a standard outerwear garment around the world has occurred with minimal contact between Americans and the global patrons of T-shirt shops. However, colonial or neocolonial situations, where rulers and ruled do have contact and have very different cultural inventories, have furnished the most common social fields in which anthropologists have studied acculturation. In these situations, the cultural movement is nearly always only in one direction: the ruled take on varying amounts of the culture of the rulers. Anthropologists (and often the people themselves) regard this process as difficult: native language must be replaced by the rulers' lingua franca; cash economy makes subsistence strategies obsolete or impossible; learned pathways to health, personal dignity and integrity, and communication with the divine are devalued and other ones must be acquired; how social acceptance is defined and political decisions made cease to be matters under local control; and pagan religions are replaced with Christianity.

Western Shoshoni Acculturation

Western Shoshonis had such a colonial situation imposed on them in varying degrees, depending on community and time period. Yet in his discussion, Steward (1951, 1955b) makes three unusual assumptions: Western Shoshonis had undergone what amounted to complete acculturation; it was a generally painless, easy process; and the process was uniform on all individuals. Some key phrases in this discussion are "most Western Shoshoni . . . were only loosely tied to any definable locality or cohesive social group"; "association with rural whites has not been very sustained, but it has been sufficient to acculturate the Shoshoni toward the Great Basin American ranching and mining subculture"; "the Shoshoni . . . retain many practices and beliefs pertaining to kinship relations, child-rearing, shamanism, supernatural powers and magic, and recreation, especially gambling games"; and "the Western Shoshoni were spared the more crucial difficulties experienced by Indians who had a fairly tightly-woven fabric of community culture" (Steward 1955a:58, 57 [1951]). Apparently, Steward attributed Shoshonis' "easy acculturation" to certain attributes of Shoshonis themselves: They lacked cohesive social groups, territorial ties, and tight communities. That these attributions were not completely accurate is not difficult to demonstrate.

The Crucial Difficulties of Acculturation

It is important to establish that we are indeed dealing with a major lacuna in Steward's work. Let us take the assertion that Western Shoshonis were spared the more crucial difficulties of acculturation. A few observations from the historic record will suffice to show that Steward's assertion is simply not true. Bowman reported in his *The Pacific Tourist* that in 1878 he saw from the window of his railroad coach a Shoshoni village "just below the town of Palisade." Although perhaps following a pattern of description generally reflective of the prejudices of the times, Bowman does not give a flattering impression of this settlement: "a dozen or so tents, discolored with smoke and besmirched with dirt and grease, revealing 6 to 10 squalid beings covered with vermin, filth, and rags" (Bowman 1883:197). Even allowing for some exaggeration, it is evident that these folks were not well off.

Palisade was a railroad town on the Humboldt River. It housed construction crews who built first the Central Pacific and then the Eureka and Palisade Railroads and later a cattle shipping depot on the Union Pacific. Indians living nearby and visible from the transcontinental trains that rumbled past may have been practicing traditional subsistence techniques: fishing, seed gathering, trapping small animals, perhaps growing a little maize. If they were, then we can infer that they had not "acculturated" to the point of participating in the cash economy, buying clothes at the local store, and living in wood-frame houses. However, thousands of emigrants—homesteaders and gold-seekers—and their animals trekking along the Humboldt Trail from the 1840s until the railroad was completed in 1869 ruined the Humboldt River as a dependable subsistence area. Much more likely responsible for the Indian camp existence was the economic dependency that the mining and ranching economy had created: Indians hoped to eke out an existence from what the new settlers cast off and from menial jobs they could get now and then. Judging from the camps' description, this effort was minimally successful. Either the Shoshonis were trying to acculturate, and were having difficulty doing so, or they were not acculturating at all. In either case, it is hard to see any basis for assessing that they were spared acculturation difficulties.

Edna Patterson states that during construction of the transcontinental railroad in the late 1860s, crews came into the Lamoille Valley on "drunken sprees." Based on an interview with Tillie Murphy (Shoshoni) in 1935, Patterson paints an unpleasant, but revealing, picture:

> Indian women of lower Lamoille were particularly terrified of being alone when the construction crews of the Central Pacific railroad went on drunken sprees and attempted to molest them. Cowboys were another enemy and a story has been told by a buckaroo that he came upon an Indian woman when she was alone and roped her with his lariat and raped her. Soldiers at Fort Halleck were disciplined severely if a sexual offense against an Indian woman could be proven. Indian women protected themselves, if they were given any warning, by putting sand and dirt into their vaginas, and from this custom they often developed infection. (Patterson 1973:9)

These incidents may attest more to the difficulties of being a woman in a violent, male-dominated world than to the difficulties of acculturation. However, Patterson's elderly Shoshoni friends and acquaintances who told her these stories were interpreting the events in terms of their Indianness as well as their femaleness. Their implication is that had they not been Indian or had they been living in stone or wood-frame houses with lockable doors, they would not have been subject to violation. Again, we do not know whether being unable to earn cash or simply preferring to live in tents and brush shelters was the crucial variable, but this much is evident: being Indian and female in a camp made one more vulnerable than being non-Indian and male on a horse. If we think about the aspects of acculturation that include face-to-face contact, that vulnerability would seem to be a crucial difficulty.

The summary of the "Life of Ira Wines" by his daughter Florence Sharp provides some insight into the pre-1900 ranching economy (Sharp ca. 1930). Wines hired cowboys, threshing crews, and a Chinese cook and launderer who "worked the year round for a dollar a day" because "Chinese labor was cheap in those days" (Sharp ca. 1930). Wines' daughter says about his relationships with Indians that "There were many Indians in the Valley and a large camp was situated about a mile from the Overland site. Mr. Wines was a great friend of the Indians and acted as counselor for them when they had trouble among themselves. If he had any difficulty settling any argument he would tell them he would send for the soldiers and they would go home in peace as they were afraid of the soldiers." It hardly sounds as if ranching in Ruby Valley provided much of a social field in which acculturation could take place. There is no mention of Indians being involved in the ranching economy at all in Sharp's manuscript, and if anything, the quote above reflects a sharp division between ranch society and Shoshoni society in Ruby Valley.

Steward's assertion that ranching provided a major social field in which acculturation took place may be true, but it is likely that it is truest only after about 1900, at least, and probably substantially true only after 1920. Ranching in the early period—the 1870s and 1880s—probably initially *displaced*

Shoshonis; it did not provide significant employment until the 1890s and early 1900s. Steward found most of his informants by consulting census rolls. He found Shoshonis living in small settlements on ranches (Crum 1996). By 1935, then, Steward could easily conclude that because Shoshonis lived on ranches and had been incorporated into the ranching economy to some extent, they had also been incorporated into the ranching subculture. However, was that really true?

"The Shoshoni Retain Many Practices and Beliefs"

It seems perplexing that Steward could perceive the Shoshonis as retaining much of their precontact culture and at the same time as being acculturated to the mining-and-ranching subculture. However, some reflection makes his perception a little less puzzling. Culture has quantifiable mass only in its technological and material object manifestations. Steward's illustration of Shoshoni culture as "meager and simple" by referring to the difference in numbers of material items between Shoshoni and American technologies is well known (see Crum, chapter 8). However, culture is more than "things" and people are not mere receptacles for culture. People have infinite capacities for learning. Thus, it is perfectly plausible that Shoshonis in the 1930s were bicultural. What is puzzling is that Steward did not see retention of practices and beliefs as a basis for Western Shoshoni collective identity, some degree of resistance to acculturation, and even a kind of Western Shoshoni ethnonationalism, that is, a movement to unite a group of people on the basis of shared cultural traits and ethnic identity (cf. Clemmer 1996).

The 1920s and 1930s were decades in which there was a resurgence of interest in Shoshoni traditions, customs, and treaty rights. A major focus of Shoshoni testimony before a subcommittee of the U.S. Senate Committee on Indian Affairs in 1932 concerned treaty rights; in fact, some Shoshonis had already hired attorney Milton Badt to represent them in pursuit of treaty rights (Crum 1991:5, 1994:103; U.S. Senate 1934:14843–14864). Basing his summary on newspaper accounts of the times, Shoshoni historian Steven Crum (1994:60) states: "In the late nineteenth and early twentieth centuries, Shoshoni culture was best expressed in the celebrations called fandangoes, which featured round dances, songs, handgames, and feasting. . . . Usually the fandangoes attracted large crowds, sometimes as many as 300 to 500 people, for the Shoshonis had an active interest in preserving their traditions."

Steward knew all this. In his report to Commissioner of Indian Affairs John Collier of 1936, he states: "There are old, non-English-speaking full-bloods who still possess native patterns of thought and behavior. . . . Their main concern is to have treaty obligations fulfilled" (Steward 1936b:4). On the surface, it seems that the Shoshoni would have provided Steward with an excellent case study of change: They had undergone a great deal of economic change; preserved certain customs and traditions; and revived, changed, and revitalized still other customs, such as turning the harvest festivals into fandangoes. Why, then, was Steward apparently totally uninterested in studying and interpreting these changes? Moreover, why did Steward insist on assigning Western Shoshonis of the period to the American ranching subculture, rather than to a general Shoshoni subculture or to several different Shoshoni subcultures? To answer these questions, we must take a brief look at Steward's two methodologies, multilinear evolution and cultural ecology, as well as at his general work with the concept of culture.

THE METHODOLOGY OF MULTILINEAR EVOLUTION AND "SUBCULTURES"

Empirically, the careful study of changes in economic and cultural and subcultural systems would seem to be demanded by Steward's methodology of multilinear evolution, which entails historic reconstruction of events in one particular place. Multilinear evolution also requires construction of at least a relative time line for those events and comparison of the events and their sequence with another historic reconstruction in another place. Ultimately, the methodology's goal is to discover "significant regularities in culture change," that is, recurrent forms, processes, and functions, and thus the existence of "cultural laws" that assign causes to the recurrence of these forms (Steward 1955b:18–19). The methodology of multilinear evolution assumes that certain predicted changes happen to groups of people over long periods of time. Population increases, technological inventions and innovations are made, surplus accumulation and competition accompany development of political hierarchies and formation of state-level administrative systems, diffusion of people and culture results in dominant traditions being established in particular regions. There is increasing occupational specialization and regional differentiation in service to standardization and uniformity. However, none of this happens if the resource base is insufficient to accommodate population increase and surplus accumulation. Moreover, the process is neither steady nor irreversible; intensive warfare, unbridled internal political competition, or poor resource management can topple the most impressive national system. Also, the process begins at different times and has very different specific attributes in different parts of the world. Thus, for example, Aztecs ruled an empire for less than 200 years and met their fate at the hands of conquerors whose political hegemony also lasted hardly another 300 years. Aztec culture became a minor theme in the Mexican nation-state. In contrast, the Roman Empire endured three times as long and its culture contributed major themes to succeeding cultures. Finally, the concept of subcultures incorporates local traditions, adaptations, and interpretations as part of the "multilinearness" of the evolutionary process.

Subcultures: Puerto Ricans and Shoshonis

It was in the very article on levels of sociocultural evolution that Steward advocated the study of regional subcultures as part of national sociocultural systems. A subculture might be termed a kind of "border culture" in today's world, that is, a collection of cultural traits carried and expressed by a group of people that are shared by many other people. Each group of people, in addition, shares a distinct set of "core" cultural features that distinguish it (Rudden and Clemmer 1998). In Steward's terms, the "different local meanings" constitute the local "cultural cores" and the "common denominator" consists of the shared traits that create shared cultural boundaries—border zones—that, for example, make all Puerto Ricans feel Puerto Rican.

In chapter four of *Theory of Culture Change,* which was written especially for that volume, Steward's summary of the Puerto Rican research (probably carried out largely by his students) asserts a complex mosaic of cultural patterns for Puerto Rico. He notes that "most shared traits—the common core or common denominator of pan–Puerto Rican culture—have a special meaning in each subculture. . . . Most features of the common denominator have different local meanings because they are functional parts of the total patterns of the different subcultures" (1955b:77). Why would this generalization not also apply to the Western Shoshoni? Why would "ranching" and "mining," as well as natural resources and land in general, not have very different meanings for Shoshonis than for whites and thus serve similar subcultural functions—that is, dividing Shoshonis from whites rather than uniting them—as the local interpretations of Puerto Rican customs do among Puerto Ricans?

Pine-nuts and child-rearing practices are cases in point. Steward (1936b:12) noted in his 1936 report to Collier that pine-nuts were in great demand by whites, but that Indians were virtually their "sole source." He even suggested that Indians should market them through "a single channel, the nuts perhaps shelled, salted and sold in small cellophane bags." In fact, as the past four decades have witnessed, the interpretation of pine-nuts and pine-nut trees has indeed been a point upon which Western Shoshoni culture and non-Indian culture part company. Even more paradoxical is Steward's identification of child-rearing practices as a subcultural indicator, again with reference to Puerto Rico. If it "is expectable that subcultural groups should differ in child-rearing just as they differ in family structure" (1955b:76), then why is cultural significance accorded to child-rearing practices and family structure for Puerto Ricans but denied to Shoshonis? How could Steward not have seen that within a few pages in the same book he had, in contradictory and illogical fashion, denied and confirmed his own theory of culture change and chosen to apply his own methodology of multilinear evolution to one case—the Puerto Rican—while utterly failing to apply it in another case—that of the Shoshoni?

To answer this question it is necessary to look briefly at how Steward treated "culture" generally in his work, how he treated it within his cultural ecological approach, and how the concept figured in his overall theory of culture change. It is also necessary to look at how Steward's thinking was evolving over time in relation to how the discipline of anthropology was evolving and how anthropology was treating culture and cultural change during the same time period.

CULTURE IN STEWARD'S WORK

Steward knew culture when he saw it, both the material and the nonmaterial aspects of it. His Ph.D. dissertation entitled *The Ceremonial Buffoon of the American Indian* (Steward 1991 [1929]) is 136 pages of discussion of nonmaterial culture. Virtually none of it touches ecology, social relations of production, or technology. Steward's "Notes on Hopi Ceremonies in their Initiatory Form in 1927–1928" (1931c) is purely a discussion of religion—ideological superstructure. His (1934b) pamphlet on the Blackfoot (Siksika) for the National Park Service devotes nearly a third of the 50-odd pages to a discussion of nonmaterial culture. Steward's articles "Myths of the Owens Valley Paiute" (1936d) and "Some Western Shoshoni Myths" (1943b) certainly deal with some aspects of subsistence and economy, but his analyses concentrate on literary elements and motifs; he does not connect the myths to ecology (cf. Crum 1991:8). Even Steward's culture-element distributions are more than half devoted to ideological superstructure and nonmaterial culture. Aside from his archaeological works, it is quite possible that a careful analysis of all of Steward's material on North American Indians would reveal more pages devoted to nonmaterial culture than to material culture, ecology, or the social relations of production.

In his "Cultures of the Intermontane (Great Basin) Area" (1940a), Steward makes a point similar to the one that he would make 15 years later about Puerto Rico: "Many elements, especially those that were imported from neighboring areas, cut across the Intermontane area with dissimilar distributions. These were unequally integrated in each local context." He then notes that "an analysis of the history and functional interrelationships of these elements and complexes will show their varying roles in Shoshonian culture. It will indicate that some features had remained relatively fixed in time and space whereas others had varied enormously" (1940a:475). Steward takes great pains to point out—as he does in his article published the same year on the Carrier Indians—that "culture change, whether through local development or borrowing, is not random but selective and somewhat directional. . . . This means that a culture is not an entirely fortuitous assemblage of unrelated elements but consists of parts which in some degree predetermine, condition, or delimit one another" (Steward 1940a:475, 480).

Cultural Ecology

Cultural ecology conceptualizes six categories of variables that mutually affect one another: *environmental resources;* the *technology* used to get them, process them, and store them; the *social* and *political organization* of producing, protecting, allocating, and distributing the resources and of marshaling human labor to do so; and the culture associated with all of the above activities, including *economic values* and *behavior patterns.* Added to these are the biological nature of human beings and psychological processes and drives. To utilize the methodology, one gathers data in all of these categories except the last two, which are regarded as "givens" and thus subject to little variation (Steward 1970a:260–261 [1938]). Steward was very careful to disassociate himself from any sort of economic determinism. "Economic determinism, though resting to an undetermined extent upon substantial truth, is, especially in such extreme interpretations as the Marxian, primarily a philosophy, not a scientifically demonstrated fact" (Steward 1970a:260 [1938]).

There is good evidence that Steward did not really formulate his theory of cultural ecology until well into the 1950s, after he had embraced multilinear evolution. However, he adumbrated it in an article in the Kroeber Festschrift entitled "The Economic and Social Basis of Primitive Bands": "Empirically and logically . . . bands fall into three types—the patrilineal band; the composite band; and the matrilineal band (actually a variant of the first type)" (1936c:331). Of course Steward was empirically wrong about these types, and he later repudiated the model. Nonetheless Steward asserted that "I shall show that the patrilineal band is most common because it is produced by recurring ecological and social factors which may be formulated into something akin to cultural law, and that the composite band occurs where there are special factors, which may readily be ascertained in each instance" (1936c:331). He was also wrong about the patrilineal band being "the most common," but the article is important for Steward's expression of what he called "the broad problem . . . to formulate the ecological and other factors which produce the primitive band" (Steward 1936c:331–332).

Steward regarded low population density, "sparse" settlement patterns, land ownership patterns, political organization, postmarriage residence patterns, existence or nonexistence of band or local exogamy, and method of reckoning land inheritance as the crucial variables that produced different kinds of bands. For a comparative database, Steward chose the Bushmen (San), Central African Negritos (Mbuti "Pygmies" or Baca), Semang, Philippine Negritos, Australian and Tasmanian Aborigines, southern California Shoshonians (Cahuilla, Serrano, etc.), Ona, Tehuelche of Patagonia, Northern Algonkians, Canadian Athabascans, Andaman Islanderas, Ojibway (Anishnabe), Montaignais, and, of course, the Owens Valley Paiute. Steward concluded, "This paper is but the first in a series which I shall devote to this general objective [the formulation of ecological and other factors that produce the primitive band]" (1936c:345). Steward's *Basin-Plateau Aboriginal Sociopolitical Groups* (1970a [1938]) was not quite the "concluding chapter of his Great Basin studies," as Fowler and Jennings (1982) have asserted, but they are certainly correct that it was not the opening one. In fact, there can be little doubt that Steward's *Basin-Plateau* is the *second paper* in the series. Steward clearly meant *Basin-Plateau* to be interpreted within the context of the problem that he had formulated in 1936 and as a detailed addition to the case studies that he summarized in his earlier cross-cultural comparison (1936c).

Steward may or may not have been surprised to find no bands among Nevada Shoshoni. However, after he found what he called the composite band among the Owens Valley Paiute (among whom he did fieldwork eight years before penetrating central Nevada), is it any wonder that he concentrated most of his effort on a study of their eastern neighbors who had no bands fitting his proposed model? Between 1934 and 1938 Steward focused on the Western Shoshoni. He utilized his findings in *Theory of Culture Change* (1955b) not because he wanted to generalize about the Great Basin, but because he wanted to demonstrate a theory and methodology utilizing cross-cultural comparisons. The Western Shoshoni were merely an example of the explanatory power of the theory and method of cultural ecology. Steward generalized from the Western Shoshoni to other Basin groups on the basis of his theory of cultural ecology, which he wanted to demonstrate.

Anyone who has read much of Steward's work will recognize the mutual compatibility of the approaches of cultural ecology and multilinear evolution. In his famous articles on the ecological aspects of southwestern society (1937f), one can certainly see the methodologies of cultural ecology and multilinear evolution working in tandem. Steward essentially dropped cultural ecology around 1940; thereafter he was interested only in the questions of large-scale change over time. Yet both cultural ecology and multilinear evolution were part of his "theory of culture change." Putting Steward's "Ecological Aspects of Southwestern Society" (1937f) together with his "Native Cultures of the Intermontane (Great Basin) Area" (1940a) yields the methodological and empirical basis for his later "Methodology of Multilinear Evolution."

Steward's Theory of Culture Change

Steward (1955b:18, 42) regarded his methodologies of cultural ecology and multilinear evolution as being empirical—that is, inductive, rather than deductive. To a large extent, they were. But Steward's theory of culture change was just that, a theory—a theory as deductive as any other theory. It was within this theory that the methodologies of cultural ecology and multilinear evolution operated.

Steward's theory of culture change can be summarized as follows. History and change are inevitable (cf. Patterson 1987:16). Adaptation determines culture, which is divisible into core and noncore culture. Core culture is technology, behavior, and social relations necessary for adaptation. Some ideological factors, such as political ideology, may be part of core culture, but Steward was doubtful on this point. Core culture is essentially the means and the relationships of production, and they determine all other aspects of culture.

Steward and the Global Capitalist System

After letting culture lie dormant in virtually every one of his analyses of North American Indian societies after 1935, Steward virtually reversed his position on culture in what is probably the last analytical paper he produced. This was a typed manuscript entitled, "Underdeveloped Nations: Predictability and Manipulability of Modernizing Trends" (1969a), which was later published in the volume *Essays on Modernization of Underdeveloped Societies* (1971).[1] Although several items were published after Steward's death in 1972, this document may be the last thing Steward actually wrote. He fell ill in the latter part of 1971, and his book on Alfred Kroeber was actually finished by his wife, Jane. So if there is a "last word from Julian Steward," this may well be it. In the conclusion to this paper, Steward makes this very interesting assertion:

> The general hypothesis of this paper is that there are two broad categories of human problems, each with hundreds of auxiliary problems. In the first category, activity is directed toward survival goals, which may be extended to include general physical and psychological well-being. These were attainable throughout more than ninety-five percent of human history by devising appropriate technologies for utilizing and adapting to different environments

> and by making the necessary social arrangements. Not all human behavior was determined by reason; for there was latitude for variation in such matters as art, religion, and details of society that were only indirectly related to survival. Many features, such as magic, were incorrect solutions, but these were possible since they rarely endangered survival.
>
> The second category of problems has arisen from the evolution of culturally-derived values which are exemplified by the existence of class-structured states that channel productive surplus to the ruling classes and have relegated survival values of the masses to a secondary position. These goals are irrational in that they evolved without foresight or planning over thousands of years, yet until recently have been generally accepted without question. (Steward 1969a:17)

Notice that it is *a certain set of cultural values* that is at fault here: the values of ruling classes that are exploiting the masses for their own gain. For Steward, *culture was inherently dangerous* because it was always possible that it might indeed assume an independent existence and turn the tables on the mode of production, thus subsuming technology, production, distribution, and social relations to a set of values and behavior patterns that were unadaptive, irrational, and potentially destructive. In Steward's view, culture easily could be an expression of psychological factors and ideology that were largely nonadaptive. Thus, culture could result in "incorrect solutions."

Local Cultural Customs and Globalization: Shoshonis Compared to Puerto Ricans

We can now return to the issue of why Steward seems to have suppressed his own observations and generally refused to recognize the vitality and continuity of Western Shoshoni culture. Steward was not being unempirical; I think that he was simply observing cultural phenomena that did not derive from an economic causality. Assimilation and acculturation were not only value-free, descriptive terms for Steward, they were also processes—cultural processes—that were, in the last instance, economically determined. Shoshonis' involvement with the mining and ranching economy *was* both assimilation and acculturation. To the extent that Shoshonis kept certain cultural customs, even language, they were irrelevant unless they were a part of the means of production. When Steward describes Shoshonian culture as essentially "gastric" and "practical," he is actually describing his theory, not the Numic peoples of the Great Basin. When he describes Shoshoni acculturation as sparing them "crucial difficulties," he means that they were incorporated into the mining and ranching economy as rural proletariat, perhaps no better or worse off than other rural proletariats around the world.

Steward failed to grasp the importance of Newe culture. He did not see that it could be a creative force, uniting people in political and social groupings that, in turn, affect their economic well-being. This is certainly the case for Western Shoshonis of the 1970s, 1980s, and 1990s (Crum 1994:179–183; Rusco 1992), and it was also the case in the 1930s when Steward did his fieldwork (Clemmer 1996; Crum 1994:127). Steward thought that the economic processes of mining and ranching would, and should, absorb Shoshonis into rural America. He did not see that the *cultural* interpretation of ranching, and of land in general (particularly the use of pinyon pines), was sufficiently different between Indians and non-Indians (Clemmer 1978, 1985) that it would be a major source of Newe identity throughout most of the twentieth century and a point of departure between Indians and non-Indians in Nevada. Steward did not see that it was *culture* that could serve as a mediating factor in Nevada's political economy. However, he could have, because it was within his theoretical paradigm of culture change to do so. In fact, one of Steward's students from Columbia University, Eric Wolf (1982), made the mediating force of culture in the recent political-economic history of the world the hallmark of his brand of anthropology.

However, Steward did see culture as an important factor in local differentiation in Puerto Rico. There he recognized a highly differentiated economy, in which customs such as the *paseo, compadrazgo,* and playing the lottery might be economically determined in financially strapped communities. In these communities a strong social support system was necessary, but might only be part of the "free-floating," recreational, psychological complex of superstructural cultural fluff among classes that had no economic worries.

Paseo is the Sunday—and sometimes daily—ritual in which people walk around the town plaza in the evening; men walk in one direction, women the other. In the 1950s, when Steward was writing, the ritual was still important for courting and marriage. Compadrazgo is the institution of a godparent loop that binds two families economically and socially. Equivalent customs in Shoshoni communities might be the Fourth of July powwows at Duck Valley and Fallon Reservations; the annual Pine-Nut Festival in Ruby Valley; the occasional meetings of ranchers' committees on the Yomba, Duckwater, Duck Valley, and South Fork Reservations; the occasional meetings to discuss the claims commission case and to oppose it; the ties that bind siblings and cousins to each other and result in frequent social gatherings among family members; and the gatherings for burying rituals held by shamans or medicine persons. Until the 1970s, at all of these gatherings Shoshoni would have been the lingua franca. My experiences at some of these gatherings led me to believe that sharing of oral histories, retelling of myths, and discussion of customs also occurred, and that this socializing and communication affirmed Newe identity.

In 1980 Western Shoshonis officially rejected the Indian Claims Commission's offer of $26 million to extinguish their land claim, preferring instead to fight a legal battle to try to get control over a portion of federally held land (see Ronaasen et al., chapter 12). In 1984 Shoshonis formed the Western Shoshone National Council, with representation from all Shoshoni communities, including the Duck Valley Timbisha, to pursue the land claim and secure hunting, gathering, and fishing rights. These events reflect a more enduring and tenacious attachment to aboriginal land and more of a cultural identity than any outsider would have predicted on the basis of Steward's assessment of Shoshoni acculturation.

Steward's theory of culture change is an evolutionary model that postulates rather rigidly defined stages (e.g., band, chiefdom, state) and transitions to them that are demographically and economically driven and politically and socially defined. Yet, the "multilinearity" of the theory makes it more flexible than the unilinear schemes of Steward's contemporaries such as Childe and White. Steward himself saw the regional and local variations in culture that could arise within the state-level stage in Puerto Rico. On the basis of Steward's perceptive insights, one could easily have predicted the strengthening of Puerto Rican identity, Puerto Ricans' reluctance to commit themselves to integration into U.S. society through statehood, and the development of a Puerto Rican independence movement. Class and regional variations in the interpretation of shared customs permitted the maintenance of those customs and thus the maintenance of a common Puerto Rican identity.

STEWARD IN HISTORY

Why, then, could Steward not have provided an equally insightful analysis of contemporary Western Shoshoni culture? In the Western Shoshoni case it was not the local variations in Newe culture or in the ranching subculture that turned out to be most significant. Rather, it was—just as in the Puerto Rican case—the maintenance of particular customs and traditions and the sharing of some aspects of the American ranching subculture *in a Shoshoni context* that proved important in uniting the Western Shoshoni.

I think several aspects of Steward's life, career, and situation in history give some clues to this question. First, it is clear from Virginia Kerns's research into Steward's early life (see chapter 1) and Joel Janetski's recapitulation of Steward's archaeological work (see chapter 2) that Steward enthusiastically embraced nature, the outdoors, and the environment. He loved being in it, working with it, thinking about it, inventorying it, appreciating human beings' dependence on it, and the "dust-to-dust" aspect of humans' attempts to grapple with the environment over long periods of time. Steward participated enthusiastically in the ranching activities of the Deep Springs Preparatory School. His ethnographies of the Owens Valley Paiute and of the sociopolitical groups of the Basin-Plateau are almost more ethnographies of the environment than they are of the people. Even though Steward dealt with nonmaterial culture in many of his publications, it seems to have been understanding the environment that animated him and inspired his ethnographic work with Numic people. If that was the case, then his discovery of Shoshonis working and living on ranches would have led him to conclude that, just as grappling with the environment would have animated Numic peoples as hunters and gatherers, so also would grappling with the environment as ranch hands. After all, doing so animated Steward, why not the Shoshoni too?

In 1935–36, when Steward did his Western Shoshoni fieldwork, he had not yet developed his methodology of multilinear evolution (see Patterson and Lauria-Perricelli, chapter 14). Although it is possible to see his concept of "levels of sociocultural integration" in his paper on bands (Steward 1936c), there is no indication that he had any interest in studying or explaining cultural change. Acculturation was a hot topic in 1936. However, "acculturation" had only recently become an anthropological buzz word, and the concept as well as the actual process were probably not generally understood. Margaret Mead had published her ground-breaking book on Omaha acculturation, *The Changing Culture of an Indian Tribe* (1932). Melville Herskovits and Ralph Linton were in the midst of formulating important insights about culture context, and their students were beginning what would have become a decades-long trend in anthropology (Herskovits 1938). In fact, Steward might have encountered one of these students in 1936, Jack Harris, who was studying culture change among the Duck Valley Shoshoni (Harris 1938, 1940). Harris's study stands in marked contrast to Steward's work on the Shoshoni.[2] Redfield, Linton, and Herskovits's (1936) "Memorandum for the Study of Acculturation" had just been published in the *American Anthropologist* earlier that year. Had Steward read it? And if he had, what had it meant to him? Steward never cited any of Herskovits's work or the "Memorandum," although he did cite Linton's very general *The Study of Man* (1936) and he liked and cited Redfield's concept of "the folk society" and the "rural-urban continuum" (Redfield 1941; Steward 1949b). It is obvious why: the concepts allowed Steward to talk about regional subcultures as variations of the larger cultural systems in which they were interpreted. However, apparently the Western Shoshoni did not even qualify for "folk culture" status. Employed by the Bureau of American Ethnology and by the University of California, Berkeley's Anthropology

Department, Steward was probably well aware of the developing trends in anthropological thinking.

The move to study cultural change was spearheaded by Boas's students at Columbia—who went on to teach at Berkeley as well—probably under the influence of Columbia sociologist Charles Ogburn. In contrast, Alfred Kroeber, Robert Lowie, and Edward Gifford, the senior ethnologists at Berkeley, were strictly salvage ethnographers who were dedicated to recovering as much information about the past and pre-reservation ways of life from elderly consultants as they possibly could. Their aim was to reconstruct pictures of vanished lifeways, not to document contemporary situations. Each summer Kroeber released a cadre of students (Steward among them) to venture into Indian communities in the West with culture-trait checklists to document the "old ways" (see Myers, chapter 9). Omer Stewart may have been the first Berkeley anthropology student to do a study of contemporary life with his dissertation on the peyote religion among the Northern Paiutes (Stewart 1939). Thus, Steward probably had neither the opportunity nor the incentive to take an interest in cultural change or to study it, and he probably lacked any close acquaintance with concepts and theories that would have enabled him to do so.

By 1949, when Steward began developing his theory of culture change, he had come a long way from his Great Basin days (see Patterson and Lauria-Perricelli, chapter 14). The fact that Steward's theory of cultural ecology fit nicely into his theory of culture change may have been fortuitous. His theory of cultural ecology, as he first presented it in 1955, is quite different from the ecological study of Basin-Plateau environmental adaptations that he presented in 1938. In fact, one could almost say that Steward did not have a theory in 1938. Certainly Alfred Kroeber, Steward's thesis advisor, who was known for his caution in proposing explanations, would not have encouraged Steward to develop a theory. Perhaps all Steward had in those early years was a priority: to persuade anthropology that the material environment should receive more attention than it was getting. By 1955, when *Theory of Culture Change* was published, a raft of cultural change and acculturation studies had been published (cf. Siegel 1955). Studies by Linton (1940) and his Columbia students had greatly clarified the anthropological conceptualization of acculturation as a process. Steward, first at Columbia (1946–1952) and then at the University of Illinois (1952–1972), could have sent any number of his students into the field to study Shoshoni cultural change. Sidney Mintz, Marvin Harris, Charles Erasmus, Robert Murphy, Eric Wolf, and Eleanor Leacock are just a few who did cultural change studies under Steward's guidance and became well known for their insights.[3]

However, the decade 1945–1955 saw the affirmation of positivism in social science and modernization in much of the world (Wolf 1972). The "Red Scare," McCarthyism, and the Hollywood blacklist discouraged all but the most polite and orderly dissent and protest. The world seemed headed in one direction: a standoff between capitalist West and communist East. When protest and dissent did erupt in the 1960s, a decade of it seemed to yield only one conclusion: things are the way they are and nothing will change that. Steward's pessimistic summing up of large-scale trends in 1970 expressed the general attitude in America that had developed over the previous two decades, namely, "the system" will prevail no matter what.

Therefore, in 1951 trends toward integrating small-scale societies into large-scale ones must have seemed inevitable. Steward saw the "save the Indian" policies of his nemesis, John Collier, completely overturned; U.S. government policy once again became one of forced acculturation, dismemberment of tribes, and termination of Indians' special treaty status. Steward (1969b) regarded the Collier era as an aberrant blip in the general trend of integration of Indians into mainstream American life (see Rusco, chapter 7). Therefore, if Shoshonis were acculturating in the 1930s (or even if they were not), they would certainly be doing so in the 1950s.

Steward was consistent in retaining his pro-assimilationist position regarding the Western Shoshoni. Also, he seems to have firmly believed that his view was not politically motivated or even historically conditioned, but that his opinion resulted from conclusions based on applying the scientific methods to the study of economy and social organization. Steward's 1936 involvement in Bureau of Indian Affairs policy matters had resulted in this "scientific" opinion being strongly criticized. His apparent unwillingness to restudy the Western Shoshoni as a case study in cultural change may have resulted from his unwillingness to compromise his earlier "scientific" finding and from the primacy of his interest in environmental matters, rather than from an assumption about the juggernaut of modernization that was shared by the general public in the 1950s.

However, toward the end of his life Steward became uncomfortable with what he apparently saw as economically driven cultural values overwhelming human adaptability; and he also became increasingly uncomfortable with the whole idea of "acculturation." In his foreword to *Contemporary Change in Traditional Societies* (1967a:2), Steward noted that acculturation was an "inadequate" concept despite many attempts to define and redefine it. To speak of "diffusion" of cultural traits may be "misleading" when applied to the modern world. He also called for a reexamination of the concept of "assimilation" and even asserted that the meaning of "evolution" had to be clarified.

Steward also rejected the categories "ethnic minorities," "subcultures," and "subsocieties," noting that they must be "broken down into useful categories" (Steward 1955b:3). Although Steward was still using the concepts of "simple" and "complex" (1967b:5) to characterize societies, he seems to have been calling for a complete restructuring of anthropological thought that, 30 years later, is still slow in taking place. It is unfortunate that he never reexamined Shoshoni cultural change in light of his ever-changing new insights. However, this probably stems from his failure to understand the process of acculturation in the first place and his ultimate realization that the concept was largely meaningless because it could not be operationalized.

CONCLUSION

Perhaps more than most social and anthropological thinkers of the twentieth century, Julian Steward is closely associated with particular themes and theories: evolution, cultural ecology, area studies, comparative studies, and sociopolitical classification. Yet a careful reading of all his work indicates that Steward rarely retained any one of these themes and theories for very long. Just as much of the anthropological community seemed to be adopting these concepts, Steward was on to something else and beginning to sow doubts about what had earlier been so convincing to him.

Therefore, I think Steward did not apply his theory of culture change toward developing an analysis and explanation of Western Shoshoni culture change for a combination of reasons. First, his anthropological interest in Shoshonis really began as an interest in the natural environment of the Great Basin, not as an interest in the people. By the time he became known for ecological studies, he had moved to area studies—Latin America to be exact. By the time he became known for area studies, he was challenging Leslie White on the concept of "general" or "unilinear" evolution as opposed to "multilinear" evolution. In 1936 he did not have the conceptual and methodological tools to study and understand acculturation—he did not become a theorist interested in change until the 1940s. In the 1950s, when Steward had become well known as a theorist, the general intellectual milieu encouraged the viewpoint that change is unidirectional, unidimensional, and ultimately monolithic. Yet by the 1960s, when the acceptance of that viewpoint was at its peak, Steward was lamenting homogenization and calling for a reexamination of the conceptual tools that had been used to document it.

The gap between Steward's theory of culture change and an assessment of Western Shoshoni culture change that takes into account the observed events and situations as well as Shoshonis' interpretations of them is really a gap between anthropological reality and anthropological theory. Steward, the great seeker of social laws and cultural causality, ultimately became the arch-revisionist, unable to justify the defense of concepts that he either developed or used with such apparent ease in earlier periods of his life. For this reason, I think Steward had a great deal of difficulty revisiting much of his past work. Future generations may learn much more about how to understand social processes and cultural change by rereading Steward as a revisionist who, rather than merely documenting cultural change and modernization in his writings, also documented the contradictions in his own thinking that led him to deconstruct concepts that he had formerly embraced. Perhaps calling him a "post-modern deconstructionist" would be going too far. However, as successors to Steward's legacy of Great Basin research, we are perhaps just now realizing in our critiques and appraisals what Steward realized long ago about theory and methodology: neither should be taken for granted or left unquestioned.

NOTES

This paper was originally presented at "Re-Reading Julian Steward," a symposium at the 25th Great Basin Anthropological Conference, October 11, 1996, at Lake Tahoe, Nevada.

1. Steward wrote on the front of it "Please return" (I did so, after making a copy) and "For India Journ. Soc. Sent 6/6/69." Someone else (probably Jane Cannon Steward), in a different handwriting, had written the address.

2. Harris left the field of anthropology shortly after earning his Ph.D. and became a prosperous businessman in San Jose, Costa Rica.

3. Steward's students Robert Murphy and Yolanda Murphy (1960) did a study of the Shoshoni-Bannock, but this was an ethnographic and ethnohistorical reconstruction much like the reconstructions Steward had done under Kroeber in the 1930s.

11

Where Were Wovoka and Wuzzie George?

Alice B. Kehoe

Julian Steward struggled to work through the incongruity between received theory and his ethnographic data. In Basin-Plateau Sociopolitical Groups *he simply called the Numa an "anomaly." By the time* Theory of Culture Change *came out in 1955, he had termed them a "family-level" society. The effort to deal with the data pushed Steward to reject the old unilinear, four-stage evolutionary schema. However, his prevailing valuation of grand theory and denigration of particularistic studies prevented Steward from considering the colonial experiences of such Numas as the great Ghost Dance prophet Wovoka and the skilled craftswoman Wuzzie George. In this short, crisp discussion, Alice Kehoe notes how much Steward's Great Basin ethnography was an effort to filter aboriginal culture out of historically situated societies in which all Steward's informants postdated conquest.*

Along with A. R. Radcliffe-Brown, Julian Steward is acknowledged as the father of "the scientific study of hunter-gatherer societies" (Burch and Ellanna 1994:viii). Willey and Sabloff (1993:178) credit Steward as "the principal figure in the environmental-evolutionary trend" in the mid-twentieth century. Bruce Trigger lauds him, "Of all the American ethnologists of this period, he had the greatest respect for archaeological data and awareness of their potential value for studying problems of human behavior over long periods" (Trigger 1989:280). Gazing from across the ocean, Malina and Vasícek (1990:80) see a somewhat different Steward: "The classical evolutionism of the nineteenth century was revived in the forties by L. A. White and E. R. Service [unilinear evolution] and in the fifties by J. H. Steward [multilinear evolution]." When I read the newly published *Theory of Culture Change* (1955b) in my senior year at Barnard, the book seemed to me a tremendous breakthrough, a watershed, the means at last of relating ecological and cultural data to obtain the essential histories of the world's peoples. Steward gave us the theoretical principles, whereas in *Star Carr* Grahame Clark had just given us a model of research. My classmate Dena Dincauze and I were inspired, raring to go into the field.

THE GENESIS OF STEWARD'S DATA

Rereading Steward, especially his *Basin-Plateau Aboriginal Sociopolitical Groups,* I feel uneasy. Is it that I must compare Steward's bloodless ethnography with Margaret Wheat's work? Is it that Steward's monograph contains nine photographs of landscapes but not a single photo of a human being? Is it the disjunction between 258 pages of description and the final few pages of generalization? I begin skimming through a second time. Where is Wovoka? How can an ethnography of the Northern Paiute, written from fieldwork three years after his death, totally omit Wovoka?

Okay, *Basin-Plateau Aboriginal Sociopolitical Groups* is about *aboriginal* Numa, and Wovoka was born after the Euro-American invasion of Nevada. But so were every one of Steward's informants. (The Mormons came to Great Salt Lake in 1847, 87 years before Steward's fieldwork.) Okay, Steward was doing salvage ethnography, looking for the *aboriginal* sociopolitical groups, but Wovoka was by heredity and conduct a traditional leader (Hittman 1990:150). Reading closely, I see that the Walker River valley is on Steward's map, but that Walker River is mentioned only on page 106 as the home of some people traveling to the festival at Austin 100 miles away—otherwise it is ignored. What appears to be a thorough survey of Shoshoni and Paiute in fact has lacunae unexplained in the text (Thomas 1983b:61).

EVOLUTIONISM, DEDUCTION, AND SCIENTISM

Rereading Steward, we must pay attention to the fact that Steward, Harold Driver, Isabel Kelly, Willard Park, and Omer Stewart were working within Kroeber's project of filling in, as Kroeber stated in 1939, "element surveys comparing the Owens Valley Northern Paiute with the tribes east and west respectively. Steward also determin[ed] the territorial bands of the Shoshone, and O[mer] Stewart those of the Northern Paiute. These works, with [Isabel] Kelly's at last give a reasonably accurate picture of the many small groups that constitute the Great Basin Shoshoneans" (Kroeber 1939c:52).

Steward's 1938 monograph came out of a research project designed not by Steward, but by Kroeber. Steward took advantage of his 1935 appointment to the Bureau of American Ethnology (BAE) to publish his share of the culture-element distributions in the form of a BAE monograph and to title it broadly as *Basin-Plateau Aboriginal Sociopolitical Groups*. The Nevada Shoshoni and Northern and Gosiute Shoshoni were the groups on which Steward and his wife focused his culture-element distribution research. To these data he added the ethnography of the Owens Valley Paiute he had studied as a graduate student, following youthful acquaintance stemming from his schooling at Deep Springs Preparatory School (Shimkin 1964:1–4; see Kerns, chapter 1).

Steward presumably expected that a review of the survey data collected by himself and his colleagues would support generalizations he had created by logical deduction. When the data did not, he declared them to constitute exceptions to the generalizations he continued to assert. In Steward's "comparative studies, the coverage achieved has been illustrative rather than comprehensive" (Shimkin 1964:10). My colleague Jim Weil uses the phrase "deductive impulse" to characterize anthropologists who seem impelled toward such logically appealing generalizations rather than prizing statements inductively derived from close adherence to data. Weil's phrase seems to fit Steward's lurches from amassed data to seductively rational hypotheses.

Rereading Steward clarifies the tension in anthropology between respect for observed data and a proclivity to construct schemata that inevitably reflect Western cultural assumptions. Steward's and Elman Service's (1962) schemata recapitulate Montesquieu's of 1748—all three premise universal regularities governed by "the nature of the terrain," as Montesquieu put it (Jones 1992:746). The belief that scientists formulate universalistic models, that one is not doing science if one does not formulate such models, confused Steward as it did so many other social scientists (Ross 1991:402, 405). Steward's contemporary, E. E. Evans-Pritchard, deplored this notion, caustically remarking, "The concepts of natural system and natural law, modelled on the constructs of the natural sciences, have been responsible for a false scholasticism which has led to one rigid and ambitious formulation after another. Released from these essentially philosophical dogmas, [social anthropology] can be really empirical and, in the true sense, scientific. The[re is a] feeling that any discipline that does not aim at formulating laws and hence predicting and planning is not worth the labour of a lifetime" (Evans-Pritchard 1963:26–27). Evans-Pritchard's contempt parallels Dorothy Ross's analysis of the scientism dominating American social sciences by the 1920s. Ross sets the stage for Steward's wavering: "The continuing force of the national ideology and its ahistoric cultural traditions led American social scientists to contain the possibility of radical change and to find a source of permanent sustenance within or outside the novelty of history" (Ross 1991:467). "America stands at the intersection of history and nature. Society was the product of interacting individuals, forming and reforming in groups the image of perpetual atomistic motion held in equilibrium" (Ross 1991:387–388).

Steward was unlikely to question the four-stage social evolution schema premised by Western intellectuals since the eighteenth century (Meek 1976) any more than he or Service (1962:30–33, 43) questioned male dominance among hunter-gatherers. Normal science gave Steward organizing concepts and he adduced concrete instances. When these instances failed to embody the predicted characteristics, Steward, and Service (1962:94–99) after him, made them fit anyway. The naive apprehension of science common in 1930s America would suggest that to have focused on the nonconforming data would have rendered *Basin-Plateau Aboriginal Sociopolitical Groups* mere local history rather than science—the sort of thing women such as Margaret Wheat and Grace Dangberg might do. Most crucially, discussing historically situated persons such as Wuzzie George and Wovoka would have negated the critical point of Steward's monograph: that it describes *aboriginal* sociopolitical groups and thus describes *natural* primitives.

Models Versus People

Wuzzie George and Jack Wilson are real people in history. We can say of Steward's monograph what Tim Ingold says of Robert Bettinger's book *Hunter-gatherers,* that "people are conspicuous by their absence from his book, figuring if at all as mere ciphers, archetypal representatives of the category of the primitive in anthropology" (Ingold 1992:796). Bettinger, of course, works in precisely the region immortalized by Steward. He chose to follow Steward's scientistic mode rather than a postcolonial engagement with the reality of history such as Michael Hittman (1973, 1990) or Stoffle et al. (1990) exemplify. Both Steward and Bettinger aimed at elucidating environmentally grounded regularities that the archaeologists, who are supposedly able to identify the environment through natural-science studies, can use to reconstruct sociopolitical groups and their economic practices. Because they sought to know a nonliterate past in which we do not necessarily recognize historic persons, Steward and Bettinger did not focus on historic Paiutes. In *Basin-Plateau Aboriginal Sociopolitical Groups* Steward mentioned a number of actual historic persons, but distilled an archaeological past out of these living Numa. This operation has been basic to prehistoric archaeology since its establishment in Daniel Wilson's 1862 *Prehistoric Man:* Obtain ethnographic analogies by drawing them out of a priori categories in the four-stage social evolution schema.

The problem, the disjunction, in *Basin-Plateau Aboriginal Sociopolitical Groups* is more than the recalcitrance of the Numa to support Steward's and

Service's nice, logical taxon of patrilocal bands. It is more than the conflict between universalizing and particular projects. The problem stems from fundamental guiding assumptions in traditional anthropology that there has been a trajectory in human history expressed in the four-stage schema and that some societies constitute living fossils—"our contemporary ancestors," as Elman Service (1962:8–10) called them.

Basin-Plateau Aboriginal Sociopolitical Groups stimulated Steward to consider the possibility that the received four-stage social evolution is simply, grossly inadequate. By 1941 he came to feel acutely the importance of actual historic data in evaluating questions of cultural process. Steward saw the issue to lie in the popularity of deliberately ahistoric correlations such as McKern's Midwest taxonomic system and Kroeber's culture-element distributions, pulled like red herrings across the trails of historic questions (Steward 1942). By 1955 the "anomaly" of the Shoshoneans was transformed, as far as Steward was concerned, into a "family level of sociocultural integration" (Steward 1955b:101), thus no longer an exception to a generalization on "all peoples in an area of low population density" (Steward 1970a:258 [1938]). Steward had come to insist on the primacy of empirical historic data (Steward 1955b:18–19). Nevertheless, he still grasped for regularities that could be held as cultural laws.

CONCLUSION: STEWARD'S STRUGGLE WITH CLASS AND SOCIETY

The mature Steward rejected the unilinear or universal evolution that had been paradigmatic to anthropology from its inception as a discipline. He correctly understood the utter incompatibility between unilinear evolution and the principles of biological evolution (Steward 1955b:2). However, one piece of heavy baggage he failed to jettison was the conventional opposition between "primitive" and "civilized." He repeated the standard line that "primitive or 'tribal' culture" is characterized by "small, simple, independent, self-contained, and homogeneous societ[ies]" exhibiting "uniformity of behavior" due to a "value system shared by all tribal members" (Steward 1955a:44–45 [1951]). Embedding the guiding assumption of John Wesley Powell, Lewis Henry Morgan (1877), and their ilk that a powerful contrast dichotomizes "primitive" from "civilized" societies, Steward's theory of culture change remains at heart, as Malina and Vasícek claim, only a variant of traditional nineteenth-century evolutionism. It nearly did break out. If Steward had gone through James Mooney's Shanty Irish School of Hard Knocks instead of Deep Springs Preparatory School, he might have been able to comprehend the full humanity of Jack Wilson. If Steward had struggled like Margaret Wheat to pursue a scientific profession in spite of being a woman, he might have been able to see the full reality of people like Wuzzie George. Given his enculturation and status within the dominant class of American society (see Kerns, chapter 1), Steward could not break the shackles of his own class's traditional knowledge.

Rereading Steward, I can understand why *Basin-Plateau Aboriginal Sociopolitical Groups* seemed of so little relevance to my study of Jack Wilson. I can recapture the excitement I felt as an undergraduate reading *Theory of Culture Change* even as I note its flaws. Steward was on to something, he struggled against the scientism so prevalent in American social sciences. He nearly succeeded in constructing the empirical foundation he realized was crucial to a truly scientific anthropology. Like Baron Montesquieu, Steward's intellect lived in a "fortified grand house surrounded by large strong ditches filled with water the colour of coffee" (Jones 1992:744). Steward could not leap over the coffee-filled moat around his study to walk as a fellow human with Wovoka and Wuzzie George. The "deductive impulse" to which he had been trained subverted his ethnography, requiring us to reread it with a highly sensitive critical eye.

12

Rethinking Cultural Ecology, Multilinear Evolution, and Expert Witnesses: Julian Steward and the Indian Claims Commission Proceedings

SHEREE RONAASEN, RICHARD O. CLEMMER, and MARY ELIZABETH RUDDEN

It is not commonly known that Julian Steward played a major role in legal proceedings relating to Indian claims. In those proceedings, he introduced key concepts of culture ecology theory and multilinear evolution as evidence against the claims of the Shoshonean Indians in the U.S. Indian Claims Commission cases. Steward prepared evidence and testified as an expert witness for the Department of Justice that because the Shoshonean Indians were not evolved beyond a "family level of sociocultural integration" they could not have rights recognizable within American law. Steward's evidence contradicted the testimony of Omer Stewart, expert witness for the petitioning Indians. The debate between Steward and Stewart that began in the Indian Claims Commission proceedings was carried over into the anthropological literature. The political, social, and historic context of the Indian Claims Commission proceedings is analyzed to provide an explanation for the Steward-Stewart debate and the Indian Claims Commission proceedings in general.

Julian Steward introduced key concepts derived from his theory of cultural ecology and his methodology of multilinear evolution as evidence against the claims of the Shoshonean Indians in the U.S. Indian Claims Commission (ICC) cases. As an expert witness for the Department of Justice, Steward prepared evidence suggesting that because the Shoshonean Indians were not evolved beyond a "family level of sociocultural integration" they could not have rights recognizable within American law. Essentially, attorneys for the government used Steward's interpretations to demonstrate that the Shoshonean Indians were not organized by economics, social networks, religion, or politics into any sort of recognizable entity that could hold legal title to territory. Steward's evidence contradicted the anthropological work of Omer Stewart, an expert witness for the petitioning Indians, who assumed that they had political organization on the "band" level and that these bands had distinct territories with boundaries. In contrast to Steward, Omer Stewart did not really have a theory of culture; his work was largely nontheoretical and heavily empirical. Whereas Steward concentrated on ecological and evolutionary theory, Stewart concentrated on the lived experiences of his informants and the logical extensions of those lived experiences in terms of concepts of groupness and land tenure. Stewart and Steward were legal opponents in cases involving the Utes, Paiutes, and Shoshones. In every case, the commission ruled in favor of the Indians.

The very nature of the ICC itself placed anthropologists in a position to legitimize the denial of indigenous rights to collectively held land and to other collective rights guaranteed by treaty with the U.S. government. Steward's development of the concept of "levels of sociocultural integration" was crucial in the government attorneys' arguments and proposed findings of fact. In this chapter we shall demonstrate how and why his concept of "levels of sociocultural integration" was easily politicized in the context of the ICC proceedings precisely because of the political nature of those proceedings. Examining the political context of Steward's interpretation of the Shoshonean Indians will help to clarify some fundamental discrepancies in the anthropological interpretations of the Great Basin Indians.

In this chapter we will review the background of Julian Steward and Omer Stewart and their recognized accomplishments in anthropology, with particular emphasis on their disagreement over whether Great Basin Indians had band-level political organization and concepts of territory and property. We will also show how this important debate in the anthropological literature grew directly out of the ICC cases. We have chosen to focus on the Northern Paiute case because, although the Great Basin cases included separate dockets involving the several Shoshonean-speaking Indian nations (e.g., the Northern Shoshone, Eastern Shoshone, Bannock, Goshute, Western Shoshone, Consolidated Ute, and Southern Paiute), in the Northern Paiute case Steward introduced into evidence the paper called "The Great Basin Shoshonean Indians: An Example of a Family Level of Socio-cultural Integration" (1955b:101-121). Although adumbrated in Steward's *Basin-Plateau Aboriginal Sociopolitical*

Groups (1970a [1938]), this paper first appeared in print as a chapter in Steward's (1955b) book *Theory of Culture Change* three years after Steward testified in the Northern Paiute case.

In a footnote Steward stated that the chapter was essentially a condensation of *Basin-Plateau Aboriginal Sociopolitical Groups;* however, it is evident that Steward had reworked the material to fit his newly developed methodology of multilinear evolution and his developing theory of culture change. Therefore the crucial position paper for the ICC proceedings was his "Levels of Sociocultural Integration: An Operational Concept" (Steward 1951). In a short comment pertaining to the ICC proceedings, Omer Stewart remarked that Steward had changed his theory (Stewart 1979:109). It is not so much that Steward *changed* his theory, but rather that he had *developed* one. This theory conceptualized property rights as a variable of land tenure, which in turn was a variable of sociopolitical organization. According to Steward's theory, only sociopolitical entities that had reached a certain level of organization on an evolutionary scale—at least the band level, which Steward used to refer to clan-based land-tenure systems as well (Steward 1951)—could have developed concepts of holding land as property. Steward's review of ethnographic material for the Ute case (decided in 1950) probably was influential in his summary presentation of the concept of "levels of sociocultural integration" in 1951. In the Northern Paiute case, Steward seems to have simply slotted the "Shoshoneans" into the schema.

In our conclusions, we offer some reflections on the degree to which anthropological concepts, theories, and issues are conditioned by historic events and on the little-known impact of the "real world" of litigation on what is often conceptualized as a "pure and objective science." Finally, we draw some parallels between the issues in the Northern Paiute case and several collective human rights issues proposed in the Draft Declaration on the Rights of Indigenous Peoples drafted by the United Nations' Working Group on Indigenous Populations (INDIGRIGHTS 1998; Sills and Morris 1993:38–45).

THE INDIAN CLAIMS COMMISSION

Congress passed the Indian Claims Commission Act in 1946. The ICC was not a new idea. Commissioner of Indian Affairs Francis Leupp had suggested it as early as 1908, as had Lewis Meriam, who headed an investigation into the Bureau of Indian Affairs (BIA) in 1928, and Commissioner of Indian Affairs John Collier in 1933 and again in 1939. The act's stipulations as to how claims could be filed were extremely liberal. Any legally constituted political entity officially recognized as an Indian tribe by the U.S. government, any tribe that had gone out of existence as a legal entity but to which some members of the political entity in question traced descent, or any "nation" that was part of a larger tribe could file a claim on behalf of its members. Congress mandated the commission "to hear and determine . . . claims against the United States on behalf of any Indian tribe, band, or Nation of American Indians" (U.S. Congress 1946:1050). One of the mandates from the BIA to its agency superintendents and field officers between 1946 and 1951 was for them to press "their" tribes to hire attorneys and file claims with the ICC. Of course, once the claim was filed, it had to proceed to its final judgment.

The commission decided early on that "it did not have the authority to return land, although it could, in response to proper arguments, declare that the Indian title to particular tracts had never been extinguished" (Clemmer and Stewart 1986:551). Instead, financial compensation was to be awarded for the value of the lands at the time of taking. The act allowed five years after August 13, 1946, for "any Indian tribe, band or other Nation" to hire attorneys and file claims petitions. The ICC specifically rejected treaties and agreements as the sole basis for claims; only in cases in which treaties had promised monetary compensation or compensation in goods and attorneys for the plaintiffs could prove that no evidence existed that the compensation had been paid, would treaties have any bearing. If treaties were not to be the basis for claims and their adjudication, then what was? The answer is expert witness testimony. Although the commission would admit evidence given by Indians themselves, attorneys quickly learned that such evidence was virtually useless. Because Indians were regarded as "interested parties," any evidence they gave had to be corroborated by "impartial witnesses." These "impartial witnesses" were invariably historians and anthropologists—scholars who had gathered information from the Indians themselves but had distilled, streamlined, interpreted, and theorized it.

An important provision of the original act of Congress that created the ICC in 1946 provided that once the award was made and the money was in the hands of the tribes, such payments "shall be a full discharge of the United States of all claims and demands touching any of the matters involved in the controversy." This provision meant that the tribes could never ask for a rehearing of a case or reopen a case, even if some grievous error had been made or their concerns had not been argued correctly by their attorneys. In one phase of the Northern Paiute case, for example, "the language used by the Commission in one phase of the . . . case, the so-called 'Snake Paiute Tract Claim,' expressly recognizes the presence of a legitimate Indian claim," but provides that

> the payment of $3,500,00 shall finally dispose of all rights, claims, or demands which said petitioners or any of them, or any group of them could

> have asserted with respect to said tract . . . and said petitioners, and each of them, and each group thereof, shall be barred thereby from asserting any such rights, claims, or demands against defendant [the U.S. government] . . . as aforesaid shall constitute a final determination of said claim . . . and shall become final on the day it is entered, the parties thereto waiving any right to appeal from or otherwise seek review of such determination. (U.S. Government Printing Office 1947:1055; cf. Forbes 1965:45)

THE ANTHROPOLOGY OF JULIAN STEWARD AND OMER STEWART

The Julian Steward and Omer Stewart story began at the University of Utah in the early 1930s, when Stewart answered an advertisement for a summer job as cook for Steward during his excavations at Promontory Point and Black Rock Cave (Rigg 1992:1). That fall, Stewart entered the University of Utah, where, expecting to study law, he changed to anthropology after a few classes from the young anthropologist Julian Steward. Stewart's undergraduate degree was guided by Steward, "who was forming the basic assumptions that would lead to his theory of multilinear evolution" (Stoffle 1991–1992:xi). In 1933 Stewart entered a graduate program in anthropology at the University of California, Berkeley, where he studied with Alfred Kroeber and Robert Lowie.

From 1935 to 1938, Omer Stewart conducted survey research in the Great Basin as part of Kroeber's culture-element distribution studies. He published "The Northern Paiute Bands" (Stewart 1939) and the "Culture Element Distribution" report (Stewart 1941). According to Stoffle (1991–1992:xi), because Stewart's data indicated that the social organization in the Great Basin was far more complex than that "postulated by Steward's new theoretical model," a rift was created between Stewart and Steward. Steward "concluded" that his former student had "broken ranks, thus committing an unforgivable heresy."

Despite Stoffle's allegations that Steward blackballed Omer, Stewart was offered a position at the University of Colorado in 1946, where he stayed until his retirement. Throughout the 1950s, 1960s, and 1970s, Stewart prepared cases and appeared as an expert witness in dozens of cases for Indian litigants, including cases for the Native American Church and the Great Basin ICC cases. Stewart evaluated his "professional work in terms of its usefulness to people" (Stoffle 1991–1992:xiii). Among other accomplishments, Stewart was awarded the Malinowski Award from the Society for Applied Anthropology in 1983. In an epitaph, Deward Walker (1991–1992:v) said that Stewart "spent his life battling racism, ethnocentrism, imperialism, and their consequences among the American Indians. Anthropology was his weapon. Conscience was his guide."

In so far as Julian Steward's background relates to this chapter, we refer the reader to this book's introduction. It should be noted that Julian Steward also studied with Kroeber at the University of California, Berkeley. Also parallel to Stewart's biography, Steward's principal ethnographic work, *Basin-Plateau Aboriginal Sociopolitical Groups* (1970a [1938]), was based in large part on surveys for Kroeber's culture-element distribution studies. In this work, Steward identified the concept of culture ecology and set its task as being to ascertain the effect that the "techno-environment" has had on "sociopolitical institutions." This approach offered the "greatest success . . . for analyzing simple hunters and gatherers" (1970a:1–2 [1938]). For Steward the Shoshonean Indians provided such an example: their "pursuits concerned with the problems of daily existence dominated their activities to an extraordinary degree," limiting and conditioning their "institutions." Although *Basin-Plateau* was regarded for decades as the "prime resource of information about the distribution and cultural characteristics" on the indigenous nations of the Great Basin, since the 1980s it has not been accepted by some anthologists as "a comprehensive ethnographic account" because the ethnographic coverage was limited mainly to the Western Shoshone of Nevada (d'Azevedo 1986:4).

In 1952, Steward accepted a special research professorship at the University of Illinois, where he prepared evidence and participated on behalf of the Department of Justice in the Great Basin Indian ICC cases. During this time Steward produced his most significant theoretical work, *Theory of Culture Change: The Methodology of Multilinear Evolution* (1955b). In this work Steward discussed his theory of levels of sociocultural integration as reflected in four specified lines of social evolution with cross-cultural regularities. The lowest level of general, cross-cultural sociocultural integration was represented by the development of the predatory band in Shoshonean society. The chapter discussing this line was a reprint of the paper "The Great Basin Shoshonean Indians: An Example of a Family Level of Sociocultural Integration" (Steward 1955b:101–121), which first appeared as evidence against the Northern Paiute Indians in the ICC cases.

However, according to Steward's anthropological interpretation of the Great Basin, before the development of the predatory band the Shoshoneans had represented "a distinctive and nonrecurrent line of development in the scheme of multilinear evolution" (Steward 1955b:120). Steward said that their economic and social relations "may be likened to a net in that each family had occasional associations with families on all sides." The net "lacked knots . . . each family was at liberty to associate with whom it pleased." The food quest dictated a family's activities and thus not even kin ties, according to Steward, gave cohesion to any definable group. It was not until the whites entered the country and introduced the horse that the Shoshonean Indians developed a "higher level of sociocultural integration and a cross-culturally significant type." With the horse, the Shoshoneans organized into "multi-family, mounted, predatory bands [that] . . . depended upon raiding and new resources brought by the whites" (Steward 1955b:121). The final phase and most advanced level of sociocultural integration and social evolution developed only after the Shoshonean Indian wars ended, when the "people who did not enter the reservations rapidly adapted themselves to a new white society by working for ranches, mines, or taking odd jobs in the new towns. The very absence of aboriginal band or community institutions made this adjustment easier" (Steward 1955b:121).

These brief summaries of the biographies of Omer Stewart and Julian Steward as well as an outline of Steward's profile of Shoshonean society shed light on the North Paiute case. Both men had similar educational backgrounds, yet they developed divergent interpretations. It is interesting that these seemingly divergent interpretations of the Great Basin social organization were used by attorneys to rigidify and elaborate the differences in legal proceedings rather than by the anthropological community.

THE NORTHERN PAIUTE NATION V. THE UNITED STATES OF AMERICA

The ICC cases had special significance for the discipline of anthropology because anthropological evidence was relied upon almost exclusively in determining "aboriginal Indian title." As noted before, in several Great Basin cases Omer Stewart was an expert witness for petitioning Indians and Julian Steward was an expert witness for the defendant, the Department of Justice. Both Stewart and Steward were considered expert witnesses because they were among the first anthropologists to conduct research in the Great Basin, primarily as part of Kroeber's culture-element distribution studies. In the Northern Paiute case, the petition was "a claim for the taking of Indian aboriginal title to the Northern Paiute land without payment of consideration" (U.S. ICC 1973a:2 [1957]). The defense put forth was that the petitioners were "inherently incapable of acquiring and/or holding 'Original Indian Title'" (U.S. ICC 1973c:1–2).

The Defendant's (Government's) Requested Findings of Fact

According to the government's defense, the so-called Northern Paiute Nation was "not an aboriginal tribe or entity united in a community under one leadership or government . . . nor did any of the so-called bands exclusively occupy a definable area." If any bands ever had existed, they ceased to exist prior to United States dominion "and there arose predatory groups which were disassociated from land use and 'ownership' and derived their principal sustenance by preying upon travelers across the claimed area and upon immigrants" (U.S. ICC 1973c:1–2). The attorney for the government based this assertion completely on two of Steward's works (which were first submitted as exhibits in 1954): "The Great Basin Shoshonean Indians: An Example of a Family Level of Sociocultural Integration" (1955b:101–121; 1968a) and testimony written with Erminie Wheeler-Voegelin (Steward and Wheeler-Voegelin 1954; U.S. ICC 1973c:1–307), which later appeared as a book called *The Paiute Indians* (1974). The evidence is summarized as it appeared in the proposed findings. Specifically, the culture ecology theory was established as the interpretational framework by attorneys for the defendant. Citing Steward, the government attorneys stated, "the existence of any kind of property rights found among any people are functions of the environment and of the technological devices for exploiting the environment" (U.S. ICC 1973c:42). Among hunting and gathering peoples, such as the Great Basin Shoshoneans including the Northern Paiute, "resources were so meager that the overall population density was low and it was difficult for more than a few families to remain in close association for any length of time" (U.S. ICC 1973c:42). Primarily, the government demonstrated that the economic fragmentation of Northern Paiute society was the result of reliance on the unstable resource pinenuts. Steward testified, "I haven't to this day discovered why it does or doesn't, but it is unpredictable. Certain years groves of it on a particular mountain might be very abundant, and the next year it might be twenty miles away" (U.S. ICC 1973c:46). Thus the "habitual use and ownership of a given grove would be impossible" (U.S. ICC 1973c:47).

In fact, the defendant argued that no economic activity led to any sort of interfamily cooperation or organization. Steward explained, "there were several reasons why [antelope and rabbit drives] did not bring about permanent integration or cohesion of territorial or social groups of fixed membership. . . . Since the place, the participants, and the leaders were never quite the same in successive years, the drives provided only temporary bonds between independent families" (U.S. ICC 1973c:55).

The defendant's findings of fact also included the following:

1. That the Northern Paiute were not organized socially, religiously, politically, or even through kinship. Referring to Steward and Wheeler-Voegelin (1974:50–51), the defending attorney denied any role for a priest or ceremonial leader because of the "complete absence of collective or group ceremonialism" (U.S. ICC 1973c:70).

2. That the Northern Paiute did not have "property or territory." Directly quoting Steward's "Cultural Ecology" paper (Steward 1955b:11–12), the defendant argued that "in an area where denial of the right to use any edible product encountered was to condemn a wandering group to starvation there could be no property right in the earth that nourished that product" (U.S. ICC 1973c:76).

3. Most importantly, the defendant (U.S. ICC 1973c:102) argued in Finding 26 that the Northern Paiute were not a nation, a band, or a tribe (Steward and Wheeler-Voegelin 1974:17; U.S. ICC 1973b). In fact, in a special attachment to Finding 15, the defendant referred to a discussion of Stewart's characterization of Northern Paiute as having bands: "The term 'band' is only a little less vague than 'tribe.' One might suppose that anthropological use of this term implies some theoretical concept of unification of local people, such as territoriality, habitual association of families in community endeavors, and recognized forms of leadership of 'chieftainship' over a designated and defined section of the population" (Steward and Wheeler-Voegelin 1954). The government attorney then relied directly on Steward to impugn Stewart's methodology: "Unfortunately, there has been a certain amount of irresponsibility in this respect. It is surprising that O. C. Stewart (1930) seemed to consider that it was sufficient merely to ask Northern Paiute informants the names of 'bands' and 'chiefs' and the territory each inhabited without analytic inquiry into the meaning of 'bands' either as an integrated social group or as phenomena in historic change" (U.S. ICC 1973c:307).

4. To ensure the defense, the government attorneys concluded with the finding that the "Northern Paiutes abandoned their old life" (U.S. ICC 1973c:292). Requested Finding 31 argued that the only bands that had ever existed were "predatory bands" that had arisen about 10 years after initial white immigration and settlement, beginning about 1845. The bands were short lived, but their existence indicated that "destruction of native vegetable foods, . . . the gradual acquisition of horses, the presence of white immigration trains and livestock herds which could be raided, and possession of firearms introduced new economic and military patterns" (U.S. ICC 1973c:230; Steward and Wheeler-Voegelin 1974:294–295).

The Petitioner's Objections to the Defendant's Proposed Findings of Fact

In response to the findings of fact put forth by the defendant, the Northern Paiute filed the "Petitioners' Objections to Defendant's Findings of Fact and a New Proposed Findings of Fact." In summary of the opening objection, the petitioners "observed" that a large part of their objections resulted from the use that the defendant had made of two writings by Dr. Julian Steward, from which "large portions of the defendant's requested findings have been lifted verbatim" (U.S. ICC 1973a:5–7 [1957]).

The Northern Paiutes' first and overall objection involved the use of Steward's two anthropological exhibits. The first "unpublished" paper, "The Great Basin Shoshonean Indians: An Example of Family Level of Sociocultural Integration," was written after Steward's "employment to testify for the Government in the Uintah Ute and other Indian cases" (U.S. ICC 1973a:5–7 [1957]). In this paper, Steward described certain cultural traits that illustrate his thesis. Based on Omer Stewart's anthropological work and other expert witness testimony, the Paiutes' attorney asserted that Steward's description was "for the most part . . . [accomplished by] elaborating or exaggerating certain features of culture that he found that to have existed among some Shoshonean-speaking Indians" (U.S. ICC 1973a:5–7 [1957]). The petitioners stated that the commission was presented with the same kind of theoretical anthropology in *Uintah Ute Indians of Utah v. The United States.* In that case, Steward "sought to attach his concept of 'family level of sociocultural integration' to the Uintah Ute Indians and the Commission found that the evidence before it on the way of life of the Uintah Utes did not support Dr. Steward's theory" (U.S. ICC 1973a:5–7 [1957]).

Against the second objectionable work, "The Northern Paiute Indians" (Steward and Wheeler-Voegelin 1974), the petitioners argued that Steward "displayed an obsession for developing arguments by which he believed the Northern Paiute Indians' claims to Indian title to land might be defeated" (U.S. ICC 1973a:5–7 [1957]). This obsession made it "impossible for him to state even the simplest evidentiary facts without lending those facts some color to flavor his arguments for the Government's defense, . . . his conclusions were rested upon only snatches of evidence while other evidence Dr. Steward would disregard or distort to remove any conflict with the conclusion he sought to draw" (U.S. ICC 1973a:5–7 [1957]). Overall, the report "contains very little that is simply description of the evidence, [but it contains a] great deal that shapes and interprets the evidence to suit the theories of the case advanced by Dr. Steward" (U.S. ICC 1973a:5–7 [1957]). In addition, the report was "prepared before the trial and without use of much of the evidence presented by the petitioners" (U.S. ICC 1973a:5–7 [1957]).

The petitioners then discussed their objections to each of the defendant's findings of fact, including a reference to exhibits of evidence and the petitioners' findings of fact:

1. The petitioners objected to Steward's anthropological proposition that "any kind of property rights found among any people are functions of the

environment and of the technological devices for exploiting the environment" (U.S. ICC 1973a:16 [1957]).

2. The petitioners objected to the notion that the Northern Paiute Indians were "necessarily nomadic, living in small groups" (U.S. ICC 1973a:16 [1957]). The finding that referred to economic fragmentation exaggerated the role of Northern Paiute "vegetable and insect foods which caused the Indians at certain times to scatter far and wide" (U.S. ICC 1973a:17 [1957]).

3. The petitioners argued that the findings exaggerated the "differences in subsistence pattern and social and community structure between the Northern Paiute Indians studied . . . by Dr. Kelly, Dr. Whiting, Dr. Park, and Dr. Stewart" (U.S. ICC 1973a:17 [1957]). Even Steward's own published works, like *Basin-Plateau Aboriginal Sociopolitical Groups,* have shown that "the Northern Paiute Indians studied by him had subsistence patterns and social and community organizations more highly developed than his theoretical concept of 'family level of sociocultural integration'" (U.S. ICC 1973a:17 [1957]).

4. The defendant's findings on religion consisted largely of "unsupported deductions and anthropological theorems in respect to the relationship between the purely social and religious ceremonies of a people and their food gathering practices" (U.S. ICC 1973a:21–22 [1957]).

5. The petitioners objected to the finding that the Northern Paiute did not have any form of political leadership. "Every ethnographer who has studied the Northern Paiute and published work on these Indians has described bands, villages, or other community groups and has described headmen or chiefs" (U.S. ICC 1973a:23 [1957]).

6. In terms of property and territoriality, the petitioners objected to Steward's theory that property rights would "condemn a wandering group to starvation" (U.S. ICC 1973a:23 [1957]). Alternatively, the evidence established that the Northern Paiute Indians had "bands or community groups, had areas within which they customarily obtained their living," and had a "sense of occupancy of their country in substantially greater degree than would be consistent with Dr. Steward's theories" (U.S. ICC 1973a:23 [1957]).

7. The petitioners objected to the defendant's assertion that the Northern Paiute were not a nation (U.S. ICC 1973a:28 [1957]). The Northern Paiute had a "name for themselves, 'Nomo', whereby they distinguished themselves from all other foreign and outside peoples" (U.S. ICC 1973a:28 [1957]). In addition, the "outer boundaries of the Northern Paiute area, with only minor exceptions, were distinct and known both to the Northern Paiute and their neighbors" (U.S. ICC 1973a:28 [1957]). In historic times, the "only occasion presented to the Northern Paiute to unite in defense of their land was that of the arrival of the white man, . . . [and] this occasion resulted in a

number of instances of widespread common defense of their land" (U.S. ICC 1973a:28 [1957]). The "skirmishes and the councils brought about by the coming of the white man demonstrated beyond any reasonable doubt that Northern Paiute Indians had a similar attitude toward their possession of their lands as has been found by this Commission to have existed among other Indian groups" (U.S. ICC 1973a:28 [1957]).

8. The concept of predatory bands was an "interpretation in large part erected out of Dr. Steward's imagination" and more than anything else it "evidences Dr. Steward's zeal for winning the case for the defendant" (U.S. ICC 1973a:30–31 [1957]). Such a concept places moral judgment against the "predatory" Indians by disregarding the "predatory" character of white men's encroachment into country being used and occupied by the Indians. It submerges the traditions and culture of the Northern Paiute by picturing the leaders and groups that participated in the events that accompanied the movement of the whites into Northern Paiute country as leaders and groups that bore no relation to the past and that neither represented nor succeeded to any of the customs or rights of the Northern Paiute Indians (U.S. ICC 1973a:30–31 [1957]).

9. The defendant made it seem, falsely, "that in these years of struggle against the arrival of the white man, the attachments of the Northern Paiute Indians to their homelands were somehow dispersed and dissipated, whereas the great weight of evidence shows that in these years these attachments of the Northern Paiute groups and leaders to the region that each considered home ground were, if anything, heightened and made specific and vocal" (U.S. ICC 1973a:30–31 [1957]).

In conclusion, the Northern Paiute again argued that Steward's interpretation was a "theoretical way of life of a primitive nomadic people living in a desert waste . . . [that] does not jibe with proven facts about the life of the Northern Paiute Indians" (U.S. ICC 1973a:38 [1957]). Alternatively, the petitioners stated that the evidence "makes clear that Indian title to the Northern Paiute area lay in the Northern Paiute Nation, being a distinct ethnic group bound together by an unbroken chain of community group interrelationships and interrelated leaders" (U.S. ICC 1973a:38 [1957]).

The Commission's Findings

Based on the exhibits, testimony, and written arguments, the "Opinion of the Commission," decided on March 24, 1959, stated that

> The Commission believes that there were within the territory claimed in this case, in aboriginal days, certain Indians who, as described by the early explorers and settlers, the government officials, and anthropologists, possessed

> certain distinct similarities. Notably the Indians of the area spoke the same language, shared a common economic life, and, in general, had a similar Indian culture. The Northern Paiute Indians are a clearly defined group of American Indians within the meaning of the term "Nation" as used under sections 2 and 10 of the Act. (U.S. ICC 1974:386–387)

The commission awarded the Northern Paiute $15,790,000 in 1965. The money was distributed in 1980.

THE ANTHROPOLOGICAL SYMPOSIUM ON THE INDIAN CLAIMS COMMISSION: JULIAN STEWARD AND ALFRED KROEBER

In 1954 a special anthropological symposium was organized in Detroit to discuss the role of anthropology in the ICC cases; both Julian Steward and Alfred Kroeber presented papers. In Steward's paper entitled "Theory and Application in a Social Science" (1955c), he argued that the differences in opinion in the ICC cases arose from the use of two basic concepts. First, in regard to the concept of property, Steward asserted that "the question is not merely whether a Nation or society occupied and maintained exclusive use of a delimitable territory" (Steward 1955c:293). Instead, property in the modern United States has several characteristics that imply "exclusive rights to the land" that are "validated by transferable title, which is registered with and protected by a higher authority, or state, which has an appropriate system of property laws" (Steward 1955c:293). Steward maintained that "no one would argue that the aboriginal Indians attached any of these features to their concept of property, despite such common and bare assertions in the ethnographic monographs as that the 'band owned the land up to certain clearly defined boundaries'" (Steward 1955c:293).

Steward said the second concept was brought out by the witnesses in the Northern Paiute case and concerned the "nature of acculturation" (Steward 1955c:298). Steward criticized Omer Stewart for assuming that "territorial bands and chiefs [were] . . . aboriginal features which continued to exist long after White occupation of the area" (Steward 1955c:298). Instead, Steward argued that these features were not aboriginal in basis; he interpreted the same evidence as "indicating that after horses were acquired predatory groups developed and lasted only during a brief phase of acculturation, when the native economy was changed by the presence of livestock and other foods that could be acquired during raiding" (Steward 1955c:298). Steward explained that "if attention is focused upon the survival of Indian features or particular cultural practices, it is easy to underestimate the extent to which White influence has directly or indirectly modified native society" (Steward 1955c:296).

In the conclusion of this paper, Steward stated:

> I would like to think that my colleagues do not hold with the allegation made by counsel by the Plaintiffs in two cases that my very credibility and my honesty were in question. The personal unpleasantness does not matter. What is crucially important is that the failure to clarify reasons for disagreement between witnesses—and in some cases to show that there is really very little disagreement—discredits Anthropology as a science, confuses anthropologists themselves, and must certainly leave the Commission in great doubt as to what the truth is. (Steward 1955c:302)

In Kroeber's symposium paper, entitled "The Nature of the Landholding Group," he proposed that "more often than not in native North America . . . land-owning and sovereign political society was not what we usually call 'the tribe,' but smaller units" (Kroeber 1955:303). Kroeber argued that the concept of tribe was an imposed white construct and, on the whole, it was smaller communities that were "independent, sovereign, and held and used territory" (Kroeber 1955:313). There were tribes that "fitted our conventional image: [in the Plains and in the East, but] the tribe [is a] minority phenomenon" (Kroeber 1955: 312). In general, Kroeber "believed" of Native American society that the "delimitation of political and land-owning units was similar to that of California," either lineage and/or tribelet organization and land ownership. Kroeber therefore implied that although applying Western legal concepts of land ownership to Native Americans might be difficult, Native American societies generally did have political organization and land ownership on their own terms.

Stewart (1961:185) maintained that in the California Indians case the commission had ruled similarly to the way it had in the Northern Paiute case. Specifically, it had rejected the "ecological theory of land use" to which the government had "presented similar defenses in other cases heard by the Commission," in the concepts of "nuclear areas" and "primary subsistence areas" (Stewart 1961:188). Instead, the commission accepted Kroeber's position that all of the claimed territory was used for some purpose. To explain, Stewart cited Associate Commissioner Louis J. O'Marr in the "Opinion of the Commission":

> We cannot accept the Government's thesis that the resources of the state or any part thereof can be determined mathematically by assigning a large percentage of subsistence derived from a small part of a given territory and reduced percentages of subsistence in other areas of a territory claimed by a particular tribelet. We believe it unrealistic and contrary to the Indian mode of life to restrict Indian territorial rights to the lands which would simply provide adequate subsistence and disallow their land claims to the areas which were of secondary importance or supplemental to the main sources of supplies. (U.S. ICC 1974:387)

THE STEWARD-STEWART DEBATE IN THE ANTHROPOLOGICAL LITERATURE

It is quite evident that the disagreement between Julian Steward and Omer Stewart over the nature of aboriginal Great Basin Shoshonean social organization began in print long before the ICC cases were assembled. Steward asserted his "no bands, no headmen, no territories" position in 1937 and 1938. Stewart had initially stated his "territorially based bands" position in 1939; it had little impact. Although not particularly in answer to Stewart, Steward asserted his interpretation again in 1940. However, his 1955 *Theory of Culture Change* was definitely an answer to Stewart (Steward 1955b:101–121). Thus, although the two men's divergent interpretations were expressed and known prior to 1946, it was really in the context of the ICC proceedings that the divergence flowered into a full-blown debate. Because a number of other anthropologists—for example, Robert Murphy, Yolanda Murphy, Robert Manners, Erminie Wheeler-Voegelin, and Isabel Kelly—were brought into the ICC Great Basin cases, the bands-headmen-territory issue began to attract wider interest. In his widely read and influential *Primitive Social Organization,* Elman Service (1962:94–99) argued vehemently against the idea that the Great Basin Shoshoneans and the Eskimo were "anomalous" in being the only hunter-gatherer peoples without bands and headmen. He directly confronted Steward with a Great Basin ethnographic survey done in the 1870s that specifically named bands, headmen, and territories.

Steward probably was unhappy with this rejection of his interpretation and the theory to which it was tied and with the fact that, for the first time, the controversy had moved from the relative obscurity of the ICC proceedings to the literature on the Great Basin culture area. Omer Stewart restated his position, which by that time the commission had accepted, in a paper presented to the Great Basin Anthropological Conference in 1964 called "Tribal Distributions and Boundaries in the Great Basin" (Stewart 1966). He discussed the material in support of the tribal territories and boundaries given in connection with the ICC cases, which included the maps defining territories. Stewart noted that in published work in 1937 and 1938, Steward himself had drawn territorial boundaries on maps showing the distribution of Paiute, Shoshone, Ute, and Bannock populations, but later minimized their significance in the ICC proceedings. Stewart said that because the ICC *did* accept territories in about the same size and form as "anthropologists had mapped them long before the Indian Claims cases started is, in my estimation, vindication of the general process of mapping tribal areas whether they are primarily linguistic groups, or whether they are ethnic groups or cultural entities of other types" (Stewart 1966:203). Stewart also gave the opinion that "the attempt by the Department of Justice to avoid payment by emphasizing the diversity of tribal uses and the fact that different peoples were sometimes present in the territories claimed for their neighbors was not sufficient to justify failure to pay the Indians for their tribal lands as they had been defined by anthropologists during their research long before the beginning of the ICC cases" (Stewart 1966:203).

In those days, the Great Basin Anthropological Conference drew barely 300 people, and the 1966 volume of conference papers was not widely distributed. However, Steward chose to bring the debate with Stewart into the mainstream of anthropological literature by reviewing the volume in what was then the secondmost widely read anthropological journal published in the United States, *American Antiquity.* Steward (1968b) strongly denied any validity to Stewart's interpretation, implying that he had been taken in by what contemporary Paiutes had told him about what their precontact social organization had been like, and Stewart had simply elaborated upon this "error" for the ICC. Concerning his testimony in the claims cases, Steward further asserted that "in the interest of fairness and accuracy," the Department of Justice had not attempted "'to avoid payment' to the Indians as O. C. Stewart alleges (p. 203), and that anthropologists, of whom I am one, who questioned the value of boundaries they themselves had drawn, were not changing their opinions for a fee. Stewart seemingly fails to understand that boundaries are merely an artifice for showing gross distributions" (Steward 1968b). In a special footnote, Steward addressed the point made that the

> plaintiffs and defendants tended to enlist expert witnesses whose views supported their positions, and denied the very serious charge [that] the witnesses altered their views at the request of the attorneys—in blunt terms, that we were bought. . . . It must be remembered that attorneys for the plaintiffs received a percentage of the settlement as their fee, while attorneys for the defendants worked on a fixed salary. In my own experience, the Department of Justice asked only that I present and interpret the facts according to my own understandings. Differences between anthropologists are very real in some cases, and I would prefer to view them as matters of scientific fact and theory. There is no question, however, that attempts to discuss scientific propositions which have been forced into terms of American legal principles and to have discourse between scientists mediated through attorneys badly clouded the areas of genuine scientific disagreement. The lack of direct discussion between anthropologists tended to exaggerate and entrench some long standing anthropological presuppositions. (Steward 1968b:197)

In 1970 Steward published his fullest explication and defense of his "no bands, no headmen, no territories" position in "The Foundations of Basin-Plateau Shoshonean Society" (Steward 1970b). It appeared in a Festschrift dedicated to the doyen of Great Basin ethnographic and linguistic studies, Sven Liljeblad. Ironically, Stewart had also been invited to contribute a chapter (Stewart 1970). Stewart's contribution was not a riposte to Steward; instead, it was an explanation for why the commission had not awarded exclusive rights to the Bannock for their territory. With Robert Murphy as the primary expert witness, the case might have been interpreted as the only one in which the "Steward contingent" had prevailed, because Murphy was Steward's student from Columbia University. But Stewart carefully explained the commission's decision: The Bannock and Northern Shoshone, allied for a century or more, jointly shared the territory despite maintaining their distinct identities and social lives; thus, neither could claim exclusive rights to it.

Stewart eventually had the final word in the debate. Just a few months after Steward's death, he presented "The Western Shoshone of Nevada and the U.S. Government, 1863–1950" (Stewart 1974) at the Great Basin Anthropological Conference, where he made a point of noting Shoshones' tenacious attachment to their land. Also, in "Temoke Band of Shoshone and the Oasis Concept" (1980) Stewart used, ironically, an ecological analysis to demonstrate territoriality and "bandness."

Because the ICC proceedings were responsible for generating a substantial scholarly debate, it is useful to review the arguments as they were expressed in the anthropological literature as well as some of the data used to support them. It will be evident that the anthropological arguments correspond completely to the legal arguments expressed in the ICC proceedings summarized above.

Aboriginal Social Organization: Steward's View

According to Steward, in the precontact period Numic people, including the Northern Paiute, lived in two kinds of aggregates: families and villages or camps. A family group might be an extended family, but was more likely to be a nuclear or stem family. At certain times, families came together and lived in villages, but village composition changed constantly. Occasionally villages and/or families got together for festivals, but these associations were also very flexible, and families frequently changed village and festival affiliations if they so desired. Group endeavors as well as social cohesion were accomplished entirely through cooperation among individual components, and only a network of kin relationships bound Western Shoshone families, villages, and festival associations together.

According to Steward (1937d, 1940a, 1955a, 1970a [1938]) the basis of this very simple, loose, and egalitarian social structure was the environment and techniques of drawing sustenance from it. During the spring and fall, families hunted and gathered berries, nuts, roots, insects, seeds, grasses, and wild vegetables and fruits. Steward felt that the pine-nut crop was of primary importance in determining a family's movements, although families more or less tended to stay in one general locality. In the late fall, after deer, antelope, and maybe an occasional buffalo obtained in southern Idaho had been killed or a crop of pine-nuts had been harvested and stored, families usually came together in camps or villages for the season. In summer, groups came together again, often in large numbers, for *Gwini* festivals celebrating good harvests of edibles, mostly pine-nuts. Village populations seem to have rarely numbered more than 300, although *Gwini* festivals undoubtedly drew close to a thousand people in more thickly populated areas such as Reese River and Ruby Valley. Rather than a cluster of dwellings, winter encampments generally consisted of perhaps 20 or 30 families within easy visiting distance of one another.

Political control of a group or of villages was vested in the community, not in one individual or group of individuals. Warfare was unknown until the contact era, except for family feuds. The only major decisions that had to be made were those involving future points of encampment, localities of abundant food sources, and division of forage territories. Thus, there were no absolute authorities and not even any war chiefs in this precontact period. Chiefs functioned only in certain situations and with certain clear mandates for particular action. The most important cooperative effort of a village was the collective hunt (usually a rabbit hunt but often a grasshopper drive) or an antelope drive involving only men. A leader was selected or simply acknowledged as director of activities on the basis of his competence on such matters. He had no power to coerce families or individuals to participate in communal hunts. However, anyone who did not participate would not partake of the yield, which was always much greater when divided among villagers than any one group or individual could hope to obtain by himself.

Besides the hunt chiefs, there was usually a village headman who had a spokesman, or "talker," and a *Gwini tegwani,* a "festival talker," who was in charge of festivals, led prayers for abundance and good harvests, and orated during the round dances at the festivals. Smaller villages might have only one man who filled all three roles or might combine at least two roles in the same person. Like the hunt chiefs, a village headman had no coercive authority; he acted primarily as a clearing house of information on adaptive strategies. He was expected to know where the best and most abundant crops could be gathered and where animals could best be hunted. In some areas, he also determined times of communal hunts and festivals. In general, the village chief or headman functioned as an advisor, spokesman, coordinator of activities, and reflector of Shoshone values, and his talker, if he had one, functioned as his assistant. A chief was usually succeeded by his son or another relative, but another man might take over if he proved a more suitable candidate. The chief always appointed his own talker. It is unclear whether chiefs from various groups were always ranked, but Steward (1970a:143 [1938]) says that there were four chiefs for the Pine Creek and Diamond Valley people, of which the head chief was a director of festivals and rabbit drives, the second chief was an assistant on antelope hunts and dances, the third was a local village chief, and the fourth was a talker at festivals and prayed especially for abundant food resources.

Steward implied a general uniformity and simplicity of kinship and social organization throughout the Great Basin, except for Owens and Surprise Valleys, California, where he suggested nascent band organization. Other than these areas, Steward suggested that a family level of social organization combined with constant mobility mitigated against any significant identification with distinct territories. This family level of social organization was conditioned by the subsistence resources and the technology that Shoshones used to obtain them. Steward (1955b:105) summarized the situation as a "socially fragmenting cultural ecology," which made Shoshone culture itself "gastric in orientation" (Steward 1970a:46 [1938]) and its material component "meagre in content" (Steward 1940a:474, 1970a:261 [1938]).

Aboriginal Social Organization: Stewart's View

The articulation of Shoshone cultural complexity to the Great Basin ecosystem can be easily inferred from Steward's own work (1970a [1938]). Omer Stewart did not have to go to great lengths to accomplish such inference. Steward's *Basin-Plateau* makes it quite clear that throughout the Great Basin groups of people living in specific areas were called by a specific name—an identity—associated with that area, whether it was a food source, an item of technology, or a characteristic of the area. For example, Railroad Valley Shoshone called Southern Paiute "Tavinai" (*Tapaineeh*), "sun-direction" or "eastern-dwellers" (Steward 1970a:71 [1938]). *Tepitekka,* "pine-nut eaters," was applied not only to the Grouse Creek Shoshone in northern Utah, but also to Shoshone in the Reese River–Austin area and by Owens Valley Shoshone to the Tubatulabal. Some, or perhaps most, of the groups also applied the names to themselves, although it is not clear from Steward's ethnography whether the custom was universal. Others include Goshute, or *Kusiutta,*

"Dusty Utes," named for the frequent dry dust storms in their territory and for their proximity to the Utes; *Tosawihi*, "white chert carriers," named for their penchant for white flint from the Tosawihi quarry area and for their frequent habitation of that area; *Akaitekka*, "eaters of northern salmon"; *Watatekka*, "seed-eaters"; and *Tokoitekka*, "snake-eaters."

Although stopping short of insisting that Numic-speaking Indians were all organized into full-scale bands with distinct chiefs (cf. Eggan 1980; Stewart 1980), Omer Stewart (1939, 1942:235–236, 1966) ascribed a localized territoriality to Northern Paiutes, Utes, Southern Paiutes, and Western Shoshones. Stewart set down his initial doubts about Steward's categories of Great Basin sociopolitical organization in a short paper that accompanied his CED on Ute and Southern Paiute culture (Stewart 1942). Although this work was not published until 1942, Omer wrote it in 1938, just prior to publication of Steward's (1970a [1938]) *Basin-Plateau*. Steward had published a short piece (Steward 1937f) in which he distinguished between "village" organization and "band" organization. According to Steward, "village" organization characterized the Nevada Shoshone and Paiute. Later he elaborated his view on the nonbandness of Nevada groups by designating their level of social organization as "family." Omer Stewart essentially credited Steward as having constructed a clever argument, but asserted that the distinction was not valid: "Steward convincingly demonstrates that two types of political organization existed, but that they were distinct or that most of the Shoshoneans of the Great Basin can be placed definitely under either type, I very much doubt. . . . I discovered that [the Northern Paiutes] lived scattered along the shores of rivers and lakes in their area and claimed a well-defined territory" (Stewart 1942:235).

Stewart also disagreed with an assertion that would later loom prominently in the ICC testimony: that band organization, and therefore territoriality, had developed only when Great Basin people acquired the horse and, in Steward's words (1955b:112), formed "predatory" bands. In contrast, Stewart asserted that "with the acquisition of the horse, bands became mobile and old boundaries were soon lost" (Stewart 1942:235). In Stewart's opinion, the horse was the main factor in destroying the sense of solidarity that inhabitants of a well-defined territory may have had and thus *destroyed* bandness, not *caused* it. That is, Stewart effectively turned Steward's model on its head.

Stewart presented a paper to the Great Basin Anthropological Conference in 1964 called "Tribal Distributions and Boundaries in the Great Basin" (Stewart 1966). In it he discussed the material in support of the tribal territories and boundaries given in connection with the ICC cases, which included the maps defining territories. The fact that the ICC accepted territories in about the same size and form as "anthropologists had mapped them long before the Indian Claims cases started is . . . vindication of the general process of mapping tribal areas whether they are primarily linguistic groups, or whether they are ethnic groups or cultural entities of other types." It was Stewart's general opinion that "the attempt by the Department of Justice to avoid payment by emphasizing the diversity of tribal uses and the fact that different peoples were sometimes present in the territories claimed for their neighbors was not sufficient to justify failure to pay the Indians for their tribal lands as they had been defined by anthropologists during their research long before the beginning of the ICC cases" (Stewart 1966:203).

In his paper presented at the Great Basin Anthropological Conference in 1974, two years after Steward's death, Stewart noted that

> Although the physical and material conditions of Western Shoshone life were nearly [completely] and permanently changed by occupation of their territory as ranches and mines reached to the limits of their territory and particularly the better valleys, some ancient Shoshone emotional, social, and psychological values and behavior patterns appear to have persisted in spite of material changes. . . . One such value which appears excessively strong among the Western Shoshone Indians, and which has usually been overlooked or ignored by nearly all of the peripatetic, migrating whites they have had to deal with, is the strong attachment they have to their home territory, [which is] very narrowly defined. (Stewart 1978:80–81)

At the 16th Great Basin Anthropological Conference, Stewart (1980) gave his final assessment of his differences with Steward. These differences rested on two points. Great Basin peoples used vast areas for occasional habitation and resource gathering, but they used certain areas much more frequently than others, which resulted in a relatively compact settlement pattern during much of any one seasonal cycle. Also, because of this pattern, a particular group would have had a distinct territory with which its identity was strongest.

Steward's Denial

Steward (1970a:248 [1938]) flatly denied any significance to these identities and territories. Steward (1968b) asserted that the fundamentally different conclusions reached by himself and Stewart resulted from Stewart's clinging to the old anthropological presupposition that hunters and gatherers had bands. Stewart's bands were "probably no more than food or other names of any people who lived in the regions, and his chiefs are those who led the people in war against the white settlers" (Steward 1968b). As for Stewart's assertion of tribal identity and territoriality, Steward said: "I need only mention that 40 years ago the Owens Valley and Mono Lake Northern Paiute had no idea of the existence in northern Nevada or Oregon of people of the same speech." In 1970, Steward's basic argument remained intact, namely, that the prehorse Shoshonean Indians were clusters of families that did not have bands, chiefs, or property relating to territory. In addition, after 1840 "warring predatory bands—or, more accurately, recruited resistance and marauding parties" (Steward 1970b:230) emerged among the Northern Paiute, but, "owing to their fluctuating membership and shifting territories, could not be bounded and were not aboriginal" (Steward 1970b:224). Again, Steward maintained that the disagreement was based on the "traditional tendency to begin analysis with the largest social units—the 'tribes' and 'bands'—and accept the presuppositions that they own and defend territory, have cohesion based on common interests and identification, and submit to an overall chief" (Steward 1970b:197).

Expert Witnesses: Scholars or Advocates?

In 1977, Lawrence Rosen published a paper that discussed the ethics of the adversary of the court and anthropological evidence. One of the examples he referred to was the Steward-Stewart debate, to which Omer Stewart responded. Highlighting the sharp difference in anthropological interpretation between Steward and Stewart, Rosen cited Steward's position that the Northern Paiute case illustrated the difficulty of using the basic anthropological concepts of tribe, band, chief, and property (Rosen 1977:555–578). Moreover, Rosen asserted more strongly the ethical dilemma that anthropologists faced in having their scholarship used to defend or deny Indian land rights. Rosen implied that political motivations of anthropologists on different sides of the ICC proceedings might have influenced them to "choose" to testify on one side or the other. This implication was, of course, one that Steward had so vigorously denied in his 1968(b) publication. In his response, Omer Stewart (1979) took exception to Rosen's statement that "there are few roles that confront conscientious anthropologists with more serious scholarly and ethical problems than those posed by their appearance in legal proceedings as expert witnesses." Stewart echoed Steward a decade earlier in remarking:

> Sorry! In 25 years as an expert witness I have never experienced any problems of scholarly or ethical nature. The above assertion seems to imply that an anthropologist as expert witness somehow behaves differently from the way he does while engaged in purely scholarly activities. That does not happen. My scholarly writings were the same before and after I testified as an expert witness for the Northern Paiute, for example, I express my opinions with vigor in meetings of scientific societies, as I do in the courts, and they are the same opinions, reached by the same processes. (Stewart 1979:109)

Stewart affirmed that the difference of opinion with Julian Steward was something that existed long before the ICC cases. "I could do little but present objective data and base my opinion on the data" (Stewart 1979:110). Steward, however, was a "great and honored theoretician." From the time of his first publication on the Northern Paiute Steward developed his theories, and when questioned by the attorneys for the Indians as to the discrepancies between his earlier statements and those on the witness stand, the answer was, "in effect, that Julian had changed his theory." However, as already noted, it is rather that in the intervening years he had *developed* a theory: the theory of culture change, based on the concepts and methods of cultural ecology and the methodology of multilinear evolution. These were the components of his theory that Steward introduced into the ICC cases and that he used to interpret, or perhaps reinterpret, the data he had gathered in a total of only ten months in 1935 and 1936 and had framed in terms of "cultural ecology" in 1938. He would not actually summarize and present his theory of cultural ecology until 1955, in a specially written chapter of *Theory of Culture Change.* Therefore it is possible that the ICC proceedings had indeed provided Steward with an opportunity to refine and streamline his multifaceted theory of change and the role of environmental conditions in that theory.

MOTIVATIONS FOR THE INDIAN CLAIMS COMMISSION ACT

Before concluding this analysis of Steward's role in the Northern Paiute case, the following fundamental questions must be addressed: Why would the U.S. government affirm title of lands within its boundaries, which either it or its citizens or its states coveted, to peoples who were alien and, in many cases, had recently been "the enemy"? Why should the United States not simply take whatever lands it wanted, affirming only those property rights that it wanted to, or which it declared to exist by virtue of the formation of states and territories? Why should it recognize such a thing as "aboriginal title," when at the time, no other group of U.S. citizens possessed such title? In other words, why recognize Indian title at all, let alone spend millions of dollars compensating it? The answers to these questions lie first of all in a recognition of what else was going on at the time and secondly in some theories that might explain the historic events.

By the end of 1945, the wartime cutting of budgets and programs and the moving of the BIA from Washington, D.C., to Chicago resulted in Commissioner John Collier, who was the most recent proponent of the idea of the ICC, deciding to leave office (Parman 1976:289). The federal government decided to stop bothering about the "Indian problem." Collier had become frustrated and disillusioned by the end of 1944 and had actually submitted his resignation to President Roosevelt in January 1945, which Roosevelt accepted, to be effective at the end of the year.

Congress subsequently formed the Hoover Commission, chaired by former president Herbert Hoover. The Hoover Commission suggested a complete reversal of Collier's policy. It proposed steps "to integrate the Indians into the rest of the population as the best solution to 'the Indian problem.'" Assimilation was to be the dominant goal of public policy. The new policy represented a return to the past, an abandonment of bilateralism; thus, it proceeded without Indian cooperation. "In an effort to relieve itself once and for all of the financial and moral burden of Indian affairs, the federal government reasserted full control of Indian lives and fortunes and fit them into its plan. It was a lousy plan" (Cornell 1988:122–125). The plan was called "termination" because federal services to Indians, federal trusteeship over Indians and their resources, reservations, and eventually recognition of the tribes themselves would be terminated. Steward had been in complete agreement with this policy of assimilation back in the 1930s before Collier had reversed it (cf. Manners 1973:892); in fact, his agreement with it was a large part of the contentiousness of his relationships with Collier and other BIA personnel (see Blackhawk, chapter 13; Rusco, chapter 7). To gain some perspective on the degree to which Steward might have been biased in favor of denying the existence of land-tenure rights to Great Basin Indians and harnessed his theories to that bias, it is necessary to examine the motivations of those who sponsored the Indian Claims Commission Act.

Inferring motivations from what people say or do is always risky. Yet it seems that there was some degree of concordance in the aims of those who wanted termination and the aims of those who established the ICC. Senators Patrick McCarran (Nevada) and Arthur B. Watkins (Utah) were among those who pushed hardest for termination legislation. Watkins phrased the aim in terms of "freeing" the Indians from the "yoke of federal supervision" (Watkins 1957). Remarks in the *Congressional Record* (1946:5312–5317) reflect some legislators' thinking that disbursement of claims monies would aid the termination process by either enabling tribes to finance all their own programs or by providing individuals with sufficient capital and investment funds to make them economically self-sufficient.

Congressman Henry M. Jackson (Washington) and Senator Karl Mundt (South Dakota) jointly sponsored the Indian Claims Commission Act. Jackson argued that the United States should simply pay its "just debts" to the Indians via the ICC instead of spending large sums on special services that would not be needed if the Indians just had wads of money; the United States had an obligation to apply "standards of fair and honorable dealings" to Indian tribes; and as long as Indians had claims pending and received services by staying on the reservation, "they will never want to leave it." Mundt added another reason: Settlement of claims would encourage Indians to leave their reservations and encourage the "progress of the Indians who desire to be rehabilitated at the white man's level in the white man's economy." Finally, Jackson argued that if the claims were not settled, continuation of this unsettled situation would "perpetuate clouds on white men's titles that interfere with the proper development of our public domain" (*Congressional Record* 1946: 5312–5317).

THE POLITICAL CONTEXT OF THE CLAIMS CASES: FOUR THEORIES

Anthropology has never developed a theory that would explain the existence of the ICC or the compensation of Indian claims as a cultural custom of the United States. Political scientists and sociologists have also rarely addressed the question directly. However, a number of theories from political science and sociology might be applicable to explaining not only the ICC's existence, but also Steward's role in it. In this section we review four theories that might move us toward explanation.

The Commodity-Capitalist Theory

Although claimed by Marxists, the theory that everything—people and their labor, culture, land, social status—will eventually become cash-valued commodities in any capitalist system is also informed by the value-oriented work of Max Weber. Marx and Engels focused on the relationship of people to the means of production as the prime mover of politics. At the height of capitalism, accumulated labor becomes a commodity with monetary value, and there is almost nothing in society that is not a commodity (Marx and Engels 1932:28–30). The ruling class are capitalists who can manipulate this accumulated labor. However, as industrialization grows, the strength of the capitalist ruling class weakens until it can no longer maintain its position and workers: Those who procure the labor that is capitalism's manipulatable commodity grow in power. Of course, it is obvious that this utopian prediction is far from coming true.

Weber's theory of capitalism is closer to that of Marx than many Marxists would probably like to admit, but differs in not having dialectical analysis and lacking any prophecies about the future of capitalism and the dictatorship of the proletariat in industrial societies. Weber (1930) noted that two of the most important characteristics of capitalism are rational capital accounting and calculable law. Such accounting involves the appropriation of all physical means of production—land, machinery, etcetera—as disposable property for the potential use of autonomous, private industrial enterprises.

To fit such a theory, the ICC proceedings would have to result in the increase in disposable property of autonomous, private individuals. Clearly, the proceedings did: Each individual received a per-capita payment of several thousand dollars and tribal governments received much larger sums (e.g., see Callaway et al. 1986:362–363). That is, the U.S. government shifted a relatively small amount of capital from one sector to another: from the government sector to the private sector. Nothing was lost to the capitalist system. In fact, the disbursement should have stimulated the economy, because that money was ultimately spent, either by Indian tribal governments or by individuals. Money spent by the Indians actually increased the power of the bourgeois and capitalist classes, because that money was used either to make large capital improvements in local Indian communities—which resulted in large expenditures and, in some cases, borrowing—or for consumer items, thus stimulating the production of hard goods. Therefore, disbursement of claims monies turned aboriginal titles into commodities with exchange value equivalent to wage-labor values. Thus, in a sense, commodities were "invented" for Indian populations that otherwise had no products to sell and little labor to be hired.

The Elite-Concession Theory

This theory stems from Marx but owes its development to C. Wright Mills (1956), E. Digby Baltzell (1964), and G. William Domhoff (1970). Mills, the infamous leather-jacketed, Harley-Davidson-mounted sociologist from Columbia University, saw the American ruling class growing stronger in the 1950s through the growing power of the military technocrats, the "masters of war" who allied their strength with that of the industrialists to form the "military-industrial complex" (Mills 1956:198–224, 269–297).

Some years later, Domhoff (1970:20–52) modified Mills's theory by demonstrating that, rather than an entire class ruling America, economic and political power was concentrated in the hands of a few ruling families, an oligarchy akin to a Brahmin caste. Domhoff dismissed the power of the military as unimportant. Philadelphia main-liner E. Digby Baltzell provided insider's data to support Domhoff's theory when he betrayed his class and exposed the workings of this small clique of ruling families of which he was a part. These ruling families maintained their "cliqueness" and their power by practicing and mandating caste endogamy and by carefully regulating social interactions by controlling private clubs and maintaining social registers as caste privileges. Baltzell noted and accounted for the gradual increase in the numbers of individuals of "ethnic minorities" of "low origins," such as Irish-Americans, Polish-Americans, and Jewish-Americans, by demonstrating that the American ruling class regularly granted concessions to lower classes by elevating "acceptable eligible candidates" into its ranks through marriage and political and economic appointments in corporations and government offices that it controlled. Baltzell approved of this increased democratization of the ruling elite, advocating what he saw as the "vital role" of the modern corporation "in gradually creating a world community," and arguing for increased ethnic heterogeneity of the corporate elite (Baltzell 1964:320–334).

The ICC would have functioned as one of these concessions by the elite to a marginalized and little-understood class. Not only was the ICC a special creation of Congress, but also it privileged American Indians by allocating a certain amount of time and money at a high level—the level of the Department of Justice—to attending to an Indian problem. It would have drawn Indians further into the larger society by forcing them to become acquainted with U.S. law, legal procedures, and the American custom of hiring attorneys to solve personal, social, and economic problems. It would have emphasized the service-oriented nature of the U.S. government and its willingness to accommodate special problems of particular ethnic minorities. Also, it would have accomplished philosophical and cultural integration of Indians into American society by downplaying the historic and cultural distinctiveness of Indians with "treaty rights" and by instead favoring "land rights," "just compensation for damages and injustice" over those treaty rights.

Like the commodity-capitalist theory, this explanation has a certain amount of logical persuasiveness to it. Although it is hard to see why such a powerful bloc, such as a ruling elite, would bother to pay off a few hundred thousand Indians, the symbolic value of doing so would have resonated with many of the American elite who mourned the passing of the "noble savage" (cf. Rudnick 1984).

The Pluralism-Polyarchy Theory

Robert A. Dahl regards U.S. politics as a "polyarchical" situation, in which elites may control certain spheres of economics and politics in particular regions, but can be and are restricted by vigorous use of various political strategies (Dahl 1967:22–25, 1971:1–32, 105–123). Labor unions, activist coalitions, and special-interest groups are the primary players in polyarchical situations, and ethnic minorities certainly constitute one category of special-interest group that exercise powerful influence in certain contexts. In a study of New Haven, where Dahl lives and teaches, Warner (1963) demonstrates that a cadre of elite families did indeed shape the economic, political, and social life of New Haven until about 1900. However, after 1900 the elite moved to the suburbs, and after World War I it ceased to be involved in New Haven politics. Political dynamics shifted to ethnic minorities, who had little economic power (Dahl 1961).

If New Haven is typical of most urban regions in America, then economic and political control is a variable of the solidarity and alliance-making capabilities of various special-interest groups, including ethnic minorities. It would be possible for any particular special-interest group to effect political and economic change in its favor as long as it did not result in that group absolutely dominating anything more than a limited regional or political sphere. These situations are what Dahl means by "polyarchy": the sharing of power between elites and special-interest groups to varying degrees in varying situations. Presumably, because elites no longer form a monolithic bloc, alliances between upper-class liberals and American Indians could result in a political situation favorable to American Indians and not antithetical to the general position and specific interest of the elite.

In fact, "cultural radicals" who associated with the "political radical elite" of Greenwich Village—the radical elite who championed the working class, fought against the repression of Native American religions, and demonstrated for women's rights—were instrumental in developing and implementing pro-Indian policies. John Collier associated with these "cultural radicals" and was, of course, the main proponent of the ICC (Luhan 1936:140–170; Rudnick 1984: 59–96, 172–182, 1996:27–30, 91–94). These cultural radicals believed that the continual revival and revitalization of good things—art, pagan religion, ancient philosophy—from the past was the hallmark of a true civilization. Their pro-Indian stance rarely went beyond the level of seeing anything that seemed to dispense justice to the Indians as "good" and also rarely questioned what seemed to be idealistic motivations of those they considered political allies in Congress and elsewhere. Thus, the ICC fit the "pro-Indian" stance of a small but powerful radical elite that approved of sharing its power with approved special-interest groups.

The Nationalist-Sovereignty Theory

There is much to recommend the pluralism-polyarchy theory. However, it must be considered in tandem with a theory that rests more on legal history than on political philosophy. This legal history is too lengthy for complete discussion here. However, the important aspect is that a rational political doctrine based on the economic and political conditions prevalent at the time of the founding of the United States was responsible for establishing a cultural custom enshrined in law by 1832: the custom of recognizing nationhood of collectivities of people on the basis of collective use and occupancy of territory (cf. Gellner 1983).[1] This custom accords with a political philosophy, growing out of the Enlightenment, that eschewed that sovereignty derived from the "divine right of kings" and embraced the idea that the users and occupiers of land hold collective jurisdiction over that land, no matter who actually owns it. In the United States, this political philosophy resulted in Indian nations being recognized as having "aboriginal occupancy" and therefore possession of most of the land in North America (Deloria and Lytle 1984; Morris 1986). The recognition of Indian rights of aboriginal possession in Anglo-American law was thus a logical step in the evolution of ideas of nationhood and sovereignty. The primary basis for creation of the ICC came from the legal recognition of this distinction. The recognition of Indian land rights is neither perfunctory nor benevolent; it is a crucial component of United States law and the process by which the United States legitimated its nationhood and its sovereignty.

All four of these theories have some cogency with regard to the Northern Paiute claims case discussed here and, indeed, to all of the claims lawsuits brought within the framework of the ICC. Certainly recognition, or the construction of a legal fiction, of aboriginal occupants of the United States as collective land-holding groups is consistent with the kind of "due process" mandate that permeates U.S. tort law and the legitimacy of the U.S. legal system to adjudicate land-tenure conflicts. At the same time, the ICC accomplished the necessary task of rationalizing how Indian land was converted from a resource-use function to a commodity function within a capitalist framework without appearing to parallel the kind of property confiscation characteristic of command economies such as Communism. It was John Collier, commissioner of the BIA during the 1930s, who pushed hardest for legislation setting up the ICC. Collier was hardly a champion of capitalism. However, just prior to becoming Indian commissioner he associated closely with movers and shakers in the radical elite such as Mabel Dodge, John Reed, John Dewey, and Stella Atwood in promoting various social causes, including the welfare of American Indians (Kelly 1983). Although no evidence exists to suggest that these and other elite radicals saw their championing of the underprivileged as a concession, the symbolic value of paying off a few hundred thousand Indians would have resonated with many of the American elite who mourned the passing of the "noble savage" including some of the radical elite who were Collier's former associates. Finally, it is evident from the congressional hearings on the Wheeler-Howard Bill from which the Indian Reorganization Act was born in 1934–1935 (and which originally contained a provision setting up a land claims commission) that Collier and his supporters forged an uneasy "polyarchical" coalition among supporters of Indians, New Dealers, and old guard "get-the-Indians-off-the-government-dole" ideologues to get the legislation passed (Philp 1977). Eleven years later, a similar coalition plus a small but influential cadre of attorneys pushed the Indian Claims Commission Act through Congress.

CONCLUSION

We now can return to an assessment of Julian Steward's role in the ICC proceedings and the importation of the debate over the nature of Paiute political organization and territoriality into the anthropological literature. Based on the above discussion, we propose that many factors were at work. Concessions to American Indians as a disadvantaged minority, the desire to integrate Indians into the capitalist system, the patronization of Indians as "partners" in an elite-orchestrated liberalizing agenda, and the affirmation of an important legal tradition linking sovereignty to the collective power of individuals and their jurisdiction over land were all at work in the ICC proceedings. It can be seen that in the long run, both Omer Stewart as an expert witness for plaintiff Indians and Julian Steward as an expert witness for the government as defendant were crucial to the ICC's overall goals.

The meanings that the attorneys attached to the concepts of property and acculturation that Steward presented in his interpretation of the Shoshonean Indians were clearly politically motivated and framed in the legal context of affirming U.S. legal doctrine. The effect was to deny indigenous rights because property was construed in such a way as to exclude Shoshonean concepts of land use from the realm of validity.

The degree of Paiute social organization that existed in precolonial times beyond the family level is still a disputed issue. Apart from the ambiguity of these terms, it seems that most scholars maintain that an overarching politically organized tribe did not exist in the various Great Basin nations, but that such political organization was a feature that emerged after Euro-American contact. For example, Catherine S. Fowler and Sven Liljeblad (1986:435) said that the recognition of the Northern Paiute people was based on linguistic evidence. "They were not for any practical purpose politically integrated, nor did they constitute a single 'tribe.'" The Western Shoshone probably were never a tribe aboriginally, but the "treaty making began a process of creating a political and ethnic nation where there had been none before" (Clemmer 1996:218–219). d'Azevedo mentioned that, apart from the contending anthropological viewpoints on the existence of bands, tribes, nations, the imposition of these alien concepts has become inextricably interwoven in government parlance and popular media. As a consequence, Native Americans themselves have "adopted these designations in long established reference to their societies, and it was largely on such legally validated categories that they have successfully justified demands for federal compensation for former lands" (d'Azevedo 1986:13). Today, for example, many Great Basin peoples identify and use the terms "band," "tribe," and "nation" (e.g., the Western Shoshone National Council).

In hindsight discussion of the ICC, Vine Deloria has stated that because it required that the Indian nations had to allege that the United States had taken its lands, the effect of the commission was to retroactively transfer many large areas of land that had not been formerly or formally ceded by the Indian nations to the United States. In essence, "deprived of the right to sue for title to their lands, the Indian nations were simply stripped of their legal status for pittance" (Deloria 1992:289). This effect is most strikingly evident in the case of the Western Shoshone, who are still today involved in serious legal grievances over their land. For the Northern Paiute, the distribution of claims monies in the 1980s meant that the claim submitted on their behalf by their attorney had the effect of preventing any of them from ever initiating legal proceedings that might actually result in return of land currently under the jurisdiction of a federal agency other than the BIA, such as the Bureau of Land Management or the U.S. Forest Service. Gone forever is the option of filing a case based on refusing the money in favor of having the actual land.

As summarized by the Western Shoshone Sacred Lands Association (1985:132–140), Western Shoshone country was defined at about 24 million acres by the treaty of 1863, which was ratified by Congress in 1868. Subsequently, white settlement reduced the territory to 18 million acres. When it came time to file for claims with the ICC, initially the representatives from the Western Shoshone Nation were told by their attorneys that they were seeking compensation for lands lost to white settlement and for "damages"; however, the attorneys filed a claim that *all* Western Shoshone lands had been taken, when in fact only a quarter of the treaty lands had been lost to white settlement. (The attorneys noted that the legal fee is determined after the dollar value is awarded.) In 1974 the Western Shoshone Sacred Lands Association (1985) was formed and hired its own attorney to try to stop the proceedings or reduce the claim. However, the action was without success. In 1977 the ICC awarded $24 million for the value of the land in 1872. The Western Shoshone have refused by majority to accept payment and officially extinguish the rights to their treaty lands. The issue has been addressed in various courts without any conclusive or just results (for a complete review of the history of Western Shoshone litigation see Rusco 1992).

The fight for the recognition of indigenous rights is one of the most pressing issues facing peoples of the world today. As a discipline of knowledge, anthropology has been tightly bound up in this political situation and in the theoretical positions that both legitimize and deny indigenous rights within the colonial state. However, unlike the past and in a way to avoid Julian Steward's politics, today's anthropology is founded upon a global human consciousness and contemporary notions of human justice, including self-determination and the political movement toward decolonialization. For example, this is clearly reflected in these three statements from the United Nations' Draft Declaration on the Rights of Indigenous Peoples:

> 3. [Affirming further] that all doctrines, policies and practices based on advocating superiority of peoples or individuals on the basis of national origin, racial, religious, ethnic or cultural differences are racist, scientifically false, legally invalid, morally condemnable and socially unjust.
>
> 6. [Recognizing] the urgent need to respect and promote the inherent rights and characteristics of indigenous peoples, especially their rights to lands, territories and resources, which derive from their political, economic and social structures and from their cultures, spiritual traditions, histories and philosophies.
>
> 12. [Recognizing also] that indigenous peoples have the right freely to determine their relationship with States in a spirit of coexistence, mutual benefit and full respect. (United Nations 1996)

Hindsight can generate any amount of speculation concerning the relationship between a historic political period and scholarly pursuits. However, a conclusion that seems unavoidable is that political agendas often have more influence on the ostensible objectivity of anthropological theory than is apparent at first glance. Julian Steward's theories are no exception. It is clear that Steward truly regarded his picture of the Numic peoples' "family level" of social organization to be empirically accurate. It is also quite clear that he regarded that level of social organization as precluding them from having collective land-tenure rights within the American legal system. Steward generally advocated assimilation for most American Indians, particularly those in the Great Basin.

Although Steward himself never expressed such a position, his overall theoretical framework leads easily to an ethnocentric judgment characterizing the Shoshonean Indians as aboriginally less socially evolved than, and by implication inferior to, modern American society (cf. Steward 1937e). Steward's assimilationist position toward the Shoshonean people denied such an implication of inferiority, yet, ironically, it effectively denied them indigenous rights as a collective land-holding group. However, it was the politically charged ICC proceedings that brought these aspects of Steward's thinking together into a political-legal position informed by anthropological scholarship. The extent to which attorneys for the two opposing sides might have created this political position within an anthropological context, and also created much more of a rift between Steward and Stewart than there had been initially, remains an open question. However, it is clear that the legal-political pressures on Steward and Stewart and their interpretations generated by the ICC proceedings must be fully taken into account when considering the theoretical points of the "bands/no bands" controversy within the anthropological literature.

With nation-states disintegrating or turning into arenas for ethnically based power struggles or multinational corporate profitmaking, it is easy to see how the movement for collective indigenous rights has become entwined with scholarly theories about the nature of nationhood, sovereignty, and the philosophy of land and resource control (e.g., Morris 1986, 1992). Anthropological theory, scholarship, and interpretations in any time period are never born in a vacuum. Despite Stewart's and Steward's demurrings to the contrary, there can be no doubt that Steward's theory of culture change, theory of cultural ecology, and concept of "levels of sociocultural integration" were honed in contexts that were as much political as they were scholarly.

NOTES

This chapter is based largely on Ronaasen's research for her master's degree (1993) at the University of Alberta, Canada. She extends much appreciation to her thesis advisor, Michael Asch, for his initial insight, theoretical direction, and generous assistance; to Henry Lewis for his many conversations and for sharing his bibliographic research on Omer Stewart's work; and to Ruth Gruhn for support and inspiration. Also, thanks to David Hundman, University of Queensland, and Ian Keen, Australian National University, for reading and commenting on an earlier version of this chapter. We are also grateful to Deward Walker, University of Colorado, Boulder; Elmer Rusco, University of Nevada, Reno; Larry Schiffer, a practicing attorney in New York City; and the late Michael Dorris, Dartmouth College.

1. The legal path involved a series of U.S. Supreme Court decisions over a period of about 10 years: *Johnson & Graham's Lessee v. McIntosh,* 21 U.S. 240. Wheat 542 (1823); *Cherokee Nation v. Georgia,* 30 U.S. 9. 5 Pet. 1 (1831); and *Worchester v. Georgia,* 31 U.S. 350. 6 Pet. 515 (1832). The cases essentially said that the Indians had the rightful occupancy of the soil, distinct original and natural rights as undisputed possessors of the soil, and distinct independent status as nations. However, Indian nations were domestic, dependent nations with limited sovereignty—in relation to the United States as wards to a guardian. Indian nations could not dispose of the land except to the discoverer of them and their lands or its successor (the United States), because discovery gave the exclusive right to the "discoverer" of extinguishing Indian title of occupancy, either by purchase or conquest. Subsequent cases affirming this legal doctrine include *Holden v. Joy,* 84 U.S. 211 (1872); *U.S. v. Gemmill,* 535.F.2d 1445 (9th Circuit) cert. Den. 429 U.S. 982 (1976); and *Strong v. U.S.,* 518.F.2d 556, 207 Ct. Cl. 254, cert. Den. 423 U.S. 1015 (1975). These cases essentially stated that Indian title is a permissive right of occupancy granted by the federal government to aboriginal possessors of the land and that the concept of recognized title comes from Congress either by treaty or statute. Thus, the Indian Claims Commission Act de facto recognized title and sovereignty of any and all Indian groups that were permitted to file claims with the ICC.

13

Julian Steward and the Politics of Representation

Ned Blackhawk

Historian Ned Blackhawk brings recently developed, reflexive ethnographic perspectives to bear on a specific analysis of Steward's Great Basin work. Blackhawk suggests that not only did Steward's categorization of Great Basin peoples within a certain stage of sociocultural evolution reify them as a stereotype within the discipline of anthropology, but also that the authority of his ethnographic description may have actually shaped the political and social world of some indigenous Great Basin societies. Blackhawk attributes powerful influence to the narrative voice of Steward's ethnography. He suggests that the effect of Steward's work was to emphasize the "otherness" of Great Basin peoples. This "otherness" derived from Steward's characterization of them in largely ecological terms, rather than within a framework that Western scholars might have used to understand their own societies. Thus, in Blackhawk's view, Steward's ethnography is just as important as an expression of the power of narrative to shape the image of a people as much as it is a presentation of information about peoples' adaptation to ecological conditions.

The expansive region of the American Great Basin and its indigenous peoples hardly appear in most renditions of American history. The indigenous population of the Great Basin represents only a tiny fraction of the continent's aboriginal population, and the histories of the lands and peoples of this vast region remain largely excluded from the broader narratives of North American history. However, unlike historians, for the past century anthropologists have maintained considerable interest in the Indians of the Great Basin. This chapter examines the representations of Great Basin Indians by Julian Steward, the preeminent anthropologist of the region. By developing theories of cultural change that have influenced generations of anthropologists, Steward pioneered both the study of the Great Basin Indians and American anthropology with his ethnographic research of the 1930s.

From the time of Franz Boas, virtually all professionally trained American anthropologists have used conceptual and methodological theories developed during fieldwork among Great Basin Indians. Both Robert Lowie and Alfred L. Kroeber, who helped solidify anthropology as an established academic discipline, based much of their linguistic and cultural theories on ethnographic fieldwork in the region (e.g., Kroeber 1907, 1925; Lowie 1924a). Julian Steward, a graduate student of Kroeber and Lowie at the University of California, Berkeley, developed what became a major field of anthropology, cultural ecology, and modified evolutionary theory to include the variant multilinear evolution.

In this chapter I will show that Steward developed his studies of Great Basin Indians under a paradigm of cultural evolution and thereby misconstrued the complexity of indigenous history and cosmology. By locating Great Basin indigenous societies in a teleology of cultural development, Steward's ethnographic representations fundamentally naturalize his indigenous subjects. I intend to challenge this naturalization and to critique Steward's theories and ethnographic authority and base this critique in part on the work of critical ethnographic theorists such as Johannes Fabian and James Clifford. I will show that Steward's portrayals of Great Basin Indians have powerfully shaped, and are implicated in, not only the academic discourses about the Great Basin, but also the political and social world of various Great Basin societies. I will rely heavily on Steward's 1936 report as a "consultant anthropologist" to the Bureau of Indian Affairs (BIA) to situate his academic understandings of Great Basin Indians in a broader discussion of power relations in the region. I shall also offer conceptual and methodological approaches for using Steward's works for studying Great Basin indigenous peoples.

Because Steward's assumptions about Great Basin cultures remain so problematic, formulating alternative uses for his ethnographies is imperative. This chapter analyzes Steward's works and influences in two ways. First and foremost, it challenges Steward's ethnographic authority on Great Basin Indian culture. A textual critique of Steward's ethnographies alone, however, fails to convey the broader implications of his portrayals of Great Basin Indians. Not only are Steward's ethnographic representations fundamentally flawed, but they also are implicated in broader relations of power between Indians and non-Indians in this region. By portraying Great Basin Indian societies in such a timeless and simplistic fashion, Steward's texts implicitly help legitimize the dispossession and impoverishment of the Native peoples in the region. As the last section of this paper shows, Steward's ethnographic authority and conceptions of Great Basin culture gave intellectual justification in the 1930s for attempts to deny federal recognition and treaty rights to different Western Shoshone peoples in Nevada.

The second primary goal of this chapter is to develop more constructive use of Steward's ethnographic and empirical information. Although conceptually troubling, Steward's ethnographies provide a wealth of ethnographic, historic, and cultural information. I have found that critically investigating and exposing a few of the numerous inherent contradictions and tensions in Steward's ethnographies demystifies the purported timelessness of his texts and offers alternative ways of conceptualizing Great Basin Indian history. These texts contain examples of indigenous cultural adaptation and resiliency that contradict some of Steward's value-laden interpretations. These contradictions reveal brief moments of contestation that can serve as heuristic guides for illuminating the broader colonial relations that characterize the history of Indian-white relations in the Great Basin. Many more alternative approaches to Steward's work are needed to fully reassess his significance and legacy, but unfortunately, without access to Steward's early field notes and journals, this obstacle may prove especially difficult.

STEWARD'S WORK AND INFLUENCE IN ANTHROPOLOGY

Steward compiled several major ethnographies of different "Shoshonean" groups by identifying nearly every indigenous population settlement throughout eastern California, Nevada, and Idaho in the 1930s and selectively visiting a number of them. Steward focused on the relationship between the social organizations of these different societies and the environment of the Great Basin. He theorized that the sparse ecological conditions of the region preconditioned the levels of cultural development among the various Indian societies. Succinctly summarizing this view, he wrote, "The Shoshonean culture was simple in structure and meager in content. . . . Their culture was essentially practical, being orientated toward physical survival in an area of extreme insecurity and frequent starvation. It centered around a set of hunting and gathering devices adapted to the exigencies of the environment" (Steward 1940a:474–475). This ecologically based interpretation of Great Basin cultural organization provided the basis for Steward's emerging theories of cultural change.

Steward did not originate the correlation between environment and sociocultural organization; it was an integral aspect of early anthropological theory prior to his research. Early Marxist social theory also held that structural and environmental conditions influenced social and cultural organization. As

Marvin Harris indicates in his massive *The Rise of Anthropological Theory*, however, these earlier "anthropological discussions of the influence of environment on culture . . . were carried out within the particularist frame of culture area classifications, and hence did not rise to nomothetic [universal] status" (Harris 1968:663). Although previous anthropologists and ethnographers, including Clark Wissler, had recognized the centrality of environmental factors in the determination of social organization, Steward became the first to systematically theorize and explore such determinations.

Steward rejected the cultural relativism and descriptive ethnography of the Boasian tradition. He instead sought more universal and quantifiable standards with which to measure and predict cultural change within particular societies. Steward called this search for reoccurring, cross-cultural phenomena "multilinear evolution." This methodological approach "assumes that certain basic types of culture may develop in similar ways under similar conditions but that few concrete aspects of culture will appear among all groups of mankind in a regular sequence" (Steward 1955b:4). Identifying these "basic types of culture," the environments in which they developed, and the causal sequence between them remained Steward's foci throughout his career.

Steward's multilinear evolution and search for universal environmental conditions for cultural organization became known as "cultural ecology," and it influenced American anthropology and cultural anthropology for nearly half a century:

> Even to give summary treatment to the work carried out by those who have been directly influenced by Steward—Sidney Mintz, Eric Wolf, Morton Fried, Elman Service, René Millon, Andrew Vayda, Robert Manners, F. Lehman—could prove an exhausting task. The list of anthropologists who have benefited indirectly from Steward's treatment . . . is proportionally larger and includes . . . many . . . who take their cultural ecology for granted. . . . The recent prominence of ecological studies [is] a result of Steward's personal influence. [This] mounting interest . . . reflects a broad movement aimed at strengthening the scientific credentials of cultural anthropology within the prestigious and well-funded natural sciences. Cultural ecology . . . strengthens the association between social science and the "harder" disciplines. (Harris 1968:654–655)

As the unofficial dean of cultural ecology, Steward helped solidify the discipline of anthropology as a "scientific" social science and became one of the world's leading anthropological authorities on indigenous cultures.

Using Steward's anthropological texts to attempt to understand the Shoshonean people of the region presents significant challenges. His theories of cultural ecology and assumptions about Shoshonean culture remain predicated upon numerous flawed conceptions. By presuming that environmental conditions of this region preconditioned the cultural behavior and institutions of the region's indigenous peoples, Steward's works fail to recognize the multiple ways in which different Great Basin peoples understand and give meaning to their own worlds. Steward's privileging of an ecological interpretation of culture and his fundamental inability to see the complex cultural meanings of his many subjects ultimately deny Great Basin societies the human capacities for historic and cultural change.

STEWARD'S ETHNOGRAPHIC WORK

Steward first developed an interest in Great Basin peoples at the age of 16 when he attended the Deep Springs Preparatory School in eastern California (Manners 1973:888–889; Murphy 1977:1–2). In 1927 and 1928 he returned to this region along the eastern slope of the Sierra Nevada to collect ethnographic information. Having recently researched his dissertation, which was based primarily on secondary ethnographic texts, Steward now conducted the fieldwork for his first ethnography. Steward interviewed numerous local informants and classified various aspects of Northern Paiute society between Owens Valley and Lake Mono, California, and identified the themes he shortly thereafter expanded into theories of cultural change.

"The Owens Valley Paiute are the southernmost of that widely distributed Shoshonean group, the Northern Paiute, which occupies most of northern Nevada" (Steward 1933a:235). Steward collected a wide array of information about the different Indian groups in Owens Valley. He organized his text around 35 operative categories beginning with "tribal distributions" and including everything from "seed-gathering and preparation" to "houses," "domesticated animals," and "kinship usages." Each section offered basic descriptions of various Paiute practices and occasionally included Paiute informants' comments as well as "theoretical aspects" from Steward. Steward described the Paiute almost entirely in the past tense, which reflected anthropology's earliest attempts to "salvage as much data as possible on the native life of the Indian tribes" (Murphy 1977:2). A few examples from the text illustrate these intentions and some of their contradictions.

Under the category of "seasonal occupations," Steward categorizes the Paiute's daily activities: "People arose before daybreak. Hunters in bed after sunrise had bad luck. Two meals a day were eaten, one at early morning and one in the afternoon. Women gathered seeds and men hunted, when food could be had, to lay up supplies for future use. Leisure time was spent gambling. Winter evenings were devoted to relating myths. In valley villages, old and young men lived at sweat-houses, smoking, talking, and gambling" (Steward

1933a:239). All aspects of this summation are most likely substantially correct, because they are corroborated by Steward's field research. However, they are also full of conceptual problems. By presenting a timeless, homogeneous understanding of Paiute society, Steward not only excludes Paiute self-representation of their "daily activities," but in the process defines their lives in a continuous stasis, or unbroken cycle of existence. Repeatedly throughout Steward's text, the Paiute exist outside of time, irrevocably tied to a primeval past.

Even when Steward portrays the Paiute in the present tense, they remain relics of the past. In another illustrative passage, he states: "Present native art products include: the summer willow house, baskets, some rabbitskin blankets, cradles, metates, and mullers. Doctoring by the shaman and use of herbs continues. The remainder of Paiute culture has practically disappeared" (Steward 1933a:238). With nearly all of their culture "disappeared," the Paiutes' existence appears ominously precarious. Steward explicitly assumes that Paiute culture is both incompatible with modern Euro-American society and inflexible and subject to eventual disappearance. From this perspective, definitive ethnographic understandings of their existence must be conducted prior to their impending demise, and Steward clearly viewed himself as the qualified recorder of the Paiutes' vanishing ethnographic characteristics. Although his first ethnography offers a few broader theoretical positions, it remains laden with the problematic definitions of "culture" common to early ethnography.

In his attempt to record Paiute characteristics, Steward showed meticulous concern for the spatial dimensions of both the territorial boundaries of the Paiute and the internal spatialized mechanisms of Paiute society and culture. These quantified representations were part of his attempts to establish measurable standards not only of the relationship between the environment and cultural organization among the Great Basin Indians, but also of the exact practices of their daily activities. Detailing a Paiute basketmaker, for instance, he writes:

> Strips [of willow] about ⅛ inch wide and 1⁄16 to 1⁄32 inch thick were moistened in her mouth or by her finger dipped in a pan of water as used, then drawn by her left hand across a knife edge against which the right thumb held it pressed. The strip was then passed through successively smaller holes, ranging from ¼ to 1⁄32 inch in diameter, punched in a can top with a nail, to shave it down. . . . The coil ran clockwise as seen from the basket bottom, the basket being held open side up, in the left hand, the hole punched with a steel awl, right hand, and the weft pushed through from the outside. (Steward 1933a:271)

In this seemingly innocuous description, Steward describes a recently observed practice. However, this measured example includes numerous tensions. Although Steward chooses to measure the specifics of basketmaking, the "knife edge," "pan," and "steel awl" are obviously recently introduced material items for the Paiute. Such instances of obvious cultural adaptation are repeatedly unrecognized throughout Steward's narratives. Furthermore, the basketmaker, similar to all his informants, here remains voiceless, nameless, and powerless to define her practice in her own terms. Although the basketmaker is silenced, in this brief example Paiute "culture" does appear momentarily fluid and compatible with Euro-American society.

This Paiute incorporation of industrial materials into existing cultural practices contradicts Steward's conception of Paiute culture as "practically disappear[ing]." Such incorporation also provides an example of potential cultural resiliency that challenges the general ahistoricism of the text. Steward fails to recognize the possible flexibility of Paiute culture. He assumes that the few metal objects—the knife, pan, and nail—are simply replacing previous indigenous tools; however, making a basket, as he suggests, requires a great deal of labor. Because this example, like all his others, is presented completely without cultural and historic context, the implied assumption is that this is a vestige of former traditions, not potentially a telling example of indigenous creativity and/or cultural adaptation. Basketmaking could indicate the Paiutes' economic integration into a regional arts-and-crafts economy, the production of gifts for various cultural ceremonies, and/or the teaching of various gender-specific songs and activities to younger women—basketmaking being, as Steward details, a "woman's" activity. More complicated understandings involving economic, religious, or gender relations within Paiute society are lost in this example and throughout Steward's "Ethnography of the Owens Valley Paiute."

In another publication, Steward charted the "Linguistic Distributions and Political Groups of the Great Basin Shoshoneans" (1937c). More concerned with outlining the territorial boundaries of all Great Basin societies than with internal social relations, Steward systematized and mapped different Shoshone groups. "Present data make it possible to bound the main linguistic divisions of the Great Basin with some accuracy and to define and locate most [of] the political divisions of the Shoshoni and their neighbors" (Steward 1937c:625). Steward conducted over 40 "test vocabularies of one hundred words . . . from Shoshoni of California, Nevada, Utah, Idaho and from Northern Paiute, Bannock, Gosiute, Ute, and Southern Paiute" (1937c:625 fn.) and placed all these various groups into three major divisions of the Shoshonean linguistic family. However, the main focus of this text was the identification of the different territorial and political boundaries of various Shoshonean groups: "It is not wholly revealing to record merely that a group had a chief or considered itself a band, for neither the nature and extent of the authority delegated to the chief nor the kind of solidarity among members of the band is self-evident. . . . Among the Nevada Shoshoni, restriction of political organization to the village is a function of social and economic activities. These Shoshoni were primarily gatherers. . . . From fall to spring, individual families, or at most two or three related families, wandered together foraging for food" (Steward 1937c:628–629).

According to Steward, as opposed to more "sedentary" groups such as the Owens Valley Paiute or the Northern Shoshone of Wyoming, the Western Shoshone of Nevada lacked any cohesive political organization. Because their subsistence patterns were so disparate and varied annually depending on irregular fall pine-nut harvests, these "gatherers" simply could not maintain extended large-scale territorial organization: "The pine nut, therefore, induced a comparatively unsettled life; a family journeyed each year to areas where the crop was most convenient or the harvest most promising . . . it found itself wintering . . . in widely separated localities" (Steward 1937c:629). These "separate localities" varied annually depending on the ecological variation in subsistence patterns. Because of their fluctuating, inconsistent composition, the winter villages in which numerous families banded together for a few months did not constitute political organizations. Consequently, the nuclear family remained for the entire year the primary system of sociopolitical organization for the Shoshone. Thus, for Steward the designations of "tribe," let alone "nation," were entirely inapplicable to the Nevada Shoshone because "Shoshoni society resembled a vast net" (Steward 1937c:630) of interrelated but separated family units.

In his ethnography *Basin-Plateau Aboriginal Sociopolitical Groups* (1970a [1938]), Steward comprehensively elaborated on his ideas about the composition of Great Basin Indian political organization. He employed a comparative approach to the entire Basin-Plateau peoples and developed systematic explanations for the presence of differing political organizations throughout the "Intermontane area." Steward based these explanations of the social structures among linguistically similar but organizationally different "Shoshonean" peoples on the differences in specific environmental conditions affecting the different groups. He argued that the fundamental attributes for these institutional variances were numerous "ecological determinants."

"Most of the Basin-Plateau people lived at a bare subsistence level. Their culture was meager in content and simple in structure. Pursuits concerned with the problems of daily existence dominated their activities to an extraordinary degree and limited and conditioned their institutions" (Steward 1970a:1–2 [1938]). For Steward, the problems of daily existence revolved around a continuous subsistence cycle—their unending food quest. Unlike his previous study of the Owens Valley, Steward organized this ethnography conceptually around the relationship between "culture" and the "environment." Although *Basin-Plateau* included similar ethnographic categories and descriptions, they all centered around this operative idea.

Throughout this ethnography, Steward identified how specific different ecological variables helped to determine the composition of various Great Basin Indian social institutions. For example, regular festivals, in which previously dispersed family groups would gather to socialize and hold dances, "were made possible in most of the western area by the temporarily increased food supply produced by rabbit drives, pine-nut trips, antelope hunts, or other communal economic affairs" (Steward 1970a:237 [1938]). Unlike the Owens Valley Paiute who lived in a more fertile area, many of the other Great Basin peoples remained too "unsettled" because of harsh environmental conditions to construct and maintain "sweat-houses" or other communal edifices. According to Steward, marital practices in the Great Basin also had ecological determinants:

> Marriage created an economic unit which insured survival of the individual, a biological unit which somewhat insured certain sex privileges, and a social unit which guaranteed security for children and which united kinship groups. Though none of these was distinctive of the area, it is possible to show that many features of them were delimited and patterned by local conditions. . . . In a region where the burden of subsistence overshadowed all other activities [marriage] was extremely important. Although any particular marriage might be of brief duration, a person could not, in the interest of self-preservation, afford to remain long single. He was generally wed to one person or another during most of his adult life. (Steward 1970a:241–242 [1938])

Steward also interpreted instances of polygyny and polyandry along similar economic lines.

This description of the rationale behind Great Basin marriage presents another telling example of the limitations of Steward's understandings of culture. Minimizing the legitimacy of his subjects' cultural motivations and emotive experiences, Steward attempts to structure the most intimate aspects of his subjects' personal lives along environmentally conditioned lines. Although these marriage patterns were invariably influenced by "local conditions," to suggest that "the burden of subsistence . . . delimited and patterned" all marital relations throughout the region is clearly an oversimplification. Such oversimplifications recur throughout Steward's ethnography. For Steward, not only marriage, but also child-rearing practices, instances of infanticide, and gambling patterns all had ecological determinants that superseded all other potential explanations. With his own categories biasing his interpretations, it became difficult for Steward to gain any alternative insights into the intricacies and variances of Great Basin indigenous societies.

In *Basin-Plateau Aboriginal Sociopolitical Groups* and a culture-element list published shortly thereafter (1941b; see Myers, chapter 9), Steward solidified his ideas about cultural ecology as the basis of Great Basin sociopolitical organization. His text also solidified his emerging interpretive paradigm linking cultural development with ecological variances. Its meticulous concern for ethnographic data, however, did not preclude its usefulness for Steward's interests in cross-cultural comparisons. Two years earlier, Steward had drawn together his research among Great Basin peoples with other ethnographers' works on the Aborigines of Australia and the Eskimos of the subarctic and presented "The Economic and Social Basis of Primitive Bands" in honor of Kroeber's birthday (Steward 1936c:331–345). Steward systemized the classification of culture types and then issued his first call for cross-cultural taxonomy based on environmental criteria. He categorized the Great Basin Indians among the least developed "primitive bands" in the taxonomy of world cultures, and equated these and other cultures' taxonomic status explicitly with ecological influences. As Marvin Harris remarks about this seminal text in cultural ecology:

> *[Basin-Plateau Aboriginal Sociopolitical Groups]* constitutes the first coherent statement of how the interaction between culture and environment could be studied in causal terms. . . . This achievement has a double focus: first, the identification of a cross-culturally valid form of social organization, the "primitive band"; second, its explanation. The band occurs among widely separated hunting and gathering peoples. . . . It is a type of social organization distinguished in its most general form by political autonomy and a small population, in that it consists of several nuclear families whose access to land is controlled by ownership privileges vested in the larger group. (Harris 1968:666)

The concept that "cross-culturally valid forms of social organization" exist, such as the "primitive band," has irrevocably transformed the study of world cultures. As Harris suggests, generations of anthropologists have employed versions of Steward's concepts of cultural ecology to draw comparisons between various different societies throughout the world. In the study of American Indians, anthropologists have grouped, categorized, and defined Indian societies and cultures based on perceived commonalities in social organization and natural environments. By establishing measurable standards with which to identify and study these "valid forms," Steward significantly influenced these transformations. However, these ethnographic theories and categories of analysis have been severely challenged by numerous recent ethnographic and cultural theorists. Outlining the nature of these critiques provides a framework for exploring the broader implications of Steward's representations of Great Basin Indians.

STEWARD'S ETHNOGRAPHY AND POSTMODERN CRITIQUE

It is now en vogue and relatively easy to critique "classic" ethnographic works such as Steward's. Recent critical ethnographic theory has questioned the many biases in traditional anthropology and has produced a series of epistemological "crises" concerning the fate of the discipline. Many of these critiques focus on broader trends in anthropology and the social sciences and are themselves, paradoxically, quite abstract with little reference to the peoples under study—peoples whose lives were the raw material for classic ethnography. For those attempting not only to question the authority of traditional ethnographic texts, but also to illustrate exactly how these texts have functioned to subordinate their "objects," this paradox remains especially difficult.

The attempts by traditional ethnographers, such as Steward, to construct "scientific" anthropological theories of culture and social organization also have been severely challenged in recent years. The disciplinary discourse that claimed both to represent accurately (and authoritatively) the lived experiences of other peoples and to systematize this knowledge for other anthropological specialists has come under severe criticism by recent cultural theorists who systematically challenge the essentialized, categorical representations of non-Western societies. James Clifford (1988:8) rightly asks, "Who has the authority to speak for a group's identity or authenticity?" This question, as well as what exactly constitutes "identity," has triggered fundamental reevaluations of the fate of ethnography.

"The predominant metaphors in anthropological research have been participant-observation, data collection, and cultural description, all of which presuppose a standpoint outside—looking at, objectifying, or, somewhat closer, 'reading' a given reality" (Clifford 1986:11). These ethnographic methods of objectification have become a central focus of many critics of anthropology who, like Clifford, examine the theoretical assumptions of such processes. Of the many contradictions in traditional ethnography, Vincent Crapanzano (1986:51) identifies two fundamental paradoxes. First, "the ethnographer does not recognize the provisional nature of his presentations. They are [for the ethnographer] definitive." Expressed interpretively in writing, this definitiveness, paradoxically, limits any reinterpretation and produces fixed, static understandings. Second, the ethnographer must "render the foreign familiar and preserve its foreignness at one and the same time" (Crapanzano

1986:52). This second, seemingly inescapable conundrum represents a fundamental challenge to traditional ethnographic legitimacy. Not only does ethnography ascribe presumed difference between peoples, but it then attempts to capture and maintain it.

The emergence of various postmodern theories challenges the legitimacy of traditional ethnographic assumptions of difference. Many critical theorists now argue that certain dialectics revolving around understandings of difference pervade Western and Euro-American metaphysics. Designations of "self" become possible, they argue, only when constructed in reference to specifically designated nonselves, or "others." Tzvetan Todorov summarizes this well: "Self-knowledge develops through the knowledge of the Other" (Todorov 1984:254). Dating back to Martin Heiddeger, many antipositivist theorists have questioned these processes of self-differentiation and revealed how such notions of difference function to replicate and support asymmetric relations of power between Western and non-Western societies. This realization of the defining power of ethnographic discourses has been extremely pronounced in the study of peoples and cultures, the purported raison d'etre of anthropology.

In the face of such challenges, anthropologists have attempted to formulate less troubling and contradictory methodologies. Like Clifford, Todorov, and Crapanzano, other scholars have examined the ways in which ethnographers (as well as novelists, travelers, and artists) have problematically represented designated "others." However, such examinations generally fail to convey the profound implications of such representations on their "objects." As Paul Rabinow (1986:241) suggests: "[Anthropologists] need to anthropologize the West: show how exotic its constitution of reality has been; emphasize those domains most taken for granted as universal; make them seem as historically peculiar as possible; show how their claims to truth are linked to social practices and have hence become effective forces in the social world." This suggestion has been slow in coming.

This brief discussion of the emergent critiques of traditional ethnographic authority illustrates the limiting nature of the many of the practices and assumptions of traditional ethnography. Julian Steward embodies many of these classical techniques. Analyzed not only for what they say about anthropology, or Steward himself, Steward's texts are remarkable for what they do not say about the Shoshone Indians of Nevada.

An analysis or summation of the silences within Steward's texts is beyond the parameters of this chapter. Clearly, despite Steward's emphasis, neither the Great Basin Indians themselves nor the environment of the region can be understood so monolithically and simplistically. To further apply the arguments that Steward employed problematic representations of Great Basin

Indians based on troubling conceptions of cultural ecology and that these representations can potentially influence and narrow the possible choices for these various indigenous societies, this final section analyzes Steward's involvement with the Indian Reorganization Act (IRA) of 1934.

STEWARD'S "SHOSHONEAN TRIBES"

Contacted in 1936 by BIA Commissioner John Collier, Steward argued against granting federal status to various groups of the Western Shoshone Indians of Nevada. As a consultant anthropologist to the bureau, Steward (1936b) issued his report "Shoshonean Tribes: Utah, Idaho, Nevada, Eastern California" in December 1936. The BIA had asked Steward for his recommendations on its efforts to restructure existing American Indian tribal governments and in certain instances to create reservation lands as called for by the IRA of 1934. The restructuring of tribal governments was one of the principal tenets of the IRA, which reversed the assimilative federal Indian policy instituted in the nineteenth century and also repealed the 1887 Dawes Severalty, or "General Allotment," Act. Because most members of Western Shoshone communities in 1934 had not been granted reservations in Nevada, the creation of reservation lands was a potentially important provision of the IRA for them. The BIA labeled these off-reservation Indians as "landless." In his 18-page report, Steward stated, "My facts have been gathered during ten years' work among Shoshonean tribes. . . . My statements are supported by several published monographs and papers and about 1,000 pages of manuscript" (1936b:1). Despite his many interactions with the Shoshone, Steward strenuously opposed Collier's and the BIA's attempts to provide reservation lands and federal recognition for the "landless" Western Shoshone Indians of Nevada.

"Do not segregate them as a racial group," Steward (1936b:11) suggested. "Do not complicate and endanger them with a tribal council, do not baffle them with a constitution and charter. . . . Segregating Shoshoni in large groups will . . . lessen race and cultural contacts and increase the difficulties of assimilation." Prefiguring themes that he later developed into his broader theories of cultural ecology, Steward based his observations of contemporary Western Shoshone Indians on his understanding of "traditional" Shoshone culture and social organization. He argued, "The Nevada and southern Idaho Shoshoni had no bands or other tribal groupings. . . . Their native culture was so meager and their socio-political groupings so tenuous that no well-defined and stable patterns had emerged. Shoshoneans had a loose society, in which an individual's social horizon extended scarcely beyond his family and in which his motivation was largely the acquisition of subsistence from day to day" (Steward 1936b:9, 7). As Steward interpreted it, because the Western

Shoshone had always lacked political structures due to the sparseness of their local ecology, federal attempts to recognize and create different Western Shoshone reservations and tribal governments contradicted existing patterns in Shoshone society. "The implication of these facts for the Indian Office program is that there were no native divisions among the Nevada and southwest Idaho Shoshoni which afford a logical basis for present segregation of the people. . . . It must be recognized therefore that the present program . . . is completely illogical and unwarranted in terms of native conditions" (Steward 1936b:9). Steward's prodigious research and academic prestige should have brought considerable credibility to his recommendations against bringing the IRA to Nevada.

However, Steward's suggestions did not go unchallenged and they were eventually rejected by the BIA. Superintendent Alida Bowler of the Carson Indian Agency, which administered Indian policy in Nevada, campaigned heavily against the report. She told Collier in a 1937 memorandum, "The interpretations and opinions of the members of your own field organization are . . . diametrically opposed to those of the Consultant Anthropologist" (Bowler 1937:1). Bowler maintained that Steward had misinterpreted not only the administration's policy objectives but also the nature of Shoshone culture. "He made no contacts at the agency to inquire into the program or to learn what we hoped to accomplish or how we proposed to go about it." In response to "the report's comments on native culture. These are hard to understand. One can only assume that the writer failed to catch many glimpses of the inner life, the heart and soul of the Indian. . . . We have no reason to conclude that it [Shoshone culture] does not have living values and satisfactions for the people out of whose past it grew. . . . No one who merely brushes the surface of Indian life in a cursory, inquisitive, exploratory manner suspects [its] existence" (Bowler 1937:3, 5). Summing up her feelings on Steward, she expressed in a "confidential" letter to Collier: "I am unshakably skeptical about the scientific thoroughness of [his] work . . . what I have heard of his work among the Shoshones here makes me doubt anything he might publish in that field" (1936b:1).

Although the Western Shoshones sporadically received various government entitlements, unlike most other American Indians at the time, their legal status as an identifiable tribe or tribes remained unclear to the federal government. Moreover, federal Indian policy was less effective in dealing with Indians who did not live on recognized reservation lands and thus did not have federally recognized tribal governments. The IRA was principally designed to restructure existing tribal governments, but with "landless" Indian groups such as many of the Nevada Shoshone, the IRA offered conditions for federal recognition and reservation lands. The IRA consequently offered many Western Shoshone the opportunity to become federally recognized American Indian tribes.

Many Indian groups, including the Nevada Shoshone, greeted Collier's reform efforts with skepticism, seeing the creation of reservations as a way for the BIA to avoid dealing with their outstanding land claims case (cf. Crum 1994; see also Ronaasen et al., chapter 12). For instance, many groups resented the imposition of new tribal governments and constitutions. However, Steward opposed the IRA more on the theoretical basis that Great Basin Shoshone culture and social organization remained fundamentally diffused with no ethnographically definable individual groups eligible for the status of "tribe." For Steward, organizing and granting political status to unorganized, former nomadic hunters and gathers was completely illogical. Reservations and federal recognition would bestow upon the Western Shoshone inapplicable and overly complicated political systems that contradicted existing patterns in their culture and social organization. In his final view, if the Nevada Shoshone became concentrated on reservations, they would ultimately fall deeper into economic and social deprivation and come to rely further on the government for assistance.

Steward's opposition to the creation of reservations and new tribal governments for the Shoshone in Nevada was at odds with many of the Western Shoshone groups' efforts to secure a firmer land basis and relationship with the federal government. As Steven Crum indicates in his pioneering tribal history of the Western Shoshone, "The IRA provision that had the greatest impact on the nonreservation Western Shoshones was the purchase of lands to create new reservations. . . . [The BIA] accepted the Shoshones' cultural trait of deep attachment to the land and took the initiative in creating reservations in some native Shoshone valleys" (Crum 1994:91–92, 97). Ultimately, the BIA rejected Steward's suggestions, officially recognized several previously unclassified Indian groups, and granted them reservation lands and federal recognition.

CONCLUSION

The broader implications of Steward's report for the BIA suggest that his ideas about Great Basin Indian peoples have had potentially powerful results in addition to shaping academic debates about the region and its people. His role as a preeminent narrator of a region and its peoples reflects much broader assumptions and relations of power that characterize much of the history of Indian peoples and Euro-Americans in the Great Basin. As Edward Said suggests, "The main battle in imperialism is over land, of course; but when it came to who owned the land, who had the right to settle and work it, who kept it going, who won it back, and who now plans its future—these issues were reflected, contested, and even for a time decided in narrative" (Said 1993:xii–xiii). Steward's works and representations of these peoples cannot be excluded from these broader imperial and colonial contexts.

With his study of the Great Basin, Steward began an entire new field of anthropological study. His theory of cultural ecology paved the way for numerous other researchers and positioned Steward to dominate the study of the Great Basin as well as much of American anthropology for over a generation. However, this theory remains predicated on problematic assumptions about the nature of Great Basin society. Scholars who critique problems of ethnographic authority need to recognize not only how such representations serve to exclude and silence their objects of study, but also how these studies themselves can potentially shape the conditions in which native peoples must operate.

Steward's texts produced fixed, categorical understandings of the Great Basin Indians and reduced vibrant, resilient, and infinitely complex peoples to static, materially and ecologically determined generalizations. Such generalizations fundamentally obscure the innumerable ways in which these Indian peoples express and represent themselves. The meanings, beliefs, and values they give to themselves, their lands, and their histories never enter into Steward's works. Their philosophy, cosmology, and hermeneutics are thus denied both contemporaneity and past as well as future existence. Interpreting how Steward accomplishes this does not warrant the same attention as what it is he silences. Although they are the subject of literally hundreds of sentences, the Great Basin Indians do not speak in Steward's texts.

14

Julian Steward and the Construction of Area-Studies Research in the United States

Thomas C. Patterson and
Antonio Lauria-Perricelli

Exploring Julian Steward's role in the formation of area studies in the United States between the late 1930s and the 1960s reveals a number of little-known and surprising influences. For example, his "Area Research: Theory and Practice" (1950) drew inspiration not only from the Puerto Rico Project that he organized in the 1940s, but also from the Virú Valley Project that Steward helped organize with Wendell C. Bennett, William D. Strong, and Gordon R. Willey. Steward also drew on Robert Redfield's Carnegie-sponsored research in the Yucatán and from various other area studies organized during and after World War II. Patterson and Lauria-Perricelli round out this appraisal and critique of Steward and his work by giving us a glimpse into Steward's activities after he left Great Basin research. In doing so, they also give us some insight into why Steward never returned to the area and the research that has framed so much anthropological work in the Great Basin.

To explore the role that Steward played in the formation of area studies in the United States between the late 1930s and the 1960s, we suggest specific scholars, research projects, and contexts that caused him to virtually abandon his research on North American native peoples. Instead he emerged as a significant figure in organizing research that was regionally focused on Latin America and driven by a concern for deriving universally valid, theoretical formulations and understandings of cultural change.

In the 1940s Julian Steward edited the *Handbook of South American Indians.* This major ethnographic undertaking involved dozens of authors and constituted a precedent-setting collection of area studies. It set the stage for the myriad strategic "area handbooks" published by the U.S. Information Service in subsequent decades and for institutionalization of Latin American and other area studies in universities. Knowledge of foreign areas was poorly developed in the United States before World War II. Most of the research conducted by U.S. anthropologists in the prewar years had been carried out within the continental United States. Furthermore, most of the individuals with detailed knowledge of areas outside the United States were not academics. As a result, area studies were virtually nonexistent in U.S. colleges and universities before the outbreak of the war in the late 1930s (McCaughey 1984).

We propose that Steward drew inspiration not only from the Puerto Rico Project but also from Robert Redfield's Carnegie-sponsored research in the Yucatán; the Virú Valley Project that Steward coorganized with Wendell C. Bennett, William D. Strong, and Gordon R. Willey; the Peruvian archaeological aficionado Rafael Larco Hoyle; and from various area-studies programs organized during and after World War II. We will also discuss how Steward's views about area studies developed between the late 1930s and the late 1960s and identify the issues that influenced his views.

THE HISTORY OF AREA STUDIES AND THE ROLE OF THE ANTHROPOLOGIST

In the years immediately preceding World War II, the Social Science Research Council (SSRC) and the American Council of Learned Societies (ACLS) began to play important roles in advocating the need for foreign multi- and interdisciplinary area studies in the United States. In the early 1930s, the ACLS created a number of committees to coordinate research and resources in the traditional Orientalist areas.[1] During the 1920s, the foreign-area emphasis of ACLS and SSRC activity was on China and Japan—regions of strategic and commercial importance to the United States. However, despite the critical importance of Pacific trade, colonies, and geopolitics, the preponderance of U.S. foreign interests lay in its own hemisphere. It is in Latin American studies that the most significant innovations took place during the 1930s and 1940s. The ACLS created a committee in 1931–1932. The following year, the SSRC International Relations Committee commissioned Frank Tannenbaum of the Brookings Institution to survey Latin America on a Guggenheim fellowship. As a result, the council sponsored a conference of 15 scholars interested in Latin American studies in 1935 and established a Committee on Latin American Studies with 29 members, seven of whom were anthropologists: John M. Cooper, Carl Guthe, Clark Wissler, A. V. Kidder, A. L. Kroeber, Robert Redfield, and Alfred M. Tozzer.

At the same time as the ACLS initiative, the Advisory Committee for the *Handbook of Latin Studies* was established, with input from the ACLS, SSRC, American Geographical Society, and the Universities of Chicago and Michigan. The handbook was a unique innovation, a periodic survey of knowledge in all fields on a major world area, shepherded by an ad hoc area-studies committee linking two of the major interdisciplinary research councils. Toward the end of the 1930s, the Rockefeller Foundation increased its support for work on Latin America, evidently commensurate with Nelson Rockefeller's initiative concerning the area. Other philanthropists had already been active: Huntington in research and libraries; Carnegie in pan-American relations; Guggenheim in support of individual scientists and scholars in various countries.

In 1940, the ACLS-SSRC Joint Committee on Latin American Studies (JCLAS) was established; it was the first formal joint research-council committee to promote the study of a major world area. The National Research Council (NRC) also formed its own, much more specialized Committee on Latin American Anthropology at the end of that year to coordinate research, resources, and government needs. In 1942, shortly after the United States entered the war, the NRC group joined the JCLAS to create the first regionally focused committee that involved all of the major research councils. During its eight years of existence, the JCLAS was the only instrumentality of its kind.[2]

Rockefeller Foundation funding played an important role in these joint-committee ventures, as it did in the specialized language-training programs already emerging by 1940. Furthermore, as shown later in this chapter, the creation of the Office of the Coordinator of Interamerican Affairs (OCIAA) under Nelson Rockefeller in August 1940 provided the federal funding for the many new initiatives in Latin American anthropology.

Government officials recognized the importance of area studies as the United States entered World War II. The Ethnogeographic Board, with anthropologist William D. Strong as chair, was established in 1942 by the NRC, ACLS, SSRC, and Smithsonian Institution "to make readily accessible to Washington military and war agencies such specific regional information and evaluated personnel data as may be available to the sponsoring institutions and the numerous other governmental and outside scientific organizations with which they are affiliated or in contact" (Bennett 1947:v). In 1943, the War Department established foreign area and language studies as part of the Army's Specialized Training Program in 55 universities and colleges; 13,185 enlisted men were enrolled in this program by December, 1943. The Army's Civil Affairs Training Schools, established in 10 universities at the same time, trained officers to administer occupied territories after the war (Fenton 1947:v–vi).

The Holistic Perspective

Anthropologists played prominent roles in the formation of these and other area-studies programs, as well as a number of regionally specialized research and practical efforts in the wartime agencies, for example, the Bureau of Economic Warfare, the Foreign and Domestic Morale branches of the Office of War Information, and the Office of Strategic Services. At the time, most U.S. cultural anthropologists were specialists in North American native peoples. Although anthropologists provided specific cross-cultural and regional expertise, the major reason for their utility in the multiple wartime and area studies lay elsewhere: in their anthropological holism.[3] Anthropology was a discipline whose practitioners possessed a vision and a conceptual scheme for grasping a totality and the interrelations of its parts. Their holistic perspective allowed them to bring together and synthesize the fragmented data collected by scholars from other fields—like economics—that lacked this vision (Lauria-Perricelli 1989:64–66).

Steward as Federal Researcher and Technocrat

After seven years of teaching and research at publicly funded universities in Michigan (1928–1930), Utah (1930–1933), and California (1933–1934) and fieldwork in the Great Basin (1935–1936), Steward took a position at the Bureau of American Ethnology (BAE) of the Smithsonian Institution. Here he returned to his childhood milieu—his father and maternal uncle were both members of an earlier generation of federal scientific cadres, his father in the Patent Office, his uncle in the Weather Bureau. However, by the 1930s this federal establishment had enormously expanded technocratic functions and personnel.

Within 1936, Steward was seconded to the Bureau of Indian Affairs (BIA), and we believe that certain critical elements of Steward's thinking crystallized at this time. These concerned the effects of hierarchical relations between national sociocultural systems and dependent indigenous subcultures, the long-term irreversible effects of top-down modernizing/acculturating forces on local cultures, and the futility of all but the most carefully "scientifically" calibrated program to reassert or vitalize cultural or national values. This experience perhaps reinforced and was reified by the technoenvironmental economism we see at work in his earlier Great Basin studies (e.g., see Black- hawk, chapter 13; Crum, chapter 8; Rusco, chapter 7).

During these years in Washington, D.C., Steward also explored fieldwork possibilities in northwestern South America. Although Steward's activities during this period are not entirely clear, it is known that by 1940 he was well positioned to take advantage of budgetary support for many anthropological projects—some in abeyance for many years, some springing from his own perspective on social research and social change. These projects were aimed at Central and South America, after the OCIAA was opened, and the Interdepartmental/International Committee on Cultural and Scientific Cooperation (IDC) was established in the Department of State. The committee was one of the minor instruments in the broad-gauged area policy that OCIAA implemented, itself the first comprehensive model of foreign assistance and intervention that, after World War II, would be generalized to each of the major world regions (Lauria-Perricelli 1989).

During the next six years, Steward played a key role in the major social science activities of the IDC, although his projects were not the only major anthropological projects. His network of collaborators, contacts—and antagonists—in these ventures included all the major academic and quasi-academic Latin Americanists in the United States at the time. Steward was not himself a member of the major committees linking the federal state to the foundations, research councils, and universities. Indeed, in later years, he never took on this role. However, this does not belie his obvious role in attempting to develop and push research projects through the bureaucracy and the budget process.

The well-known list of Steward's Washington ventures includes editing the *Handbook of South American Indians,* creating and directing the Institute for Social Anthropology (ISA), and helping Ralph Beals organize the Sociedad Interamericana de Antropología e Historia and its journal *Acta Americana.* He was close to Wendell Bennett's projects carried out through the Institute of Andean Research (funded during the war by the OCIAA) and to the Ethnogeographic Board. In 1945, Steward proposed the creation of an American Society of Professional Anthropologists and formed part of the Temporary Organizing Committee set up in Washington, D.C., to carry this out. The committee's programmatic statement was written in that same Washington, D.C., atmosphere and was cosigned by Clyde Kluckhohn (Office of Strategic Services, Office of War Information), Frank Roberts (BAE), John Provinse (Soil Conservation Service, BIA, War Relocation Authority, and later many overseas development projects in a succession of Department of State instruments), and Homer Barnett (Ethnogeographic Board and later the Trust Territory of the Pacific administrative studies). Later, Steward chaired the committee to reorganize the American Anthropological Association that emerged from the ensuing political struggle within the profession. Steward was involved in efforts to plan the proposed National Science Foundation; he was also part of a team of anthropologists that successfully lobbied Congress for expanding salvage archaeology appropriations.

Handbook of South American Indians: Ethnographic and Political Motivations

In 1932, a committee of the NRC's Division of Anthropology and Psychology—composed of anthropologists Robert H. Lowie, John M. Cooper, and Leslie Spier—indicated that there was a need for a compendium of information about the indigenous peoples of South America. The project had two major goals. The first was to bring together and make accessible widely scattered information about the native peoples of South America. In this regard, the handbook would not only be a resource for research, but it would also help to identify the kinds of investigations needed in the future. The second goal was political: "[to] serve as a symbol of scientific amity between the United States and the Republics of South and Central America" (Steward 1940b:228).

The NRC did not give high priority to the proposed *Handbook of South American Indians,* and the project languished during the Depression years. The enterprise was revived in 1940, when funds to begin the project were obtained through a special congressional appropriation obtained by the IDC with the American republics. This committee was organized through the efforts of the OCIAA headed by Nelson Rockefeller. The BAE at the Smithsonian Institution was assigned the task of preparing the volumes, and Steward was selected to edit this compendium.

When Steward submitted the first volume of the handbook to the U.S. Government Printing Office in 1944, he did not mention its role as a symbol of hemispheric amity. Instead he emphasized its role as "a concise summary of existing data that will serve as a standard reference work for the scholar, a textbook for the student, and a guide for the general reader. At the same time, it is intended to take stock of the present state of knowledge, revealing deficiencies and suggesting problems that will stimulate further research in both the field and library" (Steward 1946:2 [1944]).

Steward used a series of four cultural types to organize the handbook and to present a vast amount of disparate archaeological, ethnographic, and historic information. Each type reduced "the bewildering variety of cultural data to categories which have a real and historical meaning" (Steward 1949a:669 [1947]). Each type was based on an interpretation of economic practices, sociopolitical organization, and ritual activities rather than on historically or socially contingent cultural elements that produced diversity. Steward viewed the economic, sociopolitical, and ritual patterns that served as the basis for this classification as the ones "which integrate the institutions of the sociopolitical unit. The unit is the cohesive group whose members live in more or less permanent association with one another, participate in the same economic, social, and religious activities, and submit to the same in-group sanctions and political control" (Steward 1949a:672 [1947]). Here we see Steward giving the same priority to sociopolitical organizations and the social relations of production and distribution as he did in *Basin-Plateau Aboriginal Sociopolitical Groups* (1970a [1938]).

Steward used each cultural type to organize one of the first four volumes of the handbook: *The Marginal Tribes* (vol. 1), *The Andean Civilizations* (vol. 2), *The Tropical Forest Peoples* (vol. 3), and *The Circum-Caribbean Peoples* (vol. 4). In defining the cultural types, Steward elaborated and added to the earlier classification of South American peoples proposed by John M. Cooper (1941, 1942). The marginal tribes (vol. 1) were nomadic peoples who relied on hunting, fishing, and gathering to satisfy their subsistence needs; their sociopolitical units consisted of a single or a few loosely organized kin groups whose members were differentiated according to age, gender, kinship, and economic activities. Custom rather than law regulated the behavior of the members of these kin-organized communities (Steward 1949a:672 [1947]). The tropical forest tribes (vol. 3) were farming peoples whose members lived in permanent villages. These sociopolitical units consisted of kin groups whose members were distinguished from one another by age, gender, and association. Custom rather than law also regulated the behavior of these communities, except when special chiefs organized certain communal activities, such as warfare (Steward 1949a:672–673 [1947]). The circum-Caribbean groups (vol. 4) had more effective subsistence practices that supported denser populations in larger, permanent villages. The sociopolitical units were class stratified, and warfare was the primary vehicle for achieving membership in the upper classes; war captives constituted a slave class. Chiefs, warriors, and shamans had special powers in particular contexts (Steward 1949a:673 [1947]). Finally, the Andean civilizations (vol. 2) had the most productive agricultural systems, the most dense populations, and efficient transportation. This allowed the development of cities and states that exercised control over large areas. These groups were characterized by hereditary class systems, war for conquest, temple cults, public ceremonies, and rule by law rather than custom. "These institutions overshadowed and to some degree replaced the behavior patterns pertaining essentially to the kin group and community" (Steward 1949a:673 [1947]).

The four cultural types were related to one another in historically specific ways. Steward believed the classification had "developmental implications in that some institutions and practices were necessarily antecedent to others, but it is not a unilinear scheme" (Steward 1949a:674 [1947]). In this statement, he foreshadowed his theory of multilinear evolution (Steward 1953a). History was to be reconstructed using the age-area method, which postulates that the most widespread cultural traits are the oldest ones.

Let us outline schematically Steward's historic scheme:

1. "The patterns found among the Marginal peoples clearly stemmed from local adaptations beginning in early post-Glacial times. . . . Those of the remaining tribes, includ[ing] the civilized peoples of México and Perú, acquired distinctive American patterns at a very early time" (Steward 1949a:744 [1947]).

2. Someplace between Mexico and the central Andes was "the center of origin of an early ill-defined, Formative Period culture from which the main complexes and patterns found among all farming tribes were derived. During subsequent development, both México and Perú became specialized secondary centers" (Steward 1949a:745, 769 [1947]).

3. An interamerican Formative Period culture preceded the circum-Caribbean culture in the northern Andes and in Central America; however, the latter was not entirely derived from the former (Steward 1949a:758–759 [1947]).

4. There were two streams of historic influence from the Andes. One current carried "central Andean traits southward, especially after the *Inca* conquest, to Chile and Northwest Argentina, . . . the other carr[ied] Circum-Caribbean traits down the Atlantic Coast and up the great rivers, representing coastal, riparian, and rain forest adaptations" (Steward 1949a:697 [1947]).

5. The historic development of tropical forest culture and its relations with Andean and circum-Caribbean culture were complex. For example, Steward argued that "at some early period or periods, Andean culture may have spread with considerable vigor into the tropical rain forest areas, where it subsequently diminished or disappeared" (Steward 1949a:759 [1947]). He also suggested that circum-Caribbean religious patterns might represent the elaboration of tropical forest practices under Andean influence (Steward 1949a:760 [1947]). Steward then suggested that "Tropical Forest culture derived its essential technology from the Circum-Caribbean culture [which spread via the main waterways] and that it also acquired certain rain forest traits, but failed to borrow the Circum-Caribbean sociopolitical and religious patterns" (Steward 1949a:762 [1947]).

In the concluding pages of his interpretative summary, Steward shifted his attention to the acculturation and assimilation of South American peoples. In his view, the marginal and tropical forest tribes were exterminated or absorbed along the coast, but their cultures survived in much modified forms in the interior. The circum-Caribbean peoples—stripped of their class structure, temple-idol cult, and organized warfare—were degraded to a generalized tropical forest level. The central Andean civilizations were hard hit by epidemics, and the European minorities were able "to exploit the existing labor supply through adapting their methods to preexisting native sociopolitical patterns than to completely uproot, recast, and finally replace the people. . . . The effect of the Conquest as a whole was similar to that on the Circum-Caribbean area. The more organized and distinctive forms of the Central Andean patterns were replaced by European forms while the folk culture remained more intact" (Steward 1949a:766–767 [1947]). Steward (1947) subsequently used the historic-analytical framework he developed in the *Handbook of South American Indians* to explore cultural development in both North and South America.

The Institute of Social Anthropology

In the early 1940s, Steward recognized the need for studies of culture change, acculturation, and assimilation in various kinds of Indian communities in Latin America (1943a, 1943b, 1943c). In 1943, he helped to establish the ISA within the Smithsonian Institution and served as its first director. The institute was founded under the auspices of the Department of State's IDC. It was "one of the many tangible responses to the growing sense of a need for closer cooperation and greater understanding between the peoples of the United States and of the other American Republics" (Steward 1944a:ix).

The explicit goal of the ISA was to send personnel to those Latin American countries that wished to undertake cooperative research and teaching programs in cultural or social anthropology. The institute sponsored collaborative research in Indian communities and regions in Mexico, Peru, Guatemala, and Brazil with organizations or institutions in those countries. Although the research projects focused on subjects that were of practical interest to the host countries—such as economics, land-use patterns, or land tenure—they would also lay the foundations for studying the processes by which communities either had been incorporated or were being incorporated into the modern state (Manners 1973:893; Murphy 1977:7–8). That they would be incorporated, more or less totally, constituted one of Steward's primary assumptions (for further discussion of this point see Clemmer, chapter 10).

Steward's postwar letters to former ISA collaborators express his ideal conception of the unit. He had acted in the belief that the U.S. government should possess within the Smithsonian Institution the capacity to carry out "our" basic multidisciplinary research of both "scientific" and "practical" value on the populations of world areas, concerning topics of importance to the welfare of the host countries. Steward had even hoped to extend the ISA's purview to research in China. Steward (1949a:677) was vitally interested in using ISA to turn ethnological attention away from "traditional" indigenous communities and cultures toward "mestizo" populations and the process of transformation of people uprooted from their villages into a "national proletariat." Despite that precedent-setting importance of introducing the term "national proletariat" into the ethnographic literature of the time, it was not really Steward who did so—he introduced the concept on the basis of John Murra's paper "The Historic Tribes of Ecuador," which was prepared for the *Handbook of South American Indians* (Lauria-Perricelli 1989:248 n. 305; Murra 1946:819–820). This vision of turning ethnological attention toward the formation of "national proletariats" would underlie all of his later empirical research projects.

According to Lawrence Kelly's (1985:128–129) discussion of internal BIA memos and other unpublished documents by Steward and Scudder Mekeel, Steward had worked out key features of this vision while on loan to the BIA (for discussion of the extent to which Steward's new interest diverted him from the task assigned to him by the BIA see Blackhawk, chapter 13; Rusco, chapter 7). To be useful to administrators, anthropologists needed to study acculturation among contemporary native peoples in association with allied disciplines such as economics and rural sociology. The missing elements were international collaborative research and training.

THE POLITICS OF ETHNOGRAPHY AND ACCULTURATION STUDIES

Steward's choice of themes and of areas of international collaboration for the ISA efforts reflect both his maturing understanding of cultural change and the transformation of indigenous peoples and cultures and a shrewd molding of research objectives with the essential interests involved in the OCIAA and other aspects of U.S. wartime policy toward Latin America. Of course, this was true of many other initiatives that Steward and his network (including Bennett at the Ethnogeographic Board) developed for Latin America. The critical objectives were to eliminate all possible interimperial competitors for access to or control over hemispheric production, markets, and sociopolitical forces. Possible Axis-inspired appeals to indigenous peoples were to be discovered and blocked; political stability and social peace were necessary to guarantee the right kind of agricultural production to permit the Latin American countries to maintain their populations while guaranteeing the delivery of the appropriate products and raw materials for the wartime U.S. market. Thus, it was no accident that the themes of agricultural development and production, land tenure, rural labor, and mining recur in the ISA and other research, development, and training efforts sponsored by the OCIAA. Although the research was officially conducted "independently," the "cooperative" aspects of ISA and IDC programs were aimed at creating technical cadres within the host countries that could expand required state functions and allow the United States to tap into the capacities and knowledge of local intellectuals.

One impetus for Steward's formulation of the practical and theoretical stances of the ISA was the crystallization of the concept of acculturation in the United States in the late 1930s. A second was clearly the ethnographic studies made by British social anthropologists concerned with the problems of colonial administration in Africa, even though Steward apparently never cited any of their works. A third impetus was community and regional studies that were already being carried out in Mexico, notably the University of California's Tarascan Project directed by Ralph Beals and Robert Redfield's Carnegie-funded comparative study of four communities in the Yucatán. Two of Beals's studies on the Tarascan region appeared in the ISA's publications during Steward's tenure as director. However, it was Redfield's (1941) study of modernization in the Yucatán region, summarized in *The Folk Culture of Yucatán,* that seems to have had a more profound impact on Steward's thinking. Nevertheless, Steward criticized the fact that Redfield made no effort to articulate the community studies with the vast amount of archaeological and historic information available in the region (Steward 1944b).

What did grab Steward's attention was how Redfield conceptualized and explained the "gradations recorded from Indian village through peasant village and town to city as though the comparison represented a process illustrated at four stages of its course" (Steward 1944b:147). Redfield portrayed the process in Durkheimian terms: the breakdown of the homogeneous community rooted in "mechanical solidarity" and the emergence of the heterogeneous society based on "organic solidarity." For Steward, the weakness of this explanation was that Redfield described a historic process without making reference to history.

In 1943, Steward (1943a, 1943b, 1943c) intervened in the debate between Sol Tax, Robert Redfield, John Collier, and Emil Haury concerning acculturation, the future of indigenous peoples, and hemispheric *indigenista* policy published in *América Indígena.* Steward's view, as we discover from his late-life text on the "Indian New Deal" (Steward 1969b), expressed thinking that had crystallized as early as 1935 or 1936 (see Rusco, chapter 7). It would characterize Steward's theoretical approach to culture change and processes throughout his career, and explain his peculiar affinity for Redfield. In Steward's view, culture change was a one-way street: Modernization would inevitably steamroll any traditional society, and underlying the fate of specific cultural forms, patterns, and practices were ineluctable macrohistoric trends (see Clemmer, chapter 10). This was Redfield's position as well, although, to be sure, the two men differed significantly. Steward's heuristics privileged a base-superstructure method, whereas Redfield's perhaps more pessimistic dualism concerned the relation between the "moral" and the "technical" orders. Furthermore, their views on the relationship between anthropological inquiry as scientific discipline and the forms of social action differed. Here, the contrast was perhaps grounded in Steward's natural science/natural history orientation to anthropology versus Redfield's grounding in law as a tool for social action. The result was that Steward was always caught in what he himself saw as a potential contradiction between action as scientist and action as citizen. Although he did act and use his name, Steward felt that he would have been more effective through what he defined as true applied anthropology, the use of scientific generalizations and predictions concerning practical and ethical problems, without advocating or taking specific steps to actually apply them. Redfield, no less a liberal than Steward, thought and wrote otherwise.

In 1950 and 1951, Steward returned to the problem of how tribal communities were incorporated into modern nation-states in his article "Levels of Sociocultural Integration: An Operational Concept" (Steward 1955a [1951]). He argued that anthropologists needed to conceptualize "sociocultural systems above the tribal levels," that is, at the regional and national levels. He argued that the growth continuum of any culture was marked by a succession of increasingly complex, emergent forms (Steward 1950:106–114). "In culture, simple forms, such as those represented by the family or band do not wholly disappear when a more complex stage of development is reached, nor do they merely survive fossil-like. . . . They gradually become modified as specialized, dependent parts of new kinds of total configurations. The many-faceted national culture . . . represents a very high developmental level" (Steward 1955a:51 [1951]). Steward argued that Redfield's concepts of folk society and folk culture represented a level of sociocultural integration that contrasted with the urban society of Merida, the largest city in Yucatán. He proceeded to suggest that, although some folk societies are integrated into larger sociocultural systems through urbanization, others "are incorporated into states and nations as regionally specialized subcultures which do not undergo urbanization at all and which are readapted rather than transformed" (Steward 1955a:53 [1951]).

THE VIRÚ VALLEY PROJECT: INSPIRATION FOR THE CONCEPTS OF "CAUSALITY" AND "LAW" IN THE STUDY OF CULTURE

Although most of the participants in the Virú Valley Project were archaeologists, ethnographic and geographic studies had already been conducted in the vicinity by personnel affiliated with the ISA (Gillin 1945; Steward 1950:36–37). As archaeology, the project employed a method that Steward had come to consider as fundamental to progress in ethnography: the combination of problem-oriented regional or even national-level studies of specific sites or communities. This scheme allowed Steward—true, paradoxically, to the tradition of Americanist culture history in which he had been trained—to visualize both long-term as well as contemporaneous studies of processes of change in a single framework. Thus, Steward could attempt to express the entire culture history of the Central and South American peoples or the totality of Puerto Rican subcultures as a very complex image of socio-spatial distributions, relations, and gradients along dimensions of change.

From Steward's perspective, the Virú Valley Project overcame a major limitation of Redfield's research in the Yucatán. The outlines of the project were sketched by Steward and three archaeologists with whom he had collaborated in various ways in the 1930s and 1940s: Wendell C. Bennett, William D. Strong, and Gordon R. Willey. They proposed "to make a complete [archaeological,] historical, ethnographic, and geographic study of the Viru Valley in northern Peru. . . . The general purpose was to study the valley's cultural development from the time of its earliest inhabitants through aboriginal empires and the Spanish Colonial Period to the present day" (Steward 1950:36).

The archaeologists who participated in the Virú Valley Project used the cultural sequence they constructed on the basis of their investigations as a keyhole through which they could view cultural development throughout the central Andes (cf. Bennett 1948). The cultural evolutionary frameworks they adopted were derived from the one proposed in 1946 by the influential Peruvian agrarian capitalist and aficionado of archaeology, Rafael Larco Hoyle (Patterson 1989; Willey 1946).

Larco Hoyle (1948) argued that the cultures of the north coast of Peru evolved through a series of stages: hunter-gatherer, evolutionist, classic, fusion, and imperial. He argued that the expansion of the productive forces, especially the development of irrigation systems during the classic stage, was the motor driving cultural evolution in northern coastal Peru. Larco Hoyle's views were ultimately derived from and an elaboration of those of V. Gordon Childe.

By late 1946, Steward (1948) had adopted and modified Larco Hoyle's conceptual scheme and terminology, which differed from his culture historic analysis of American cultural development that was published in 1947 (Steward 1947). Within a year, he extended this framework in "Cultural Causality and Law: A Trial Formulation of the Development of Early Civilizations" to consider the development of early civilizations in both the Old and New Worlds (Steward 1949b). This evolutionary framework served as the foundation for a very elaborate theory of human history that he outlined in *Area Research: Theory and Practice.* In this framework

> The rise and fall of kingdoms . . . in Egypt, Mesopotamia, India, China, Meso-America, and the Andes is often described as the rise and fall of civilization. . . . [Although particular kinds of societies did not survive,] most of the basic cultural achievements, the essential features of civilization, were passed on to other nations. In each of these centers both culture and society changed rather considerably during the early periods, and everywhere the developmental processes were about the same. At first there were small communities of incipient farmers. Later the communities cooperated in the construction of irrigation works and populations became larger and more settled. Villages amalgamated into states under theocratic rulers. Finally, culture ceased to develop as the states of each area entered into competition with one another. . . .
>
> [Following the stagnation of these early theocratically ruled states in each area,] each state began to compete with others for tribute and advantages. One or another state succeeded in dominating the others, that is, in building an empire, but such empires ran their course and collapsed after some . . . years only to be succeeded by another empire not very different from the first. (Steward 1950:103–104)

Steward contrasted the view of the historian in which each "era of cyclical conquests is filled with great men, wars and battle strategy, shifting power centers, and other social events" with that of "the culture historian" who was concerned with the development of "basic civilizations" and with the changes that occurred when the centers of civilization shifted to new areas.

Steward also saw recent history in terms of processes, causes, and "laws": "The industrial revolution brought profound cultural change to Western Europe and caused competition for colonies and for areas of exploitation. Japan entered the competition as soon as she acquired the general pattern. The realignments of power caused by Germany's losses in the first world war and by Italy's and Japan's in the second are of a social order. What new cultural patterns will result from these remains to be seen" (Steward 1950:104–105).

Steward rejected the assumption that the "spread of communism" would necessarily cause "basic cultural changes" that were ipso facto dangerous. "Russia acquired drastically new cultural patterns as a result of her revolution. . . . Whether communism has the same meaning in other nations has still to be determined" (Steward 1950:105).

STEWARD AND THE POSTWAR AREA-STUDIES ESTABLISHMENT

Steward took a position as professor of anthropology at Columbia University in the fall of 1946. For the next few years, his agenda involved the pursuit of both public and foundation-sector funding for area-related research. His position in the wartime Washington, D.C., agencies had given him a good grasp of the participants, issues, forces, and tactics involved. Steward maintained an advisory relationship to the ISA, from which he apparently unsuccessfully attempted to influence the unit's operations. However, by March 1947 his differences with the direction that the ISA was taking (apparently with George Foster and perhaps other officials at the Smithsonian) led him to resign and sever this linkage. Steward's correspondence shows him alert to the potentialities of foreign area research under the Fulbright program. He was also apparently involved in drafting a proposal to the Office of Naval Research concerning the "cultural patterns of Latin America."

During his first year at Columbia, Steward conducted a seminar in which he clarified his analyses of the weaknesses in anthropological and sociological community-study methods. By early 1947, if not earlier, he had crystallized a model for research (see above), whose implementation he sought at every opportunity, and Steward explored possibilities in many countries—Peru, Brazil, Mexico, Paraguay, and China. Although Steward was not the only player in area studies, Latin American or elsewhere, he had close ties to major participants in the efforts to create area-studies instrumentalities that centered on the SSRC. His key ally here was again Wendell C. Bennett, now returned to Yale; others were Charles Wagley and the sociologist Donald Young, who was the executive secretary of the SSRC. Since the middle of the war, the SSRC had acted as the principal secretariat for the Joint Research Council efforts to develop an area-studies apparatus in the universities and to insure its ties with the public policy bloc of the state and the foundations.

Steward was one of many senior scholars who returned to the universities at this time. Although their views on Cold War politics would later vary, there was a widely shared consensus—not empty rhetoric—among these men concerning the honorable relationship between service to the state, the use of science as a liberating tool for creating a social order, and the appropriateness of the state's working as a rational force. Even the individuals whom Steward viewed as antagonists (e.g., Leslie White, John Collier, and Scudder Mekeel) worked within this framework.

For Steward, there was no immediate contradiction between the purposes and national goals of the interventionist state, general human welfare, and the ability of carrying out basic scientific research that was simultaneously of scientific and practical value. The appearance and reappearance of these phrases in his research proposals of the period were in no way mere cant or empty rhetoric.

THE PUERTO RICO PROJECT: AN OBJECT AND MODEL FOR INTERPRETING AREA STUDIES OF COMPLEX SOCIETIES

Harry Shapiro, a physical anthropologist at the American Museum of Natural History and a colleague at Columbia, had been discussing research possibilities with the Social Science Research Center of the University of Puerto Rico (UPR). In April 1947 Shapiro approached Steward concerning the community-study aspect of a joint cultural/biological anthropological study of Puerto Rico. The project, which was to be financed as part of UPR's policy-oriented research program, would require additional funding. Steward assimilated this research possibility into his ongoing projections. After an unsuccessful approach to the Viking Fund for the additional monies, he adopted another strategy, one which he had evidently been pursuing with the developing area-studies network. The strategy paid off with three research grants: Rockefeller Foundation funding for the UPR Social Anthropology Project study of the effects of 50 years of American culture contact on Puerto Ricans and Puerto Rican communities (1948–1949); a second Rockefeller grant, mediated through the SSRC and Columbia University, to clarify "research effort and procedures" in planned interdisciplinary area studies, using the Puerto Rico Project as a basis for the pilot study; and an SSRC commission for Steward to write a monograph appraising the methodologies for area studies and for editing a bulletin of area studies. This bulletin would pull together information on existing efforts, including those of the research fellows who were being funded by the SSRC and ACLS.

The Rockefeller Foundation believed that the Puerto Rico Project would contribute information useful for guiding and assessing the foundation's programs of social and economic transformation/stabilization abroad and at home and would further the development of universal theories of change. The foundation officers supported the SSRC's interest in the project. The search began for models for conducting interdisciplinary, synthetic studies of complex contemporary societies throughout the world. Within the SSRC Committee on World Area Research, Wendell Bennett had been promoting the idea of performing a pilot—an integrated area-studies project using a Latin American country as the focus. Given the developments sketched earlier in this chapter, by 1947 the area-studies apparatus concerning Latin America was the most mature. The Puerto Rico Project was chosen because it appeared to offer the possibility of appraising and expanding the efforts of an ongoing, comprehensive program of social, demographic, and economic research that combined U.S. models and investigators with in-country researchers and expertise. The possibility combined the extractive, synthetic, and self-expanding elements central to the imperial design of area studies.

The UPR's social-science research program had been conceived within a field of basic research and theory already molded by the strategies of the Rockefeller Foundation, other influential funding sources, and consumers of knowledge from the emerging "foreign area-study apparatus." Here, Puerto Rico became an object—not without caution and reservations—for interlocking funding agencies seeking to resolve certain problems for one of their strategies of research development. Casting Puerto Rico in the role of interamerican or international pilot project *object* was nothing new, and it would soon become more important during the 1950s.

For the Rockefeller Foundation and SSRC officials and advisors, Julian Steward's record attested to his competence to direct such a project. Not the least important would have been his experience with the *Handbook of South Americans,* which mobilized and incorporated knowledge produced by "Latin American" intellectuals and scholars into a U.S. government–promoted regional compendium. So too was his work at the ISA organizing in-country research projects cooperating with local universities, with mixed research teams of U.S. and local researchers. However, it is the irony of the arrogance, as well as the limitations of such "imperial designs," that such a complex negotiation in Puerto Rico was entrusted to the direction of an anthropologist who spoke no Spanish, who had never been in Puerto Rico, and who had an exceedingly limited control of the literatures about the island.

The results of the investigations carried out by Steward and his associates appeared in 1956 in *The People of Puerto Rico* (Steward 1972 [1956]; Steward et al. 1972 [1956]). It was one of the first attempts by anthropologists to study and portray a national society (Lauria-Perricelli 1989:1). Steward wrote that the aim of the Puerto Rico Project was to study the social anthropology of an area "with modern civilizations of different kinds or with folk cultures and societies that have come under some form of Euro-American or Russian dominance. . . . [It was concerned with finding out] how the influences emanating from a highly industrialized society [like the United States] affected the local and regional varieties of culture found in one of its agrarian dependencies" (Steward 1950:154). Steward described Puerto Rico as a U.S. colony, "agrarian, rural, and economically part of a capitalist world in that it depends upon an export crop and imports nearly all of its manufactured goods and about half of its food" (Steward 1950:129). The cultural heterogeneity was due to the differential penetration of "the processes by which production, social patterns, and related modes of life are selectively borrowed from the outside and adapted to local needs" (Steward 1950:133–134).

In his view, the social structure of the island was composed of two interdependent features. One consists of a series of distinctive, localized sociocultural subgroups, which are crosscut by class, ethnic, and other social categories that are arranged hierarchically throughout the island. The other consists of a set of formal institutions, such as economic relationships or the legal and government system, that constitute binding and regulating forces. "These institutions have aspects which are national and sometimes international in scope and which must be understood apart from the behavior of the individuals connected with them" (Steward 1955b:47). "The most important factors in Puerto Rico's cultural change . . . appeared to penetrate the Island along axes of these basic institutions" (Steward 1950:145).

The Puerto Rico Project did not become the multidisciplinary project that Steward sought to make it. Even though the appraisal of area studies was a significant methodological statement for an anthropology concerned with situating modern communities in their national/international context (Steward 1950), from the perspective of the area-studies establishment and its central concern with international power relations *The People of Puerto Rico* had a number of limitations (Shimkin 1964:6). Steward paid little attention to national resource bases, manpower, spatial organization, political power, and industrialization. In the end, the point of view was too restricted.

CONTEMPORARY CHANGE IN TRADITIONAL SOCIETIES

In 1952 Steward accepted a research professorship at the University of Illinois. By this time, his ties with the area-studies establishment and its networks had become more tenuous. He was to embark on an even more ambitious series of comparative projects aimed at documenting and analyzing cross-cultural regularities in processes of social change. Of these, the most ambitious was funded by the Ford Foundation, whose massive intervention in international development, modernization, and Cold War policy began in 1953.

In 1956 Steward (1967a, 1967b) and his associates addressed the kinds of contemporary changes that were taking place in the postwar era through a series of cross-cultural studies of modernization in different traditional societies, including one Native American society, the Hopi (Nagata 1966:x, 1970). They believed that the participation of several persons, each studying a different society "would better clarify the underlying problems and yield more comparable data than the findings of independent studies of single cases of modernization" (Steward 1967a:v).

For Steward, modernization referred to the distinctive kinds of sociocultural changes that were taking place in the postwar era. In his view, modernization was an evolutionary rather than a cumulative process. He regarded modernization as the "sociocultural transformations that result from factors and processes that are distinctive of the contemporary industrial world" that resulted in "basic structures and patterns" qualitatively changed (Steward 1967b:4). Again Steward waxed universally evolutionistic, postulating a kind of unremitting globalization in which modernization "processes unique to the modern world affect any component of urban or rural populations." He wrote of a "contemporary world culture" that had a vast repertory of scientific knowledge; technological applications of science in industry, transportation, communications, health, and other fields; and international economic institutions, religions, political alliances, and humanistic achievements. "All nations contribute in some degree to this culture, and under certain preconditions, any may potentially draw from it." Assuming that this evolutionary process pertained solely to the nation-state level, he noted that "each nation has a combination of modernizing factors that provides a new context of change for its basic populations" (Steward 1967b:7).

Steward believed that the traditional ethnographic accounts of anthropologists told us relatively little about the effects of modernization, because they did not situate or relate the local communities or societies they studied to the wider national and international contexts. Furthermore, social scientists from other disciplines—economics, sociology, and political science, to name only a few—had also become interested in the processes of change occurring in traditional societies, and "a common interdisciplinary interest in cross-cultural comparisons is emerging, but methodologically the more delimited problems, conceptualizations of data, and particular methods tend to be those traditional to each discipline" (Steward 1967b:6). Steward suggested a new approach for dealing with the issues of modernization, a "cause-and-effect" model in which there might be "differential evolution of the components of a culture . . . [and] various particular lines of evolution must be inferred from the empirical data of substantive cases" (Steward 1967b:3). Steward also advocated dismantling "the very generalized concepts of ethnic minorities, subcultures, and subcultural groups or subsocieties" as well as breaking down "rural" and "urban" into "useful categories" derived from the modernization process (Steward 1967b:3).

This "cause-and-effect" model assumed a top-down process of change in which "state-level agencies" mediate "institutional factors" to the "local societies."

However, some local input was envisioned in the form of "local societies and local associations which represent these institutions on a community level." Steward also acknowledged "features of the natural environment that not only facilitate or inhibit change but that require cultural ecological adaptations" (Steward 1967b:4–5).

Steward believed that the data accumulated by the participants in the Cross-Cultural Regularities Project showed that "one of the most common consequences of modernization has been that members of the society have acquired an incentive for private gain" (Steward 1967b:9). He also pointed out that another common trend involved "a reduction of the percentage of the population that operates as 'free individual enterprise' and an increase in the number of salaried workers" (Steward 1967b:10). Although the project members did not compare modernization in capitalist and socialist settings, Steward believed their data showed that capitalist and socialist systems were becoming more similar. That is, "convergent evolution is occurring in the modernization of both capitalist and socialist systems, and this is particularly evident in many aspects of change in contemporary Russia. The basic incentive to produce more goods in both systems will probably be increased salaries" (Steward 1967b:10).

The success of Steward's cross-cultural regularities approach ultimately hinged on the degree to which its features as a model enabled it to deal with historic contingency and also to distinguish the "modern" features associated with industrialization and urbanization from those that were integral to capitalism. The model never achieved that capability. Because Steward's view of capitalism was visceral rather than theoretically informed, he was never able to accomplish either in a satisfactory manner. On the one hand, the categories of his scientific materialism were those of capitalist political economy. On the other, his approach minimized the importance of cultural tradition and meaning; it could neither theorize them nor deal with elites in Third World countries who were not cosmopolitan comprador mediators of industrializing trends elsewhere.

CONCLUSIONS: STEWARDIAN MODELS OF CHANGE

Steward's importance and influence in anthropological circles grew steadily after the late 1930s. The strength of his research program in the late 1940s and early 1950s was that he formulated a comparative method for analyzing the cultural and social changes that accompanied economic growth. He produced it at a time when the United States dominated the world economy and pursued its national and international interests as if they were identical. The dominant political needs of the U.S. economy during the

Truman years were maintaining high domestic employment; implementing and guiding the economic recovery of Western Europe and Japan; containing the left and the Soviet Union, which were incorrectly linked by many; and determining the role of Great Britain in the postwar world.

The weaknesses of Steward's research program emerged only after 1952 when the locus of U.S. foreign-aid programs shifted to Asia, Africa, and the Middle East and when questions of decolonization and modernization rather than reconstruction came to the fore. These weaknesses became more apparent in 1955 after the Bandung Conference of nonaligned nations and the emergence of the Soviet Union as a source of foreign aid to the emerging Third World. The division of the world into two realms was broken, and the United States perceived the nonaligned nations of the Third World as an arena for competition. As the decade progressed, it was no longer so certain that these nations would automatically or naturally follow a path of capitalist economic development—like the United States, Japan, and the countries of Western Europe. In this context, the crucial question was no longer how to promote economic growth. Instead it became how to promote capitalist economic and social development and to ensure that the recipient nations remain firmly committed to this process in spite of increasingly frequent and intense social and political reactions against it. Thus, Steward's role as a functional intellectual in the United States waned after 1953 (Patterson 1987:19). He did not address the problem that arose increasingly during the 1950s as a result of decolonization and social and political opposition to capitalist development in the nonaligned nations: The problem was how to identify and support those groups that would promote capitalist economic development in the Third World. Steward could not address this question.

NOTES

1. Chinese Studies/Materials on Chinese Studies, 1929; Japanese Studies, 1930; and Indic-Iranian Studies, 1930. In 1931–1932, the ACLS formed its Committees on Latin-American Studies, Byzantine Studies, and Mediterranean and Near Eastern Studies. In 1936, the Committees on Near Eastern and Arabic and Islamic Studies were created. In 1937–1938, the Committees on Slavic Studies and American Culture Studies were both formed.

2. The next two joint regional committees, concerned with Southern Asia and Slavic Studies, respectively, came into being only in 1949, as the postwar/early Cold War area-studies apparatus was being developed. The Joint Exploratory Committee on Latin American Studies (ACLS, NRC, SSRC, and the American Council on Education), which was empowered in 1947–1948, determined that little more was left to achieve in developing the nature and infrastructure for Latin American studies. Accordingly the JCLAS was laid down in 1947–1948. It was only in 1959 that a new joint committee was created, when hemispheric hegemony was again problematic after the Cuban Revolution.

3. The value of the holistic approach was emphasized in the results of an unpublished survey of anthropological activities in wartime service, "Anthropology during the War and After," NRC, Division of Anthropology and Psychology, Committee on War Services of Anthropologists, 10-III-1943. A copy is in the Steward Archive at the University of Illinois, Urbana. Ralph Beals chaired the committee and Steward was a member.

References

DOCUMENTARY SOURCES

DSC Deep Springs College, Correspondence and Records. Deep Springs, California.

JHS Julian H. Steward Papers. University Archives, University of Illinois, Urbana.

JJJS Journal of Julian and Jane Steward, 1934–1936.

TA Telluride Association Papers. Ithaca, New York.

UCMDA University of California, Museum and Department of Anthropology, Correspondence and Records. Bancroft Library, University of California, Berkeley.

Aikens, C. M.

1966 *Fremont-Promontory Relationships in Northern Utah.* Anthropological Papers No. 82. Salt Lake City: University of Utah Press.

Ambler, R. J.

1966 *Caldwell Village and Fremont Prehistory.* Unpublished Ph.D. dissertation, Department of Anthropology, University of Colorado, Boulder.

American Society for Ethnohistory

1988 *Conference Program of the American Society for Ethnohistory, November 11–13.* American Society for Ethnohistory.

Ames, Kenneth

1982 *Management Report: Archaeological Excavations at Site 10-AA-17, Swan Falls, Idaho.* Manuscript in Department of Anthropology, Boise State University, Boise.

Anastasio, Angelo

1972 The Southern Plateau: An Ecological Analysis of Intergroup Relations. *Northwest Anthropological Research Notes* 6(2):109–229.

Anderson, D. C.

1983 Models of Fremont Culture History: An Evaluation. *Journal of Intermountain Archaeology* 2:1–27.

Arkush, Brooke S.
1986 Aboriginal Exploitation of Pronghorn in the Great Basin. *Journal of Ethnobiology* 6(2):239–255.
1995 The Archaeology of CA-MNO-2122: A Study of Pre-Contact and Post-Contact Lifeways among the Mono Basin Paiute. *University of California Anthropological Records* 31:1–199.
1998 *An Archaeological Assessment of White Horse Pass, Elko County, Nevada.* Report on file at Nevada State Historic Preservation Office, Carson City.

Asbury, Calvin
1912 Letter to the Commissioner of Indian Affairs, December 26, 1912. Western Shoshone Agency, Record Group 75, National Archives, San Bruno, California.

Baltzell, E. Digby
1964 *The Protestant Establishment: Aristocracy and Caste in America.* New York: Random House.

Bancroft, Hubert Howe
1883 *The Native Races: Wild Tribes,* vol. 1. San Francisco: A. L. Bancroft Company.

Barnett, H. G.
1937 Culture Element Distributions: VII. Oregon Coast. *University of California Anthropological Records* 1(3):155–203.

Barrett, S. W.
1980 Indians and Fire. *Western Wildlands* 6(3):17–21.

Battle Mountain Messenger
1880 Indian Talk. 17 April:3. Battle Mountain, Nevada.

Battle Mountain Scout
1922 Shoshone Indians Elect New Chief. 7 October:1. Battle Mountain, Nevada.
1947 Shoshones Want Aid from Whites. 25 December:1. Battle Mountain, Nevada.

Beale, Donald M., and Arthur D. Smith
1970 Forage Use, Water Consumption, and Productivity of Pronghorn Antelope in Western Utah. *Journal of Wildlife Management* 34(3)570–582.

Benedict, Ruth
1934 *Patterns of Culture.* Boston: Little, Brown.

Bennett, Wendell C.
1947 *The Ethnogeographic Board.* Smithsonian Miscellaneous Collections Vol. 107, No. 1. Washington, D.C.: Smithsonian Institution.

Bennett, Wendell C., assembler

1948 *A Reappraisal of Peruvian Archaeology.* Memoirs of the Society for American Archaeology No. 4. Salt Lake City: Society for American Archaeology.

Birnie, Lieut. R., Jr.

1876 Executive Report of Lieutenant R. Birnie, Jr. In *Annual Report upon the Geographical Surveys West of the One Hundredth Meridian, Annual Report of the Chief Engineers for 1876,* pp. 130–135, Appendix JJ. Washington, D.C.: U.S. Government Printing Office.

Bowler, Alida C.

1936a Letter to John Collier, March 7, 1936. Record Group 75, 1907–1939, Organization Division, File 9571A-1936-Carson-068-TeMoak, National Archives, San Bruno, California. Also in JHS Box 10.

1936b Letter to John Collier, March 21, 1936. Records of the Bureau of Indian Affairs, Record Group 75, Collier Office File, Folder Alida C. Bowler (Miss) 1934–1937 Supt. Carson Agency, National Archives, San Bruno, California.

1936c Letter to Scudder Mekeel, November 12, 1936. Box 9038-43-Carson-042, Record Group 75, National Archives, San Bruno, California.

1937 Memorandum: To Commissioner Collier, March 7, 1937. JHS Box 10, File Indian Reorganization, 1937.

Bowman, J. R.

1883 *The Pacific Tourist: J. R. Bowman's Illustrated Trans-Continental Guide of Travel from the Atlantic to the Pacific Ocean, 1882–83.* New York: H. T. Williams.

Brandon, William

1985 *Indians.* Boston: Houghton Mifflin.

Breiseth, Chris, and Brad Edmonston

1987 Interview transcript for oral history project, TA.

Burch, Ernest S., Jr., and Linda J. Ellanna (editors)

1994 *Key Issues in Hunter-Gatherer Research.* Oxford: Berg.

Butler, B. Robert

1978 *A Guide to Understanding Idaho Archaeology: The Upper Snake and Salmon River Country.* 3rd ed. Pocatello: Idaho Museum of Natural History.

1981 Late Period Cultural Sequences in the Northern Great Basin Subarea and Their Implications for the Upper Snake and Salmon River Country. *Journal of California and Great Basin Anthropology* 3(2):245–256.

1986 Prehistory of the Snake and Salmon River Area. In *Handbook of North American Indians: 11. Great Basin,* edited by Warren L. d'Azevedo, pp. 135–148. Washington, D.C.: Smithsonian Institution.

Byers, John A.
1997 *American Pronghorn: Social Adaptations and the Ghosts of Predators Past.* Chicago: University of Chicago Press.

Cahalane, Victor H.
1947 *Mammals of North America.* New York: Macmillan.

Callaway, Donald, Joel Janetski, and Omer Stewart
1986 Ute. In *Handbook of North American Indians: 11. Great Basin,* edited by Warren L. d'Azevedo, pp. 336–367. Washington, D.C.: Smithsonian Institution.

Carson Agency
1927 An interview with members of the Te-moak Band of homeless Indians, January 17, 1927. Box 9038-43-Carson-042, Record Group 75, National Archives, San Bruno, California.

Chance, John K.
1969 Julian H. Steward: An Appreciation. *Journal of the Steward Anthropological Society* 1(1):i–iii.

Childe, V. G.
1951 *Social Evolution.* New York: H. Schumann.

Chrétien, C. Douglas
1945 Culture Element Distributions: XXV. Reliability of Statistical Procedures and Result. *University of California Anthropological Record* 8(5):469–490.

Christensen, Earl M., and Hyrum B. Johnson
1964 *Presettlement Vegetation and Vegetational Change in Three Valleys in Central Utah.* Brigham Young University Science Bulletin Biological Series Vol. 4, No. 4. Provo: Brigham Young University.

Clemmer, Richard O.
1972 *Directed Resistance to Acculturation: A Comparative Study of the Effects of Non-Indian Jurisdiction on Hopi and Western Shoshone Communities.* Ph.D. dissertation, Department of Anthropology, University of Illinois, Urbana-Champaign. Ann Arbor: University Microfilms.

1974 Land Use Patterns and Aboriginal Rights, Northern and Eastern Nevada: 1858–1971. *Indian Historian* 7(1):24–47.

1978 Pine Nuts, Cattle and the Ely Chain: Rip-off Resource Replacement Vs. Homeostatic Equilibrium. In *Selected Papers from the 14th Great Basin Conference,* edited by Don D. Tuohy, pp. 62–75. Socorro, New Mexico: Ballena Press.

1985 The Pinon-Pine: Western Shoshone Indians Versus the Bureau of Land Management. *Environmental Review* 9(2):131–149.

1987 The Tail of the Elephant: Indians in Emigrant Diaries, 1844–1862. *Nevada Historical Society Quarterly* 30(4):269–290.

1996 Ideology and Identity: Western Shoshoni "Cannibal Myth" as Ethnonational Narrative. *Journal of Anthropological Research* 52:207–223.

Clemmer, Richard O., and Omer C. Stewart

1986 Treaties, Reservations, and Claims. In *Handbook of North American Indians: 11. Great Basin,* edited by Warren L. d'Azevedo, pp. 525–557. Washington, D.C.: Smithsonian Institution.

Cleveland, Doris

1932 Letter to Tasker Oddie, February 28, 1932. Tasker Oddie Papers, Nevada Historical Society, Reno.

Clifford, James

1986 Introduction. In *Writing Culture: The Poetics and Politics of Ethnography,* edited by James Clifford and George E. Marcus, pp. 1–26. Berkeley: University of California Press.

1988 *The Predicament of Culture: Twentieth-Century Ethnography, Literature, and Art.* Cambridge: Harvard University Press.

Collier, John

1936a Letter to Alida C. Bowler, March 26, 1936. Records of the Bureau of Indian Affairs, Record Group 75, Collier Office File, Folder Alida C. Bowler (Miss) 1934–1937 Supt. Carson Agency, National Archives, San Bruno, California.

1936b Memorandum: To Dr. Scudder Mekeel, December 22, 1936. Records of the Bureau of Indian Affairs, Record Group 75, Collier Office File, Folder Alida C. Bowler (Miss) 1934–1937 Supt. Carson Agency, National Archives, San Bruno, California.

1963 *From Every Zenith: A Memoir and Some Essays on Life and Thought.* Denver: Sage Books.

Colville, Ruth Marie

1996 *La Vereda: A Trail through Time.* Alamosa, Colorado: San Luis Valley Historical Society.

Congressional Record

1946 Indian Claims Commission. Proceedings and Debates of the 79th Congress, 2nd session. *Congressional Record* Vol. 92, Pt. 4.

Cooper, John M.

1941 *Temporal Sequences and the Marginal Cultures.* Catholic University of America Anthropological Series No. 10. Washington, D.C.: Catholic University of America.

1942 Areal and Temporal Aspects of Aboriginal South American Culture. *Primitive Man* 15 (1/2):1–38.

Cornell, Stephen I.

1988 *Return of the Native.* New York: Oxford University Press.

Coville, F. V.

1892 The Panamint Indians of California. *American Anthropologist* (o.s.) 5(4):351–356.

Cramton, Louis

1932 Report of Facts with Relation to Water Rights of the Indians of the Western Shoshone (Duck Valley) Indian Reservation, January 28, 1932. Indian Irrigation Service Records, Department of the Interior, Record Group 48, National Archives, College Park, Maryland.

Crapanzano, Vincent

1986 Hermes' Dilemma: The Masking of Subversion in Ethnographic Description. In *Writing Culture: The Poetics and Politics of Ethnography,* edited by James Clifford and George E. Marcus, pp. 51–76. Berkeley: University of California Press.

Creek, Darwin E.

1967 *A Summary of Pronghorn Antelope Investigations.* Cheyenne: Wyoming Game and Fish Commission.

Crum, Beverly

ca. 1975 Antelope Song. Transcribed and translated by Beverly Crum, a Shoshone speaker and linguist from the Duck Valley Reservation in Nevada. Copy in Steven Crum's possession, Native American Studies, University of California, Davis.

ca. 1975 Imma Hupia (The Early Morning Song). Transcribed and translated by Beverly Crum.

ca. 1975 Uppi Katete (There, in a Distant Place). Transcribed and translated by Beverly Crum.

1980 Newe Hupia-Shoshone Poetry Songs. *Journal of California and Great Basin Anthropology, Papers in Linguistics* 2(1980):3–23.

Crum, Steven J.

1991 Julian Steward's Vision of the Great Basin: A Response. Paper presented at the 84th Annual Meeting of the Organization of American Historians.

1994 *The Road on Which We Came: A History of the Western Shoshone.* Salt Lake City: University of Utah Press.

1996 Discussant's Comments. *Symposium 14: Re-reading Julian Steward.* 25th Great Basin Anthropological Conference, Kings Beach, California.

Dahl, Robert A.

1961 *Who Governs? Democracy and Power in an American City.* New Haven: Yale University Press.

1967 *Pluralist Democracy in the United States: Conflict and Consent.* Chicago: Rand McNally.

1971 *Polyarchy, Participation and Opposition.* New Haven: Yale University Press.

Daubenmire, R. F.

1943 Vegetation Zonation in the Rocky Mountains. *The Botanical Review* 9(6):325–393.

d'Azevedo, Warren L. (editor)

1986 *Handbook of North American Indians: 11. Great Basin.* Washington, D.C.: Smithsonian Institution.

d'Azevedo, Warren L., Wilbur H. Davis, Don D. Fowler, and Wayne Suttles (editors)

1966 *The Current Status of Anthropological Research in the Great Basin, 1964.* Desert Research Institute Social Sciences and Humanities Publications No. 1. Reno: University of Nevada.

Deloria, Vine, Jr.

1992 The Application of the Constitution to American Indians. In *Democracy, Indian Nations and the U.S. Constitution,* edited by Oren R. Lyons and John C. Mohawk, pp. 281–315. Santa Fe: Clear Light Publishing.

Deloria, Vine, Jr., and Clifford Lytle

1984 *The Nations Within: The Past and Future of American Indian Sovereignty.* New York: Pantheon.

Domhoff, G. William

1970 *The Higher Circles: The Governing Class in America.* New York: Random House.

Dominguez, Steve, and Deward E. Walker Jr.

1981 Tukeda Subsistence. Unpublished manuscript. Anthropology Department, University of Colorado, Boulder.

Driver, Harold E.

1938 Culture Element Distributions: VII. The Reliability of Culture Element Data. *University of California Anthropological Records* 1(4):205–219.

1939 Culture Element Distributions: X. Northwestern California. *University of California Anthropological Records* 1(6):297–433.

Driver, Harold E., and Alfred L. Kroeber

1932 Quantitative Expression of Cultural Relationship. *University of California Publications in American Archaeology and Ethnology* 31(4):211–258.

Durkheim, E.
1915 *The Elementary Forms of the Religious Life.* New York: Free Press.
Eastman, Carol M.
1990 *Aspects of Language and Culture.* 2nd ed. Novato, California: Chandler and Sharp.
Egan, Howard R.
1917 *Pioneering the West, 1846–1878.* Richmond, Utah: Howard R. Egan Estate.
Eggan, Fred
1980 Shoshone Kinship Structures and Their Significance for Anthropological Theory. *Journal of the Steward Anthropological Society* 11(2):165–193.
Elko Free Press
1929 1867 Agreement Never Kept Temoaks State. 17 May:1. Elko, Nevada.
Evans-Pritchard, E. E.
1963 *Essays in Social Anthropology.* Glencoe, Illinois: Free Press.
Fabian, Johannes
1983 *Time and the Other: How Anthropology Constructs Its Object.* New York: Columbia University Press.
Fenton, William N.
1947 *Area Studies in American Universities.* Washington, D.C.: Commission on Implications of Armed Services Education Programs, American Council on Education.
Firth, Raymond
1973 *Symbols: Public and Private.* Ithaca: Cornell University Press.
Forbes, Jack D.
1965 The "Public Domain" of Nevada and Its Relationship to Indian Property Rights. *Nevada State Bar Journal* 30(3)16–47.
Foster, George
1986 Changing Culture of the Anthropological Profession. Paper presented at the 57th Annual Meeting of the Southwestern Anthropological Association.
Fowler, Catherine S.
1972 Some Ecological Clues to Proto-Numic Homelands. In *Great Basin Cultural Ecology: A Symposium,* edited by Don D. Fowler, pp. 105–121. Desert Research Institute Publications in the Social Sciences No. 8. Reno: University of Nevada.
1982 Settlement Patterns and Subsistence Systems in the Great Basin: The Ethnographic Record. In *Man and Environment in the Great*

Basin, edited by D. B. Madsen and J. F. O'Connell, pp. 121–138. SAA Papers No. 2. Washington, D.C.: Society for American Archaeology.

Fowler, Catherine S., and Sven Liljeblad
1986 Northern Paiute. In *Handbook of North American Indians: 11. Great Basin,* edited by Warren L. d'Azevedo, pp. 435–465. Washington, D.C.: Smithsonian Institution.

Fowler, Catherine S., Molly Dufort, and Mary K. Rusco
1995 *Timbisha Shoshone Tribe's Land Acquisition Program: Anthropological Data on Twelve Study Areas.* Submitted to the Timbisha Shoshone Tribe, Death Valley, California.

Fowler, Catherine S., Molly Dufort, Mary K. Rusco, and the Historic Preservation Committee Timbisha Shoshone Tribe (Pauline Esteves, Grace Goad, Ed Esteves, and Ken Watterson)
1995 *Residence without Reservation: Ethnographic Overview and Traditional Land Use Study, Timbisha Shoshone, Death Valley National Park, California (Phase 1).* Submitted to the National Park Service, Washington, D.C.

Fowler, Don D.
1977 *Models in Great Basin Prehistory: A Symposium.* Desert Research Institute Publications in Social Sciences No. 12. Reno: University of Nevada.
1980 History of Great Basin Anthropological Research, 1776–1979. *Journal of California and Great Basin Anthropology* 2(1):8–36.

Fowler, Don D., and Jesse D. Jennings
1982 Great Basin Archaeology: A Historical Overview. In *Man and the Environment in the Great Basin,* edited by D. B. Madsen and J. F. O'Connell, pp. 105–120. SAA Papers No. 2. Washington, D.C.: Society for American Archaeology.

Fowler, Don D., David B. Madsen, and Eugene M. Hattori
1973 *Prehistory of Southeastern Nevada.* Desert Research Institute Publications in the Social Sciences No. 6. Reno: University of Nevada.
1986 History of Research. In *Handbook of North American Indians: 11. Great Basin,* edited by Warren L. d'Azevedo, pp. 15–30. Washington, D.C.: Smithsonian Institution.

Frison, George C.
1991 *Prehistoric Hunters of the High Plains.* 2nd ed. San Diego: Academic Press.

Geertz, Clifford
1963 *Agricultural Involution.* Berkeley: University of California Press.
1973 *The Interpretation of Cultures.* New York: Basic Books.

1983 *Local Knowledge: Further Essays in Interpretative Anthropology.* New York: Basic Books.

Gellner, Ernest

1983 *Nations and Nationalism.* Ithaca: Cornell University Press.

Georgetta, Clel E.

1972 *Golden Fleece in Nevada.* Reno: Venture Publishing.

Gheen, Levi

1873 *Statistical Report of Estimated Enumeration of Western Bands of Shoshone and Other Indians in White Pine, Lander, Nye, Elko and Lincoln Counties, 1873.* Western Shoshone Agency, Record Group 75, National Archives, San Bruno, California.

Gibson, Arrell Morgan

1980 *The American Indian: Prehistory to the Present.* Lexington, Massachusetts: D. C. Heath and Company.

Gillin, John

1945 *Moche: A Peruvian Coastal Community.* Institute of Social Anthropology Publication No. 3. Washington, D.C.: Smithsonian Institution.

Gold Field Weekly News

1905 A Card from Chief Toi Toi. 27 October:2. Gold Field, Nevada.

Goss, James A.

1964 Internal Diversity in Southern Numic. Paper presented at the Great Basin Anthropological Conference, Reno.

1968 Culture-Historical Inference from Utaztekan Linguistic Evidence. In *Utaztekan Prehistory,* edited by Earl Swanson, pp. 1–42. Occasional Papers of the Idaho State University Museum No. 22. Pocatello: Idaho State University Museum.

1977 Linguistic Tools for the Great Basin Prehistorian. In *Models in Great Basin Prehistory,* edited by Don D. Fowler, pp. 49–70. Desert Research Institute Publications in the Social Sciences No. 12. Reno: University of Nevada.

Grayson, Donald K.

1993 *The Desert's Past: A Natural Prehistory of the Great Basin.* Washington, D.C.: Smithsonian Institution.

Green, Thomas J.

1982 House Form and Variability at Givens Hot Springs, Southwest Idaho. *Idaho Archaeologist* 6(1/2):33–44.

1992 Aboriginal Residential Structures in Southern Idaho. *Journal of California and Great Basin Anthropology* 15(1):58–72.

Grosscup, Gordon L.

1977 Notes on Boundaries and Culture of the Panamint Shoshone and Owens Valley Paiute. *Contributions of the University of California Archaeological Research Facility* 35:109–150.

Gruhn, Ruth

1987 Aboriginal Culture History through Linguistics and Archaeology in the Great Basin. *Idaho Archaeologist* 10(1):3–8.

Gunnerson, James H.

1962 Plateau Shoshonean Prehistory: A Suggested Reconstruction. *American Antiquity* 28(1):41–45.

1969 *The Fremont Culture: A Study in Culture Dynamics on the Northern Anasazi Frontier.* Papers of the Peabody Museum of American Archaeology and Ethnology Vol. 59, No. 2. Cambridge: Harvard University.

Hall, Matthew C.

1990 The OXBOW Archaeological Incident: Investigations at Twenty-three Locations between Owens Valley, Eastern California, and Walker Basin, Southwestern Nevada. Report on file, Eastern California Information Center, Archaeological Research Unit, University of California, Riverside.

Hall, Matthew C., and Amy Dansie

1990 Archaeology and Bone Taphonomy of an Antelope Butchering Site, Southwestern Mineral County, Nevada. Paper presented at the 22nd Biennial Great Basin Anthropological Conference, Reno.

Hanley, Thomas A., and Kathleen A. Hanley

1982 Food Resource Partitioning by Sympatric Ungulates on Great Basin Rangeland. *Journal of Range Management* 35(2):152–158.

Harper, Kimball T.

1986 Historical Environments. In *Handbook of North American Indians: 11. Great Basin,* edited by Warren L. d'Azevedo, pp. 51–63. Washington, D.C.: Smithsonian Institution.

Harris, Jack

1938 The Western Shoshone. *American Anthropologist* 40:407–411.

1940 The White Knife Shoshoni of Nevada. In *Acculturation in Seven American Indian Tribes,* edited by Ralph Linton, pp. 39–111. New York: D. Appleton-Century.

Harris, Marvin

1968 *The Rise of Anthropological Theory.* New York: Crowell.

Hatch, Elvin

1973a *Theories of Man and Culture.* New York: Columbia University Press.

1973b The Growth of Economics, Subsistence, and Ecological Studies in American Anthropology. *Journal of Anthropological Research* 29(4):221–243.

Heizer, Robert F.

1978 History of Research. In *Handbook of North American Indians: 8. California,* edited by Robert F. Heizer, pp. 6–15. Washington, D.C.: Smithsonian Institution.

Herskovits, Melville

1938 *Acculturation: The Study of Culture Contact.* New York: Augustin.

Hewes, Gordon W.

1947 *Aboriginal Use of Fishery Resources in Northwestern North America.* Unpublished Ph.D. dissertation, Anthropology Department, University of California, Berkeley.

1973 Indian Fisheries Productivity in Pre-Contact Times in the Pacific Salmon Area. *Northwest Anthropological Research Notes* 7(2):133–155.

Hibbard, C. W., and W. W. Dalquest

1960 A New Antilocaprid from the Pleistocene of Knox County, Texas. *Journal of Mammalogy* 41:20–23.

Hittman, Michael

1973 *Ghost Dances, Disillusionment and Opiate Addiction: An Ethnohistory of Smith and Mason Valley Paiutes.* Unpublished Ph.D. dissertation, Department of Anthropology, University of New Mexico, Albuquerque.

1990 *Wovoka and the Ghost Dance.* Yerington: Yerington Paiute Tribe.

Hogan, P., and L. Sebastian

1980 The Variants of the Fremont: A Methodological Evaluation. In *Fremont Perspectives,* edited by D. B. Madsen, pp. 13–16. Antiquities Selected Papers Vol. VII, No. 16. Salt Lake City: Utah State Historical Society.

Holmer, Richard N., et al.

1986 *Shoshone-Bannock Culture History: Reports of Investigation.* Pocatello: Idaho State University, Swanson/Crabtree Anthropological Research Laboratory.

Hoover, Robert L., C. E. Till, and Stanley Ogilvie

1959 *The Antelope of Colorado: A Research and Management Study.* Colorado Department of Fish and Game Technical Bulletin No. 4. Denver: Colorado Department of Fish and Game.

Hopkins, Nicholas A.

1965 Great Basin Prehistory and Uto-Aztecan. *American Antiquity* 31(1):48–60.

Hultkrantz, Ake
1986 Mythology and Religious Concepts. In *Handbook of North American Indians: 11. Great Basin,* edited by Warren L. d'Azevedo, pp. 630–640. Washington, D.C.: Smithsonian Institution.

INDIGRIGHTS
1998 *United Nations Draft Declaration on the Rights of Indigenous Peoples* http://biopark.org/INDIGRIGHTS.HTML

Ingold, Tim
1992 Foraging for Data, Camping with Theories: Hunter-Gatherers and Nomadic Pastoralists in Archaeology and Anthropology. *Antiquity* 66(252):790–803.

Janetski, Joel C.
1994 Recent Transitions in the Eastern Great Basin: The Archaeological Record. In *Across the West: Human Population Movement and the Expansion of the Numa,* edited by D. B. Madsen and D. Rhode, pp. 157–178. Salt Lake City: University of Utah Press.

Janetski, J. C., and D. B. Madsen (editors)
1990 *Wetland Adaptations in the Great Basin.* Museum of Peoples and Cultures Occasional Papers No. 1. Provo: Brigham Young University.

Janetski, J. C., R. K. Talbot, D. E. Newman, L. D. Richens, J. D. Wilde, S. A. Baker, and S. E. Billat
1996 *Clear Creek Canyon Archeological Project: 5. Results and Synthesis.* Museum of Peoples and Cultures Technical Series No. 95-9. Provo: Brigham Young University.

Janis, C.
1982 Evolution of Horns in Ungulates: Ecology and Paleoecology. *Biological Review* 57:261–318.

Jefferson, James, Robert W. Delaney, and Gregory C. Thompson
1972 *The Southern Utes: A Tribal History.* Ignacio, Colorado: Southern Ute Tribe.

Jennings, Jesse D.
1953 Danger Cave: A Progress Summary. *El Palacio* 60(5):179–213.
1956 The American Southwest: A Problem in Cultural Isolation. In *Seminars in Archaeology, 1955,* edited by Robert Wauchope, pp. 59–127. Memoirs of the Society for American Archeology No. 11. Salt Lake City: Society for American Archeology.
1957 *Danger Cave.* Anthropological Papers No. 27. Salt Lake City: University of Utah Press.
1968 *Prehistory of North America.* New York: McGraw-Hill.
1973 The Short Useful Life of a Simple Hypothesis. *Tebiwa* 13(1):1–9.

1978 *Prehistory of Utah and the Eastern Great Basin.* Anthropological Papers No. 98. Salt Lake City: University of Utah Press.

Jones, Ryhs

1992 Philosophical Time Travellers. *American Antiquity* 66(252):744–757.

Jorgensen, Joseph G.

1980 *Western Indians: Comparative Environments, Languages, and Cultures of 172 Western American Indian Tribes.* San Francisco: W. H. Freeman and Company.

Judd, N. M.

1926 *Archaeological Observations North of the Rio Colorado.* Bureau of American Ethnology Bulletin No. 82. Washington, D.C.: Smithsonian Institution.

Kahrl, William

1982 *Water and Power: The Conflict over Los Angeles' Water Supply in the Owens Valley.* Berkeley: University of California Press.

Keesing, Roger

1974 Theories of Culture. *Annual Review of Anthropology* 3:75–97.

Kelly, Isabel T.

1932 Ethnography of the Surprise Valley Paiute. *University of California Publications in American Archaeology and Ethnology* 31(3):67–210.

Kelly, Lawrence C.

1980 Anthropology and Anthropologists in the Indian New Deal. *History of the Behavioral Sciences* 16:6–24.

1983 *The Assault on Assimilation: John Collier and the Origins of Indian Policy Reform.* Albuquerque: University of New Mexico Press.

1985 Why Applied Anthropology Developed When It Did: A Commentary on People, Money, and Changing Times, 1930–1945. In *Social Contexts of American Ethnology, 1930–1945,* edited by June Helm, pp. 122–138. Washington, D.C.: American Ethnological Society.

Kelly, Robert L.

1995 *The Foraging Spectrum.* New York: Smithsonian Institution Press.

Kessler, Ronald E. (editor)

1994 *Anza's 1779 Comanche Campaign.* Translated by Alfred B. Thomas. Monte Vista, Colorado: Ronald E. Kessler.

Kroeber, Alfred L.

1901 Ute Tales. *Journal of American Folklore* 14(35):252–285.

1907 Shoshonean Dialects of California. *University of California Publications in American Archaeology and Ethnology* 4(3):65–165.

1908a Notes on the Ute Language. *American Anthropologist* 10(1):74–87.

1908b Origin Tradition of the Chemehuevi Indians. *Journal of American Folklore* 21(81/82):240–242.

1909a Notes on Shoshonean Dialects of Southern California. *University of California Publications in American Archaeology and Ethnology* 8(5):235–269.

1909b The Bannock and Shoshoni Languages. *American Anthropologist* 11(2):266–277.

1922 Elements of Culture in Native California. *University of California Publications in American Archaeology and Ethnology* 13(8):259–328.

1925 *Handbook of the Indians of California.* Bureau of American Ethnology Bulletin No. 78. Washington, D.C.: Bureau of American Ethnology.

1939a Preface. In The Structure of California Indian Culture. *University of California Publications in American Archaeology and Ethnology* 37(1):1–11.

1939b Culture Element Distributions: III. Area and Climax. *University of California Publications in American Archaeology and Ethnology* 37(3):101–116.

1939c Culture Element Distributions: XI. Tribes Surveyed. *University of California Anthropological Records* 1(7):435–440.

1939d Cultural and Natural Areas of Native North America. *University of California Publications in American Archaeology and Ethnology* 38(1):1–242.

1941 Preface. In Culture Element Distribution: XIII. Nevada Shoshone. *University of California Anthropological Records* 4(2):209–360.

1955 The Nature of the Landholding Group. *Ethnohistory* 2:303–314.

1963 *Configurations of Cultural Growth.* Berkeley: University of California Press.

Kuhn, Thomas S.

1970 [1962] *The Structure of Scientific Revolutions.* 2nd ed. Chicago: University of Chicago Press.

Lamb, Sydney M.

1958 Linguistic Prehistory in the Great Basin. *International Journal of American Linguistics* 24(2):95–100.

Larco Hoyle, Rafael

1948 *Cronología arqueológica del norte del Perú.* Buenos Aires: Sociedad Geográfica Americana.

Larsen, Parry

1964 *Antelope Physiological Studies.* Albuquerque: New Mexico Department of Fish and Game.

Lauria-Perricelli, Antonio
1989 *A Study in Historical and Cultural Anthropology: The Making of "The People of Puerto Rico."* Ph.D. dissertation, Department of Anthropology, New School for Social Research. Ann Arbor: University Microfilms.

Lee, Richard B., and Irven Devore
1968 Problems in the Study of Hunters and Gatherers. In *Man the Hunter,* edited by Richard B. Lee and Irven Devore, pp. 3–12. Chicago: Aldine.

Leone, Mark P.
1972 Issues in Anthropological Archaeology. In *Contemporary Archaeology,* edited by Mark P. Leone, pp. 14–27. Carbondale: Southern Illinois University Press.

Levi-Strauss, Claude
1963 *Structural Anthropology.* New York: Basic Books.
1966 *The Savage Mind.* London: Weidenfeld and Nicolson.
1967 The Story of Asdiwal. In *The Structural Study of Myth and Totemism,* edited by E. Leach, pp. 1–48. London: Tavistock.
1969 *The Raw and the Cooked.* New York: Harper and Row.
1973 *From Honey to Ashes.* New York: Harper and Row.
1979 *The Origin of Table Manners.* New York: Harper and Row.
1981 *The Naked Man.* New York: Harper and Row.

Liljeblad, Sven
1957 Indian Peoples in Idaho. Mimeo in Anthropology Department, Idaho State College, Pocatello.
1971 The History of Indian Tribes in Idaho: Languages. Manuscript in Liljeblad's Papers, Special Collections, University of Nevada, Reno.
1986 Oral Tradition: Content and Style of Verbal Arts. In *Handbook of North American Indians: 11. Great Basin,* edited by Warren L. d'Azevedo, pp. 641–659. Washington, D.C.: Smithsonian Institution.

Lingenfelter, Richard E.
1986 *Death Valley and the Amargosa: A Land of Illusion.* Berkeley: University of California Press.

Linton, Ralph
1936 *The Study of Man.* New York: D. Appleton-Century.

Linton, Ralph (editor)
1940 *Acculturation in Seven American Indian Tribes.* New York: D. Appleton-Century.

Lowie, Robert
1909a The Northern Shoshoni. *Anthropological Papers of the American Museum of Natural History* 2(2):165–306.
1909b Shoshone and Comanche Tales. *Journal of American Folklore* 22(85):265–282.
1915 Dances and Societies of the Plain Shoshone. *Anthropological Papers of the American Museum of Natural History* 11(10):803–835.
1919 Sun Dance of the Shoshoni, Ute, and Hidatsa. *Anthropological Papers of the American Museum of Natural History* 16(5):387–431.
1923 The Cultural Connection of California and Plateau Shoshonean Tribes. *University of California Publications in American Archaeology and Ethnology* 20(9):145–156.
1924a Notes in Shoshonean Ethnography. *Anthropological Papers of the American Museum of Natural History* 20(3):185–314.
1924b Shoshonean Tales. *Journal of American Folklore* 37(143/144):12–42.
1930 The Kinship Terminology of the Bannock Indians. *American Anthropologist* 32(2):294–299.

Lubinski, Patrick M.
1997 *Pronghorn Intensification in the Wyoming Basin: A Study of Mortality Patterns and Prehistoric Hunting Strategies.* Unpublished Ph.D. dissertation, Anthropology Department, University of Wisconsin, Madison.

Luhan, Mabel Dodge
1936 *Movers and Shakers.* New York: Harcourt, Brace.

McCaughey, Robert A.
1984 *International Studies and Academic Enterprise: A Chapter in the Enclosure of American Learning.* New York: Columbia University Press.

Madsen, Brigham D.
1980 *The Northern Shoshone.* Caldwell, Idaho: Caxton Printers.
1986 *Chief Pocatello: The "White Plume."* Salt Lake City: University of Utah Press.

Madsen, David B.
1979 The Fremont and the Sevier: Defining Prehistoric Agriculturalists North of the Anasazi. *American Antiquity* 44(4):711–722.
1982 Get It Where the Gettin's Good: A Variable Model of Great Basin Subsistence and Settlement Based on Data from the Eastern Great Basin. In *Man and Environment in the Great Basin,* edited by D. B. Madsen and J. F. O'Connell, pp. 207–226. SAA Papers No. 2. Washington, D.C.: Society for American Archaeology.

1989 *Exploring the Fremont.* University of Utah Occasional Publications No. 8. Salt Lake City: Utah Museum of Natural History.

Madsen, David B., and J. F. O'Connell (editors)

1982 *Man and Environment in the Great Basin.* SAA Papers No. 2. Washington, D.C.: Society for American Archaeology.

Madsen, David B., and David Rhode

1994 *Across the West: Human Population Movement and the Expansion of the Numa.* Salt Lake City: University of Utah Press.

Malina, Jaroslav, and Zdenek Vasícek

1990 *Archaeology Yesterday and Today.* Cambridge: Cambridge University Press.

Malouf, Carling

1974 The Gosiute Indians. In *Shoshone Indians, American Indian Ethnohistory: California and Basin-Plateau Indians,* edited by D. A. Horr, pp. 25–172. New York: Garland.

Manners, Robert

1973 Julian Haynes Steward 1902–1972. *American Anthropologist* 75:886–903.

Marwitt, J. P.

1970 *Median Village and Fremont Culture Regional Variation.* Anthropological Papers No. 95. Salt Lake City: University of Utah Press.

Marx, Karl, and Friedrich Engels

1932 *Capital, The Communist Manifesto, and Other Writings.* Edited by Max Eastman. New York: Carlton House.

Mason, Ellis

1952 Food Habits and Measurements of Hart Mountain Antelope. *Journal of Wildlife Management* 16(3):387–389.

Mayhugh, John S.

1884 Letter to the Commissioner of Indian Affairs, September 8, 1884. In *Annual Report of the Commissioner of Indian Affairs, 1884,* p. 130. Washington, D.C.: U.S. Government Printing Office.

Mead, Margaret

1932 *The Changing Culture of an Indian Tribe.* New York: Columbia University Press.

Meatte, Daniel S.

1986 Evidence for the Historic Occurrence and Aboriginal Utilization of Caribou in Southern Idaho. *Idaho Archaeologist* 9(2):41–42.

Meek, Ronald L.

1976 *Social Sciences and the Ignoble Savage.* Cambridge: Cambridge University Press.

Mekeel, Scudder

1936a Letter to Alida C. Bowler, October 28, 1936. Box 9038-43-Carson-042, Record Group 75, Bureau of Indian Affairs National Archives, San Bruno, California.

1936b Letter to Alida C. Bowler, December 16, 1936. Box 9038-43-Carson-042, Record Group 75, Bureau of Indian Affairs National Archives, San Bruno, California.

1938 Letter to Alida C. Bowler, November 18, 1938. Box 9038-43-Carson-042, Record Group 75, Bureau of Indian Affairs National Archives, San Bruno, California.

Merriam, C. Hart

1955 *Studies of California Indians.* Berkeley: University of California Press.

1963 *Ethnographic Notes on California Indian Tribes.* Edited by Robert Heizer. Report No. 68. Berkeley: University of California Archaeological Research Facility.

Miller, Wick R.

1966 Anthropological Linguistics in the Great Basin. In *The Current Status of Anthropological Research in the Great Basin, 1964,* edited by Warren L. d'Azevedo, Wilbur H. Davis, Don D. Fowler, and Wayne Suttles, pp. 75–112. Desert Research Institute Social Sciences Social Sciences and Humanities Publications No. 1. Reno: University of Nevada.

1986 Numic Languages. In *Handbook of North American Indians: 11. Great Basin,* edited by Warren L. d'Azevedo, pp. 98–106. Washington, D.C.: Smithsonian Institution.

Mills, C. Wright

1956 *The Power Elite.* New York: Oxford University Press.

Mintz, Sidney

1979 The Role of Water in Steward's Cultural Ecology. *Journal of the Steward Anthropological Society* 11(1):17–32.

Morgan, Lewis H.

1877 *Ancient Society.* New York: Holt.

Morss, Noel

1931 *The Ancient Culture of the Fremont River in Utah.* Peabody Museum of American Archaeology and Ethnology Papers Vol. 12, No. 3. Cambridge: Harvard University.

Murphy, Robert F.

1970 Basin Ethnography and Ecological Theory. In *Language and Culture of Western North America: Essays in Honor of Sven S.*

Liljeblad, edited by Earl H. Swanson Jr., pp. 152–171. Pocatello: Idaho State University Press.

1977 Introduction: The Anthropological Theories of Julian H. Steward. In *Evolution and Ecology: Essays on Social Transformation,* edited by Jane Cannon Steward and R. F. Murphy, pp. 1–40. Urbana: University of Illinois Press.

1981 Julian Steward. In *Totems and Teachers,* edited by Sydel Silverman, pp. 171–204. New York: Columbia University Press.

1987 American Anthropology. In *Perspectives in Cultural Anthropology,* edited by Herbert Applebaum. Albany: State University of New York Press.

Murphy, Robert, and Yolanda Murphy

1960 Shoshone-Bannock Subsistence and Society. *University of California Anthropological Records* 16(7):293–338.

1986 Northern Shoshone and Bannock. In *Handbook of North American Indians: 11. Great Basin,* edited by Warren L. d'Azevedo, pp. 284–307. Washington, D.C.: Smithsonian Institution.

Murphy, Timothy W., and Fred P. Frampton

1986 Aboriginal Antelope Traps on Bureau of Land Management Lands in the Elko Area, Northeastern Nevada. Paper presented at the 20th Biennial Great Basin Anthropological Conference, Las Vegas, Nevada.

Murra, John

1946 The Historic Tribes of Ecuador. In *Handbook of South American Indians: 2. The Andean Civilizations,* edited by Julian H. Steward, pp. 785–822. Washington, D.C.: Smithsonian Institution.

Myers, L. Daniel

1987 *Levels of Context: A Symbolic Analysis of Numic Origin Myth.* Unpublished Ph.D. dissertation, Anthropology Department, Rutgers University, New Brunswick, New Jersey.

1988 Hunters and Gatherers as Anthropological Exemplars: An Illustration from the American Great Basin. Paper presented at the 5th International Conference on Hunting and Gathering Societies, Darwin, Australia.

1990a Towards a Natural History of the Numa: A Symbolic Analysis of the Numic Origin Myths. Paper presented at the 22nd Great Basin Anthropological Conference, Reno.

1990b Cannibalism and Incest as Metaphor among the Numa: A Symbolic Analysis of Numic Origin Myths. Paper presented at the American Anthropological Association Annual Meeting, New Orleans.

1992 Myth as Ritual: Thoughts from a Symbolic Analysis of Numic Origin Myths. Paper presented at the Great Basin Anthropological Conference, Boise.

Nagata, Shuichi

1966 *Modern Transformations of Moenkopi Pueblo.* Unpublished Ph.D. disser- tation, Department of Anthropology, University of Illinois, Urbana.

1970 *Modern Transformations of Moenkopi Pueblo.* Urbana: University of Illinois Press.

Nelson, E. W.

1891 The Panamint and Saline Valley (Calif.) Indians. *American Anthropologist* (o.s.) 4(4):371–372.

Nelson, Edward W.

1925 *Status of the Pronghorned Antelope, 1922–1924.* USDA Department Bulletin No. 1346. Washington, D.C.: U.S. Government Printing Office.

Noon, F. C.

1917 Chancellor's Report: Minutes of the 1917 Convention. TA.

Nunn, L. L.

ca. 1925 Constitution of Deep Springs and the Deed of Trust. DSC.

Opler, Marvin K.

1943 The Origin of Comanche and Ute. *American Anthropologist* 45:155–158.

Palmer, E.

1876 Exploration of a Mound in Utah. *American Naturalist* 10:410–414.

Parker, Patricia L., and Thomas F. King

1990 *Guidelines for the Identification and Evaluation of Traditional Cultural Properties.* National Register Bulletin No. 38. Washington, D.C.: U.S. Government Printing Office.

Parman, Donald L.

1976 *The Navajos and the New Deal.* New Haven: Yale University Press.

Parr, Robert E.

1989 *Archaeological Investigation of the Huntoon Pronghorn Trap Complex, Mineral County, Nevada.* Master's thesis, Anthropology Department, University of California, Riverside.

Patterson, Edna B.

1973 *This Land Was Ours: An In-Depth Study of a Frontier Community.* Springville, Utah: Art City Publishing.

1985 Mary Hall: Western Shoshone Basketmaker. *Northeastern Nevada Historical Society Quarterly* 85(4):103.

Patterson, Thomas
1987 Development, Ecology, and Marginal Utility in Anthropology. *Dialectical Anthropology* 12:15–31.
1989 Political Economy and a Discourse Called "Peruvian Archeology." *Culture and History* 4:35–64.

Pavesic, Max
1987 Anadromous Fish Remains from Schellback Cave No. 1, Southwestern Idaho. *Idaho Archaeologist* 10:23–26.
1988 Archaeological Evidence of Shoshonean Sturgeon Exploitation in Western Idaho: Preliminary Findings. Paper presented at the 15th Annual Idaho Archaeological Society Meeting, Boise.
1997 Aboriginal Sturgeon Exploitation on the Middle Snake River. *North American Archaeologist* 18(3):277–288.

Philp, Kenneth R.
1977 *John Collier's Crusade for Indian Reform, 1920–1954*. Tucson: University of Arizona Press.

Plew, Mark G.
1980 Fish Remains from Nahas Cave: Archaeological Evidence of Anadromous Fishes in Southwestern Idaho. *Journal of California and Great Basin Anthropology* 6:129–132.

Rabinow, Paul
1986 Representations Are Social Facts: Modernity and Post-Modernity. In *Writing Culture: The Poetics and Politics of Ethnography*, edited by James Clifford and George E. Marcus, pp. 234–261. Berkeley: University of California Press.

Ray, Verne
1939 *Cultural Relations in the Plateau of Northwestern America.* Publications of the Frederick Webb Hodge Anniversary Publication Fund Vol. 3. Los Angeles: Southwestern Museum.
1960 The Columbia Indian Confederacy. In *Culture in History: Essays in Honor of Paul Radin,* edited by Stanley Diamond, pp. 771–789. New York: Columbia University Press.

Reagan, Albert B.
1935 Archaeological Report of Field Work Done in Utah in 1934 and 1935. *Proceedings Utah Academy of Science* 12:50–88.

Redfield, Robert
1941 *The Folk Culture of Yucatán.* Chicago: University of Chicago Press.

Redfield, Robert, Ralph Linton, and Melville Herskovits
1936 A Memorandum on the Study of Acculturation. *American Anthropologist* 38:149–152.

Reese River Reveille
1897 Death of the Shoshone Chief. 21 April:3. Austin, Nevada.
Reich, Herbert
1974 Early Recollections of Deep Springs. *Deep Springs Newsletter* 19: 1–3.
Rigg, Larry P.
1992 Omer Call Stewart, Ph.D. (1908–1991). *Southwestern Lore* 58:1–4.
Ronaasen, Sheree L.
1993 *Culture Ecology and Functionalism: Social Theory Framed by a Colonial Political Context.* Master's thesis, Department of Anthropology, University of Alberta, Edmonton.
Rosen, Lawrence
1977 The Anthropologist as Expert Witness. *American Anthropologist* 79:555–578.
Ross, Dorothy
1991 *The Origins of American Social Science.* Cambridge: Cambridge University Press.
Rudden, Mary Elizabeth, and Richard O. Clemmer
1998 Acculturation Is Meaningless. Manuscript submitted for publication.
Rudnick, Lois Palken
1984 *Mabel Dodge Luhan: New Woman, New Worlds.* Albuquerque: University of New Mexico Press.
1996 *Utopian Vistas.* Albuquerque: University of New Mexico Press.
Rudolph, Teresa
1995 *The Hetrick Site: 11,000 Years of Prehistory in the Weiser River Valley, Idaho.* Boise: Science Applications International.
Rudy, Jack R.
1953 *An Archaeological Survey of Western Utah.* Anthropological Papers No. 12. Salt Lake City: University of Utah Press.
Rusco, Elmer R.
1982 The Organization of the Te-Moak Bands of Western Shoshone. *Nevada Historical Society Quarterly* 25(3):174–196.
1986 The Formation of the Constitutions of the Reno-Sparks Colony. Paper presented at the 20th Great Basin Anthropological Conference, Las Vegas, Nevada.
1992 Historic Change in Western Shoshone Country: The Establishment of the Western Shoshone National Council and Traditionalist Land Claims. *American Indian Quarterly* XVI(Summer):337–360.
1996 *A Fateful Time: The Background and Legislative History of the Indian Reorganization Act.* Manuscript submitted for publication.

Sahlins, Marshall, and Elman Service
1960 *Evolution and Culture.* Ann Arbor: University of Michigan Press.

Said, Edward W.
1993 *Culture and Imperialism.* New York: Knopf.

Sauer, Carl O.
1950 Grassland Climax, Fire and Man. *Journal of Range Management* 3(10):16–21.

Schoenherr, Allan A.
1992 *A Natural History of California.* Berkeley: University of California Press.

Service, Elman R.
1962 *Primitive Social Organization: An Evolutionary Perspective.* New York: Random House.

Sharp, Florence
ca. 1930 Life of Ira Wines. Manuscript in Nevada Historical Society Library, Reno.

Shimkin, Demitri B.
1947 Wind River Shoshone Ethnogeography. *University of California Anthropological Records* 5(4):245–288.
1964 Julian H. Steward: A Contributor to Fact and Theory in Cultural Anthropology. In *Process and Pattern in Culture: Essays in Honor of Julian H. Steward,* edited by Robert A. Manners, pp. 1–17. Chicago: Aldine.
1986 Eastern Shoshone. In *Handbook of North American Indians: 11. Great Basin,* edited by Warren L. d'Azevedo, pp. 308–335. Washington, D.C.: Smithsonian Institution.

Short, Shelton H.
1965 *A History of the Nevada Livestock Industry Prior to 1900.* Master's thesis, Department of History, University of Nevada, Reno.

Siegel, Bernard J. (editor)
1955 *Acculturation: Critical Abstracts, North America.* Stanford: Stanford University Press.

Sills, Marc. A., and Glenn T. Morris (editors)
1993 *Indigenous Peoples' Politics: An Introduction.* Vol. I. Denver: University of Colorado Fourth World Center for the Study of Indigenous Law and Politics.

Simms, S. R.
1986 New Evidence for Fremont Adaptive Diversity. *Journal of California and Great Basin Anthropology* 8(2):204–216.
1990 Fremont Transitions. *Utah Archaeology* 3(1):1–18.

Simms, Steven R., and Kathleen M. Heath

1990 Site Structure of the Orbit Inn: An Application of Ethnoarchaeology. *American Antiquity* 55:797–813.

Smith, Arthur D., and Donald M. Beale

1980 *Pronghorn Antelope in Utah: Some Research and Observations.* Utah Division of Wildlife Resources Publication No. 80-13. Salt Lake City: Utah Division of Wildlife Resources.

Snyder, Fredrick

1926a Letter to Emmett McNeilly, February 1, 1926. Carson Agency Records, Record Group 75, National Archives, San Bruno, California.

1926b Letter to John Worden, August 12, 1926. Reno Agency, Box 287, Record Group 75, National Archives, San Bruno, California.

Sperber, Dan

1975 *Rethinking Symbolism.* Cambridge: Cambridge University Press.

1982 *On Anthropological Knowledge.* Cambridge Studies in Social Anthropology No. 54. Cambridge: Cambridge University Press.

Statham, Dawn Strain

1982 *Camas and the Northern Shoshoni: A Biographic and Socioeconomic Analysis.* Boise State University Archaeological Reports No. 10. Boise: Boise State University.

Stearns, S., and F. Peterson

1987 *Investigation of a Possible Archaic Antelope Trap, Clover Valley, Nevada.* Nevada Department of Transportation Archaeological Technical Report Series No. 4. Carson City: Nevada Department of Transportation.

Stegner, Wallace

1954 *Beyond the Hundredth Meridian: John Wesley Powell and the Second Opening of the West.* Boston: Houghton Mifflin.

Steward, Jane C., and Robert F. Murphy

1977 *Evolution and Ecology: Essays on Social Transformation.* Urbana: University of Illinois Press.

Steward, Julian H.

1918a Letter to F. C. Noon, January 7, 1918. TA.

1918b Information form, May 31, 1918. TA.

1920 Academic records. DSC.

1921a Academic records. DSC.

1921b Letter to E. A. Thornhill, July 15, 1921. TA.

1925 Steward's undergraduate transcript. Cornell University, Ithaca, New York.

1928a Letter to Alfred L. Kroeber, July 26, 1928. UCMDA Box 43.

1928b Pottery from Deep Springs Valley, Inyo County, California. *American Anthropologist* 30:348.

1929 Petroglyphs of California and Adjoining States. *University of California Publications in American Archaeology and Ethnology* 24:47–238.

1931a Letter to Edward W. Gifford, November 5, 1931. UCMDA Box 43.

1931b Archaeological Discoveries at Kanosh in Utah. *El Palacio* 300:121–130.

1931c Notes on Hopi Ceremonies in Their Initiatory Form in 1927–1928. *American Anthropologist* 33:56–79.

1933a Ethnography of the Owens Valley Paiute. *University of California Publications in American Archaeology and Ethnology* 33:233–350.

1933b *Early Inhabitants of Western Utah: I. Mounds and House Types.* Bulletin of the University of Utah. Vol. 23, No. 7, pp. 1–34. Salt Lake City: University of Utah.

1933c *Archaeological Problems of the Northern Periphery of the Southwest.* Museum of Northern Arizona Bulletin No. 5. Flagstaff: Museum of Northern Arizona.

1934a Two Paiute Autobiographies. *University of California Publications in American Archaeology and Ethnology* 33(5):423–438.

1934b *The Blackfoot.* Berkeley: Field Division of Education, National Park Service, U.S. Department of the Interior.

1936a *Pueblo Material Culture in Western Utah.* Anthropological Series Vol. 1, No. 3, University of New Mexico Bulletin No. 287, pp. 1–64. Albuquerque: University of New Mexico.

1936b *Shoshonean Tribes: Utah, Idaho, Nevada, Eastern California.* Report prepared for the Bureau of Indian Affairs. JHS Box 10, File Indian Reorganization, 1937.

1936c The Economic and Social Basis of Primitive Bands. In *Essays in Anthropology Presented to Alfred L. Kroeber,* edited by Robert H. Lowie, pp. 331–350. Berkeley: University of California Press.

1936d Myths of the Owens Valley Paiute. *University of California Publications in American Archaeology and Ethnology* 34(5):335–440.

1936e Shoshoni Polyandry. *American Anthropologist* 38(4):561–564.

1937a *Ancient Caves of the Great Salt Lake Region.* Bureau of American Ethnology Bulletin No. II 6. Washington D.C.: Bureau of American Ethnology.

1937b Applied Anthropology in America. Unpublished paper, JHS Box 10, File Indian Reorganization, 1937.

1937c Linguistic Distributions and Political Groups of the Great Basin Shoshoneans. *American Anthropologist* 39:625–634.

1937d World's Most Primitive Indians Inhabit Utah, Says Savant: Anthropologist Declares Goshutes' Habits Once More Simple Than That of Cavemen. *Salt Lake Tribune* 24 October:2B.

1937e Letter to Scudder Mekeel, March 27, 1937. JHS Box 10.

1937f Ecological Aspects of Southwestern Society. *Anthropos* 32(1):87–104.

1939 Some Observations on Shoshonean Distribution. *American Anthropologist* 41:261–265.

1940a Native Cultures of the Intermontane (Great Basin) Area. In *Essays in Historical Anthropology of North America Published in Honor of J. R. Swanton.* Smithsonian Miscellaneous Collections No. 100, pp. 445–502. Washington D.C.: Smithsonian Institution.

1940b Handbook of South American Indians. *Boletín bibliográfico de antropología americana* 4(3):227–230.

1941a *Archaeological Reconnaissance of Southern Utah.* Anthropological Papers No. 18, Bureau of American Ethnology Bulletin No. 128. Washington D.C.: Bureau of American Ethnology.

1941b Culture Element Distributions: XIII. Nevada Shoshone. *University of California Anthropological Records* 4(2):209–359.

1941c Recording Culture Changes among the Carrier Indians of British Columbia. In *Explorations and Fieldwork of the Smithsonian Institution in 1940,* pp. 83–90. Washington, D.C.: Smithsonian Institution.

1942 The Direct Historical Approach to Archaeology. *American Antiquity* 7:337–343.

1943a Culture Element Distributions: XXIII. Northern and Gosiute Shoshoni. *University of California Anthropological Records* 8(3):263–392.

1943b *Some Western Shoshone Myths.* Anthropological Papers, Bureau of American Ethnology Bulletin No. 136, pp. 249–299. Washington, D.C.: Bureau of American Ethnology.

1943c Acculturation Studies in Latin America: Some Needs and Problems. *American Anthropologist* 45:198–204.

1943d Acculturation and the Indian Problem. *América Indígena* 3(4):323–328.

1943e Anthropological Research Needs and Opportunities in South America. *Acta Americana* I(1):20–37.

1944a Preface. In *Houses and House Use of the Sierra Tarascans,* by Ralph L. Beals, Pedro Carrasco, and Thomas McCorkle, pp. ix–x.

Institute of Social Anthropology Publication No. 1. Washington, D.C.: Smithsonian Institution.

1944b Review of *The Folk Culture of Yucatán,* by Robert Redfield. *Journal of American Folklore* 57(2):146–148.

1946 [1944] Introduction. In *Handbook of South American Indians: The Marginal Tribes,* edited by Julian H. Steward, pp. 1–9. Bureau of American Ethnology Bulletin Vol. 1, No. 143. Washington, D.C.: Bureau of American Ethnology.

1947 American Culture History in the Light of South America. *Southwestern Journal of Anthropology* III(2):85–107.

1948 A Functional-Developmental Classification of American High Culture. In *A Reappraisal of Peruvian Archaeology,* assembled by Wendell C. Bennett, pp. 103–104. Memoirs of the Society for American Archaeology No. 4. Salt Lake City: Society for American Archaeology.

1949a [1947] South American Cultures: An Interpretive Summary. In *Handbook of South American Indians: The Comparative Ethnology of South American Indians,* edited by Julian H. Steward, pp. 669–677. Bureau of American Ethnology Bulletin Vol. 5(2), No. 143. Washington, D.C.: Bureau of American Ethnology.

1949b Cultural Causality and Law: A Trial Formulation of the Development of Early Civilizations. *American Anthropologist* 51:1–27.

1950 Area Research: Theory and Practice. *Social Science Research Council Bulletin* 63:1–164.

1951 Levels of Sociocultural Integration: An Operational Concept. *Southwestern Journal of Anthropology* 7:374–390.

1953a Evolution and Process. In *Anthropology Today,* edited by Alfred Kroeber, pp. 313–325. Chicago: University of Chicago Press.

1953b Aboriginal and Historic Groups of the Ute Indians of Utah: An Analysis and Native Components of the White River Ute Indians. Mimeo in U.S. Department of Justice, Washington, D.C.

1954a Letter to Wetmore. JHS Box 6.

1954b Autobiographical appraisal. JHS Box 6.

1955a [1951] Levels of Sociocultural Integration: An Operational Concept. In *Theory of Culture Change,* by Julian H. Steward, pp. 43–63. Urbana: University of Illinois Press.

1955b *Theory of Culture Change: The Methodology of Multilinear Evolution.* Urbana: University of Illinois Press.

1955c Theory and Application in a Social Science. *Ethnohistory* 2:291–302.

1961 Letter to Deep Springs College, May 17, 1961. DSC.

1962 Letter. *Science* 135:964–966.

1967a Foreword. In *Contemporary Change in Traditional Societies,* vol. 1, edited by Julian H. Steward, pp. v–x. Urbana: University of Illinois Press.

1967b Perspectives on Modernization: Introduction to the Studies. In *Contemporary Change in Traditional Societies,* vol. 1, edited by Julian H. Steward, pp. 1–55. Urbana: University of Illinois Press.

1968a The Great Basin Shoshonean Indians: An Example of a Family Level of Socio-cultural Integration. In *Man in Adaptation: The Cultural Present,* edited by Y. A. Cohen, pp. 68–81. Chicago: Aldine.

1968b Review of the Current Status of Anthropological Research in the Great Basin: 1964, edited by Warren d'Azevedo, Wilbur Davis, Don D. Fowler, and Wayne Suttles. *American Antiquity* 33:264–267.

1969a Underdeveloped Nations: Predictability and Manipulability of Modernizing Trends. Unpublished manuscript. Copy in Richard Clemmer's possession, Anthropology Department, University of Denver.

1969b The Limitations of Applied Anthropology: The Case of the Indian New Deal. *Journal of the Steward Anthropological Society* 1:1–17.

1969c *Observations on Bands.* Natural Museum of Canada Bulletin No. 230. Ottawa: Natural Museum of Canada.

1969d Letter to Herbert Reich, November 25, 1969. JHS Box 3.

1969e Letter to Marvin Harris, March 8, 1969. JHS Box 3.

1969f Letter to John Chance, March 23, 1969. JHS Box 3.

1970a [1938] *Basin-Plateau Aboriginal Sociopolitical Groups.* Bureau of American Ethnology Bulletin No. 120. Washington, D.C.: U.S. Government Printing Office. Reprinted 1970. Salt Lake City: University of Utah Press.

1970b The Foundations of Basin-Plateau Shoshonean Society. In *Languages and Cultures of Western North America,* edited by Earl H. Swanson, pp. 113–151. Pocatello: Idaho State University Press.

1971 Underdeveloped Nations: Predictability and Manipulability of Modernizing Trends. In *Essays on Modernization of Underdeveloped Societies,* edited by A. R. Desai, pp. 138–148. Bombay: University of Bombay Department of Sociology.

1972 [1956] Introduction. In *The People of Puerto Rico,* 4th printing, edited by Julian H. Steward, Robert A. Manners, Eric R. Wolf, Elena Padilla Seda, Sidney W. Mintz, and Raymond L. Scheele, pp. 1–27. Urbana: University of Illinois Press.

1973 *Alfred Kroeber.* New York: Columbia University Press.
1991 [1929] *The Ceremonial Buffoon of the American Indian.* New York: Garland. Originally published as Steward's Ph.D. dissertation, Department of Anthropology, University of California, Berkeley.
Steward, Julian H., and Robert Manners
1953 The Cultural Study of Contemporary Societies: Puerto Rico. *American Journal of Sociology* 59:123–130.
Steward, Julian H., and Robert Murphy
1977 [1956] Tappers and Trappers. In *Evolution and Ecology: Essays on Social Transformation,* edited by Jane Cannon Steward and Robert F. Murphy, pp. 151–179. Urbana: University of Illinois Press.
Steward, Julian H., and F. M. Seltzer
1938 Function and Configuration in Archaeology. *American Antiquity* 4:4–10.
Steward, Julian H., and Erminie Wheeler-Voegelin
1954 The Northern Paiute Indians. Mimeo in U.S. Department of Justice, Washington, D.C.
1974 The Northern Paiute Indians. In *Paiute Indians,* vol. III, pp. 9–328. American Indian Ethnohistory: California and Basin-Plateau Indians No. 1 New York: Garland.
Steward, Julian H., Robert A. Manners, Eric R. Wolf, Elena Padilla Seda, Sidney W. Mintz, and Raymond L. Scheele (editors)
1972 [1956] *The People of Puerto Rico.* 4th printing. Urbana: University of Illinois Press.
Stewart, Omer C.
1939 The Northern Paiute Bands. *University of California Anthropological Records* 2(3):127–149.
1941 Culture Element Distributions: XIV. Northern Paiute. *University of California Anthropological Records* 4(3):361–446.
1942 Culture Element Distributions: XVIII. Ute–Southern Paiute. *University of California Anthropological Records* 6(4):231–356.
1955 Forest and Grass Burning in the Mountain West. *Southwestern Lore* 21(1):5–9.
1959 Anthropology and the Indian Claims. *The Delphian Quarterly* 42(3):8–13, 21.
1961 Kroeber and the Indian Claims Commission Cases. In *Alfred Kroeber: A Memorial,* pp. 181–191. Kroeber Anthropological Society Papers No. 25. Berkeley: Kroeber Anthropological Society.
1965 The Shoshone: Their History and Social Organization. *Idaho Yesterdays* 9(3):2–5, 28.

1966 Tribal Distributions and Boundaries in the Great Basin. In *The Current Status of Anthropological Research in the Great Basin, 1964,* edited by Warren L. d'Azevedo, Wilbur H. Davis, Don D. Fowler, and Wayne Suttles, pp. 167–238. Desert Research Institute Social Sciences and Humanities Publications No. 1. Reno: University of Nevada.

1970 The Question of Bannock Territory. In *Languages and Cultures of Western North America: Essays in Honor of Sven S. Liljeblad,* edited by Earl H. Swanson Jr., pp. 201–231. Pocatello: Idaho State University.

1974 The Western Shoshone of Nevada and the U.S. Government, 1863–1950. In *Selected Papers of the 14th Great Basin Anthropological Conference,* edited by Donald R. Tuohy, pp. 77–114. Socorro, New Mexico: Ballena Press.

1979 An Expert Witness Answers Rosen. *American Anthropologist* 81:108–111.

1980 Temoke Band of Shoshone and the Oasis Concept. *Nevada Historical Society Quarterly* 23:246–261.

1991 Fishing and the Wind River Shoshone Indians. *Northwest Anthropological Research Notes* 25(1):13–30.

Stocking, George W., Jr.

1968 *Race, Culture, and Evolution: Essays in the History of Anthropology.* New York: Free Press.

1983 *Observers Observed: Essays on Ethnographic Fieldwork.* Madison: University of Wisconsin Press.

Stoffle, Richard W., Jr.

1991–1992 Epitaph for Omer Call Stewart. *High Plains Anthropologist* 11/12:ix–xxiii.

Stoffle, Richard W., David B. Halmo, John E. Olmstead, and Michael J. Evans

1990 ISR Institute Report. Ann Arbor: Institute for Social Research, University of Michigan.

Stuiver, M., and P. J. Reimer

1987 CALIB and DISPLAY: Radiocarbon Calibration Program. Rev. 2.0. Seattle: University of Washington Quaternary Isotope Laboratory.

Swanson, Earl H., Jr.

1966 The Geographic Foundations of the Desert Culture. In *The Current Status of Anthropological Research in the Great Basin: 1964,* edited by Warren L. d'Azevedo, Wilbur H. Davis, Don D. Fowler, and Wayne Suttles, pp. 137–146. Desert Research Institute Social Sciences and Humanities Publications No. 1. Reno: University of Nevada.

1972 *Birch Creek: Human Ecology in the Cool Desert of the Northern Rocky Mountains, 9000 B.C.–A.D. 1850.* Pocatello: Idaho State University Press.

Tagg, Martyn D.

1984 *The Timba-sha Survey and Boundary Fencing Project: Archaeological Investigations at Death Valley National Monument.* Western Archeological and Conservation Center Publications in Anthropology No. 27. Tucson: University of Arizona.

Taylor, Graham D.

1975 Anthropologists, Reformers, and the Indian New Deal. *Prologue* 7(Fall):151–162.

1980 *The New Deal and American Indian Tribalism: The Administration of the Indian Reorganization Act, 1934–35.* Lincoln: University of Nebraska Press.

Thomas, David H.

1973 An Empirical Test for Steward's Model of Great Basin Settlement Patterns. *American Antiquity* 38(2):155–176.

1974 An Archeological Perspective on Shoshonean Bands. *American Anthropologist* 76(1):11–25.

1983a The Archaeology of Monitor Valley: I. Epistemology. *Anthropological Papers of the American Museum of Natural History* 58(1):1–194.

1983b On Steward's Model of Shoshonean Sociopolitical Organization: A Great Bias in the Basin? In *The Development of Political Organization in Native North America,* edited by Elizabeth Tooker and Morton H. Fried, pp. 59–67. Washington, D.C.: American Ethnological Society.

Thomas, David Hurst, Lorann S. A. Pendleton, and Stephen C. Cappannari

1986 Western Shoshone. In *Handbook of North American Indians: 11. Great Basin,* edited by Warren L. d'Azevedo, pp. 262–283. Washington, D.C.: Smithsonian Institution.

Thomas, Earl

1966 The Pronghorn Antelope. *Wyoming Wildlife* 30(6):12–14.

Thompson, Johnny

1932 Letter to Tasker Oddie, August 15, 1932. Tasker Oddie Papers, Nevada Historical Society, Reno.

Todorov, Tzvetan

1984 *The Conquest of America: The Question of the Other.* New York: Harper and Row.

Tremholm, Virginia C., and Maurine Carley

1964 *The Shoshoni: Sentinels of the Rockies.* Norman: University of Oklahoma Press.

Trigger, Bruce G.
1981 Archaeology and the Ethnographic Present. *Anthropologica* 23:3–17.
1989 *A History of Anthropological Thought.* Cambridge: Cambridge University Press.
Tsukamoto, George K.
1983 *Pronghorn Antelope Species Management Plan.* Reno: Nevada Department of Wildlife.
United Nations
1996 *Draft Declaration on the Rights of Indigenous Peoples.* United Nations Commission on Human Rights. Internet, March 15 Version. (For Web site address, see INDIGRIGHTS entry.)
U.S. Congress
1946 *Indian Claims Commission Act.* 79th Congress, 2nd session 60 Stat. 1049. August 13, 1946.
U.S. Government Printing Office
1947 Statutes at Large: 1946. Vol. 60. Pt. I. Washington, D.C.: U.S. Government Printing Office.
U.S. Indian Claims Commission
1973a [1957] *Northern Paiute Nation, Petitioner, before the Indian Claims Commission, Washington, D.C. The Northern Paiute Nation, et al., Petitioner v. the United States of America, Petitioners. Petitioner's Proposed Findings of Fact and Accompanying Brief.* Microfiche, Briefs, Testimony, Transcripts, Decisions. New York: Clearwater Publishing.
1973b *Expert Testimony before the Indian Claims Commission: Anthropology Report on the Northern Paiute in Nevada, Oregon, and California, 1826 to 1880.* New York: Clearwater Publishing.
1973c *Defendant's Requested Findings of Fact. Northern Paiute Identifiable Group v. The United States of America. Indian Claims Commission. Docket 87.* New York: Clearwater Publishing.
1974 *Commission Findings on the Paiute Indians.* New York: Garland.
U.S. Senate
1934 Hearings before a Subcommittee of the Committee on Indian Affairs. *Survey of Indians in United States.* 72nd Congress, lst session. September 16–20, 1932. Washington, D.C.: U.S. Government Printing Office.
Voegelin, Charles F., Florence M. Voegelin, and Kenneth L. Hale
1962 *Typological and Comparative Grammar of Uto-Aztecan. I. Phonology.* International Journal of American Linguistics Memoir No. 17.

Walker, Deward E., Jr.

1967 *Mutual Cross-Utilization of Economic Resources in the Plateau: An Example from Aboriginal Nez Perce Fishing Practices.* Washington State University, Laboratory of Anthropology, Report of Investigations No. 41. Pullman: Washington State University.

1968a American Anthropological Association Symposium on American Indian Fishing and Hunting Rights. November 1968. Proceedings. *Northwest Anthropological Research Notes* 2(2):1–43.

1968b *Conflict and Schism in Nez Perce Acculturation.* Pullman: Washington State University Press.

1978 *Indians of Idaho.* Moscow: University of Idaho Press.

1991–1992 Dedication to Omer C. Stewart. *High Plains Anthropologist* 11/12:v–viii.

1992 Productivity of Tribal Dipnet Fisherman at Celilo Falls: Analysis of the Joe Pinkham Fish Buying Records. *Northwest Anthropological Research Notes* 26(2):123–135.

1993a The Shoshone-Bannock: An Anthropological Reassessment. *Northwest Anthropological Research Notes* 27(2):139–160.

1993b Lemhi Shoshone-Bannock Reliance on Anadromous and Other Fish Resources. *Northwest Anthropological Research Notes* 27(2):215–250.

Wallace, Earnest, and E. Adamson Hoebel

1952 *The Comanches: Lords of the South Plains.* Norman: University of Oklahoma Press.

Warner, Ted J. (editor)

1976 *The Dominguez-Escalante Journal.* Translated by Fray Angelico Chavez. Provo: Brigham Young University Press.

Warner, W. Lloyd

1963 *Yankee City.* New Haven: Yale University Press.

Watkins, Arthur V.

1957 Termination of Federal Supervision: The Removal of Restrictions over Indian Property and Person. *Annals of the American Academy of Political and Social Sciences* 311:47–55.

Webb, S. D.

1973 Pliocene Pronghorns of Florida. *Journal of Mammalogy* 54:203–221.

1977 A History of Savanna Vertebrates in the New World. Part I. North America. *Annual Review of Ecological Systems* 8:355–380.

Weber, Max

1930 *The Protestant Ethic and the Spirit of Capitalism.* London: G. Allen and Unwin.

Wedertz, Frank S.

1978 *Mono Diggings.* Bishop, California: Chalfant Press.

Western Shoshone Sacred Lands Association

1985 Case of the Western Shoshone. In *Native Peoples in Struggle: Cases from the Fourth Russell Tribunal and Other International Forums,* edited by Esmaelillo and Robin Wright, pp. 132–140. Cambridge: Akwesasne Notes and Anthropology Resource Center.

Wilke, Philip J.

1986 Aboriginal Game Drive Complexes at and near Little Whisky Flat, Mineral County, Nevada. Paper presented at the 20th Biennial Meeting of the Great Basin Anthropological Conference, Las Vegas, Nevada.

Willey, Gordon R.

1946 The Chiclín Conference for Peruvian Archaeology. *American Antiquity* XII(1):132–134.

1988 *Portraits in American Archaeology: Remembrances of Some Distinguished Americanists.* Albuquerque: University of New Mexico Press.

Willey, Gordon R., and J. A. Sabloff

1993 *A History of American Archaeology.* San Francisco: W. H. Freeman and Company.

Willis, Roy

1974 *Man and Beast.* New York: Basic Books.

Wobst, Martin H.

1978 The Archaeo-Ethnology of Hunter-Gatherers Or the Tyranny of the Ethnographic Record in Archaeology. *American Antiquity* 43(2):303–309.

Wolf, Eric

1972 American Anthropologists and American Society. In *Reinventing Anthropology,* edited by Dell H. Hymes, pp. 251–263. New York: Vintage.

1982 *Europe and the People without History.* Berkeley: University of California Press.

Wood, W. Raymond

1980 Plains Trade in Prehistoric and Protohistoric Intertribal Relations. In *Anthropology on the Great Plains,* edited by Margot Liberty, pp. 98–109. Lincoln: University of Nebraska Press.

Wood, W. Raymond, and Margot Liberty (editors)

1980 Plains Trade in Prehistoric and Protohistoric Intertribal Relations. In *Anthropology on the Great Plains,* edited by W. Raymond Wood and Margot Liberty. Lincoln: University of Nebraska Press.

Wormington, H. Marie
1955 *A Reappraisal of the Fremont Culture with a Summary of the Archaeology of the Northern Periphery.* Denver Museum of Natural History Proceedings No. 1. Denver: Denver Museum of Natural History.

Worthington, Keith N.
1958 *A Century of Life in Nephi and Juab Valley, 1851–1951.* Master's thesis, Department of History, Brigham Young University, Provo.

Wright, Gary A., et al.
1980 High Country Adaptations. *Plains Anthropologist* 25(89):181–197.

Yoakum, James D.
1978 Pronghorn. In *Big Game of North America: Ecology and Management,* edited by J. L. Schmidt and D. C. Gilbert, pp. 103–109. Harrisburg, Pennsylvania: Stackpole Books.
1986 Trends in Pronghorn Population, 1800–1983. In *Proceedings of the Twelfth Pronghorn Antelope Workshop,* edited by M. Hess, pp. 77–85. Reno: Nevada Department of Wildlife.

Young, James A., Raymond A. Evans, and Paul T. Tueller
1976 Great Basin Plant Communities—Pristine and Grazed. In *Holocene Environmental Change in the Great Basin,* edited by R. Elston and P. Headrick, pp. 187–216. Nevada Archaeological Survey Research Paper No. 6. Reno: Nevada Archaeological Survey.

Zeveloff, Samuel I.
1988 *Mammals of the Intermountain West.* Salt Lake City: University of Utah Press.

Contributors

Brooke S. Arkush, Ph.D., Department of Sociology and Anthropology, Weber State University, Ogden, Utah

Ned Blackhawk, B.A., Department of History, University of Washington, Seattle

Richard O. Clemmer, Ph.D., Department of Anthropology, University of Denver, Colorado

Steven J. Crum, Ph.D., Native American Studies, University of California, Davis

Molly Dufort, M.A., Department of Anthropology, University of Nevada, Reno

Pauline Esteves, Timbisha Shoshone Community, Death Valley, California

Catherine S. Fowler, Ph.D., Department of Anthropology, University of Nevada, Reno

James A. Goss, Ph.D., Department of Anthropology, Sociology and Social Work, Texas Tech University, Lubbock

Joel C. Janetski, Ph.D., Museum of Peoples and Cultures, Brigham Young University, Provo, Utah

Alice B. Kehoe, Ph.D., Department of Social and Cultural Sciences, Marquette University, Milwaukee, Wisconsin

Virginia Kerns, Ph.D., Department of Anthropology, College of William and Mary, Williamsburg, Virginia

Antonio Lauria-Perricelli, Ph.D., Department of Anthropology, New School for Social Research, New York

L. Daniel Myers, Ph.D., Epochs Past, Dunkirk, Maryland

Thomas C. Patterson, Ph.D., Department of Anthropology, Temple University, Philadelphia, Pennsylvania

Sheree Ronaasen, M.A., Department of Anthropology, University of Queensland, Brisbane, Australia

Mary Elizabeth Rudden, M.A., Lakeland, Florida

Elmer R. Rusco, Ph.D., Department of Political Science, University of Nevada, Reno

Mary K. Rusco, M.A., Reno, Nevada

Deward E. Walker Jr., Ph.D., Department of Anthropology, University of Colorado, Boulder

Index